A Trinitarian Theology of Law

In Conversation with Jürgen Moltmann, Oliver O'Donovan,
and Thomas Aquinas

A Trinitarian Theology of Law

In Conversation with Jürgen Moltmann, Oliver O'Donovan, and Thomas Aquinas

David H. McIlroy

Foreword by Nigel G. Wright

WIPF & STOCK · Eugene, Oregon

Wipf and Stock Publishers
199 W 8th Ave, Suite 3
Eugene, OR 97401

A Trinitarian Theology of Law
In Conversation with Jurgen Moltmann, Oliver O'Donovan and Thomas Aquinas
By McIlroy, David H. and Wright, Nigel G.
Copyright©2009 by McIlroy, David H.
ISBN 13: 978-1-49825-424-3
Publication date 7/2/2009
Previously published by Paternoster, 2009

To my parents, Bill and Tricia,
who taught me the love of God by example
and theology by osmosis

CONTENTS

Foreword by Nigel G. Wright   xv
Preface   xvii
Acknowledgments   xix
Abbreviations   xxi

Chapter 1 The Necessity of a Trinitarian Theology of Law   1
Introduction   1
Law   5
    The Idea of Law in Theology   5
    The Relationship between Law and Morality in Philosophy and
    Theology   6
The Derivation and the Role of the Trinity in Contemporary Theology   9
    The Derivation of the Trinity in Contemporary Theology   9
    The Role of the Trinity in Contemporary Social Theology   14
The Problem of the Trinity in the Western Theology of Law   16

Chapter 2 The Social Trinitarianism of Jürgen Moltmann   22
Introduction   22
The Shape of Moltmann's Trinitarianism   24
    The Revelation of God the Son   28
    The Place of the Holy Spirit within the Trinity   29
    The Role of God the Father in Moltmann's Trinitarianism   35
Moltmann's Theology of Power   36
    The Nature of Christ's Lordship and Rule   36
    The Authority of God the Father   39
    Authority and Law as Hostile Powers   40
    The Work of the Holy Spirit: Law as a Taming and an Ordering
    Power   45

Moltmann's View of History and Eschatology   48
   Moltmann's View of History   48
   Law and Eschatology   51
   The Last Judgment   52
   Salvation and Shalom   55
   The Nature of Anticipations   57
Law, Solidarity, Liberation and Human Rights   58
   Solidarity and Social Justice   59
   Liberation: Freedom and Authority   60
   Human Rights and Christian Ethics   64
   The Spiritual Nature of Justice   70
Criticisms of Moltmann's Trinitarianism   71
Towards a Synthesis of Moltmann's View of Law   73
   Law as a Negative Power   73
   Law as an Ordering Power   75
   Integrating Solidarity, Liberation and Human Rights into
   a Theology of Law: Law as Creative Justice   79
   Synthesising Moltmann's Visions of Law   81
Conclusion   82
   A Critique of the Powers-That-Be   82
   Justice as the Calling of Human Law   83
   Righteousness beyond Justice   84

**Chapter 3 Oliver O'Donovan: Political Authority in the Light
of the Ascended Christ**   87
Introduction   87
Trinitarian Considerations in O'Donovan's Account of Political
Theology   87
   The Kingship of God   87
   The Centrality of Christ   92
      THE CENTRALITY OF CHRIST TO THE MORAL ORDER   94
      CHRIST'S KINGSHIP AND THE *ESSE* OF POLITICAL AUTHORITY 98
      CHRIST'S KINGSHIP AND THE *BENE ESSE* OF POLITICAL
      AUTHORITY   104
   The Place of the Spirit in O'Donovan's Thought   110
      THE ROLE OF THE SPIRIT IN O'DONOVAN'S ACCOUNT OF THE
      MORAL ORDER   110

THE WORK OF THE SPIRIT AND POLITICAL AUTHORITY 113
Law and the Trinity in O'Donovan's Thought 117
The Priority of the Church's Mission 118
The Trinity and the Necessary Task of Delivering Judgment 120
THE IMPERATIVE OF JUSTICE 120
NATURAL LAW AND HUMAN LAW 124
THE TORAH AS A POTENTIAL SOURCE OF ILLUMINATION
FOR HUMAN LAW 126
COLLECTIVE IDENTITY AND SOCIAL ORDER 129
COLLECTIVE IDENTITY, SOLIDARITY AND THE
COMMON GOOD 132
The Trinity and the Limits of Human Justice 135
THE LIMITATIONS OF HUMAN FINITUDE AND SINFULNESS 136
HUMAN JUDGMENT AND THE SON 138
HUMAN JUDGMENT AND THE POWER OF THE SPIRIT 140
*The Trinity and the Possible Task of Consciously Facilitating
the Church's Mission* 142
The Grace of God and the Preservation of Political Authority 148
Conclusion 150

**Chapter 4 Thomas Aquinas's Theology of the Holy Spirit
as the New Law** **152**
Introduction 152
The Context and Contours of Aquinas's Thought 154
The Context of Aquinas's Thought 154
Aquinas the Biblical Theologian 155
Aquinas the Trinitarian Theologian 157
Aquinas's Account of the Role of Law in Salvation 164
The Eternal Law and God's Providence 164
Aquinas and the Mosaic Law 167
WHY THE TORAH? 168
CHRIST'S FULFILMENT OF TORAH AND TEMPLE 171
The Role of Natural Law in Aquinas's Thought 174
Aquinas on the New Law 180
Aquinas the Virtue Ethicist 185
Aquinas on Glorification 187
The Place of Human Law after the Drama of Salvation 191

Aristotelian Optimism   192
Limitations on the Role of Human Law   195
Thinking about Human Law with, and beyond, Aquinas   200
   HUMAN LAW AS SUBMITTED TO CHRIST   201
   THE WORKINGS OF THE HOLY SPIRIT   202
   A SHARP DISTINCTION BETWEEN NATURAL GOODS AND
   THE *SUMMUM BONUM*   203
   TEMPERING HUMAN LAW IN THE LIGHT OF SOTERIOLOGY
   AND THEODICY   204
Aquinas and O'Donovan   205
Conclusion   206

**Chapter 5 Human Law in Relation to the Work of the Son
and the Spirit**   **208**
Methodology   208
The Trinity and Law in the Doctrine of Creation   213
Law and the Fall   214
The Trinity and the Doctrine of Providence   214
Law and the Work of Christ   217
   Law and the Incarnation   217
   Law and the Crucifixion   218
   Law and the Resurrection   219
Law and the Work of the Holy Spirit   219
   The Holy Spirit and the Torah   219
   Overcoming Alienation through Free Obedience in the Spirit 221
The Last Judgment   226
Summary   226
The Limited Role of Human Law   227
   *The Ambivalent Relationship between Human Government
   and Divine Government*   227
   The Role of Human Law in the Light of Redemption   227
   Human Freedom and the Image of God   229
   The Need to Restrain Evil   230
   On the Relationship between Human Justice and Divine Justice 231
Conclusion   233

Chapter 6 Conclusion   **235**

Envoi   238

Bibliography   **239**

Index   **259**

FOREWORD

There are two trends in contemporary theology that are captured in this
excellent book by David McIlroy. One is the close attention that has been given
over some time now to a fully and properly Trinitarian theology. The other is a
more recent renewal of a long tradition of Christian reflection on the civil order
that is currently experiencing fresh impetus. Both these tendencies are greatly
to be welcomed and in the current volume are brought together in a compelling
and effective way to make a substantial contribution to Christian engagement
with society.

As a barrister by training and profession Dr McIlroy is able to draw upon
considerable resources in the history of Christian thought, not least in the
conversation partners he has chosen to engage with in this study, although
many others could have served a similar purpose. A passing acquaintance with
the Hebrew Scriptures should be enough to demonstrate that understandings of
law are deeply ingrained in the faith of the people of Israel. The continuing
biblical drama demonstrates thereafter the mark that such understandings have
left on Christian life and practice as well, although truth to tell the relationship
between law and grace is one that has been often misconstrued and
misrepresented. As the Christian faith has made its impress upon the societies it
has helped to shape, it has consistently shown its potential for informing the
legal systems of those societies. Conversely, legal systems have been useful in
influencing the form and content of doctrinal formulations. What ought to be
clear from this book is that the practice of law is in principle an honourable
one, and that it is entirely right to think and speak of a Christian vocation to
practise law, most especially when the skills of the lawyer are placed at the
service of the powerless. Dr McIlroy would be the first to point out that if the
temptation of the law is that it be used to bolster the interests of those who least
need it, its potential is that it be used to deliver, albeit it in the faltering way
which is true of all human systems, justice for the oppressed.

We all have an interest in living in well-ordered communities in which right
and just dealings are put at a premium. The Christian lawyer serves this interest
and should be encouraged never to lose sight of it. In a world where it is
possible to be highly skilled and educated in one area while remaining
relatively, and sometimes startlingly, untutored in many others, it is imperative

that learned lawyers be as educated as they can make themselves in the ways of theology. David McIlroy has certainly achieved this for himself and by means of his writing provides a means by which colleagues who share his concerns, of which there are many, may gain access to the understanding he has achieved.

This book is a valuable contribution to the public theologies that are now emerging with vigour and energy.

Dr Nigel G. Wright
Principal, Spurgeon's College, London

PREFACE

My previous book *A Biblical View of Law and Justice* began where I think all Christian theology should begin, with the Bible. I sought to explore what the Bible says about law and about justice, treating its material in sections relating to different aspects of the biblical message, whilst working on the assumption that the Bible in its canonical form has been God-given, and therefore to do holistic biblical theology is to do canonical theology.

If the first book was canonical theology, the present book is systematic theology. The particular aspect of systematic theology which I have chosen to address is the Trinity. The reason for this is that I am a Nicene Christian. The Nicene Creed, *pace* the dispute over the *filioque*, represents, it seems to me, the faith once delivered to the saints. Here is the core of mature Christian belief, and at its heart stands the conviction that in the revelation of Christ God has shown Himself to be Father, Son and Holy Spirit.

Turning then to my particular theme, Colin Gunton has argued that Western Christian thought has failed to integrate its doctrine of the Trinity with its other theological convictions. If that claim is true, then thinking in trinitarian terms may enable us to achieve significant clarification in a number of areas, including our theology of law. This book is an attempt to do so.

Through the interaction of my own thought with that of Jürgen Moltmann, Oliver O'Donovan and Thomas Aquinas, I seek to demonstrate that the understanding of the place of human law and the role of human justice in God's purposes which I have developed in my first book is not only canonically supported but also justifiable in terms of a systemic theology which gives full weight to the Christian vision of the triune God.

ACKNOWLEDGMENTS

My debts in this book are even more numerous than those in my earlier writings. I am especially grateful, however, to my *doktorvater* Nigel G. Wright, Principal of Spurgeon's College, and to John E. Colwell, who was Director of Post-Graduate Research during my doctoral studies, for their wise guidance and for the opportunities they gave me to develop my thought. I also want to thank David J. Southall and Terry J. Wright, fellow travellers on the doctoral path whose support and encouragement was invaluable.

I have especially benefited from the friendship of Peter Grant, International Director of TEAR Fund, and of Terry Tennens, Director of International Justice Mission UK, who have given me opportunities to relate my theories to practical situations of injustice around the world.

Finally, I want to say thank you again to my wife, Rebecca, and to my children, Emily and Joshua, for their love, patience, and support during the long days of study.

David H. McIlroy
Spurgeon's College, London
August 2008

ABBREVIATIONS

BOI	O'Donovan and Lockwood O'Donovan, *Bonds of Imperfection*
BVLJ	McIlroy, *A Biblical View of Law and Justice*
CD	Barth, *Church Dogmatics*
CG	Moltmann, *The Crucified God*
CJF	Moltmann, *Creating A Just Future*
Comp. Theol.	Aquinas, *Compendium Theologiae*
CPS	Moltmann, *The Church in the Power of the Spirit*
De Potentia	Aquinas, *Quaestiones disputatae de potentia*
De Regno	Aquinas, *On Kingship – To the King of Cyprus*
De Veritate	Aquinas, *Quaestiones disputatae de veritate*
DON	O'Donovan, *Desire of the Nations*
EH	Moltmann, *The Experiment Hope*
Future	Moltmann, *The Future of Creation*
GIC	Moltmann, *God In Creation*
GSS	Moltmann, *God for a Secular Society*
IG	O'Donovan and Lockwood O'Donovan, *From Irenaeus to Grotius*
In Heb.	Aquinas, *Super Epistolam ad Hebraeos*
In Ioan.	Aquinas, *Super Evangelium S. Ioannis Lectura*
In Matt.	Aquinas, *Super Evangelium S. Matthaei Lectura*
JWR	O'Donovan, *The Just War Revisited*
On Job	Aquinas, *The Literal Exposition on Job*
Problem	O'Donovan, *The Problem of Self-Love in St. Augustine*
RMO	O'Donovan, *Resurrection and Moral Order*
RP	Bartholomew et al., eds., *A Royal Priesthood?*
RPS	Moltmann et al., eds., *Religion and Political Society*
ScG	Aquinas, *Summa contra Gentiles*
Sent.	Aquinas, *Scriptum super libros sententiarum Magistri Petri Lombardi*
SL	Moltmann, *The Spirit of Life*
Source	Moltmann, *The Source of Life*
ST	Aquinas, *Summa Theologiae*
TKG	Moltmann, *The Trinity and the Kingdom of God*
TOH	Moltmann, *Theology of Hope*

WJC   Moltmann, *The Way of Jesus Christ*
WOJ   O'Donovan, *The Ways of Judgment*

CHAPTER I

The Necessity of a Trinitarian Theology of Law

Introduction

Joan Lockwood O'Donovan opens her *Theology of Law and Authority in the English Reformation* with the dramatic claim that 'From a theological perspective, it is arguable that all public disagreement is about authority and law, divine and human, whatever may be the ostensible issues.'[1] If this is correct, then adopting a proper theological approach to the question of law is of fundamental importance.

In the latter half of the twentieth century and beyond, Barth's claim that the Trinity must be the starting point for Christian theology has won wide acceptance. Gunton has argued that the doctrine of the Trinity has decisive implications for every sphere of life.[2] The present thesis seeks to explore the implications of the doctrine of the Trinity for a theology of law.

However, if there is a consensus about the importance of the doctrine of the Trinity for all areas of theology, there is disagreement about what that doctrine of the Trinity should look like. Contemporary theology has three different models of the Trinity from which to choose: there is a 'Western' model, which emphasises that God is a single subject. This is the Barthian model, defended by Paul S. Molnar.[3] It is also the model of those Thomists such as Emery and Levering who assert that Aquinas is a trinitarian theologian.[4] There is an 'Eastern' model, which emphasises that the triune God is three persons in perfect communion. This model has supporters in the West such as Gunton and T.F. Torrance.[5] Thirdly, there is the model of a social Trinity, which differs

---

[1] J. Lockwood O'Donovan, *Theology of Law and Authority in the English Reformation* (Atlanta, GA: Scholars Press, 1991) 1.
[2] C.E. Gunton, *The Promise of Trinitarian Theology* (Edinburgh: T&T Clark, 1991) 12.
[3] P.D. Molnar, *Divine Freedom and the Doctrine of the Immanent Trinity: In Dialogue with Karl Barth and Contemporary Theology* (Edinburgh: T & T Clark, 2002).
[4] G. Emery, *Trinity in Aquinas Trinity in Aquinas* (Ypsilanti, Michigan: Sapientia Press, 2003)165-208; M. Levering, *Scripture and Metaphysics: Aquinas and the Renewal of Trinitarian Theology* (Oxford: Blackwell, 2004) 228-34, especially footnote 108.
[5] Gunton, *Promise*, 38-42; T.F. Torrance, *Christian Doctrine of God: One Being, Three Persons* (Edinburgh: T&T Clark, 1996) 102-4.

from the Eastern model in that it lacks the *taxis* which is characteristic of the Eastern model. The social Trinity model is the model used by Moltmann and feminist theologians such as Catherine LaCugna.[6]

At the methodological stage of the inquiry, however, what is more important than the model of the Trinity being proposed is how that model is being deployed. At this point, there are two different strategies. The first, exemplified by Moltmann and LaCugna, is the programmatic use of a particular model of the Trinity from which there are direct correlations to tangible social conclusions. The second strategy is to reflect on the biblical narrative which reveals the Trinity and to reflect on the Trinity which illuminates the biblical narrative and so to situate present societies within that biblical narrative and in relation to the triune God. In schematic terms, the first strategy privileges the immanent Trinity as the resource for social theory; the second strategy privileges the economic Trinity.

The present study begins, in the next chapter, by considering the implications of Moltmann's social trinitarianism for a theology of law. It concludes that, notwithstanding the dialectic of cross and resurrection which is its ostensible starting point, Moltmann ends up abstracting from the biblical self-revelation of God in God's dealings with humankind.[7] The result is a strategy which privileges the immanent Trinity as the source for conclusions about human society and is prone to projectionism. The second strategy, which gives primary weight to the biblical narrative, is therefore preferable.

The third chapter therefore turns to the pre-eminent contemporary political theologian, Oliver O'Donovan, whose work has been commended for its careful attention to the biblical narrative. O'Donovan is significant for three reasons. First, for the way in which he seeks to shape his political theology in the light of the biblical revelation. Second, because he has acted self-consciously to revive the tradition of Western Christian political theology, and stands in a continuing line from Augustine. Third, because in his most recent book, he has announced that political theology has a trinitarian structure (*WOJ* 239).

Gunton's plea for trinitarian theology comes against a background of

---

[6] C. LaCugna, *God for Us: The Trinity and the Christian Life* (New York: Harper Collins, 1991).

[7] In the present study, the author has adopted the following convention. Although attempts have been made to minimise them, personal pronouns for God will not be avoided entirely. 'His' in capitalised form will be used, in an attempt to strike a balance between God's self-revelation as Father and Son on the one hand, and the recognition that the use of such pronouns with regard to God is not univocal but rather equivocal. The Spirit will also be referred to as 'His', not in order to imply any particular gender to the Spirit but rather to avoid the de-personalisation which inevitably results in the English language if the word 'Its' is employed instead. Within quotations, corrections have not been made to the use of pronouns for God nor to conform to current norms for gender-inclusive language.

accusation that theology in the West has suffered from a trinitarian deficit, ultimately attributable to Aquinas and Augustine.[8] The question to be put to O'Donovan is whether, despite his best intentions, his immersion in the Western tradition has left his own work insufficiently informed by God's self-revelation in the Bible as the triune God. The study concludes that there is an extent to which this is indeed the case, as O'Donovan has yet to offer a developed account of the Spirit's actions as preparations for the witness of the Church.

It therefore remains necessary to identify a theologian who prioritises the biblical narrative and the economic Trinity in his understanding of the role of human law in social relations. The fourth chapter contends that Aquinas is in fact such a theologian. This assertion is *prima facie* surprising, since Aquinas has typically been read, by both friend and foe, as prioritising the unity of God over the distinction between the Persons, with the result that the Trinity is nothing more than an appendix to his monotheism. This reading of Aquinas has, however, been decisively challenged by Thomists such as Gilles Emery in Switzerland and Matthew Levering in America. For Levering, Aquinas takes the Trinity seriously and the doctrine shapes his account of salvation. Building on these readings, the present thesis contends that Aquinas' account of the roles of natural law and human law has been fundamentally misread, precisely because the importance of the Holy Spirit as the agent of the New Law has been ignored or excised from his thought.

In the fifth chapter, it will be argued that Aquinas's account can be built on, integrating the best insights of Moltmann and O'Donovan, to offer an account of human law as a means through which the triune God graciously works by the Holy Spirit, for limited but important purposes, preserving a relative justice and peace, leaving space for people to respond to the Son, in accordance with the will of and to the glory of God the Father.

In the fifth chapter also, the place of human law is established by considering the category of law in relation to creation, the Fall, providence, the incarnation, crucifixion, resurrection, the giving of the Spirit and the *eschaton*. These themes are explored from an Irenaean perspective, drawing out in relation to them the work of the Son and the Spirit as the two hands of the Father.

Law is understood to be a created reality but human law as we now know it differs from the divine command in that it is a temporary ordinance given for the time of humanity's rebellion against God. Human law can only point to but not attain the original good order of creation or the *shalom* of the eternal city.

---

[8] For K. Rahner, the culprit is Aquinas: *The Trinity* (London: Burns and Oates, 1970) 17; although Gunton in his early work was of the same opinion, he later came to regard Augustine as primarily responsible for the West's problems with the doctrine: 'Augustine, the Trinity and the Theological Crisis of the West', *Scottish Journal of Theology* 43 (1990) 33-58.

That human law is even able to point towards these realities is due to the grace of the Holy Spirit, understood as the Spirit's action in all places and at all times in human history. This grace is to be found both in the Spirit's involvement in the ordering of human societies and also in enabling what is termed 'shallow justice' to be done. 'Shallow justice' is that limited form of justice, concerned with temporal goods and external actions, which human rulers may enact, to however limited and imperfect a degree. In this pneumatologically oriented account of an aspect of divine providence, what is affirmed is necessarily affirmed by faith rather than being perspicacious.

Christ is presented as the eternal law incarnate, the one who claimed authority over the Torah and who fulfilled it in all its aspects. The one who embodied God's definitive appeal to the world was crucified by human rulers in a reiteration of humanity's choice to reject God. Thus, Jesus identifies with all the victims of the injustice of earthly regimes, whilst demonstrating through His resurrection that such regimes will not have the last word.

The Torah must not only be related to Christ but also to the Spirit. Following Aquinas, and the account given in my book *BVLJ*, it is argued that the historical books from Joshua to 2 Kings tell a story about the repetitive rejection by God's people of God's lordship over them and of the inveteracy of human sinfulness. This, it is argued, is the context in which Jeremiah and Ezekiel prophesied about the need for God to write God's laws on the hearts of God's people.

The Holy Spirit is the fulfilment of those prophecies, the one through whom 'deep justice' is effected, as human beings are transformed through the Spirit's work of sanctification, into Christ-likeness. The efficacy of the internal law given by the Spirit is thus contrasted with the inadequacy of external human laws, even if God-given. This work of sanctification is presented as a solution to the problem of alienation from authority, and is understood to culminate in glorification, in the perfect conformity of human beings to Christ through the power of the Spirit who brings them into perfect communion with the Father in eternity.

Finally, the Last Judgment is understood to relativise all human judgment by demonstrating its provisionality; to urge human judges to temper their judgments with mercy; and thus to enable them to perform a limited task conscientiously.

Overall, the superiority and finality of the work of the Son and the Spirit bounds the role of human law. Human law does not possess the necessary tools to be redemptive, but should be informed by the fact that God has acted to redeem humanity. In particular, it is argued that the triune God who is free to love seeks to enter into a relationship of love with human beings, who therefore cannot be coerced into such a relationship through laws which compel them to attend Christian rituals. What is given to human law to do is to restrain evil and, by so doing, in some sense to anticipate the justice which the triune God has enacted through the cross and resurrection and will enact finally in the Last

Judgment.

Human law is therefore ordered to justice, albeit 'shallow justice', and those involved in its administration are accountable to God when it is misused for other purposes. It is by grace that, in the performance of its limited tasks, human law is used providentially to witness indirectly to the justice of God in Christ and to prepare a space for the direct witness of the Church to Christ.

What is offered is not an account of human law as a self-sustaining institution, but rather one which affirms that human legal systems are simultaneously under the judgment of God in so far as they fall short in their pursuit of 'shallow justice' and are sustained by the grace of God in so far as God uses them to preserve human societies. Human law is therefore overshadowed by the work of the Son, included in the purposes of the Father, and used as an instrument by the Holy Spirit.

Finally, in a brief concluding chapter, the possibilities for future work building on this thesis will be identified and sketched.

Before turning to the substantive consideration of the three thinkers identified, it is necessary, however, to define the debate. This must be done in three respects. First, the usage of 'law' for the purposes of this thesis must be defined. Second, more must be said about the way in which doctrines of the Trinity are derived and deployed in contemporary theology. Third, there must be reference to the tradition of Western political theology, in order that the intellectual context for the thought of Moltmann, O'Donovan and Aquinas may be understood.

Law

The Idea of Law in Theology

The word 'Law' is used in Christian theology in relation to Grace and Gospel. Its meaning in this context is the commands of God or the demands of God. It is also used, either with or without a capital L, to mean the *Torah*, the Law of Moses, as in 'the Law and the Prophets', and sometimes as a summarising expression for the Old Testament as a whole. Without capitalisation, the word 'law' is used to mean human law, what O'Donovan describes as 'positive community law'. [9] The phrase 'moral law' refers to Christian moral teaching, understood as law because it corresponds to the commands of God.

Recently Bernard Jackson, Joseph Blenkinsopp, C.J.H. Wright and others have done work which argues that the Torah was not intended primarily as a law code for implementation by the courts but rather as a guidebook, meditation upon which would lead the people of Israel to lead righteous lives. [10]

---

[9] O'Donovan, *RMO*, 155.

[10] B.S. Jackson, '"Law" and "Justice" in the Bible', *Journal of Jewish Studies* 49 (1998) 218-29; J. Blenkinsopp, *Wisdom and Law in the Old Testament: The Ordering of Life in Israel and Early Judaism*, revd. edn. (Oxford: OUP, 1995) 84-87, 92-93, 118; C.J.H.

This provides the background for the Christian usage of the term 'law' in the New Testament and beyond. In the light of this work, two significant and related advances are made. First, legalism is seen to be a misunderstanding of Torah rather than an inevitable outcome of Torah. Second, Christian ethics, with their emphasis on character and virtue as well as right actions, are shown to be in continuity with rather than in opposition to Old Testament ethics.

Beyond the general distinctions between the Torah, human law and moral law, each of the writers under consideration refers to law from a particular perspective. When Moltmann talks of law, he means legalism or retributive justice, both of which he sees as oppressive powers over against human beings. For O'Donovan, although he draws careful distinctions between moral law, positive community law, and the *Torah*, in his political theology human law is generally seen through the lens of politics and sometimes appears somewhat in the far distance.

For Aquinas, 'law' is a category made up of a number of realities which have analogous characteristics. He distinguishes between the eternal law, the natural law, the divine law, and human law. Eternal law is, in the final analysis, nothing other than God, the One who is fully Act, acting in the world God has created to bring it to the good end God has purposed for it. Natural law is what human beings understand of the purpose for which they were made, as related to the natural goods given in creation. Divine Law is subdivided into the Old Law and the New Law. The Old Law is the *Torah*. The New Law is the grace of the Holy Spirit. Finally, human law is the equivalent of O'Donovan's positive community law.

The focus of the present thesis is on human law, but accounting for the proper role of human law in the light of the Trinity necessarily involves discussion of the other types of law identified. It will be contended that law, as a category, is more fundamental than human politics, but that human law is a function of human rule necessitated by humankind's rejection of God's rule and defiance of God's laws.

The Relationship between Law and Morality in Philosophy and Theology

The status of human law has been considerably debated over the past 150 years by legal philosophers. The legal positivists have asserted that human law is nothing more or less than that which is declared to be law by those that have the power to do so. In Austin's account, law is simply the commands of the sovereign. This voluntarist explanation is plausible enough with regard to legislation, but has been derailed by the brute facts of Nazism. Its horrors necessitated the reiteration that human legislators are not free to legislate

Wright, *Living as the People of God: The Relevance of Old Testament Ethics* (Carlisle: Paternoster, 1990) 113; *Walking in the Ways of the Lord: The Ethical Authority of the Old Testament* (Leicester: Apollos, 1995) 104; McIlroy, *BVLJ*, 50-51.

whatever they will, but are answerable to some higher, more fundamental, laws. International law has been asserted as giving rise to legal obligations, based on the assumptions of civilization, the customary practices of nations and Treaty obligations. Human rights have been 'declared' in international conventions and made directly enforceable in national legal systems. Some Christian theologians have embraced human rights, whilst others have been cautious, if not sceptical, of this 'religion without God'.[11] An alternative strategy, though not necessarily incompatible with a commitment to human rights, has taken shape in the New Natural Law, of Grisez,[12] Finnis[13] and George.[14] This is a revival of the Thomist tradition, but at a high level of abstraction, in which the self-evident truths on which the ethical superstructure is constructed are vaguely defined.[15]

That which is implausible in the natural law case is the assertion that bad laws are no laws.[16] That which is implausible in the positivist case is the assertion that positive laws have nothing necessarily to do with morality. This aspect of the positivist case fails on two grounds. Firstly, it fails on the ground, advanced by Tony Honoré, that it is inherent to the nature of law that it incorporates the claim not only that obedience to it is morally justified, but that it is itself 'morally in order.'[17] For a command to qualify as law, implicit in the sovereign's 'Because I say so' is the assertion 'and I am right to say so'. Law therefore forms a category of publicly pronounced, enforceable moral rights and duties. Honoré argues that, in consequence, laws may be validly interpreted and challenged in accordance with certain moral values which are inherent in law such as fairness, equity, justice, honesty, humanity, dignity, prudence, and other similar values which 'conduce to co-operation and co-existence'.[18]

Secondly, the positivist case fails on the ground that there is something about the rule of law, about the processes of the public promulgation and adjudication regarding human laws, which tends towards making them conducive to good laws and inimical to bad ones. The argument on this point

---

[11] J-M. Berthoud, *Une Réligion Sans Dieu: Les Droits de l'Homme contre l'Evangile* (Paris: Editions l'Age de l'Homme, 1993).

[12] G. Grisez, 'The First Principle of Practical Reason', *Natural Law Forum* 10 (1965) 168-96.

[13] J. Finnis, *Natural Law and Natural Rights* (Oxford: Clarendon, 1980); *The Fundamentals of Ethics* (Oxford: Clarendon, 1983).

[14] R.P. George, *In Defense of Natural Law* (Oxford: OUP, 1999).

[15] J.W. Montgomery, 'Why a Christian Philosophy of Law?' in P. Beaumont, ed., *Christian Perspectives on Human Rights and Legal Philosophy* (Carlisle: Paternoster, 1998), 84-85.

[16] T. Honoré, 'The Necessary Connection between Law and Morality', *Oxford Journal of Legal Studies* 22 (2002) 490.

[17] Honoré, 'The Necessary Connection', 490-91.

[18] Honoré, 'The Necessary Connection', 492, 494.

was begun by Lon Fuller[19] and H.L.A. Hart.[20] It has been continued by Matthew Kramer[21] and Nigel Simmonds.[22] Simmonds has convincingly demonstrated that although the discipline of the rule of law does not prevent many kinds of serious evil, it does restrain some.[23]

Both these points against legal positivism can be regarded in theological terms as evidence of the fact that law is ordered to justice. This ordering of law to justice is expressed in biblical terms in the concepts of *mishpat* and *tsedeq*.[24] O'Donovan prioritises *mishpat* because he, following Augustine, wants to distinguish absolutely between God's perfect justice and the inevitably prudential attempts of human rulers to maintain a tolerable restraint on socially intolerable evil. I prioritise *tsedeq* because, following Aquinas, I want to assert that the 'shallow justice' which human rulers are called to uphold is a relative good, and is really good in so far as it is commissioned by God who gracefully uses it to fulfil God's purposes.[25] As O'Donovan says, at *DON* 36, the conceptual distinction need not lead to a disagreement, provided the integration of *tsedeq* into the *mishpatim* is recognised. I have argued in *BVLJ* and elsewhere that *tsedeq* is most helpfully translated as justice, not because it is something other than righteousness, but because it is not personal moral rectitude divorced from a practical concern for social justice.[26]

John Warwick Montgomery argues that natural law and legal positivism have corresponding strengths and weaknesses. He draws from the Bible a legal philosophy which agrees with natural law that there is an ideal standard of judgment above human law, but asserts with legal positivism that 'all societal rules with the formal, official sanction of the body politic are law'.[27] On Montgomery's account, which is broadly Lutheran in this regard, disobedience to a human law is always an evil, although it may on occasions be a lesser evil.[28]

Jacques Ellul, who, following Barth, radically rejects the possibility of any

---

[19] L.L. Fuller, *The Morality of Law* revd. edn. (New Haven: Yale University Press, 1977).

[20] H.L.A. Hart, *The Concept of Law* 2nd edn. (Oxford: Clarendon Press, 1994).

[21] M.H. Kramer, *In Defense of Legal Positivism* (Oxford: OUP, 1999); 'On the Moral Status of the Rule of Law', *Cambridge Law Journal* 63 (2004) 65-97.

[22] N.E. Simmonds, *Central Issues in Jurisprudence: Justice, Law and Rights* 2nd edn. (London: Sweet & Maxwell, 2002); 'Straightforwardly False: The Collapse of Kramer's Positivism', *Cambridge Law Journal* 63 (2004) 98-131; *Law as a Moral Idea* (Oxford: OUP, 2007) chapter 3.

[23] D. Priel, 'Review of Matthew H. Kramer *Where Law and Morality Meet*', *Modern Law Review* (2006) 116-17.

[24] Jackson, '"Law" and "Justice" in the Bible', 219 footnote 4.

[25] McIlroy, *BVLJ*, 78-81, 132.

[26] McIlroy, *BVLJ*, 78-81; 'A Prophetic Vision of Justice', *Engage* 7 (2004) 4-5.

[27] J.W. Montgomery, 'Law and Justice', *Law & Justice* 120 (1994) 16.

[28] Montgomery, 'Law and Justice', 25.

stable God-given natural law for fear that this is taken to be the limit of human obligations, offers a different foundation for human law. On his account, 'The world is ... preserved not by man's action, but by God's mercy. ... [Human] Law is commissioned to make life possible for man and to organise society in such a way that God may maintain it.'[29] The validity of this essential point, however, need not result in denying that God, in God's mercy, has revealed the natural law as a means through which human societies may be sustained.

Montgomery offers an account of human law which relates it to judgment. Because human law is bound to reflect created values to some extent, it can act as a schoolmaster to lead people to Christ, as those who violate it come to see their own unrighteousness. Ellul, on the other hand, relates human law to God's grace. The existence of human law preserves a space within which people can respond to the gospel. Both the notes of human law as judgment and human law as grace have to be sounded in any adequate theology of human law.

The Derivation and the Role of the Trinity in Contemporary Theology

The Derivation of the Trinity in Contemporary Theology

The contemporary revival of interest in the Trinity has coincided with, or gone hand in hand with, depending on your point of view, an assault on the metaphysical construction of the doctrine of God.

In his efforts to provide a new point of departure for trinitarian theology, Colin Gunton made at least two major criticisms of Western theism, both of which he argued were the result of too much emphasis on Greek philosophy and too little attention to the nature of the trinitarian God revealed in salvation history.

The first of those criticisms is a dominant theme of his book *The Promise of Trinitarian Theology*, which he describes as a 'quest for ontology, an understanding of the kind of being that God is.'[30] He accuses Augustine of failing to understand the richness of the trinitarian insight of the Cappadocian Fathers[31] and of bequeathing to his successors in the West a theology in which the Trinity was seen as a problem rather than a solution, and as an appendix to the doctrine of the one God.[32] Instead of the Trinity and the interrelationships of Father, Son and Holy Spirit constituting the very being of God, the implication of Augustine's theology, argues Gunton, is that there is an underlying substratum behind the Trinitarian faces of God which represents the true, unknowable being of God.[33] Furthermore, in naming the Spirit Love and Gift, Augustine abstracts from the role of the Spirit revealed in Scripture, to the

---

[29] J. Ellul, *The Theological Foundation of Law* (London: SCM, 1961) 103-104.
[30] Gunton, *Promise*, vii.
[31] Gunton, *Promise*, 9-10, 38, 54, 74, 97
[32] Gunton, *Promise*, 3, 32, 163.
[33] Gunton, *Promise*, 3-4, 33, 36, 41-3, 53-4.

particular detriment of the eschatological dimension of the work of the Holy Spirit, an omission which Gunton describes as one of Augustine's worst legacies to the Western tradition.[34]

The second criticism is nascent in *The Promise of Trinitarian Theology*[35] but comes to fuller expression in Gunton's book *Act and Being*. It is that the Greek conclusions about the metaphysical attributes of God have taken priority in Christian theology over the characteristics of God revealed in the Bible. There are two consequences of this: one is an underemphasis on biblical categories without philosophical equivalents: thus the holiness and graciousness of God have been underplayed in the theological tradition.[36] Secondly, there has been a marked tendency to see God as a static being, not just a union of *hypostases* but also as in *stasis*.[37] Instead, building on his earlier emphasis on the interplay of the relationships within the Godhead,[38] Gunton argues for a dynamic vision of God,[39] with dramatic consequences for, amongst other things, the doctrine of impassibility.[40] In order to do justice to such a dynamic vision, as well as being understood as subsisting from eternity to eternity, the Trinity must be understood in the light of salvation history.[41]

This approach to the Trinity highlights another inadequacy in Augustine's thought which is its spiritualising tendencies, which leave the Trinity as an irrelevance to the material world.[42] It is this suspicion of matter, argues Gunton, which draws Augustine's 'attention away from the concrete historical events in which God is present to the world in the economy of creation and salvation'[43] and thereby paves the way for abstract philosophising about the nature of God.

---

[34] Gunton, *Promise*, 50; 'Augustine, the Trinity and the Theological Crisis of the West' 52-54.

[35] Gunton, *Promise*, 51.

[36] C.E. Gunton, *Act and Being* (London: SCM, 2002) 15, 34, 36, 67, 90, 93, 155.

[37] Gunton, *Promise*, 150; *Act and Being* at 101, where he quotes Barth with approval: '[W]e must not make any mistake: the pure *immobile* is – death.': *Church Dogmatics* (Edinburgh: T. & T. Clark, 1956-77) II/1, 494.

[38] Gunton, *Promise*, 9-10, 51

[39] Gunton, *Promise*, 73, 150; *Act and Being*, 16-8, 21, 34.

[40] Gunton, *Act and Being*, 23, 125-132. T. Weinandy offers the best defence of the doctrine of impassibility against contemporary attacks in *Does God Suffer?* (Edinburgh: T & T Clark, 2000).

[41] Gunton, *Promise*, 34, 39, 66. Also at 33, where Gunton discusses Rahner's insight in *The Trinity* 17 that 'It looks as if everything which matters for us in God has already been said in the treatise *On the One God*', with the consequence that 'salvation history comes to appear irrelevant to the doctrine of God.' This led to a tendency in Western theology to treat the Greek philosophers as having received revealed wisdom or made 'natural' discoveries about the nature of God which are at least of equal value to the Old Testament. This thesis is drawn out in *Act and Being* at 3, 76-93.

[42] Gunton, *Promise*, 35, 38.

[43] Gunton, *Promise*, 48.

Augustine is thereby held responsible for starting the trend which made the doctrine of the Trinity the subject of metaphysical speculation divorced from God's self-revelation in salvation history.

If Gunton is right in his criticisms, then the Trinity has been for far too long in Christian theology a doctrine with nowhere to go. It has been a theory lacking a *praxis*. Gunton contends that what Augustine bequeaths to the Western tradition is a view that: 'Because the differences between the [divine] persons become effectively redundant, they no longer bear upon the shape of thought about the realities of life in the world ... and a kind of monism results.'[44]

Against this neglect of the Trinity, Gunton uses the example of ecclesiology to demonstrate the possibilities for theological clarification resulting from a renewed attention to the doctrine. He contends that:

> the doctrine of the church ... is immediately illuminated if seen in the light of the Trinity. It is remarkable how often Paul, for example, uses the word *koinonia*, communion or community, when speaking of the church and its way of being in the world. The church is the human institution which is called in Christ and the Spirit to reflect or echo ... on earth the communion that God is eternally. The church is therefore called to be a being of persons-in-relation which receives its character as communion by virtue of its relation to God, and so is enabled to reflect something of that being in the world.

> But the doctrine of the Trinity is not restricted to the religious sphere, for if what is said about God is true the same kind of implications must be spelled out for other spheres of life also.[45]

With regard to political theology, if Gunton's observations are correct, then what one would expect to find is a tradition in which the Trinity is either not present; or to which only lip-service is paid whilst the driving forces are coming from elsewhere; or if present and weight-bearing, is denied transforming power because it is conceived of in static terms. Examination of the predominant Christian theopolitical tradition suggests that Gunton's contention is at least plausible, albeit not wholly validated. If Gunton is right, then a renewed attention to the Trinity will offer invaluable insights in this realm of Christian thought too.

Against this neglect of the Trinity, Jürgen Moltmann's social trinitarianism appears to adopt precisely the point of departure which Gunton would endorse. For Moltmann, 'Anyone who really talks of the Trinity talks of the cross of Jesus, and does not speculate in heavenly riddles.'[46] Moltmann, with characteristic exaggeration, goes so far as to claim: 'the doctrine of the Trinity

---

[44] Gunton, *Promise*, 59.
[45] Gunton, *Promise*, 12.
[46] Moltmann, *CG*, 213, 249.

... is nothing other than a shorter version of the passion narrative of Christ ... The content of the doctrine of the Trinity is the real cross of Christ himself.'[47] While this is an overstatement, the truth in Moltmann's point can be acknowledged if it is understood as a claim that the events from Gethsemane to Easter Sunday are the apogee of a series of divine actions which begin with the Incarnation and end with the *parousia*.[48] To alter the brackets, the passion can be seen as the crux (literally!) of a series of events which begins with the Holy Spirit coming upon Mary and ends with the Holy Spirit coming on Pentecost Sunday; or which begins with God the Father initiating the creation of the world and ends with Christ handing over the kingdom to God the Father so that God may be all in all (1 Cor. 15:24-28).

What Moltmann means, however, is that the crucifixion and resurrection are constitutive for God. It is not just that the cross and resurrection reveal who God is, it is that they affect and change who God is.

Even for those theologians who find such a suggestion unacceptable, however, there is a clear realisation that it is 'in the light of the Cross, the Resurrection, and the sending of the Holy Spirit at Pentecost, [that] we can see that God is inherently triune.'[49] Trinitarian theology has therefore been recalled to its origins, to a recognition that it is the Easter events which drove the Church to the doctrine of the Trinity.

If, however, the Trinity is supremely revealed in the Easter events, it also gives shape to and is shaped by the whole of salvation history. Dych says that 'The Trinity ... is the most comprehensive doctrine elaborated in the Christian tradition to express all the elements of the experience of God in salvation history'.[50] Letham similarly argues that

From its beginning in the eternal counsel of God to its completion at the eschaton, our salvation is rooted in the Trinity. The Father chose us in Christ before the foundation of the world, and to him is attributed the beginning of action. In the Incarnation, the Son takes human nature, lives, dies on the cross, is raised from the dead, ascends to the right hand of the Father, and will return to consummate our salvation. In turn, the Holy Spirit is sent at Pentecost to indwell and to pervade his people, to render us suitable for union and communion with God. Thus, the grand sweep of salvation follows a Trinitarian structure.[51]

The Christian doctrine of the Trinity has to be approached from the perspective

---

[47] Moltmann, *CG*, 254.

[48] J.E. Colwell, *Living the Christian Story: The Distinctiveness of Christian Ethics* (Edinburgh: T. & T. Clark, 2001) 91.

[49] R. Letham, *The Holy Trinity: In Scripture, History, Theology, and Worship* (Phillipsburg, N.J.: P&R, 2004) 69; J.E. Colwell, *Promise and Presence: An Exploration of Sacramental Theology* (Carlisle: Paternoster, 2005) 17.

[50] W. Dych, *Karl Rahner* (London: Continuum, 1992) 148.

[51] Letham, *The Holy Trinity*, 404-5.

of salvation history. Gunton follows W.J. Hill in seeing 'the doctrine of the Trinity as the articulation of the doctrine of God under the impact of the Christian scheme of salvation.'[52] The Trinity is always mysterious, arguably nonsensical, apart from that salvation history. Therefore, it will not do to interpret the Trinity apart from salvation history, nor is it possible to arrive at an authentically Christian view of salvation history without constantly understanding it in terms of the actions of the Trinitarian God.

Seeing the Trinity in the light of salvation history reveals grace and holiness to be fundamental attributes of God's character, manifest in all God's actions towards God's creation.[53] Understanding the Trinity as demanded by the course of salvation history, necessarily requires a reflection on the interaction between the Trinity and the other schema which have been used to view that history.

However, even trinitarianism conceived of in terms of salvation history can fail to reflect adequately the subtleties of the biblical revelation about the actions and being of God if like many theologians, including Barth according to Gunton, distinctions are drawn between the Trinity on the basis that creation is attributable to the Father, redemption to the Son, with the Spirit merely acting as the motive power for the Father's and the Son's action in the world; or alternatively, in terms of creation, redemption and sanctification, with each stage attributed to the sole action of a single Divine Person.[54] Such a separation out of the approach of God to the world risks opening the door to a Marcionite opposition between the Creator God of the Old Testament, exuding law and judgment, and the Redeemer God of the New Testament, exhibiting grace and goodness.[55]

Instead of separating out creation, redemption and sanctification, argues Gunton following Irenaeus, 'all three of those actions are attributed to the Father and mediated by both the Son and the Spirit. The Father is the one who creates, reconciles, sanctifies and the rest, but he does so in every case by the actions of his two hands.'[56]

If the intimate link between the Trinity and the Easter events has been re-established, this latter point, on the necessary relationship of the Trinity and the whole of salvation history is, as yet, an area in which contemporary theologians, perhaps inhibited by the divisions between the specialisms of biblical theology and systematic theology, have work to do.

With regard to the three theologians whose thought is being explored in the present thesis, Moltmann does attempt to relate Jesus to Israel's history but his

---

[52] Gunton, *Promise*, 27, 4, 10, 39, 48; W.J. Hill, *The Three-Personed God: The Trinity as a Mystery of Salvation* (Washington DC: Catholic University of America Press, 1982) 28, 274.
[53] Gunton, *Act and Being*, 117-121.
[54] Gunton, *Act and Being*, 139.
[55] O'Donovan and Lockwood O'Donovan, *IG*, 24.
[56] Gunton, *Act and Being*, 139.

ideas regarding the Spirit are not similarly anchored. O'Donovan pays close attention to the narrative of salvation history, but the Spirit appears to be the possession of the Church rather than vice versa. Despite the usual criticisms of him, Aquinas can be shown to have carefully related the Spirit and the Son to salvation history, recognising their roles in the creation, preservation and salvation of the world.

The Role of the Trinity in Contemporary Social Theology

The implications of the Trinity for human social life can be derived in one of two different ways. On the one hand, there is the model of God standing on one side and human beings on the other. That which is to be found on one side of the divide must be mirrored on the other side. On the other hand, significance may be drawn from the way in which the triune God invites human beings to participate in God's triune life. On this account, God the Holy Spirit seeks to transform human beings into the likeness of God the Son and to bring them into relationship with God the Father.[57]

Among political theologians, the first model tends to be associated with an emphasis on the immanent Trinity as determinative for political theology. The second model, by contrast, pays primary attention to the economic Trinity. Put crudely, the first approach treats the Trinity as an image to be appropriated, whereas the second regards it as a reality to which human beings are invited to respond.

The first approach carries with it two dangers. It carries with it the danger of modalism. If the relationship is always conceived of as being between God on the one hand and human beings on the other, then constant effort must be made to insist that the Divine Persons are of real importance in the nature of that relationship. Second, it carries with it the danger of projection.

This is the particular danger to which those who hold to a social vision of the Trinity are prey. The Trinity becomes an image to be appropriated. It will be argued in the second chapter that Moltmann deploys the Trinity as a vision to be wielded in pursuit of ideological goals. If the desired social outcome, predetermined in advance, is what is in fact driving the account of the Trinity, then Moltmann is caught by Milbank's accusation that all too often what passes for Christian social theology is nothing other than the baptism of pagan or heretical accounts.[58] Similar complaints can be made about LaCugna's approach to and use of the Trinity.

Kathryn Tanner objects that it is not possible simply to read off a given social order from a theological image. Describing God as king may lead to

---

[57] I am grateful to Tom Smail for pointing out that it is not necessary to adopt one approach exclusively.

[58] J. Milbank, *Theology & Social Theory: Beyond Secular Reason* (Oxford: Blackwell, 1990) 1-6.

making human kings into gods, or alternatively, to stripping them of their authority by reserving legitimate kingship to God alone. What Tanner sees happening is that contemporary political debates are incorporated into theological accounts of the Trinity and then the description of the Trinity so constructed is read back into desired social outcomes.[59] Contrary to the claims of Moltmann and others that the doctrine of the Trinity is conducive to respect for diversity and to non-authoritarian politics,[60] Tanner argues that one could just as easily conclude that the doctrine of the Trinity teaches the need for homogeneity and hierarchy in society.[61]

If, however, the Trinity is a reality we respond to, then this demands an attention to what the Trinity means for us. Therefore the focus is on the economic Trinity as revealed by the economy of salvation. Nonetheless, while a return to an emphasis on the economic Trinity in place of speculation regarding the immanent Trinity alleviates the problem of projection to some extent, reflections on Jesus' relationship with His Father could still be used to justify social models of hierarchy and paternalism.[62]

Reading off conclusions for human relations from particular accounts of the inner life of the Trinity is therefore problematic, and conservatives as well as radicals can be criticised in this regard. Tanner's conclusion is that 'trinitarianism can be every bit as dangerous as monotheism; everything depends on how that trinitarianism (or monotheism) is developed and applied.'[63]

Tanner argues that because our knowledge of the inner life of God is necessarily incomplete and because our, inevitably partial, descriptions of that inner life rely on conceptual analogies it is difficult to draw definite conclusions from such descriptions and therefore inevitably theologians end up importing the content of social and political prescriptions into the discussion rather than inferring it from the Trinity.[64] Human life as it presently is, is so different from the inner life of the Trinity that inferring conclusions about the shape of the former from speculation regarding the shape of the latter is a perilous exercise.[65]

A better approach, suggests Tanner, is one which seeks to understand the triune God not as someone on whom we are to model human relationships but rather as the One who invites us to participate in God's triune life.[66] The God

---

[59] K. Tanner, 'Trinity' in P. Scott and W.T. Cavanaugh, eds., *The Blackwell Companion to Political Theology* (Oxford: Blackwell, 2004) 319-332 at 320-21.

[60] Moltmann, *TKG*, 192-202.

[61] Tanner, 'Trinity', 322.

[62] Tanner, 'Trinity', 322-23.

[63] Tanner, 'Trinity', 323.

[64] Tanner, 'Trinity', 324-25.

[65] Tanner, 'Trinity', 325-27.

[66] Tanner, 'Trinity', 328-331; *Jesus, Humanity and the Trinity: A Brief Systematic Theology* (Edinburgh: T&T Clark, 2001) 1-95.

who reveals Godself in the economic Trinity joins us to Christ in the Spirit and thereby brings us to share in Jesus' own relations with the Father and the Spirit.[67] On this approach, 'Humans do not attain the heights of trinitarian relations by reproducing them, but by being incorporated into them as the very creatures they are.'[68]

This requires a doctrine of 'deification', the point of which is both to include us by the Spirit in Jesus' relationship to the Father, and also to insist that we are so included as mere humans *in Christ* and are never *interchangeable* with Christ.[69] The doctrine may be labelled *theosis*, deification, divinization, or glorification. Of course, not all versions of the doctrine are the same. The label that will generally be used in this thesis is that of glorification. This term is suitably apophatic and avoids the misunderstanding that Christianity gives us an eschatological expectation of becoming somehow autonomous gods. It also has the potential advantage of securing the truth that the eschatological glorification of humankind in fellowship with the triune God does not make us less human but, to the contrary, is a flowering of our full humanity.

It will be argued in the second chapter of this thesis that Tanner's criticisms of Moltmann's approach are well-founded and in the fourth chapter that Aquinas offers, through his doctrine of glorification, an account of human participation in the life of the triune God which is valuable for a theology of law because precisely this approach yields genuine theological insights for human life from the doctrine of the Trinity. In the third chapter it will be contended that O'Donovan's careful attention to the biblical economy would benefit from a greater focus on the persons of the triune God. The fifth chapter therefore seeks to build upon the reading of Aquinas proposed, whilst integrating the best insights of Moltmann and O'Donovan in order to offer an account of human law in the light of the actions of the triune God in the economy of salvation.

The Problem of the Trinity in the Western Theology of Law

For the present study to be worthwhile, however, there needs to be a certain plausibility about the contention that Western theology has not yet said everything that needs to be said about a theology of law in the light of the doctrine of the Trinity. For the purposes of the present study that could be established in one of two ways. An attempt could be made to demonstrate that the Western Church has habitually paid lip-service to the doctrine of the Trinity

---

[67] Tanner, 'Trinity', 328.

[68] Tanner, 'Trinity', 329.

[69] A.N. Williams, 'Deification in the *Summa Theologiae*: A Structural Interpretation of the *Prima Pars*', *The Thomist* 61 (1997) 221; Tanner, 'Trinity', 331; E.J. Rybarczyk, *Beyond Salvation: Eastern Orthodoxy and Classical Pentecostalism on Becoming Like Christ* (Carlisle: Paternoster, 2004) 97.

while allowing it no substantive role in its doctrine of God. Even sketching such a grand claim would require a thesis of its own.

A more circumspect claim would be that, even assuming that the Western Church has had an adequately trinitarian doctrine of God, that doctrine has not been sufficiently joined up with its thinking about human law.

In order to explore the truth of that more modest claim, it is appropriate to turn to the encyclopaedic digest of classical Christian political thought, O'Donovan and Lockwood O'Donovan's *From Irenaeus to Grotius*. One of the striking features of the selections in that volume is the relative absence of reflection on the Trinity. Some thinkers focus on God the Father as a paradigm for human authority; others take the Lordship of Christ as the key theme. There is a constant reference to the law of nature, and hence to God as Creator, and a considerable controversy over the impact of the redemptive actions of God in Christ, and who can properly claim to be heir to them – the Christian bishops/ bishop of Rome or the Christian kings/ emperor. But for few of the thinkers cited is the Trinity central to their reflections on politics and law. As is usual in the West, the person of the Trinity who disappears from view in consequence is the Holy Spirit.

In fact, the neglect of the Holy Spirit in political theology is to be found in both East and West, albeit with different causes. The absence is, in the West, part of the legacy of the way in which Augustine's conception of the Trinity was handled by the subsequent tradition. In the East, it is instead a consequence of caesaropapism, in which the mediating role of the Son and the Spirit is collapsed into the person of the emperor.

A further explanation for the failure of trinitarian thinking to make an impact on political theology can be found in the equation of secular power and ecclesiastical power which took place. While there might have been useful analogies to have been drawn between the two, the problem was that the ecclesiological conception of authority was not informed by trinitarian considerations, but instead modelled after the worldly pattern. Far from the Church consistently exhibiting a distinctive character as community, the Church too often took its lead from the world.[70]

The shape of the discussion in the Constantinian era was also dominated by the premise, the assumption, that the ruler was a Christian. The sense of the biblical texts having to deal with the reality of rulers who were not Christian and emperors who were, in terms of the claims they made, AntiChrist, was lost on many of the medieval interpreters. The contrast between the claims of Christ

---

[70] Gunton, *Promise*, 60-61. Both Barth and Yoder stress the importance of the church standing out as a counter-culture and seeing political change as the world follows its example: R.E. Hood, *Contemporary Political Orders and Christ: Karl Barth's Christology and Political Praxis* (Allison Park, PA: Pickwick, 1985) 175-77; J.H. Yoder, *Body Politics: Five Practices of the Christian Community before the Watching World* (Scottdale: Herald Press, 2001).

and the claims of Caesar was sometimes softened by the argument that Rome had had a divine destiny to conquer the world (cf. Eusebius of Caesarea);[71] or alternatively the claims of Christ were equated with those of the Pope, who asserted his primacy over the rights of the secular rulers.

Where the Trinity or particular persons of the Godhead do feature in Christian political theology, and either the Father or the Son appear regularly, theologians are guilty of purporting to derive direct and logical equivalences.[72]

The inaugurator of the sequence is Eusebius of Caesarea. For Eusebius, Jesus, the Word of God and the second person of the Trinity, is the bringer of the kingdom of God, the mediator of the kingship of God, who therefore facilitates and legitimates the exercise of kingship by humankind. Eusebius' political theology is christomonist in nature: the incarnate Christ is the only person of the Trinity who matters. The mantle of the incarnate Christ is then bestowed on the emperor who 'embodies at once God's kingship, as its "image" and man's.'[73] In his 'Speech for the Thirtieth Anniversary of Constantine's Accession', monotheism (in para.3) becomes practical christomonism (para.4).

The heavenly kingdom of the Divine Word is to be expressed by the similitude of an earthly kingdom (para.4), which Eusebius' theology has already declared in 'The Speech on the Dedication of the Holy Sepulchre Church' to be the divinely appointed function of the Roman Empire. All that remained was for the divinely chosen emperor to take his seat as the earthly simulacrum, and this role Constantine fulfilled perfectly in Eusebius' eyes.[74]

Christ then disappears from sight behind Constantine. In Eusebius' eulogy, Constantine is become the Platonic Philosopher-King. It is no longer Christ but Constantine who is the mediator on earth between God and humankind. He is the Lord's Anointed.[75] It is Constantine who is become the Second Adam, the Redeemed One who exercises the divine right to rule! He rules on earth after the manner of Jesus Christ who rules in heaven. As Duncan Forrester recognises, Eusebius effectively translated the pagan emperor cult into Christian terms.[76]

Eusebius offers a theology of the divine monarch in Christian garb. It is monarchical christology in which the king is God's Christ; or monarchical pneumatology in which the king is the man exhibiting in perfect fullness the

---

[71] Eusebius, 'A Speech on the Dedication of the Holy Sepulchre Church' in O'Donovan and Lockwood O'Donovan, *IG*, 58-9.

[72] A charge identified by Gunton with regard to ecclesiology in *Promise* at 72-4.

[73] O'Donovan and Lockwood O'Donovan, *IG*, 57.

[74] Tanner, 'Trinity', 322.

[75] O'Donovan and Lockwood O'Donovan, *IG*, 62.

[76] D.B. Forrester, *Christian Justice and Public Policy* (Cambridge: CUP, 1997) 21-3; N.G. Wright, *Power and Discipleship: Towards a Baptist Theology of the State* The Whitley Lecture 1996-97 (Oxford: Whitley, 1996) 8.

royal fruit of the Spirit, with the absolutising consequences which necessarily follow from such a claim.

These consequences are made plain in the writings of Agapetos (fl. 530), for whom the emperor stands in the place of Christ, mediating the presence of God to his subjects and representing his subjects to God.[77]

The danger with the Eastern view of the emperor as the God-man or the representative man-before-God is that although Christology provides its derivation, the conception outgrows its origins, enabling Christology to be discarded like the husk which contained the wheatgerm. This, write O'Donovan and Lockwood O'Donovan, is what in fact happened over the course of time.[78]

Western theology takes its starting point from Augustine. However, assessing either his trinitarian thought or his political thought is a complex affair. Gunton's criticisms of Augustine have already been noted earlier in this chapter. Letham considers that Augustine may himself be acquitted of many of the accusations levelled at him by Gunton.[79] 'However, Augustine's legacy is a different thing. Succeeding generations in the West would develop a powerful focus on the divine essence, driven by the psychological illustrations. Here Gunton's criticisms have weight.'[80] A similar view is taken by Bobrinskoy, whose view is that the psychological analogy of the Trinity was only illustrative for Augustine, but 'became a systematic criterion of later theological thought, with Anselm and in Thomism.'[81]

With regard to Augustine's political thought, interpretations have been manifold. Two contemporary political theologians lay serious claim to be his heirs. Oliver O'Donovan is one; John Milbank is the other. In Milbank's thought, his Augustinianism is combined with a highly metaphysical view of the Trinity and a Platonic view of reality.[82] The strengths and weaknesses of this approach must be discussed elsewhere. O'Donovan, on the other hand, anchors his theology concretely in the biblical narratives and his trinitarian theology is derived from there. For the reasons set out above, this is likely to be the more promising approach.

In the West, there are some echoes of the Eastern view in the position of the Norman Anonymous (fl. ca.1100). For the Norman Anonymous, the two

---

[77] O'Donovan and Lockwood O'Donovan, *IG*, 180-1.

[78] O'Donovan and Lockwood O'Donovan, *IG*, 236.

[79] B. Green mounts a similar defence of Augustine in 'The Proto-modern Augustine? Colin Gunton and the Failure of Augustine', *International Journal of Systematic Theology* 9 (2007) 328-41.

[80] Letham, *The Holy Trinity*, 198.

[81] B. Bobrinskoy, *The Mystery of the Trinity: Trinitarian Experience and Vision in the Biblical and Patristic Tradition* (Crestwood: N.Y.: St Vladimir's Seminary Press, 1999) 284.

[82] Milbank, *Theology & Social Theory*, 290; J.K.A. Smith, *Introducing Radical Orthodoxy: Mapping a Post-secular Theology* (Grand Rapids, Michigan: Baker Academic, 2004) 48.

natures of Christ – divine and human – are imaged on earth by king and priest respectively. The king therefore images Christ's divine majesty; the priest his suffering and self-sacrificing humanity.[83] This imaging is made possible because both kings and priests are anointed, and therefore receive the Holy Spirit.[84] Because Christ's kingship is from eternity and represents His equality with the Father, whereas His priesthood is in time and represents His submission to the Father, so the Norman Anonymous establishes that the king has divine jurisdiction even over ecclesiastical affairs. The division of Christ's two natures effected by the Norman Anonymous divides Christ's kingship from His servanthood, thus muting the radical demands of servant leadership which the Incarnation presents to the powers-that-be. Furthermore, the anointing of the Spirit is taken by the Norman Anonymous to mean that priests and kings become

> one with God and his Christ; they are Gods and Christs through the spirit of adoption. Through them Christ and the Holy Spirit speak; in them Christ has his representatives, and does his work; in them he sacrifices, reigns, and governs his people. Each of them, therefore, is Christ and God in the Spirit; each, in fulfilling his office, has the role and image of Christ and God, the priest Christ's priestly role and image, the king Christ's kingly role and image; the priest Christ's lower, human office and nature, the king Christ's higher, divine office and nature.[85]

Thus in the political theology of the Norman Anonymous, the explicit place given to the Holy Spirit merely reinforces the representation of God to people through their human leaders.

Western theology did not embrace the Norman Anonymous's high view of human leadership. Instead, it tended to follow John of Salisbury (1115-76) for whom it is the law not the office which is primary with regards to human rulers. For him, it is 'the law' which is 'a gift of God, the likeness of equity, the norm of justice, the image of the divine will, the custodian of security, the unity and confirmation of a people, the standard of duties, the excluder and exterminator of vices' (*Policraticus*, book 8.17).[86] There are echoes here both of creation and pneumatology. Although the king is likened to the Son of God, it is his obedience to the law rather than his divine majesty which is the point of imitation (*Policraticus*, book 4.6).[87]

There are further hints of trinitarian thought in John of Salisbury's famous discussion of tyranny. The tyrant is declared by John to be 'thrice guilty of "high treason"': against the public power received from God, against the commanding laws, and against the whole body of justice (*Policraticus*, book

---

[83] O'Donovan and Lockwood O'Donovan, *IG*, 250-51.
[84] O'Donovan and Lockwood O'Donovan, *IG*, 253.
[85] O'Donovan and Lockwood O'Donovan, *IG*, 255.
[86] O'Donovan and Lockwood O'Donovan, *IG*, 277.
[87] O'Donovan and Lockwood O'Donovan, *IG*, 277.

3.15).'[88] Is it overstraining that triad to find in it power given by God the Father, commanding laws given through the Word of God, and the spirit of justice?

With regard to Aquinas, Luther and Calvin, evaluating the tradition is difficult and any outline of the position is necessarily an impressionistic sketch. There is Aquinas on the one hand and Thomism on the other. There is Luther on the one hand and Lutheranism on the other. There is Calvin on the one hand and Calvinism on the other.

There is not space in this thesis to explore whether all three could be defended against the accusation Gunton makes against the Western tradition. Aquinas is the one in respect of whom that task will be attempted. However, the defence being advanced is a defence of Aquinas and not a defence of Thomism. Indeed, the defence can be regarded as another flank in the attack on Cajetan as a misinterpreter of Aquinas.[89] It may be that a similar defence could be proposed in respect of Luther or, perhaps more probably, in respect of Calvin. If successful, such enterprises would still leave untouched Barth's conclusion that Lutheranism led to an abdication of a critical stance vis-à-vis the State and in Calvinism political theology was determined by reference to a general providence or creator rather than specific attention to the triune God.[90]

Considerable further work would be required to prove beyond reasonable doubt the case that the tradition of Western political theology has not been sufficiently informed by the doctrine of the Trinity, but there seems to be a case to answer. Such a degree of plausibility is sufficient to justify an inquiry into the ways in which a Christian theology of law could re-engage with the Trinity approached from the perspective of salvation history.

Within the field of political theology, the present study seeks to explore the interrelationship between the doctrine of the Trinity and the theology of law to be found in the thought of Moltmann, O'Donovan and Aquinas. It starts with an enquiry into Moltmann's departures from the Western tradition, before returning to O'Donovan who stands self-consciously within the tradition, and then re-evaluating Aquinas who, it will be argued, the tradition has badly misunderstood. What will then be offered is a way forward, based on this re-reading of Aquinas but incorporating the best insights of Moltmann and O'Donovan.

---

[88] O'Donovan and Lockwood O'Donovan, *IG*, 279.

[89] The challenge to Cajetan was first raised by de Lubac and has been gathering pace since: F. Kerr, *After Aquinas: Versions of Thomism* (Oxford: Blackwell, 2002) 136; G. Hyman, *The Predicament of Postmodern Theology: Radical Orthodoxy or Nihilist Textualism?* (Louisville, Kentucky: Westminster John Knox Press, 2001) 32; J. Milbank, *The Word made Strange: Theology, Language, Culture* (Oxford: Blackwell, 1997) 44.

[90] K. Barth, *Church and State* (London: SCM, 1939) 30, 5. Separate attention would have to be given to the neo-Calvinist thought of Abraham Kuyper because of his book on the Holy Spirit and because of his development of the idea of common grace.

Chapter 2

The Social Trinitarianism of Jürgen Moltmann

Introduction

Moltmann's thought is wide-ranging and diffuse. Moltmann describes himself as an ecumenical theologian,[1] not just because of his involvement with the WCC, but because of his adoption of ideas from all parts of the Christian compass, Judaism and beyond.[2] While this renders his thought rich in suggestive possibility, there are obvious problems about the extent to which the different perspectives can be successfully integrated, and it risks, at worst, incoherence.[3] At times one feels with Moltmann that he has left no shibboleth unsaid, which makes discerning the operative lines of his thought difficult.

On the positive side, often one-sidedness or imbalance which appears from a consideration of one of his books will be corrected by a complementary emphasis in the next. Thus, the focus on the resurrection as an eschatological event in *Theology of Hope* is balanced by the focus on the cross as a present comfort in *The Crucified God*.[4] Each volume integrates new lines of thought, correcting imbalances or raising additional lines of enquiry, some of which are profitable and others merely speculative.[5]

Because of these characteristics of Moltmann's thought, it is not conducive to a clear understanding simply to rehearse his major works sequentially. Instead, different strands have to be teased out, so that the strengths and weaknesses of each can be considered, before finally the questions of synthesis or contradiction can be answered.

---

[1] A description he gives himself in *GSS* 161.
[2] R. Bauckham, *The Theology of Jürgen Moltmann* (Edinburgh: T&T Clark, 1995) 7.
[3] This is what A. Rasmussen found, writing in 1994: *The Church as Polis: From Political Theology to Theological Politics as Exemplified by Jürgen Moltmann and Stanley Hauerwas* (Lund: Lund University Press, 1994) 37, 89, 379. In 2004, D. Cosden described Moltmann's theology of work as 'at best confusing, and at worst contradictory': *A Theology of Work: Work and the New Creation* (Carlisle: Paternoster, 2004) 66.
[4] Bauckham, *The Theology of Jürgen Moltmann*, 1.
[5] Bauckham, *The Theology of Jürgen Moltmann*, 3.

On the face of it, there are three nodes to Moltmann's thought: cross, resurrection, *eschaton*. To put it more exactly, there are three events the significance of which he seeks to explore. His contention is that the Trinity is the necessary doctrinal corollary which makes sense of and gives shape to these events as and in the history of God.[6] At first sight the schema which seems appropriate is to think about the solidarity and messianism of the Son with regard to the cross, the power of the Spirit with regard to the resurrection, and the glorification and new creation of the Father with regard to the *eschaton*.

But in fact it is strongly arguable that, contrary to his protestations, Moltmann's later theology becomes increasingly dominated by a fourth node: creation, which is indwelt by the Holistic Spirit.[7] In *WJC*, it is the Spirit who is the motive power behind Jesus' life, teaching and death.[8] The suffering of the Son then becomes the quintessential demonstration of the solidarity of the Spirit with apparently godforsaken creation. It is the Spirit who is able to transform the future into what is to come, and so to vindicate the hopefulness of the early *Theology of Hope* which has been disappointed. Most significantly of all, in *Coming* it is clear that the *eschaton* is not just the consummation of the Father's kingdom and the perfection of the Son's sonship, but the coming to rest in creation of the Spirit who has always been hovering over the waters.[9]

There is no direct development of a theology of law in Moltmann's writings. Instead, his views on law have to be discerned in the light of his reflections on other matters. Among the topics to be considered are the implications of Moltmann's trinitarianism, his theology of power, his view of history and eschatology, and his political theology. With regard to Moltmann's political theology, the themes of solidarity, liberation and human rights merit separate attention. Only once these strands in his thought have been surveyed, can conclusions be reached about the ways in which Moltmann's trinitarianism influences his reflections on law as a human institution. It will be argued that Moltmann is highly equivocal about human law, which he sees as an institution continually tainted by its negative associations with power, but as potentially positive because of its orientation towards justice. However, it will also be claimed that in the final analysis the shape of Moltmann's trinitarianism is driven primarily by *a priori* commitments to particular outcomes with the result that his trinitarianism is determined by his views about the desired shape of human society rather than vice versa. Therefore, although Moltmann's reflections on justice contain valuable insights, his trinitarian model cannot be

---

[6] Moltmann, *TKG*, 95.

[7] Moltmann, *TKG*, 111; *GIC* 14; *Source* 114; Bauckham, *The Theology of Jürgen Moltmann*, 21-23. The seeds of this idea may perhaps be traced back to one of the essays in *Hope and Planning* (London: SCM, 1971) at 21-22.

[8] Moltmann, *WJC*, 73-94.

[9] Moltmann, *The Coming of God: Christian Eschatology* (London: SCM, 1996) xiii, 265-66, 317, 335; *WJC* 290.

adopted.

The Shape of Moltmann's Trinitarianism

Moltmann's doctrinal work has two principal targets: the doctrine of impassibility[10] and the Kantian view that the Trinity is an irrelevant doctrine because it is of no practical consequence.[11] The cross reveals the human, crucified God to be triune, and Moltmann's account of this requires the reformulation of both trinitarian theology and christology. His trinitarianism challenges the patriarchial monarchism which has dominated the Church's structure and thinking.[12] His christology seeks to replace the Pantocrator, the Christ enthroned in heaven,[13] with the poor, suffering, unprotected, crucified Christ.[14] It is precisely this crucified Christ whom Moltmann sees as having cosmic importance as the mediator of creation.[15]

In Moltmann's view, the Church arrived at the doctrine of the Trinity because it was bound to do so on the basis of the New Testament and the Gospels in particular, and within those Gospels, the events of the cross and the resurrection.[16] Moltmann argues that it is not a sovereign Lord God which is the datum Christian theology is called upon to interpret, but rather the history of Jesus, whom the New Testament reveals to be the Son of God the Father and through whom God the Father sends the Holy Spirit.[17]

Moltmann's own *theologia crucis* constantly emphasises that 'What happens on the cross manifests the relationships of Jesus, the Son, to the Father, and vice versa.'[18] The Christian Trinity is the Trinity of God the Son who suffered, died and was raised to life; of God the Father who gave up His Son to death and raised Him to new life; and of the Holy Spirit through whom the unity of the

---

[10] Moltmann, *TOH*, 140; *CG* 253; *TKG* 22; *In the End – the Beginning: The Life of Hope* (London: SCM, 2004) 70-71; Bauckham, *The Theology of Jürgen Moltmann*, 15; G. Müller-Fahrenholz, *The Kingdom and the Power: The Theology of Jürgen Moltmann* (London: SCM, 2000) 23.

[11] Moltmann, *TKG*, 6; see also *CG* 244 where Melanchthon and Schleiermacher are named as the villains of the piece.

[12] Moltmann, *CPS* 305; *Source* 100.

[13] For the implications of which, see Moltmann, *Coming*, 163-164.

[14] Moltmann, *CG*, 41.

[15] Moltmann, *TKG*, 102-4, 112; *GIC* 94-5.

[16] Moltmann, *TKG*, 16, 94; *WJC* 71, 74; *History and the Triune God* 70; Bauckham, *The Theology of Jürgen Moltmann*, 156, see also 166.

[17] Moltmann, *CG* 247, 249; *CPS* 209; *TKG* 64, 93; see Bauckham's "Preface" to *CG* xiii-xiv.

[18] Moltmann, *CG* 213, 249, 254; *EH* 81; Bauckham, *The Theology of Jürgen Moltmann*, 12, 15, 155; M. Douglas Meeks' foreword to *EH* xvi; Rasmussen, *The Church as Polis*, 180.

Father and Son was preserved in these passionate actions.[19]

In reflecting on the cross, Moltmann's primary question was: 'what does the cross of the Son of God mean for God himself?' (*Experiences* 305). His subsequent trinitarian enquiry has been into the history of God, which finds its centre in the Christ event, 'but whose horizons span the beginning and end of history' (*CPS* 209). His critics accuse him of historicising God.[20]

The way in which Moltmann orients his reflections means that even though Moltmann in *TKG* purports to focus on the economic Trinity, because his interest is on what is happening *to* God in the biblical economy, rather than focussing on what the Trinity in the economy is doing for human beings, the centre of his account is speculation about the inner life of God rather than on the relations of the triune God with humanity.[21] Moltmann's view is of 'the trinitarian God as three divine subjects in mutual loving relationship' who enter into 'a reciprocal relationship' with the world

> in which God in his love for the world not only affects the world but is also affected by it. ... The trinitarian history of God's relationship with the world is thus a real history for God as well as for the world: it is the history in which God includes the world within his own trinitarian relationships. All this Moltmann takes to be the meaning of the Christian claim that God is love.[22]

Bauckham identifies the 'concept of dynamic relationality' as the centrepiece of Moltmann's trinitarianism.[23] Molnar sees this as its controlling principle, jeopardising God's freedom.[24]

Moltmann's trinitarianism is a response to Kant's critique of pure reason which dismisses the Trinity as an unnecessary speculation because it is of no practical consequence. His social conception of the Trinity has, he contends, definite practical consequences not least of which is that it places God's power at the service of God's fatherly purposes rather than conceiving of God as fundamentally 'the Almighty' whose fatherhood is incidental instead of

---

[19] Moltmann, *History and the Triune* God, 78; *EH* 81; R.E. Otto, *The God of Hope: The Trinitarian Vision of Jürgen Moltmann* (Lanham, Maryland: University Press of America, 1991) 175.

[20] P.D. Molnar, 'Moltmann's Post-Modern Christology: A Review Discussion', *The Thomist* 56 (1992) 683.

[21] Tanner, 'Trinity', 328.

[22] Bauckham, *The Theology of Jürgen Moltmann*, 15, 'Jürgen Moltmann's *Trinity and the Kingdom of God* and the Question of Pluralism' in K. Vanhoozer, ed., *The Trinity in a Pluralistic Age* (Grand Rapids: Eerdmans, 1997) 157; Moltmann, *Future*, 93; *TKG* 19, 98.

[23] Bauckham, *The Theology of Jürgen Moltmann*, 15.

[24] Molnar, *Divine Freedom*, 232.

essential to God's character.[25] Moltmann consigns to the dustbin of history those forms of Christian thought about the Trinity which, in his view, owed their conception of God to Greek philosophy and natural theology.[26] Implicit in his condemnation of them is a recognition of the truth of Kant's criticism. Because the Trinity was annexed to a vision of God which had already been determined on other grounds, it was practically irrelevant. Unsurprisingly, given the foci of *TOH* and *CG,* it is the doctrines of eschatology and divine impassibility which Moltmann uses to make his case for a re-thinking of Christian trinitarianism.

In Moltmann's assessment the radical nature of the cross, the resurrection and the *eschaton* has been domesticated because God's expression (that is to say, revelation) of Godself in these events has been screened through a previously determined philosophical vision of God.[27] Whereas Greek philosophy insisted that God could not suffer because such vulnerability would detract from God's perfection, Moltmann insists that such invulnerability, such stony-heartedness is not a virtue but a vice. '[T]he one who cannot suffer cannot love either. So he is also a loveless being.'[28] Instead of the impassible deity of Greek philosophy, who enters into suffering only in the paradoxes of the two-natures christology of Jesus Christ, Moltmann thinks of God as suffering on the cross as God the Son, and as God the Father suffering the death of His Son.[29]

Moltmann also argues that Barth's trinitarianism did not go far enough, and that because Barth never really escaped the idea that God is a single subject possessing a unified lordship,[30] he developed nothing more than a trinitarian monarchy in which command-obedience is the fundamental expression of the relationship between God the Father and God the Son,[31] with the result that his thought remained supportive of authority, domination and hierarchy.[32]

By contrast, in Moltmann's own trinitarian thought there is a plurality of subjects in the Trinity; an inter-relationship between the persons of the Trinity,

---

[25] Moltmann, *GSS,* 98; *HTG* 7; *TKG* 35; *CJF* 33; Müller-Fahrenholz, *The Kingdom and the Power* 140, 145; Otto *the God of Hope* 179.

[26] Moltmann, *TKG,* 11-12.

[27] Moltmann, *CG,* 221; A. Clarke, *A Cry in the Darkness: The Forsakenness of Jesus in Scripture, Theology and Experience* (Oxford: Regent's Park College, 2002) 67, 76.

[28] Moltmann, *CG,* 229; *The Open Church: Invitation to a Messianic Lifestyle* (London: SCM, 1978) 16, 22-23; *Experiences of God* (London: SCM, 1980) 15; *Future* 93; *TKG* 37-38; *Jesus Christ for Today's World* (London: SCM, 1994) 44; Clarke, *A Cry in the Darkness,* 81, 89-91.

[29] Moltmann, *WJC,* 173.

[30] Moltmann, *Future,* 64; *TKG* 63,156; 'Gottesoffenbarung und Wahrheitsfrage' in E. Busch, ed., *Parrhesia: Karl Barth zum Achzigsten Geburtstag* (Zurich: EVZ, 1966) 158; Bauckham, *The Theology of Jürgen Moltmann,* 17.

[31] Moltmann, *TKG,* 140; *GIC* 258.

[32] Moltmann, *GIC,* 161-62.

whose fundamental nature is love.[33] Command and obedience are present at times as an expression of this love, but they are an expression of it rather than forming its basis, and in Moltmann's account are far from being its most important expression.[34] The Trinity is not in a fixed 'descending' order of Father, then Son, then Holy Spirit, but is in changing patterns of relationship with God's world. 'Behind and within these changing relationships is the enduring trinitarian fellowship, in which there is no subordination, only mutual love in freedom.'[35]

The concept of perichoresis is key to Moltmann's trinitarianism and to the way in which he extrapolates from the Trinity.[36] Perichoresis is one of the ideas he uses to avoid any hint of subordinationism in his doctrine of the Trinity.[37] Furthermore, in Moltmann's thought, 'the mutual relationships of the three Persons as a perichoretic, social Trinity are the context for understanding the reciprocal relationships of God and the world.'[38] Moltmann sees the perichoresis of the divine persons as 'the archetype of the community of human beings and all creation.'[39] Human beings in their sociality, in their community, are the image of the God who in God's triune nature is essentially social.[40] Moltmann contends that the reflection of his conception of the triune God is 'a community of women and men without privileges, a community of free and equal people, sisters and brothers.'[41]

Moltmann also seems to be grasping towards a perichoresis between the Church and the poor;[42] 'an expanded concept of the church' made up of 'the *manifest* church of believers and followers of Jesus, and the *latent* church of the poor and those who wait for Jesus' (*Experiences* 266). He also models his strong account of the interrelationship of human beings and nature on this idea of perichoresis.[43]

Most controversially of all, however, Moltmann sees God's relationship to

---

[33] Moltmann, *CG*, 256.

[34] Moltmann, *GiC*, 258.

[35] Bauckham, *The Theology of Jürgen Moltmann*, 16; *TKG* 94-95.

[36] Moltmann, *GSS*, 102; *TKG* 157.

[37] Moltmann, *TKG*, 178-79; *SL* 301-05; Müller-Fahrenholz, *The Kingdom and the Power*, 146.

[38] Bauckham, *The Theology of Jürgen Moltmann*, 6, 162; *TKG* 157, 160.

[39] Moltmann, *GiC*, 17; *WJC* 152.

[40] Moltmann, *CPS*, xix-xx; *GSS* 83; *TKG* xvi, 155; *GiC* 222-3, 241, 266; *SL* 11, 94, 160, 221.

[41] Moltmann, *Source*, 37.

[42] Moltmann, *EH*, 117; *The Open Church* 105; *SL* 245; *Future* 54; *CPS* 126, 127, 132; *Theology Today: Two Contributions towards making Theology Present* (London: SCM, 1988) 77; 'The Messiah in Christianity', *Concilium* 10 (1974) 159; *Experiences in Theology: Ways and Forms of Christian Theology* (London: SCM, 2000) 230-37; Bauckham, *The Theology of Jürgen Moltmann*, 14.

[43] Bauckham, *The Theology of Jürgen Moltmann*, 17-18.

God's creation as one of mutual indwelling, made possible by the fact that the world is both God's creation and is indwelt by God's Spirit.[44] 'God and creation are bound together in a process in which they are both reciprocally related, utterly correlative.'[45] Redemption is the perfection of this indwelling, the coming to rest of God in the new creation.[46] Müller-Fahrenholz says that in Moltmann's thought 'the Orthodox concept of perichoresis is given a panentheistic and process "loading", so that it becomes a basic structure of life generally.'[47]

The *eschaton* is therefore not only the point at which God will be all in all, but the new creation will see the birth of 'a community of peace in which all created beings are there for one another, with one another and in one another, and through the interchange of their energies [will] keep one another in life, for one another and together.'[48]

Moltmann argues for a vision of the Trinity which is outward looking. For Moltmann, 'God's being trinitarian means that he is open in love for the union of his creation with himself. In the missions of the Son and the Spirit God opens himself in seeking love and then in gathering love gathers creation into union with himself. His final unity is then one which includes the whole of his creation in an eschatological, trinitarian "panentheism".'[49] The danger inherent in his account of this is that it makes the Godhead dependent on creation.[50]

How does this view of the Trinity colour Moltmann's understanding of the role of the Persons of the Trinity?

The Revelation of God the Son

Moltmann insists that each of the three poles which reveal the Trinity – the cross, resurrection and the *eschaton* – has both saving significance and significance for God in Godself.[51] He is critical of Barth's crucicentrism,[52] in which everything of significance happens on the cross, and that what occurs subsequently in the resurrection and the *eschaton* is merely the revelation, the

---

[44] Moltmann, *Future*, 91; *TKG* 96; *GIC* xii, 10, 98, 150, 258; *SL* 77.

[45] Letham, *The Holy Trinity*, 301.

[46] Moltmann, *TKG*, 104-5, 109; *WJC* 302; *Coming* xiii, 266, 280, 290, 317; Bauckham, *The Theology of Jürgen Moltmann*, 18; Otto, *The God of Hope*, 194.

[47] Müller-Fahrenholz, *The Kingdom and the Power*, 147.

[48] Moltmann, *WJC*, 255; *Coming* 307.

[49] Bauckham, *The Theology of Jürgen Moltmann*, 158, 162; *SL* 218-19, 234, 294-95.

[50] S.R. Holmes, *Listening to the Past: The Place of Tradition in Theology* (Carlisle: Paternoster, 2002) 103-104; Letham, *The Holy Trinity*, 301.

[51] Generally, see Moltmann, *CPS*, 62; *TKG* 45, with regard to particular aspects, see *CG* 264; *TKG* 83, 88; *History and the Triune God* 82-84; *SL* 149.

[52] Moltmann, *WJC*, 230-2.

bringing to light of what had already occurred but was hidden.[53] Instead he insists that something new happens in the resurrection (*Experiences* 107) and there is further newness to come in the *eschaton*, the newness of fulfilment.[54] '[T]he promises about Jesus have been 'confirmed and validated, but not yet fulfilled. ... the Christian hope expects from the future of Christ not only unveiling, but also final fulfilment.'[55]

Pending that fulfilment, 'we ... have to say that the identity of Jesus can be understood only as an identity *in,* but not above and beyond, cross and resurrection – that is, that it must remain bound up with the dialectic of cross and resurrection.'[56] This dialectical identity of Christ, an identity constituted by the contradiction of the cross and the resurrection, 'will find its resolving synthesis only in the *eschaton* of all things.'[57] It takes trinitarian form because the exalted Son of God who is seated at the right hand of God the Father is the crucified Christ, who was raised by God the Father through the God the Holy Spirit.[58]

The Place of the Holy Spirit within the Trinity

Moltmann regards the Augustinian idea of the Holy Spirit as the *vinculum amoris* between the Father and the Son, both as turning the Trinity in on itself and as dissolving the personality of the Holy Spirit.[59] For Moltmann, it is the Spirit, who is sent, who opens the trinitarian history of God 'to the world, ... to men and women, and ... to the future.'[60] It is also the Spirit, he contends, who makes the efficacy of Christ universally relevant.

Whereas, as shall be seen in the next chapter, there is a tendency in O'Donovan to present the Spirit exclusively as the agent of the Son, for Moltmann their interrelationship is more dynamic.[61] In his use of motherly

---

[53] Moltmann, *WJC,* 231; *SL* 150-51; in *SL* at 81 he describes this as a failing of Protestantism generally.

[54] Moltmann, *WJC,* 319.

[55] Moltmann, *TOH,* 228, 206; *WJC* 304; Otto, *The God of Hope,* 67-69.

[56] Moltmann, *TOH,* 200; *WJC* 214; Bauckham, *The Theology of Jürgen Moltmann,* 33, 100.

[57] Moltmann, *TOH,* 201; R. Bauckham, 'Moltmann's Eschatology of the Cross', *Scottish Journal of Theology* 30 (1977) 302-3.

[58] Moltmann, *History and the Triune God: Contributions to Trinitarian Theology* (London: SCM, 1991) 80.

[59] Moltmann, *TKG,* 142-43; *CPS* 55; *Experiences in Theology* 317; Bauckham, *The Theology of Jürgen Moltmann,* 154.

[60] Moltmann, *TKG,* 90; *SL* 289; *Source* 91.

[61] 'The history of Christ and the history of the Holy Spirit are so interwoven that a pneumatic christology leads with inner cogency to a christological pneumatology.': *CPS* 236. See also *CPS* 388, footnote 22 to chapter 5.

language about the Holy Spirit,[62] his Spirit-christology,[63] and his mention of Zinzendorf's image of the holy family,[64] Moltmann can even speak of the Holy Spirit as the divine mother of Christ.[65]

The Spirit is, for Moltmann, the Spirit of creation and the Spirit of the resurrection.[66] It is the cosmic Spirit who brings about, sustains and gives direction to 'the reciprocal relationships of life'.[67] The Spirit is also the unseen motor of the history of liberation in the world. The Spirit creates the future from the future. As the Spirit of futurity, 'The Spirit subjects man to the tendency of the things which are latent in the resurrection of Jesus and which are the intended goal of the future of the risen Lord.'[68] However, the charge of one-sidedness must be laid against Moltmann. To accuse Moltmann of having a deficient pneumatology may seem a strange accusation to put to one who has gone beyond a subordinationist understanding of the Holy Spirit within the Trinity[69] and who claims at least to be attempting to avoid falling into the trap of detaching the Holy Spirit from the Son.[70] Nonetheless, one of the surprising things about Moltmann's pneumatology, given the way in which he develops his christology, is the limited extent to which Moltmann explores its roots in Jewish messianic expectation. Whereas he is rightly insistent on the connection between Jewish messianic hope and Jesus Christ,[71] his Old Testament references to the Spirit are to the *ruach* of God seen in the context of creation or the psalms.[72] The connection of the Spirit of God with the law and with righteousness and holiness, to be found in the link between wisdom and Torah, and most notably in the new covenant prophecies of Jeremiah and Ezekiel are notable by their *almost* total absence from Moltmann's pneumatology.[73]

---

[62] Moltmann, *History and the Triune God*, 64-5; *SL* 157-60, 271, 286; *Source* 27; 'The Fellowship of the Holy Spirit – Trinitarian Pneumatology', *Scottish Journal of Theology* 37 (1984) 294-96; Bauckham, *The Theology of Jürgen Moltmann*, 169-70.

[63] Moltmann, *CPS*, 36; *WJC* 74; *SL* 58; *Source* 15; Bauckham, *The Theology of Jürgen Moltmann*, 20.

[64] Moltmann, *SL*, 159; *Source* 36; *Experiences in Theology* 291.

[65] Moltmann, *WJC*, 83-84.

[66] Moltmann, *GIC*, 67, 270; *WJC* 264; *SL* 7-8, 35, 94-5; K. Barth, *Letters 1961-1968* (Grand Rapids, Eerdmans, 1981) 348.

[67] Moltmann, *CJF*, 57-61; Letham, *The Holy Trinity*, 302; Molnar, 'Moltmann's Post-Modern Christology', 692.

[68] Moltmann, *TOH*, 212, 223; Bauckham, *The Theology of Jürgen Moltmann*, 152; Otto, *The God of Hope*, 190-93.

[69] Moltmann, *SL*, 71; Bauckham, *The Theology of Jürgen Moltmann*, 6, 158-59.

[70] Moltmann, *SL*, 230-36.

[71] Moltmann, *TOH*, 141, 148-49; *On Human Dignity: Political Theology and Ethics* (London: SCM, 1984) 101-102; *WJC* 321-5; Rasmussen, *The Church as Polis*, 68.

[72] Moltmann, *SL*, 40-47.

[73] The exceptions which prove the rule are *SL* 45-46, 55-57 and an undeveloped reference in *In the End* 44.

In his emphasis on the Spirit indwelling creation, Moltmann draws such a close connection between creation and the new creation that he confuses the gift and the giver.[74] In consequence of this perichoresis between the Spirit and creation, 'No reality or potentiality that was in creation at the beginning is suppressed by the Spirit.'[75] 'Moltmann so concentrates on God's involvement with his creation as virtually to make that involvement his whole being.'[76] The Spirit is thus seen as giving Himself when He gives human beings life, with the result that 'Moltmann fails to distinguish consistently the Holy Spirit from the human spirit ... and believes because "God is in all things, [and] ... all things are in God ... Every experience of a creation of the Spirit is hence also an experience of the Spirit itself.'[77]

Relying heavily on 1 Corinthians 15:20-28, which he uses frequently throughout his work, Moltmann sets out a vision of eschatological panentheism – the moment when God will finally be 'all in all'.[78] While there may be some scriptural warrant for speaking in such terms, his attempt to read some degree of panentheism back into the original creation is far more speculative. Moltmann loads so much of the Holy Spirit's work onto creation that nothing new happens at Pentecost other than the manifestation of that which was already present.[79]

Whereas, as will be seen in chapter 4, Aquinas offers an integrated account of how the work of Christ and of the Spirit fulfil the Torah, Moltmann's pneumatology is not connected with his reflections on the Torah. It is only in *WJC* rather than in *SL* that Moltmann reflects on the fact that 'the messianic era cannot be a time without the Law, but must be understood as the time of the Law's perfect fulfilment'[80] and observes that Paul's meaning in Romans 10:4 is

---

[74] Moltmann, *SL*, 47. The distinction was very carefully maintained by Irenaeus, *Against the Heresies* in A.C. Coxe, ed., *The Ante-Nicene Fathers vol. 1: the Apostolic Fathers with Justin Martyr and Irenaeus* (Buffalo, NY: Christian Lit. Publ. Co, 1887) 5.12.2.

[75] Moltmann, *CPS*, 191; *WJC* 239, 242.

[76] Bauckham, 'Moltmann's Eschatology of the Cross', 310.

[77] Molnar, *Divine Freedom*, 132.

[78] Moltmann, *TOH*, 88, 224; *Hope and Planning* 50; *CPS* 350; *EH* 40, 66, 83, 120; *Future* 94, 105, 116, 166; *History and the Triune God* 83; *TKG* 104-5; *GIC* 288; *WJC* 174, 193, 283, 319; *SL* 102, 212; *Coming* 240, 335; *GSS* 185; 'The Liberating Feast', *Concilium* 10 (1974) 80; *Experiences in Theology* 50, 100, 310-11, 316, 323; *In the End* 76, 150, 155; Bauckham, *The Theology of Jürgen Moltmann*, 162; Moltmann 'The World in God or God in the World? Response to Richard Bauckham' in R. Bauckham, ed., *God Will Be All in All: The Eschatology of Jürgen Moltmann* (Edinburgh: T&T Clark, 1999) 35-41.

[79] Moltmann, *GIC*, 68-69. The one place in Moltmann's writings where he appears to hold to the classical understanding that 'A different divine presence is revealed in the history of the Holy Spirit from the presence revealed in creation from the beginning' is in the minor work *Experiences of God* at 77, published in German in 1979.

[80] Moltmann, *WJC*, 123.

that 'Christ is the *goal* of the law *(telos)*' so that 'The unconditional love which is possible through Christ and in the power of the Holy Spirit is the fulfilment of the Torah, and the form in which the Torah is carried over and translated into the messianic era.'[81] Moltmann systematically fails to follow this insight through in his other writings.

The result is that the holiness of the Holy Spirit is underplayed, and that an entire strand of biblical thinking is missed. Other than at isolated points in *WJC*, Moltmann tends to think in terms of freedom from law, rather than empowerment for righteousness and understanding of righteousness (contra Gal. 5:13; James 1:25; 1 Peter 2:16). Moltmann chooses to call the Holy Spirit the Spirit of life instead, and the emphasis of his thought is on God's Spirit as the Source of life[82] and the Spirit of Wholeness, or the Holistic Spirit.[83] The subtitle for the German edition of *The Spirit of Life* is not 'A Universal Affirmation' as in the English edition, but 'A Holistic Pneumatology'.[84] For Moltmann, the Spirit gives Himself in the original creation, and in so doing, *already* grants to creation a share in the inner life of the Trinity itself.[85]

Whilst healing and wholeness is a legitimate aspect of the work of the Spirit of God, Moltmann's thought does appear to be imbalanced in this direction with insufficient emphasis given to the work of the Holy Spirit in sanctification and glorifying God through promoting God's holiness. Part of the reason for this is the narrowness of Moltmann's interpretation of 'sin'. Sin is, for Moltmann, quintessentially violence towards other human beings and nature rather than violation of God's commands.[86] This is symbolised by his location of the Fall in Cain's killing of Abel rather than Adam and Eve's eating of the forbidden fruit.[87] Moltmann's understanding of sin is also limited by the fact that he regards self-control as the tyranny of the soul over the body.[88] In *WJC* at

---

[81] Moltmann, *WJC*, 123.
[82] The title of his popular version of *SL*.
[83] Bauckham, *The Theology of Jürgen Moltmann*, 22.
[84] Moltmann, *SL*, xiii, 37; Müller-Fahrenholz, *The Kingdom and the Power*, 182.
[85] Moltmann, *TKG*, 113.
[86] Moltmann, *History and the Triune God*, 116-17; *On Human Dignity* 30-31; *WJC* 127, 254; *SL* 132, 139, 171-73; *Coming* 90-95, 210; *Experiences in Theology* 295-96; Molnar, 'Moltmann's Post-Modern Christology', 677. See also the critique of E. Shaw, 'Beyond Political Theology' in G.M. Bryan, ed., *Communities of Faith and Radical Discipleship* (Macon: Mercer University Press, 1986) 52, where he writes: 'The Achilles heel of Moltmann's political theology is his failure to understand the radical character of sin.'
[87] Moltmann, *The Power of the Powerless* (London: SCM, 1983) 8; *WJC* 127-9; *SL* 125-26; *CJF* 42; *Coming* 94.
[88] Moltmann, *CPS*, 277; *EH* 159; *The Open Church* 38; *CJF* 73-75, 79; *GIC* 253; *History and the Triune God* 93-94; *WJC* 265-6; *SL* 90-93, 95, 166, 172-73; *Source* 73-76. Rasmussen, *The Church as Polis*, 100, 103, 107. In *SL* at 176 Moltmann omits self-control from the list of the fruits of the Spirit!

184-5, Moltmann provides a different definition of sin, as 'the condition in which a person closes himself off from the source of life, from God',[89] but the missing dimension is the same. The result is that although Moltmann recognises that 'conditions won't change *unless people change*' it is ourselves primarily rather than the Spirit that he regards as the agent of that change.[90] In short, an account of sanctification is almost entirely missing from Moltmann's work. There is an isolated reference in *Experiences* at 49 to human fulfilment in terms of holiness and happiness. But this reflection in Thomist terms is not developed elsewhere in his writings. Indeed, on the following page, he looks forward to the eschatological 'perichoresis of God and the world', which depends, 'not on a growth in faith, or progress in the sanctification of the heart, but on a new real presence of God in the kingdom of his glory, which will succeed this kingdom of grace here.' By contrast, for Aquinas, eschatological glorification is precisely the consummation of the growth in faith and progress in sanctification which the grace of the Holy Spirit has been working in Christian hearts. Moltmann occasionally uses the language of participation and deification, but in his account it is a panentheistic perichoresis between God and all that God has made, rather than a specific gift of God to humanity.[91] His panentheism is inferior to the classical doctrine of deification both because too much is pre-loaded on to creation and because Moltmann does not offer an account of sanctification as the movement which culminates in glorification.

Bauckham identifies a different deficiency in Moltmann's doctrine of the Spirit. Contrary to his own intentions elsewhere, when Moltmann reflects on the place of the Spirit within the Trinity he often does so in relation to the Father and the Son in isolation from the Spirit's place in the work of God.[92] The problem is that this leaves him dangerously short of biblical material with which to work. As Bauckham points out, both the feminine and the impersonal language applied to the Spirit are used to characterise the Spirit's relation to ourselves.

---

[89] Moltmann, *WJC*, 184; *Future* 122; *In the End* 93. At *SL* 86-7, he refers to sin as rebellion against God, but again the context is the denial of life. M. Volf sees this view of sin as influenced by 'the Eastern tradition' and the priority which it gives to death over sin as problematic: 'After Moltmann: Reflections on the Future of Eschatology' in R. Bauckham, ed., *God Will Be All in All* (Edinburgh: T&T Clark, 1999) 249-51.

[90] Moltmann, *GSS*, 244; *History and the Triune God* 122; Rasmussen, *The Church as Polis*, 100.

[91] Moltmann, *Coming*, 272; *Experiences in Theology* 310-11, 323; *In the End* 145, 155-59

[92] Bauckham, *The Theology of Jürgen Moltmann*, 162-66. See Moltmann, *TKG*, 189, 199; *History and the Triune God* 60, 88-9; *SL* 12; 'The Fellowship of the Holy Spirit', 290-1; *GIC* 235-41.

The only way in which, from the resources of Scripture and tradition, we can conceive the Spirit's personal relation to the Father and the Son is by bringing *ourselves* into the picture: the Spirit inspires *our* relationship to the Father and the Son. We cannot stand outside the trinitarian fellowship and see it as a model for our own relationships. We can only enter it and experience the Spirit's relationship to the Father and the Son as our own relationship to the Father and the Son.[93]

Moltmann's failure to apply the method he used in relation to christology to his pneumatology has the same consequence as the failure to think about the mission of the Spirit in terms of fulfilment of Old Testament promises: it downplays the mission of the Spirit in making us the adopted children of God. Though Moltmann does mention this biblical theme (*GIC* 229; *Future* 89-90) he does not offer an account of righteousness understood as Christ-likeness which is the biblical concomitant of the idea of our adoption in Christ.

Bauckham argues that Moltmann's own theology contains the resources to remedy the failing he has identified.

The perichoretic unity of the Trinity is open to us and can include us because one of the three, the Spirit, relates to the Father and the Son in such a way as to be able to be our relationship to the Father and the Son. The Spirit *is* God's ability to be an open fellowship in which his creation can be included, just as the Son is God's ability to be incarnate as a human person.[94]

Re-thinking the relationship between human beings and the Spirit in this way, Bauckham argues that

the human fellowship which the Spirit, through his indwelling, creates cannot be an image of the Trinity as it is in itself apart from us, but ... is a participation in the Trinity's history with us. It is the fellowship of sisters and brothers of Jesus, who with Jesus know his Father in the Spirit – and also, Moltmann would add, of the friends of Jesus who share with Jesus his friendship with the Father in the Spirit. Only in this differentiated relationship with the Trinity can we in any sense "reflect" the Trinity. We do so as the Spirit conforms us to the image of the incarnate Son, in both his loving obedience to the Father and his loving openness to all people.[95]

Bauckham notes that his final point, about Jesus' loving openness to all people is made by Moltmann himself in *GIC* 242-3. Developing Moltmann's thought in this direction would bring him closer to Aquinas. However, as it stands, it is telling that Moltmann does not conceive of the Spirit's mission in conforming

---

[93] Bauckham, *The Theology of Jürgen Moltmann*, 163. For a related criticism, see Müller-Fahrenholz, *The Kingdom and the Power*, 196-99.
[94] Bauckham, *The Theology of Jürgen Moltmann*, 164.
[95] Bauckham, *The Theology of Jürgen Moltmann*, 164-5.

us to the pattern of the Son's loving obedience to the Father,[96] and of enormous significance in relation to Moltmann's views on law.

The Role of God the Father in Moltmann's Trinitarianism

One of the strengths of Moltmann's trinitarianism is that God the Father is not remote from or unmoved by the death of God the Son on the cross, but is passionately involved.[97] However, more generally within Moltmann's theology, it is easier to identify what Moltmann does not think is an appropriate understanding of the role of the Father within the Trinity rather than to find him offering a positive account of it. Moltmann is keen to emphasise the involvement of each member of the Trinity in creation in order to challenge the patriarchialism which attributes creation to God the Father alone,[98] and which makes of Him 'the Almighty, maker of heaven and earth',[99] whose omnipotence is primary and whose relationship to God the Son is secondary. The practical importance of this view of the Almighty which Moltmann challenges is that God's image on earth is the image of the one ruler, rather than the image of the community.[100]

In contrast, Moltmann argues that 'In this kingdom God is not the Lord; he is the merciful Father. In this kingdom there are no servants; there are only God's free children. In this kingdom what is required is not obedience and submission; it is love and free participation.'[101] The triune God is therefore the God of loving community not the paradigm of despotic sovereignty.[102] The difficulty is that the way in which Moltmann develops his account of the love of God and his insistence that God's *modus operandi* in the world is the representative suffering of the Son and the indwelling of the Holy Spirit leaves God dangerously devoid of sovereignty and tied to the world process.[103] Instead of simply abandoning the idea of God as 'Almighty', Moltmann might have

---

[96] At *History and the Triune God* 122, Moltmann says: '[w]e should look for the Spirit where human beings become autonomous agents of their own life and take the initiative for themselves.' Compare the views of Jonathan Edwards that human freedom comes from the abandonment of the impossible attempt to live as little gods and, through the Spirit, a total commitment to God: J. Edwards, 'A Divine and Supernatural Light ...' in *The Works of Jonathan Edwards* Vol.2 (Edinburgh: Banner of Truth, 1974) 12-17; Holmes, *Listening to the Past*, 106.

[97] Moltmann, *WJC*, 173; *Experiences in Theology* 304-5.

[98] Moltmann, *WJC*, 286, 311; *GSS* 102.

[99] Moltmann, *History and the Triune God*, 7.

[100] Moltmann, *GSS*, 122, 99; *Experiences in Theology* 292.

[101] Moltmann, *TKG*, 70; Rasmussen, *The Church as Polis*, 99-100.

[102] Moltmann, *GSS*, 101; *TKG* 197; *CPS* 103.

[103] G. Hunsinger, 'Review of Jürgen Moltmann *The Trinity and the Kingdom*', *The Thomist* 47 (1983) 136; Molnar, *Divine Freedom*, 216-225; Milbank, *The Word Made Strange*, 180.

done better to refashion the idea of God's sovereignty along more Nicene and biblical lines and lay stress not on God's absolute ability to do anything whatsoever but rather on the assurance that God's divine purposes will not be thwarted.[104]

Moltmann's Theology of Power

Moltmann's early work bristles with a palpable hostility to authority, one which Letham describes as 'almost pathological'.[105] Moltmann's concern is understandable, given that he grew up in Nazi Germany and was sent as a child-soldier to fight in a senseless war which was already lost. However, the need of the hour in the West may now be for a theology which treats authority as relatively good whilst denying absolutely its pretensions to ultimacy.

Although the *eschaton* will bring, in Moltmann's view, the abolition of power, in his two main cycles of writings he appears to vacillate between arguing that, in the present, the alternative to the deadly power structures of this world is the abolition or reduction of power *tout court* and contending there is, in Jesus, a different model for wielding the power that must necessarily be wielded.

Moltmann's trinitarianism also displays the same bifurcation with regard to his view of authority. He develops his hostility to power and authority through a particular account of the kingdom of the Son and the sovereignty of the Father. His reflections on the work of the Spirit, however, open a space for the conception of authority as an ordering force which may promote liberation and justice.

The Nature of Christ's Lordship and Rule

Moltmann sees the meeting between Jesus and Pilate as central to an understanding of the relationship between the Church and the State.[106] Moltmann interprets this encounter as the juxtaposition of two postures of power in this world: the machismo of Pilate and the servanthood of Jesus. It is the latter which unmasks and withdraws 'legitimation from tyranny in the name of its victims.'[107] Jesus reveals that the way of God in history is not the way of "the Almighty" 'who is always on the side of the big battalions'.[108]

In contrast to these tyrannies, 'Christ's lordship consists in his conquest of

---

[104] E.J. Bicknell, *A Theological Introduction to the Thirty-Nine Articles of the Church of England* 2nd edn. (London: Longmans, Green & Co., 1925, 1942) 205; Otto, *The God of Hope*, 145-46.

[105] Letham, *The Holy Trinity*, 311.

[106] Moltmann, *WJC*, 154, *CPS* 90; *CG* 142; *EH* 55; *RPS* 33.

[107] Moltmann, *GSS*, 57.

[108] Moltmann, *GSS*, 182; *RPS* 35; *TKG* 35.

enmity and violence and in the spread of reconciliation and harmonious, happily lived life.'[109] The kingdom he proclaims is 'the kingdom of fatherly and motherly compassion, not the kingdom of dominating majesty and slavish subjection.'[110]

In contrast to power politics, Jesus' rule 'has nothing to do with the nature of the world ruler. It consists 'in the transformation of dominion into service, of power into love, and of demands into vicarious suffering'.[111] Moltmann sees the nature of Jesus' mission exemplified in Matthew 25, where the Son of Man identifies Himself with the poor and suffering in this world.[112]

> If the anticipation of God's future was found in the Christ who was condemned according to the law and crucified by the state, then the point in the social order at which the anticipation of Christian hope and Christian love ought to be found has been marked permanently: we must find it in the people whom Jesus, according to Matt. 25, called the least of his brethren, and with whom he identified himself.[113]

The *imago Dei* is perfected on earth not in the political god-king but in the crucified Christ.[114] He is the one to whom all authority in heaven and on earth has been given, but He came not to rule but to serve 'in order to make us free for fellowship with God and for openness for one another.'[115]

Overall the effect of Moltmann's political theology is to replace authority from above with authority from below, a claim which is theologically justified on the basis that it is the oppressed and not the powerful with whom God has been identified through the person of Christ.[116]

The coming reign of God was inaugurated by Jesus' representative suffering, through which 'He anticipate[d] the coming righteousness of God under the conditions of human injustice in the law of grace and in the justification of the godless by his death.'[117] Through His resurrection He was declared to be *Kyrios* by God the Father, but His reign is eschatologically

---

[109] Moltmann, *WJC*, 279.
[110] Moltmann, *TKG*, 71; *Experiences in Theology* 34, 97 makes the same point with regard to the Exodus.
[111] Moltmann, *Man: Christian Anthropology in the Conflicts of the Present* (London: SPCK, 1974) 113.
[112] Moltmann, *Experiences in Theology*, 132, 235; *The Open Church* 103-4; *EH* 67; *In the End* 71; Müller-Fahrenholz, *The Kingdom and the Power*, 132. For Moltmann, such poverty is multi-dimensional and 'extends from economic, social and physical poverty to psychological, moral and religious poverty': *CPS* 79.
[113] Moltmann, *Future*, 53; *Coming* 111; 'The Liberation of the Future and its Anticipations in History' in R. Bauckham, ed., *God Will Be All in All* (Edinburgh: T&T Clark, 1999) 287.
[114] Moltmann, *GIC*, 215.
[115] Moltmann, *Future*, 129; *GIC* 227.
[116] Moltmann, *TKG*, 197-98; *The Open Church* 17.
[117] Moltmann, *CG*, 190.

determined.[118] Not until the parousia will we see the fulfilment of the prophecy in Daniel 7 that 'the God of Israel will make his righteousness prevail against unjust ruling powers on earth and ... bring the nations to the peace of humanity.'[119]

In this time between the resurrection and the *parousia,* Christ's lordship is both a present reality and, an as yet unfulfilled promise.[120] This gives rise to a realism with regard to the present state of the world, and a hopefulness with regard to the possibilities of God breaking into it.

The reign of Christ is thus marked by the dialectic of cross and resurrection. Thus it is not the powers-that-be but the martyrs who testify to the coming kingdom. 'The martyrs [are] ... apocalyptic witnesses to the coming truth against the ruling lie, to coming justice and righteousness against the prevailing injustice, and to coming life against the tyranny of death.'[121] Yet their witness is meaningful because 'with Christ the general resurrection of the dead has already begun. ... New creation is beginning in Christ in the very midst of this world of violence and death.'[122]

The rule of God has to be understood both as actually present and as on its way to its fulfilment.[123] At present, it is challenged and resisted. This dual recognition protects us from both over-realised eschatology and apocalyptic resignation.[124] For all that Christ's lordship has not yet reached its fulfilment, and is therefore subject to the eschatological proviso, Moltmann insists that it is a present reality and that it is the task of Christians to work in step with the Holy Spirit to anticipate it through concrete actions for liberation.

'Generally, [Moltmann's] eschatology functions as a critical theory that de-legitimizes the present for the sake of the hoped for just, free and peaceful future. Because God has opened the future, everything can be changed.'[125] The goal is freedom and the abolition of dominion. Jesus' rule is leading, in Moltmann's view, to the moment envisioned in 1 Corinthians 15.24 when every rule and authority and power will be abolished. In that day,

> [h]uman subordination and super-ordination, and a system of justice enforced by power, is to be replaced by the brotherhood of all men with the Son of God in the atmosphere of the all-pervasive glory of the Father. Then, as the indwelling of the divine glory in all being brings protection against futility, chaos and wickedness,

---

[118] Moltmann, *CPS,* 32.

[119] Moltmann, *WJC,* 325.

[120] Moltmann, *TOH,* 217.

[121] Moltmann, *WJC,* 204; *Coming* 152.

[122] Moltmann, *WJC,* 221.

[123] Moltmann, *CPS,* 190; *WJC* 191, 304.

[124] Moltmann, *Coming,* 192; *On Human Dignity* 103-05.

[125] Rasmussen, *The Church as Polis,* 132; *CJF* 95.

earthly protective measures and human repressions become superfluous and void. Then freedom is fulfilled in the sphere of a new creation free of all dominion.[126]

Moltmann sees this outcome as total, culminating in the handing over of the kingdom by the Son to the Father, as described in 1 Corinthians 15:20-28. He therefore affirms that Christ's lordship is temporary but His Sonship is eternal.[127]

The Authority of God the Father

Moltmann will not countenance a simplistic theology which talks of God as Father as the ground for paternalism and the idea of the ruler as the *parens patriae*. He insists that the Father of Jesus Christ has nothing to do with 'those father religions which depend on the images of Jupiter, Caesar and other fathers of the fatherland or the family.'[128] He rejects the monarchial vision of God which is derived from a vision of fatherhood which 'gives protection and demands obedience.'[129] This amounts to taking a particular patriarchal model of human fatherhood and projecting it on to God, instead of meditating upon the nature of God's divine fatherhood and learning the lessons from it. Instead he argues that the Christian God is the one who invites us to 'call him "Abba", beloved Father, in the spirit of free sonship. It is freedom that distinguishes him from the universal patriarch of father religions.'[130]

It is because of the Trinity that 'God's sovereignty can then no longer be understood as the "universal monarchy" to which everything is subjected. It has to be interpreted and presented as the redeeming history of freedom.'[131] In contradistinction to the pattern of this world, in which authority equals domination,[132] Moltmann sees the royal rule of God as liberating in nature and effect, and initially expressed in 'the gathering and exodus of the people from slavery.'[133]

---

[126] Moltmann, *CPS*, 104, 178; *GIC* 233; *WJC* 193. N.G. Wright, *Disavowing Constantine: Mission, Church and the Social Order in the Theologies of John Howard Yoder and Jürgen Moltmann* (Carlisle: Paternoster, 2000) 45.

[127] Moltmann, *CG*, 266-68, 273-75, 288; *Hope and Planning* 50; *Future* 27, 30; *TKG* 88, 92; *WJC* 182, 191, 194; *Coming* 104, 306.

[128] Moltmann, *CG*, 320; *Man* 67; *History and the Triune God* 57, 89; *TKG* 163; *SL* 101 *Experiences in Theology* 325-26; see also J.B. Metz, 'Prophetic Authority' in J. Moltmann et al., eds., *Religion and Political Society* (New York: Harper and Row, 1974) at 171-209 to which Moltmann also contributed an essay.

[129] Moltmann, *Source*, 100.

[130] Moltmann, *TKG*, 163, 183; *GIC* 94; *Experiences in Theology* 280.

[131] Moltmann, *TKG*, 134.

[132] Rasmussen, *The Church as Polis*, 113, 288-89.

[133] Moltmann, *CPS*, 78; *History and the Triune God* 57-58; *SL* 271; Otto, *The God of Hope*, 66.

The problem with Moltmann's emphasis on God suffering with the oppressed and opposing worldly authorities is that on his account '[a]ny real notion of Lordship applying to God's love revealed in Christ is reinterpreted by the experience of suffering drawing God into the fluctuations of creation itself.'[134]

Authority and Law as Hostile Powers

In Moltmann's account of the trials of Jesus in chapter 4 of *CG*, there is evidence that Moltmann is suspicious, if not hostile, to law. There also appears to be an unreflective equation in his thought between authority and domination. Both these features are superseded by a more nuanced approach in *WJC*.

Moltmann's political theology is, in part, an attempt to reclaim a Christian voice in the public square which had been abandoned as a result of the (misinterpreted) Lutheran doctrine of the Two Kingdoms.[135] The Church has something to say to the powers-that-be, which will call them and their self-justifications into question.[136]

For all that Moltmann is a political theologian, the 'law' as such is not one of his major themes within his central corpus of work.[137] For the whole of the first cycle of books and up until the third book in the second cycle, Moltmann is more interested in 'power' and its uses.[138] Power is to be limited and controlled,[139] and it seems, if possible, eliminated.[140] He warns of the dangers inherent in 'the growth of human power and the progressive concentration of that power'[141] and identifies liberation from the idols of power as one of the three dimensions in which Christ's death takes on significance, along with liberation from the compulsion of sin and liberation from godforsakenness.[142] Elsewhere, when reflecting on the political consequences of the cross, Moltmann sees it as pointing the way for liberating people 'from political

---

[134] Molnar, 'Moltmann's Post-Modern Christology', 672.

[135] Moltmann, *On Human Dignity*, 61-77; *CJF* 26-27.

[136] Moltmann, *GSS*, 57.

[137] Moltmann's first cycle of major works consists of *Theology of Hope* (1965), *The Crucified God* (1972) and *The Church in the Power of the Spirit* (1975). His second cycle of major works consists of *The Trinity and the Kingdom of God* (1980), *God in Creation* (1985), *The Way of Jesus Christ* (1989), *The Spirit of Life* (1991), and *The Coming of God* (1996).

[138] Moltmann, *WJC*, 67.

[139] Moltmann, *CPS*, 177.

[140] Moltmann, *CPS*, 106.

[141] Moltmann, *Coming*, 200.

[142] Moltmann, *CPS*, 86; see also *CG* 304; *GSS* 1. N.G. Wright, *Disavowing Constantine*, 10.

idolatry, paternalism, and alienation.'[143]

In both his account of the nature of the Church and his political theology, Moltmann is often guilty of simply opposing power and authority with love and freedom, so that power and authority are equated with domination.[144] As Bauckham points out, this 'neglects the inevitability of some kind of power and authority in human society and therefore misses the opportunity to explore the way in which power and authority can be based on consent, exercised in love, and directed to fostering, rather than suppressing, freedom and responsibility.'[145]

However, in *EH*, Moltmann defines 'power' more neutrally as 'the means by which we can obtain something by force', 'violence' as the 'abuse of power' and 'law' as 'the rules which we must follow in gaining acceptance of our claims'. He grants the 'law' legitimacy provided it is constitutional, conforms to human rights, and is just, or at least does 'not make injustice the norm.'[146] Moltmann's working definition of law therefore seems to be that law is legitimate power or power which asserts its legitimacy. However, that claimed legitimacy is always subject to question in the name of Christ for the sake of the poor and the oppressed.

Moltmann is highly critical of what he regards as a Christian-imperial political theology, in which 'The authority of the emperor was secured by the idea of unity: one God – one Logos – one Nomos – one emperor – one church – one empire [whose] Christian empire was welcomed in chiliastic terms as the Christ's promised kingdom of peace.'[147]

Moltmann's trinitarianism is designed to cut the ground from under any claim by a human ruler to have a blank cheque from God. In *WJC*, Moltmann writes: 'If God reveals himself in the raising of the Christ crucified in helplessness, then God is not the quintessence of power, such as the Roman Caesars represented. Nor is he the quintessence of law, such as the Greek cosmos reflects. God is then the power that quickens into life, that makes the poor rich, that lifts up the humble and raises the dead.'[148]

Moltmann's critique of power derives from 1 Corinthians 2:6, 8. He

---

[143] Moltmann, 'The Cross and Civil Religion' in J. Moltmann et al., eds., *Religion and Political Society* (New York: Harper and Row, 1974) 35; *EH* 112.

[144] Moltmann, *GSS*, 58.

[145] Bauckham, *The Theology of Jürgen Moltmann*, 145; Rasmussen, *The Church as Polis*, 113.

[146] Moltmann, *EH*, 137.

[147] Moltmann, *CG*, 339; *RPS* 24-5; *EH* 106; *History and the Triune God* 92; *GSS* 245; *On Human Dignity* 205-07; 'Ich glaube an Gott den Vater: Patriarchalische oder nichtpatriarchialische Rede von Gott?', *Evangelische Theologie* 43 (1983) 400; *Experiences in Theology* 290, 303; *Coming* 161-162, see 183 for his view of the parallel development of papal hierarchicalism.

[148] Moltmann, *WJC*, 241; *Jesus Christ for Today's World* 80, see also *Future* 102.

understands that the powers of this age are doomed to perish[149] and that they crucified the Lord of glory. 'The gods of the power and riches of the world and world history ... belong on the other side of the cross, for it was in their name that Jesus was crucified. The God of freedom, the human God, no longer has godlike rulers as his political representatives. ... If the crucified one is Kyrios, then the Caesars must renounce this title.'[150]

Moltmann believes that whereas thoroughgoing monotheism leads to hierarchy,[151] monarchism and if pushed to the ultimate extreme, theocracy, the Trinity leads, if taken seriously, to very different conclusions.[152] Neither equation is necessarily true, however. Tanner points out that orthodox trinitarianism was nominally the dominant religious culture under European monarchies for many centuries,[153] while Otto stresses that ancient Israel combined monotheism with tribal leadership for a significant period of time and adopted a monarchy only hesitantly.[154]

Nonetheless, Moltmann maintains that far from the Trinity being practically irrelevant, as Kant thought, it makes all the difference to the shape of Church-State relations.[155] Moltmann argues that orthodox trinitarianism failed to make more of a difference precisely because it deferred too much to Greek philosophical theism and because its implications were suppressed in order to support the *pax* of christendom. However, despite that, the focus of trinitarian theology on the triune God who has come in the person of Jesus and is coming again relativises the human ruler's position and places them under God's authority rather than endowing them with God's regency.

In Moltmann's early and middle work, when he does refer to 'law' the connotations are usually negative.[156] Moltmann refers often in his writings to 'law' as part of a triad with 'sin and death' as the powers which oppress human life in the present age.[157] In *Future,* he says bluntly: 'Christian freedom is born

---

[149] Moltmann, *CPS*, 63.
[150] Moltmann, *CG*, 200; 'The Confession of Jesus Christ: A Biblical Theological Consideration', *Concilium* 118 (1979) 19; *Experiences in Theology* 176; *In the End* 91.
[151] Moltmann, *TKG*, 165, 193; *GIC* 1; Otto, *The God of Hope*, 81-83.
[152] Moltmann, *EH*, 107; Bauckham, *The Theology of Jürgen Moltmann*, 139, 172; Clarke, *A Cry in the Darkness*, 224.
[153] Tanner, 'Trinity', at 321; S.W. Sykes, 'The Dialectic of Community and Structure' in F.B. Burnham, C.S. McCoy, and M.D. Meeks, eds., *Love: The Foundation of Hope: The Theology of Jürgen Moltmann and Elisabeth Moltmann-Wendel* (San Francisco: Harper & Row, 1988) 121-22; K. Kilby, 'Perichoresis and Projection: Problems with Social Doctrines of the Trinity', *New Blackfriars* 81 (2000) 439.
[154] Otto, *The God of Hope*, 81-82.
[155] Moltmann, *CG*, 339-340; *EH* 108; *TKG* 195-99.
[156] See, for example, Moltmann, *TOH*, 315; *CG* 341.
[157] Moltmann, *Theology & Joy*, (London: SCM, 1973) 48; *CG* 306, 334; *CPS* 223, 292; *Future* 53, 54, 66, 77, 102; *The Power of the Powerless* 125; *GIC* 122; *On Human Dignity* 21.

out of the resurrection of Christ and is alive in resistance to the vicious circle of law, sin and death.'[158] In *EH*, he sets up battlelines between the powers of the past: sin, law, and death, and the forces of the future: spirit, justice, and freedom.[159] There appear to be two possible candidates for the meaning of 'law' in this context: legalism and retributive (retaliatory) justice.

'Law' as 'legalism'[160] Moltmann denounces as an aberration both in Jewish thinking about the Torah at the time of Christ and in Protestant orthodoxy.[161] Against those positions, Moltmann suggests that the Old Testament Torah should be understood in the light of 'promise'[162] and that Christian ethics should be understood as matters of joy, freedom and doxology.[163] The implication of Moltmann's thought is that 'legalism' is tantamount to idolatry; it is the transformation of the law, which is an important, but relative, value into the supreme value. In *GSS*, he expressly uses 'law' as shorthand for 'the law of self-justification'[164] and in *SL* he talks about '... the compulsion to evil, ... the law of works, and ... the violence of death'.[165] On this account, Christ was crucified because He confronted those who were self-righteous in their legalistic obedience to the Torah. The question of divine righteousness in history is therefore 'does inhuman legalism triumph over the crucified Christ, or does God's law of grace triumph over the works of the law and of power.'[166] Whilst legalism is a prominent theme in Moltmann's writing, the difficulty with identifying it with 'law' as such as part of the triad is that it is a reference to a particular religious disease rather than a universal condition. Nonetheless, Moltmann does capitalise 'the Law' in this way in *GIC* at 123. There is also something of this sense present in Moltmann's discussion of Paul's understanding of the law 'as the power in whose name he himself had persecuted the Christians' in *WJC* at 184.

The other candidate is Moltmann's understanding of 'law' as the *lex talionis* or the law of retributive (retaliatory) justice.[167] This is an idea which can be seen as axiomatic in the state of things as they are. Moltmann's description of authority as domination is then complemented by a view of law as seeking to repress evil through retributive justice, a phenomenon which only leads to further sin and death.

---

[158] Moltmann, *Future*, 102; *History and the Triune God* 58.
[159] Moltmann, *EH*, 6.
[160] Moltmann, *CG*, 128, 130, 133-137, 144-45, 151, 164, 179.
[161] Moltmann, *CPS,* 87; *Future* 95; *On Human Dignity* 210-11.
[162] Moltmann, *TOH*, 122, 145; *CG* 137; Müller-Fahrenholz, *The Kingdom and the Power*, 49.
[163] Moltmann, *Future*, 95; *CG* 14; *CPS* 137.
[164] Moltmann, *GSS*, 198.
[165] Moltmann, *SL*, 115-16.
[166] Moltmann, *CG*, 179; Otto, *The God of Hope*, 127.
[167] Moltmann, *CPS*, 87-88; *Future* 99; *Coming* 250.

This understanding of the law is not identical with the Old Testament's understanding of the *torah*. It must rather be understood as what governs the world, the foundation of the systems of life with which people try to defend themselves politically and psychologically against chaos, evil and death, and yet by doing so disseminate chaos, evil and death at the same time. We might describe this law archaically and psychologically, and in the general religious sense, as *Ananke*.[168]

At worst, the practice of retributive justice is worldly, fleshly, deadly justice.[169] The two conceptions, of legalism and retributive justice, can be seen as aspects of law designed to preserve the social order and the *status quo*, whose administrators and guardians become the oppressors of the transgressors, the outcasts and the outlaws.[170] What they have in common is the attempt to repress lawlessness,[171] but they only ever succeed in cutting off the branches without taking the axe to the root of the tree. In fact, in Moltmann's assessment, 'legalism ... was bound and is always bound to lead to retribution'.[172]

On this account law is simply the monopoly on violence, and merely the lesser of evils. At best, this understanding of the law would place it in the context of the covenant with Noah, which 'does not overcome the wickedness of acts of violence committed by one human being against another, and by human beings against animals, but ... does restrict them, and imposes the death penalty for murder, so as to protect the perpetrators of violence from themselves, and in order to preserve the life of others.'[173] Although human retributive justice harnesses powers of force and order, it can be a cloak for oppression and violence, and remains outside the perfection of Christ.

For Moltmann, the state is demythologised, accountable and limited: rulers are no longer seen as being in position of a divine blank cheque, by reason of their divine right or the empirical fact of their authority, subject only to a final drawing up of accounts at the end of history.[174] Instead, they are called into question by the example of Jesus Christ and the liberating power of the Holy Spirit.

The Work of the Holy Spirit: Law as a Taming and an Ordering Power

Moltmann understands the Holy Spirit's work in creation to have a number of

---

[168] Moltmann, *CPS*, 87-88.

[169] Moltmann, *SL*, 88.

[170] Moltmann, *CG*, 132-33, 256.

[171] Moltmann, *CG*, 306. See also *CPS* 89, where Moltmann's discussion conflates the two ideas in a way reminiscent of the early Luther.

[172] Moltmann, *CG*, 144.

[173] Moltmann, *WJC*, 128.

[174] Herbert W. Richardson 'Introduction', to *RPS* at 5; Moltmann 'The Cross and Civil Religion', 35, 40; *CG* 342-3.

dimensions. He argues, on a dubious exegetical basis and with considerable reliance on the Apocrypha that the Holy Spirit gives Himself when He gives the breath of life to created beings.[175] He also sees the Holy Spirit as giving the relationships which he regards as constitutive for beings. This means that '*the community of creation*, in which all created things exist with one another, for one another and in one another, is also *the fellowship of the Holy Spirit.*'[176] '[T]he eternal Spirit is *the divine wellspring of life* – the source of life created, life preserved and life daily renewed, and finally the source of the eternal life of all created being.'[177]

However, from this, another observation follows logically. The Holy Spirit, who is the spirit of unity and fellowship in the created order, is therefore also present 'as an ordering power immanent in the world.'[178] In addition, another biblical theme forms a very minor key in Moltmann's thought. There are brief glimpses that he appreciates that the Spirit is given in the New Covenant era in order that the people of God might fulfil God's Torah, spontaneously obey Him and keep His commandments.[179] However, this idea is suppressed on the basis that Moltmann wants to prioritise freedom and is suspicious when God is invoked in support of notions of authority and law.[180]

Although Moltmann makes mention of this idea of the Spirit as the spirit of order and the spirit of righteousness, these themes are not developed and instead his reflections on the Spirit are driven by the ideas of the Spirit as the Spirit of the original creation, the Spirit as the power of the resurrection,[181] the Spirit as the spirit of justice,[182] the Spirit of freedom,[183] and the Spirit as the

---

[175] Moltmann, *SL*, 34-35. Moltmann's three references are to Wisdom 1:7 'God's Spirit fills the world and he who holds all things together knows every sound', to Job 33:4 'The spirit of God has made me, and the breath of the Almighty gives me life', and to Psalm 104:29 which is translated 'If [God] thought only of himself, and took back to himself his spirit and his breath, all flesh would perish together, and man would return to dust.' It is far from clear that the Wisdom passage justifies Moltmann's assertion that 'It is therefore possible to experience God *in, with and beneath* each everyday experience of the world, if God is in all things, and if all things are in God, so that God himself "experiences" all things in his own way.' (*SL* 34). The Job passage is consistent with traditional theological understandings of the Spirit's work. The same is true of the third passage, though here the translation offered by Moltmann differs significantly from the NIV which renders the verse 'When you [God] take away *their* breath, they die and return to the dust.' (emphasis mine).
[176] Moltmann, *SL*, 10, italics original.
[177] Moltmann, *SL*, 82, italics original.
[178] Moltmann, *SL*, 46.
[179] Moltmann, *SL*, 45-46, 56.
[180] Moltmann, *SL*, 107.
[181] Moltmann, *SL*, 55.
[182] Moltmann, *SL*, 53-54, 143.
[183] Moltmann, *SL*, 109.

power of futurity[184] and of the new creation.[185]

Some of Moltmann's theological tenets are open to the interpretation that law-making authorities have a mediating function, restraining sin in a world in which no-one could withstand the Judgment of God. Although Moltmann does not say so in so many words, if one aspect of the last things is the sole rule of God the Father, then the present mediation of rule and presence of God the Father by God the Son and God the Holy Spirit is because, as the Israelites always feared, sinful human beings could not stand in the light of God's presence. Yet implicit in the surrender by Christ to God the Father of His mediating rule at the end of history, is the recognition that mediation of the divine purposes of God the Father is an integral and indispensable part of life in this world in which its redemption is not yet complete.

Moreover, the institution of law itself is seen by Moltmann as curbing unjust power. In *WJC* he writes 'to subject the exercise of power to law is the first stage in the conquest of violence. The second stage in conquering the rule of violence is the solidarity of the people in rejecting that rule, and their refusal to co-operate with it in any form.'[186] In *WJC*, Moltmann distinguishes between power, defined as the just use of force, and violence, defined as the unjust use of force.[187] Although social and political violence have not been abolished, Moltmann regards as a key achievement of Christianity, that it requires 'justification for every application of power – especially by the state.'[188] Human law, therefore, has a valuable place in holding human rulers accountable for the just use of their authority.

Although Moltmann demythologises law in his early work, when he turns in his later work to consider the cosmology of Ephesians and Colossians he re-mythologises 'the powers'.[189] With regard to the 'cosmic forces', Moltmann sees the theology of these epistles as demonstrating that such powers are spirits created in Christ and redeemed by Christ, who 'can be put at the service of Christ's universal peace.'[190] He recognises the reality that '[o]rdered systems which once ministered to life are toppling over into their very opposite, so that they now work for death.'[191]

In *GIC*, he talks of 'the potencies which are intended to make the life processes possible' but which have become perverted. 'Deliverance from evil therefore also means the restoration of the good in earthly potentialities for living *and* in the heavenly potencies which make these potentialities possible.

[184] Moltmann, *SL*, 103.
[185] Moltmann, *The Open Church*, 40; *SL* 67.
[186] Moltmann, *WJC*, 130.
[187] Moltmann, *WJC*, 129; *CJF* 44-45 contains substantially the same argument.
[188] Moltmann, *WJC*, 130.
[189] Moltmann, *WJC*, 282-6.
[190] Moltmann, *WJC*, 284.
[191] Moltmann, *WJC*, 185.

The very powers which have been perverted into what is destructive will themselves be redeemed; for their power is created power, and is as such good. It is only their power of destruction that was evil.'[192] Where structures have become perverted, structural reform may be required.[193]

But how are such powers to be understood? If institutions which shape human lives are to be embodied or inhabited by the spiritual powers, when we think of these power structures is the emphasis on the power or on the structure? If it is on the structure then these institutions constitute spaces in which the spiritual powers can dwell and therefore amount to a battleground in which the angels contend with the demons to determine the shape of the forces which affect human lives. Conversely, if the emphasis is on the power then these institutions are themselves *daemons*, powers which according to traditional cosmologies, must stand on one side or other of the great cosmic battle between good and evil.

It is unclear which of the two conceptions Moltmann holds. In *WJC*, he appears to be thinking in terms of institutions as powers, whereas in *CG* he talks about the fact that 'in every sphere of life the powers of the coming new creation are in conflict with the powers of a world structure which leads to death.'[194]

How do God's grace and Christian hope relate to these ordering structures infected by structural sin? Gunton suggests a helpful way forward, by thinking of demonic possession in the Gospels 'as a form of slavery endured by the created order, which is liberated to be itself by being set free by creation's Lord.'[195] There is, thanks to the providence of God, an ordering to even sinful human affairs which prevents their descent into absolute chaos and which is capable of ministering to life. Whenever the lordship of Christ is modelled, i.e. whenever power is used to serve others; whenever the Holy Spirit is allowed to blow, bringing wisdom, justice, truth and freedom, then legal authority is exercised in a way which is acceptable to God. However, even this relative acceptability is only founded in the love, grace and patience of the triune God.

Although Moltmann rejects the idea of 'orders' because such a conception is, in his view, too static, he does recognise that there are 'ordering processes' which need to be regulated and administered.[196] Such ordering is necessary and ordered systems have the potential, at least, to minister to life.[197]

Moltmann's early work tends to focus on the fact that power is in the wrong

---

[192] Moltmann, *GIC*, 169.

[193] Müller-Fahrenholz, *The Kingdom and the Power*, 192.

[194] Moltmann, *CG*, 18; *SL* 89.

[195] C.E. Gunton, *The Triune Creator: A Historical and Systematic Study* (Edinburgh University Press, 1998) 22.

[196] Moltmann, *CPS*, 164.

[197] Moltmann, *WJC*, 185.

hands,[198] while in his latter work, there seems to be an increased recognition that political authority is unavoidable,[199] and that revolution *per se* is not enough.[200] Political authority is therefore a necessity, but because of Christianity's understanding of people's dignity and equality before God, and because of 'its expectation of ... not only the abolition of death but also the abolition of every rule, authority and power (1 Cor. 15:24-6)',[201] political authority is the servant of the people and is temporal and secular rather than eternal and divine in its scope.

Moltmann's View of History and Eschatology

Moltmann's View of History

The place of law in the light of Moltmann's view of history also requires consideration. In Moltmann's thought, the shape of the cross and the resurrection is determined by the *eschaton*, the future of God, which is their origin, and towards which they point.[202] The *eschaton* brings the coming of the kingdom of God. The cross is inevitable given the hostility of the powers of this age to the coming rule of God.[203] The resurrection is the demonstration of God's power to overcome these rulers, and of God's commitment to renew the creation.[204] It is in the resurrection that the certainty of Christian hope is to be found.[205]

Precisely because its nature is radically different from that of earthly kingdoms, the kingdom of the coming God rescues people from their captivity to the enslaving and death-dealing character of worldly kingdoms and brings them into the kingdom of freedom.[206]

The kingdom of God is Moltmann's basic eschatological symbol. It is the liberating rule of God over all things and in all things in the new creation.[207] However, he insists that it has present, practical importance.[208] Moltmann's theology is not conceived in static or ontological categories, but in the light of

---

[198] Moltmann, *Religion, Revolution and the Future* (New York: Charles Scribner & Sons, 1969) 143; Rasmussen, *The Church as Polis*, 111-12.

[199] Moltmann, *CPS*, 119; *GIC* 233; *WJC* 193.

[200] Rasmussen, *The Church as Polis*, 188-89, 288-290.

[201] Moltmann, *CPS*, 178; *GIC* 233; *WJC* 193. N.G. Wright, *Disavowing Constantine*, 45.

[202] Moltmann, *Future*, 27;*WJC* 316; Bauckham, *The Theology of Jürgen Moltmann*, 3, 32.

[203] Moltmann, *GSS*, 185.

[204] Bauckham, *The Theology of Jürgen Moltmann*, 12.

[205] Moltmann, *TOH*, 90, 165, 223, 82-83, 85, 195; *CPS* 221; *Source* 81; Bauckham, *The Theology of Jürgen Moltmann*, 9.

[206] Müller-Fahrenholz, *The Kingdom and the Power*, 221-22; *SL* 111.

[207] Moltmann, *SL*, 194; *EH* 53; *Theology Today* 19.

[208] Moltmann, *Coming*, 131; *GSS* 251; Müller-Fahrenholz, *The Kingdom and the Power*, 221.

history and the Last Day which is coming to meet us.[209] The power which motivates this hope is that of the Holy Spirit. The Church is the Spirit's possession and not vice versa.[210]

The interaction between the coming kingdom of God and human history is established by the dialectic of cross and resurrection.[211] Moltmann decisively rejects the idea that the future is a matter of organic growth out of the past.[212]

In *The Theology of Hope*, Moltmann sought to rehabilitate the Christian doctrine of hope – a belief in God's inbreaking into the world, not merely in fulfilment of what was already present within it[213] nor in total contradiction with what has gone before.[214] Throughout his work, Moltmann seeks to hold the tension between the continuities and discontinuities between the God-created present and the re-created future. God's actions in the world are not merely an extrapolation of processes begun in creation but the constant *advent*, the constant inbreaking of new possibilities, of new divine actions, in the service of the goal of the new creation of all things.[215]

The God who is Lord is 'the God "who has raised Jesus from the dead" and therein shows himself to be the *creator ex nihilo*. ... His future does not result from the trends of world history. His rule is his raising of the dead and consists in calling into being the things that are not, and choosing things which are not, to bring to nothing things which are (1 Cor. 1:28).'[216]

Moltmann sets up two sides in history: the oppressed and the oppressors, or to put it another way, the 'progressive side of justice, freedom and peace' and the 'reactionary side of injustice, oppression and war.[217] The action of God in history, who has allied Godself 'with those who are dispossessed, denied and downtrodden'[218] means that the oppressed rather than the oppressors will be the ultimate victors, although both will be liberated from the dehumanising effects of oppression.[219] Those who bear the cross of suffering will experience the

---

[209] Moltmann, *Future*, 90.
[210] Moltmann, *CPS*, 36; *SL* 103, 230-31; *Source* 93; Bauckham, *The Theology of Jürgen Moltmann*, 13; Rasmussen, *The Church as Polis*, 76, 86-7.
[211] Moltmann, *Future*, 52, 66.
[212] Moltmann, *Coming*, 3, 25-29.
[213] Moltmann, *TOH*, 18, 85-86, 103; *EH* 52.
[214] Moltmann, *TOH*, 129-30.
[215] Moltmann, *Future*, 30; *WJC* 206; Müller-Fahrenholz, *The Kingdom and the Power*, 58
[216] Moltmann, *TOH*, 221.
[217] Rasmussen, *The Church as Polis*, 147; Moltmann, *Coming*, 134. Compare the very different political theology of Coleridge who seeks to hold in tension the forces of permanence and progression and ends up with a reactionary defence of the status quo: Holmes, 'Of Neoplatonism and Politics' in *Listening to the Past* 137-152.
[218] Moltmann, *Future*, 17; *SL* 129.
[219] Moltmann, *RPS*, 45; *Future* 57; *Experiences in Theology* 186, 213, 233; *In the End* 48, 56, 61; Rasmussen, *The Church as Polis*, 269.

resurrection of their hopes.[220]

Rasmussen sees the Hegelian vision of dialectical progress underlying the ebb and flow of history, in which the oppressed will be liberated in the long run, as underlying Moltmann's early thought. However, this becomes less obviously present in his later work, where an apocalyptic concern about the future of history dominates.[221] By the time of *WJC*, Moltmann is explicitly recognising that "'the God of history" is a very hidden God, whose plans and ways may after all only be manifest and comprehensible in the seeing face to face.'[222] But such agnosticism is uncharacteristic of Moltmann. Only a few pages later he writes of the 'universal eschatology of redemption [which] provides the foundation which then makes it justifiable to discern and acknowledge tendencies in the evolution of nature and in human history as being also parables and hints, anticipations and preparations for the coming of the messianic new creation.'[223]

The publication of *Coming* requires a re-evaluation of Moltmann's view of history. In that work, Moltmann develops the dialectic of cross and resurrection by talking of two times side by side at work in the world: a future time extrapolated from the present and an *advent* time breaking into the present.[224] Into this fallen, dying world God's renewing power is constantly coming.[225] Seen in this light, the history of the Church does not have to be one of unbroken success to postmillennial triumph nor one of the steadfast clinging on until premillennial rapture.[226] It is a history which can be subject to ebb and flow, which will never arrive at utopia until the *eschaton*,[227] but from which hope can never be extinguished.[228]

---

[220] Moltmann, *GSS*, 18, 58; *Future* 16-17; *WJC* 178, 206-7; Bauckham, *The Theology of Jürgen Moltmann*, 101. In his more recent work, Moltmann acknowledges that the same person can be, depending on the relation focused on, either oppressed or oppressor: *SL* 125; *Experiences in Theology* 229; *In the End* 144.

[221] Rasmussen, *The Church as Polis*, 91-92, 111, 150, 225, 339, 353. Optimism is heavily tempered by the time of Moltmann *WJC* 298-305 and *Coming* 234. See also Otto, *The God of Hope*, 17-21 for a discussion of the Hegelian influences on Moltmann's thought.

[222] Moltmann, *WJC*, 301.

[223] Moltmann, *WJC*, 304.

[224] Moltmann, *Coming*, 6, 44-46, 138; *WJC* 303; *Source* 72. Bauckham compares Moltmann's approach to time with what he called 'the modern time myth' in 'Time and Eternity' in R. Bauckham, ed., *God Will Be All in All: The Eschatology of Jürgen Moltmann* (Edinburgh: T&T Clark, 1998) 158-93.

[225] Bauckham, *The Theology of Jürgen Moltmann*, 5.

[226] Bauckham, *The Theology of Jürgen Moltmann*, 10.

[227] Moltmann, *Hope and Planning*, 108.

[228] Moltmann, *GSS*, 185; *Coming* 194.

Law and Eschatology

Moltmann's theological scheme is distinctive in his refusal to allow the pre-history of salvation or the categories of creation and preservation to dominate his assessment of God or of the Church or social institutions.[229] The *missio Dei* and the mission of the Church which is consequent upon it,[230] cannot be understood, he argues, other than by reference to their future, their goal in the consummation of God's kingdom,[231] and the eternal destiny in which God will be all in all.

Wherever possible Moltmann seeks to transform ontological categories into eschatological categories.[232] In fact, he develops a distinctive eschatological epistemology in which things are only understood in the light of the future, and that future is not determined by the inherent possibilities of the present but by the extraordinary possibilities of the *advent* of God.[233] Human knowledge is therefore necessarily incomplete because the existing realities of the world are not immutable,[234] and what they may become is still ahead of us.

In terms of law this means that a quest for timeless ideal norms is misplaced.[235] Moltmann in his early work rejects the idea of natural law and of the orders of creation, even when given forward direction by being presented as orders of preservation or as divine mandates.[236] Indeed, Moltmann believes that it was this view of the world 'as a cosmos which, ordered by eternal laws and filled with divine significance, reflected the central order of all things'[237] led to the cultural captivity of the Church which instead of seeking to anticipate the eschatological kingdom of God saw itself as one of the stabilising powers which protected order against the threat of chaos.[238]

In schematic terms, Moltmann sees the future in terms of liberation and the

---

[229] See, for example, Moltmann, *TOH*, 75-76, 303.

[230] Moltmann, *CPS*, 64; *Source* 19: 'God's mission is nothing less than the sending of the Holy Spirit from the Father through the Son into this world, so that this world should not perish but live.' See also Bauckham, *The Theology of Jürgen Moltmann*, 2, 13.

[231] Moltmann, *CPS*, xvi, 11, 84; *GSS* 211, 220, 251.

[232] So, for example, he reinterprets the doctrine that God made humankind in the image of God as expressing both destiny and promise, rather than just, or even primarily, ontological reality: *TKG* 116. In the end, because as he himself points out 'Beginning and end ... belong together and must not be separated from one another' (*WJC* 281) this merely displaces epistemological speculation from ontology to eschatology: see Müller-Fahrenholz, *The Kingdom and the Power*, 187, 218 for criticism of this aspect of Moltmann's thought.

[233] Moltmann, *TOH*, 92, 223, 282; Bauckham, *The Theology of Jürgen Moltmann*, 9; Rasmussen, *The Church as Polis*, 65.

[234] Moltmann, *TOH*, 288.

[235] Moltmann, *TOH*, 204; *Hope and Planning* 112.

[236] Moltmann, *Hope and Planning*, 112-18, 120-25.

[237] Moltmann, *CPS*, 37; *GIC* 199.

[238] Moltmann, *CPS*, 37, 16.

end of lordship. The sabbath rest of God will come when the Son of God hands over His lordship to God the Father, who will then reign in unmediated glory.[239] Human rulers and structures of power are therefore not only temporal but temporary and passing away.[240] It is these coming realities to which the Church ought to witness.

The Last Judgment

In *WJC* Moltmann arrived at a more positive understanding of law which results from his speculations about the nature of the Last Judgment, re-working ground laid in *CG* 180-84.[241] Moltmann takes injustice seriously. He recognises that the victims of injustice cry out to heaven and must not be forgotten. He also acknowledges that the perpetrators of injustice can find no rest. His vision of the Last Judgment is not, however, one of an apocalyptic day of retribution, but rather of 'the day on which peace begins [when by] passing judgment on injustice and enmity, the messiah creates the preconditions for the universal kingdom of peace.'[242] He wants God to act according to a righteousness which *creates* justice rather than merely establishing facts and handing out condemnations.[243] In 'Peace the Fruit of Justice', Moltmann asserts: 'God's justice is always saving, always brings justice and always establishes righteousness. In his righteousness God does not merely confirm what is just and what is unjust, but proffers justice to those without it and shows the doers of violence the injustice of their ways.'[244] This sort of vision of justice would be anticipated on earth by restorative justice, which seeks to reconcile victims and offenders, and by justice which rehabilitates.[245]

Moltmann posits that the nature of the Last Judgment must be consistent with Jesus' message and actions. He then asserts that Jesus taught and displayed not retributive justice but reconciling justice. The Last Judgment must therefore, he concludes, have the same character. It must be a reconciling justice not a retributive justice, and Moltmann's account of this reconciliation is universalist.

Moltmann's logic is straightforward but the premises of his argument are questionable. In *WJC* Moltmann identifies that Jesus set out his messianic mission at Nazareth by quoting from Isaiah 61.[246] But Moltmann at no point explores the significance of the fact that Jesus stopped just before 'the day of

---

[239] Moltmann, *CG*, 275; *GIC* 64;*WJC* 182-3; *Coming* 317-19.

[240] Moltmann, *TKG*, 91; *WJC* 193-4.

[241] See also Moltmann, *TOH*, 128-137; *CPS* 234.

[242] Moltmann, *WJC*, 335.

[243] Moltmann, *WJC*, 336.

[244] Moltmann, 'Peace the Fruit of Justice', *Concilium* 195 (1988) 114; *GSS* 193; *SL* 129; *WJC* 184.

[245] Moltmann, *WJC*, 338; *Man* 77.

[246] Moltmann, *WJC*, 91; *CPS* 76; *On Human Dignity* 102.

vengeance of our God'. Was Jesus revoking this word of prophecy or merely postponing it to the Last Judgment? Is Jesus' message as unequivocal as Moltmann portrays it? An examination of the synoptic gospels would suggest that Jesus in fact had more to say about the Last Judgment than anyone else, quite apart from the dislocation between Moltmann's vision of the Last Judgment and the Gospel of John's portrayal of the stark alternatives of eternal life and condemnation.

The universalist drift within Moltmann's thought is evident in *CPS* and becomes pronounced in *WJC*, but Moltmann only draws out its systematic conclusions in *Coming*. In *God Will Be All in All*, a collection of essays discussing Moltmann's eschatology, Moltmann says of himself: 'Perhaps I belong to the people whom my friend Johann Baptist Metz calls "the last universalists"'.[247] The critical questions to be put to Moltmann are whether he does not underplay the seriousness with which God takes God's own holiness and human free will. Moltmann is certainly right that Jesus is, in Christian eschatology, 'the figure of the universal judge' who 'will finally bring justice to those who have never received justice, and will make the unjust just'.[248] He is also right that '[t]he purpose of Jesus' judgment is not retaliation in all directions.'[249] The problem is that in Moltmann's account, God's creative righteousness becomes a law which God is bound to obey, even at the expense of human freewill and God's own holiness.

N.G. Wright's conclusion is that Moltmann fails to give full weight to the fact that 'The cross indicates that God's forgiveness passes through and does not deny his own wrath.'[250] The nature of God's justice which Moltmann characterises as reconciling justice rather than retributive justice might be more accurately described in biblical terms as mercy beyond wrath. Adopting these terms makes it possible to think of even the state's role in criminal justice as *in principle* capable of serving a redemptive purpose.[251]

A similar criticism could be made in terms of the fact that Moltmann's account of the Last Judgment is not pursued with the same trinitarian rigour as is evident at other points in his thought.[252] To raise just one criticism, at the moment of judgment it would appear that God is the sole determining subject, in marked contrast to the reciprocity which Moltmann insists elsewhere is an essential feature of the triune God. Moltmann cannot maintain that God loves us and will not force us to love God whilst at the same time wishing to assert

---

[247] Moltmann, 'Can Christian Eschatology become Post-Modern?' in R. Bauckham, ed., *God Will Be All in All* (Edinburgh: T&T Clark, 1999) 264.

[248] Moltmann, *WJC*, 338; *SL* 128.

[249] Moltmann, *WJC*, 338.

[250] N.G. Wright, *Disavowing Constantine*, 167.

[251] N.G. Wright, *Disavowing Constantine*, 168.

[252] Bauckham points out that explicit references to the Trinity or to Christology are surprisingly rare in *Coming*: *God Will Be All in All*, 5, 10.

that each and every thing in the universe will be redeemed.[253] Either God's love is an active power persuading us to enter into relationship with God, or it is a violent embrace which holds us against our will.

Moltmann becomes increasingly confident about the difference between God's judgments and human judgments. Moltmann is clear that the Last Judgment is not retributive in nature.[254] Instead, it is 'solely the victory of the divine righteousness that is to become the foundation of the new creation of all things.'[255]

> The Judge to be expected is the One who gave himself up for sinners and who ... will judge according to his gospel of the saving righteousness of God and according to no other law. He will not judge in order to punish the wicked and reward the good, but so as to make the saving righteousness of God prevail among them all. He will "judge" in order to raise up and to put things right.[256]

In place of the retributive justice which is the 'natural', i.e. default option used in the world, this is a messianic justice, a reconciling justice which seeks to put both the victim and the oppressor in the right.[257] This justice first justifies the victim and convicts the oppressor, but then reconciles them to one another. The oppressor is convicted but not condemned. Law has been, in effect, turned by Moltmann from an ontological reality into an eschatological reality, with dramatic consequences.

Perhaps this is overconfident. Maybe Moltmann did better in his earlier thought where he left the nature of God's righteousness as an unresolved question. Although this meant a gap at the centre of his theology, it was consistent with his rejection of totalism, the idea that any principle turned into an ideology becomes an idol (CPS 215).

Leaving that observation aside, to what extent is human law called to anticipate the reconciling justice of God? To what extent is Moltmann's view of God's reconciling justice dependent on his belief that God alone can make atonement?[258] If human law is essentially conservative, retributive and based on the possible, then what Moltmann's eschatology does is to reserve space for grace and miracle, space into which law can barely intrude. Human law is therefore necessary, but it remains unclear whether it is merely a necessary evil or has, in his view, a more positive role.

If retributive justice is as necessary for human society under our present fallen conditions as it is universal, subject to the proviso that reconciliation

---

[253] Even the devil: Moltmann, Coming, 254.
[254] Moltmann, WJC, 314.
[255] Moltmann, WJC, 315, emphasis mine.
[256] Moltmann, WJC, 315.
[257] Moltmann, CG, 183; SL 129; Coming 250; In the End 143.
[258] Moltmann, SL, 134; Jesus Christ for Today's World 40-42, 68; Müller-Fahrenholz, The Kingdom and the Power, 191-92.

ought to be fostered and encouraged,[259] then its relationship to sin and death must be reconsidered. If retributive justice is not the only face of law to be taken into account, then its relationship to liberation and grace must also be reconsidered. It is the doctrine of the Holy Spirit's action in common grace which enables the reconciling and creative possibilities of law to be accounted for as well as an appreciation of what is *relatively* good about retributive justice, compared with no justice at all.

Retributive justice is necessitated by the social consequences of sin and seeks to stem the forces of death by returning violence to the source of the outbreak. The means by which it does so are, however, perilous, and prone to abuse. The administration of retributive justice is therefore to be understood as provided for by God's common grace in order for social life to exist, and as sustained by common grace so that despite the flaws, sinfulness and perils of its use, social life is maintained.

Salvation and Shalom

An intermittent feature in Moltmann's thought is the idea of *shalom*. However, when it appears it is almost as a by-product of his reflections on salvation and the sabbath, rather than a concept in its own right.[260] Moltmann insists that salvation is about far more than rescuing souls. It is '*soteria* and *shalom*, salvation as life from the dead and the annihilation of death, and the extermination of the godless powers of futility. It is the new creation of the world on the foundation of God's righteousness – as glory.'[261] In this context, *shalom* is 'the future in which righteousness and life rule.'[262] Its presupposition is justice and its connotations both salvation and well-being.[263]

Practical liberation is an important task for Moltmann because of the nature of the new creation as an embodied creation,[264] and as the redemption of *this* creation which is in bondage to decay.[265] God has committed Godself in covenant to this world.[266] 'Christianity's hope is not directed towards "another" world, but towards the world as it is changed in the kingdom of God.'[267]

The eschatological *shalom* is achieved through the consolation of the victims of

---

[259] As restorative justice seeks to do.
[260] It appears at Moltmann, *TOH*, 329; *WJC* 304; 'Peace the Fruit of Justice', 111-2. The idea is also present, but not mentioned in terms, at *TOH* 204-5; *CPS* 291; *Coming* 70.
[261] Moltmann, *Future*, 164; *Hope and Planning* 125; *EH* 171.
[262] Moltmann, *Future*, 54; *SL* 141.
[263] Moltmann, *SL*, 154; *CJF* 39-42; *CPS* 291; *Coming* 70.
[264] Moltmann, *Religion, Revolution and the Future*, 74; *GIC* 248; *WJC* 265-6, 283; *SL* 89-90; *Coming* 58-77.
[265] Moltmann, *Coming*, 6.
[266] Moltmann, *TOH*, 121; see also *CG* 280 and *TOH* 204 where he talks in the same terms about God's righteousness as the ground of creation.
[267] Moltmann, *CPS*, 164; *SL* 89; *Source* 74-75.

history and the redemption of both them and their oppressors. 'The reconciliation of the whole cosmos through Christ (Col. 1:20) is for the justification of all created beings who have been injured and have lost their rights, and aims at the implementation of God's righteousness and justice, which alone secures the life and peace of creation.'[268]

For Moltmann, this *shalom* is to be embodied on earth in the Church.[269] Those who are aware that they have peace with God are enabled to protest against the world's peacelessness.[270]

Moltmann insists that justice is the indispensable foundation for peace.[271] Therefore, some degree of earthly anticipation of the heavenly *shalom* is essential because '[w]ithout just social and political conditions there is no peace between human beings and nations.'[272] As N.G. Wright observes, the anticipation of the divine *shalom* flows from a just social order.[273]

Moltmann is able to hope that the world will follow the Church's lead because of his conviction of the universal nature of reconciliation and redemption, which the Church anticipates now as *pars pro toto*.[274] The particular role the Church is called to play is to witness to 'the universal interests of God's kingdom and his righteousness and justice in history.'[275]

In *GIC* Moltmann envisions the new creation in terms of the sabbath rest of God.[276] While this enables him to grasp some aspects of peace covered by the idea of *shalom*, it is still a thin version of the biblical concept which appears. Although the idea of sabbath enables him to connect through the concept of rest with the values of peace and harmony,[277] it misses out on the connotation of 'ordering' and 'righteousness/justice' which is inherent in the idea of *shalom*.[278] These ideas do not receive full consideration in his other treatments of the subject, in part because *shalom* is for Moltmann a conclusion rather than a fundamental idea.

A full blooded concept of *shalom*, with its connotations of peace, unity and

---

[268] Moltmann, *WJC*, 312.

[269] Moltmann, *WJC*, 133.

[270] Moltmann, *GSS*, 194; *CJF* 6; *WJC* 187.

[271] Moltmann, *WJC*, 255; *SL* 123, 143; *CJF* 38-40; *Coming* 206, 211.

[272] Moltmann, *GSS*, 21, 60-1.

[273] N.G. Wright, *Disavowing Constantine*, 162.

[274] Moltmann, *GSS*, 105; *TKG* 124; *Experiences in Theology* 332.

[275] Moltmann, *GSS*, 220.

[276] Moltmann, *GIC*, chapter XI. See also *WJC* 290; *Coming* xiii.

[277] Moltmann, *GIC*, 277.

[278] Moltmann might disagree with this, and point to his comments in 'The Bible, the Exegete and the Theologian' in R. Bauckham, ed., *God Will Be All in All* (Edinburgh: T&T Clark, 1999) at 229 that 'The divine righteousness and justice which is to be practised in the sabbath years is, over against the usual legal norms, amnesty justice, the liberating justice which forgives sins and puts things to rights' as evidence that his understanding of the sabbath does include broader aspects of *shalom*.

righteousness[279] would enable him to think in terms of our wholeness and unity with God without dissolving our individuality, whilst recognising empowerment for righteousness as a key ministry of the Holy Spirit.

The Nature of Anticipations

Although the kingdom of God only reaches perfection in the *eschaton*, it is the coming kingdom. It 'begins in this world with the poor; the justice of God comes justifying those who are suffering from injustice.'[280] Signs of the kingdom's presence can therefore be expected in this life. These signs Moltmann calls 'anticipations'.

> The glory of God is only completed (Rom. 11:36) when the "creation at the beginning" is consummated by the "new creation at the end" ... Wherever on the way to this goal the gospel is preached to the poor, sins are forgiven, the sick are healed, the oppressed are freed and outcasts are accepted, God is glorified and creation is in part perfected.[281]

Moltmann defines 'anticipation' in the following way: 'An anticipation is not yet a fulfilment. But it is already the presence of the future in the conditions of history. It is a fragment of the coming whole. It is a payment made in advance of complete fulfilment and part-possession of what is to come.'[282] Anticipations therefore act as promises of what is to come.[283]

In *HIG*, Moltmann endorses Paul Ricoeur's description of his position: as operating with the categories of 'nevertheless', with regard to what may be expected in the present, and 'how much more', with regard to what may be hoped for in the future.[284]

Just as the quintessential eschatological event, the resurrection, occurred in history to foreshadow that final judgment, so there are also anticipations of the final accountability of rulers in their present accountability to the people they rule, and in particular, the fact that they are answerable for their treatment of the oppressed.

Moltmann continues to insist on the eschatological proviso, the recognition that the full light of dawn always lies ahead of us, as a necessary part of the

---

[279] N. Wolterstorff explores the implications for political theology of the biblical passages on *shalom* in *Until Justice and Peace Embrace* (Grand Rapids: Eerdmans, 1983) at 69-72.

[280] Moltmann, *RPS*, 42; *SL* 111.

[281] Moltmann, *CPS*, 60.

[282] Moltmann, *CPS*, 193; see also *Future* 47; *WJC* 219.

[283] Moltmann, *GIC*, 64.

[284] Moltmann, *History and the Triune God*, 67; P. Ricoeur, *Le Conflit des Interpretations: Essais d'Hermeneutique* (Paris : Seuil, 1969) 393.

Church's hope.[285] Elsewhere he says 'Hope is realized in history, but it also transcends its own incarnations.'[286] Moltmann wants to guard against a repeat of the error which led to the Hellenization of Christianity: the belief that the *eschaton* had arrived in the conquest of the Roman Empire by the Church.[287] Bauckham has drawn attention to the way in which Moltmann uses the idea of the millennium of Christ's universal earthly rule as a means of exposing as presumptuous any claims of Christian states or churches to embody Christ's rule.[288] Moltmann insists that

> the present world of sin and violence cannot sustain the new world of God's righteousness and justice. That is why this righteousness of God's is going to create a new world, and will be manifested only at the end of the time of this world, and in the daybreak of the new creation. Only then will "the glory of the Lord appear". But even in the history of this world there are already revelations of the new world to come, revelations ahead of time.[289]

In the meantime, because the rule of Christ is contested, the path to our resurrection remains the same path that Jesus walked: the path of the cross (*Theology & Joy* 52). The dialectic of cross and resurrection marks the path of the Church in this world. Only the *parousia* will bring the crises of the world to an end.[290]

Law, Solidarity, Liberation and Human Rights

Moltmann's idea of justice is given content in three key concepts in his thought: solidarity,[291] liberation and human rights.[292] All three are controversial. Solidarity is controversial because as a concept which is deep-rooted in Catholicism and liberation theology, it is regarded as suspect by those adhering to the dogma of Protestant individualism. Liberation requires definition because freedom is such a controverted concept. Human rights are problematic because in their secular conception they are seen by some thinkers,

---

[285] Moltmann, *WJC*, 191, 219, 304; *Theology Today* 34.
[286] Moltmann, *CPS*, 25.
[287] Moltmann, *TOH*, 157; Rasmussen, *The Church as Polis*, 86.
[288] R. Bauckham, 'The Millennium' in R. Bauckham, ed., *God Will Be All in All: The Eschatology of Jürgen Moltmann* (Edinburgh: T&T Clark, 1998) 136. The remainder of the article raises questions as to whether Moltmann's use of the millennium is either necessary in order to safeguard the concerns about the relationship between the present and the future which he raises, or whether his development of the concept is in fact effective in achieving that goal.
[289] Moltmann, *WJC*, 219.
[290] Moltmann, *CPS*, 50.
[291] Moltmann, *CG*, 45, 60; *CPS* 97.
[292] Moltmann, *CPS*, 178.

both Christian and non-Christian, as amounting to a religion without God.[293]

Solidarity and Social Justice

Moltmann's belief in solidarity arises from his affirmation that individualism is deficient in its view of human beings and that relationality is fundamental to what it means to be human.[294] Solidarity is necessary because of the truth of that relationality. Solidarity is connected to Moltmann's trinitarianism because of the idea of relationality which Moltmann sees as essential both to what it means for God to be God and to what it means for human beings to be human.

Solidarity manifests itself in social justice, which 'is the form of authentic interdependence between people, and between society and the environment.'[295] Reciprocal dependence, interdependence is, therefore, unavoidable and good, but one-sided dependence leads to domination and helplessness and is stifling.[296]

Solidarity is neighbourly love (*The Power of the Powerless* 109); it means fellowship, especially with those who 'are visibly living in the shadow of the cross: the poor, the handicapped, the people society has rejected, the prisoners and the persecuted.'[297] This has socialist and egalitarian overtones.[298] In Moltmann's view, 'It is only injustice that turns want into a torment, and being deprived of one's rights that turns poverty into a hell.'[299] Consequently, it is justice, which occurs when everyone receives as each has any need,[300] rather than prosperity, which Moltmann sees as the prime social goal.

The idea of solidarity is developed in *CPS* though the concept of 'symbiotic life', which is a lifestyle in which the satisfaction of the needs of the community is preferred to the heedless forcing through of private claims.[301] Moltmann argues that such a recognition of 'symbiosis' would enable due primacy to be given to the claims of social justice and solidarity.[302] As will become evident, if this is fundamental to Moltmann's political and legal thought, then serious work needs to be done to integrate this with his declared commitment to human rights and his operative definition of freedom.

---

[293] Berthoud, *Une Réligion Sans Dieu*, and F. Klug, *Values for a Godless Age: The History of the Human Rights Act and its Political and Legal Consequences* (Harmondsworth: Penguin, 2000).
[294] Moltmann, *GIC*, 188.
[295] Moltmann, *Future*, 130.
[296] Moltmann, *SL*, 125.
[297] Moltmann, *CPS*, 97.
[298] Moltmann, *The Power of the Powerless*, 107; *GSS* 69, 224; *SL* 194; *CJF* 39.
[299] Moltmann, *The Power of the Powerless*, 133; *Source* 108.
[300] Moltmann, *Source*, 110.
[301] Moltmann, *CPS*, 174; Müller-Fahrenholz, *The Kingdom and the Power*, 92.
[302] Moltmann, *CPS*, 175; *Future* 130.

Liberation: Freedom and Authority

Liberation is clearly one of Moltmann's key concepts. Müller-Fahrenholz describes it as a 'code word' which has a number of dimensions and operates in Moltmann's thought as 'the hallmark and seal of God's history in which human history and the history of our world are hidden. The kingdom of God breathes freedom.'[303]

Moltmann sees 'the resurrection of the crucified Christ as the foundation, goal and praxis of a history of liberation.'[304] In terms of political theology, Moltmann sees liberation at work against five "vicious cycles", the cycles of poverty and economic injustice, violence and oppression, alienation, the industrial pollution of nature and, senselessness and godforsakenness.[305]

Moltmann frequently talks in terms of liberation. But what does this mean? For Moltmann, an action is liberating if it ministers to life.[306] True liberation is a divine action, but it manifests itself in political consequences – in release from the prisons of capitalism, racism and technocracy.[307] In an essay first published in 1991, 'Political Theology and the Theology of Liberation', he writes: '... the intention of our political theology is undoubtedly to make people who are the humiliated objects of the power and violence of others the free determining subjects of their own lives.'[308] Liberation is therefore about autonomy, about enabling people to live their lives for themselves.

At some points in his thought, Moltmann appears to be arguing for freedom as autonomy in its liberal conception. Freedom is freedom *from-* from rules, from taboos, from oppression, from subjugation. All of this is implied by Moltmann's understanding of autonomy as the space 'to realize one's inner potential without external restrictions.'[309] However, there are moments in his writings where Moltmann seems to realise the insufficiency of this notion and therefore seeks to establish a moral direction to liberation in terms of 'justice, peace and the integrity of creation, in expectation of the coming kingdom of God, which will complete history and put everything to rights.'[310] The difficulty is that such a suggestion is not developed through an account of what

---

[303] Müller-Fahrenholz, *The Kingdom and the Power*, 25; *EH* 51; *SL* 99.

[304] Moltmann, *WJC*, 215, 237; *TKG* 134; *History and the Triune God* xi.

[305] Moltmann, *Future*, 109-113; *CG* 344-346; *RPS* 40; *EH* 176, 180-184; *On Human Dignity* 110; *SL* 112; Otto, *The God of Hope*, 110-11.

[306] Moltmann, *CG*, 316; in *Source* he talks about the mission of life: 21-22, 54. In *Experiences* at 149-50 he spells out eight aspects of what furthers life.

[307] Moltmann, *CG*, 334.

[308] Moltmann, *GSS*, 58.

[309] Rasmussen, *The Church as Polis*, 98 footnote 40, see also 281-82.

[310] Moltmann, *Experiences in Theology*, 297-98; *TOH* 329; *Gospel of Liberation* (Waco: Word, 1973) 89; *GIC* 35; *GSS* 240.

personal and social moral righteousness would look like.[311] At the crux of his theology, when pressed to give an account of the pathos of God the Father and God's commitment to God's creation, Moltmann seeks to redefine freedom. In relation to God in Godself, he argues, freedom is not to be understood as absolutist freedom of choice.[312] The appropriate frame of meaning is rather participation in community, in which aspects like hospitality, friendliness and friendship are important.[313] God is free because God is always able to act in accordance with God's nature, and God's nature is love.[314] This means that God's freedom 'lies in the *friendship* which he offers men and women, and through which he makes them his friends.'[315]

Reasoning back, if divine freedom is God's freedom to act in accordance with God's nature in favour of other people, who are all the objects of God's love, then human freedom is our freedom to act in accordance with our created (rather than fallen) nature, in favour of other people, who are all the objects of God's love. On this account, freedom is not the liberal nirvana of being left to oneself, it is a virtue to be practised in community. '... [F]reedom [is] fellowship with God, man and nature.'[316]

This definition of 'freedom' sounds like it is the equivalent of what is meant in English by the concept of 'fraternity'.[317] Participation in and submission to communal values are therefore not inimical to freedom, provided that those communal values themselves are liberating in that they minister to life. Besides, as Moltmann himself says, pluralism without community is undoubtedly anarchy.

Moltmann's position takes a further twist in two essays in *GSS*, in which he offers a possibility of moving beyond the view of freedom as autonomy, on the basis that our promises, and our faithfulness to them, give us identity in time.[318] It is on the basis of our commitment to our promises, that we and others, know where we stand in the community.[319] It then becomes possible to think of faithfulness and fraternity as the essence of freedom in the Spirit. This emphasis on promises also chimes with his idea that covenant is the basis for

---

[311] Whereas Moltmann seeks to retain the rhetoric of freedom, Milbank challenges it and argues that peace is a more fundamental concept for human flourishing: *Theology & Social Theory*, 314; N. Lash, 'Not Exactly Politics or Power', *Modern Theology* 8 (1992) 359. The problem with Milbank's account, like Moltmann's, is that insufficient substance and meaning is given to sanctification.

[312] Moltmann, *GIC*, 83; *GSS* 182-3; *TKG* 52-56, 107-08.

[313] Moltmann, *GSS*, 206-7; *The Open Church* 52-53; *TKG* 56; Müller-Fahrenholz, *The Kingdom and the Power*, 144.

[314] Moltmann, *GIC*, 75.

[315] Moltmann, *TKG*, 56.

[316] Moltmann, *SL*, 106; *Experiences in Theology* 240.

[317] Moltmann, *SL*, 117-19; *History and the Triune God* 64; *TKG* 215-16.

[318] Moltmann, *GSS*, 87; *Experiences in Theology* 95.

[319] Moltmann, *GSS*, 157.

the legitimation of political authority.[320]

However, in its purportedly communitarian aspect, freedom is being appreciated and accepted *as oneself* by the community of which one is part.[321] But even this, Rasmussen argues, is on Moltmann's account, primarily 'a question of accepting and being accepted as one is, not of being formed through the community.'[322] This means that Moltmann's emphasis on community is insufficient to effect a paradigm shift in the meaning of freedom. Ultimately, he still places significant weight on the idea of freedom as autonomy, which explains his equation of authority with domination.[323]

Confirmation that Moltmann's view of freedom remains heavily marked by the idea of freedom as autonomy is evident in the way he portrays the Spirit of God as the Spirit of freedom. In *SL*, he defines true freedom as 'being possessed by the divine energy of life, and participation in that energy.'[324] Elsewhere, commenting on the relationship between the Holy Spirit and freedom, he says: '... the power of the Spirit is manifested in the fact that it gives the believer freedom, opens the way to the future, to the eternal, to life. For freedom is nothing else than being open for the genuine future, letting oneself be determined by the future. So Spirit may be called the power of futurity.'[325] This sounds more like the language of self-fulfilment than that of biblical discipleship and obedience to righteousness.

As Rasmussen remarks:

> In an interesting way Moltmann's distinction between his political ethics of freedom and justice and his account of personal life in terms of spontaneous self-realization fits the sharp division between the public and the private spheres in liberal societies and theory. He develops a political ethics, but can give no account of how virtuous people are formed more than in terms of liberation.[326]

Although Moltmann talks at various times of freedom understood as rule, community and project,[327] the controlling idea which orients and gives shape to

---

[320] Moltmann, 'Covenant or Leviathan? Political Theology for Modern Times', *Scottish Journal of Theology* 47 (1994); 'Revolution, Religion and the Future: German Reactions', *Concilium* 201 (1989) 49-50; *On Human Dignity* 155-158.

[321] Moltmann, *GSS*, 207; *SL* 104-5, 255-59, 262.

[322] Rasmussen, *The Church as Polis*, 98.

[323] Rasmussen, *The Church as Polis*, 288; S. Hauerwas, *Suffering Presence: Theological Reflections on Medicine, the Mentally Handicapped, and the Church* (Notre Dame, 1986) 56, 41f, 52; *A Community of Character: Toward a Constructive Christian Social Ethic* (Notre Dame, 1981) 84.

[324] Moltmann, *SL*, 115.

[325] Moltmann, *TOH*, 212, quoting R. Bultmann, *Theologie des Neuen Testamentes*, 1953, p.331 (Eng. Tr. pp.334-35); *CPS* 34.

[326] Rasmussen, *The Church as Polis*, 269; *SL* 128.

[327] Moltmann, *History and the Triune God*, 55-69; *TKG* 213-218; *SL* 117-120; *GSS* 155-161; Rasmussen, *The Church as Polis*, 96-98.

the other conceptions of freedom which he explores is that of freedom as liberation from oppression.[328] This has serious consequences for Moltmann's apparent communitarianism, because it means that the idea that persons are constituted in their relationships is never integrated as well into his thought about human societies as it is in his trinitarianism. Too much remains of the liberal idea that individuals should be free to be themselves, with the consequence that their relationships are considered to be external to their personhood.

Charry makes a similar critique to that of Rasmussen. For her, Moltmann's invocation of 'liberation' as a theme justifying the re-orientation of Christian theology towards movements like environmentalism and feminism is dangerous, because the crisis which 'liberation' seeks to solve is one which has been caused by our emancipation from God. Given that we are all affected by human sinfulness, '[s]imple emancipation from external authority is insufficient to fit us for the new life required by and for life in Christ. ... [I]t is under the guidance of God that we are transformed and outfitted to confront the crises of our day that are of our own making.'[329]

Instead of Moltmann's naïve adoption of the modern demonisation of authority as the desire to dominate, Charry argues that the Christian is called to flourish under the call and the cross of Christ and to be transformed by being taken up into the divine life.[330] She argues for a return to Paul's theology, in which freedom from the powers of the world is also freedom directed by God in which Christians become slaves to righteousness.[331] This freedom takes its form as we belong to the body of Christ. Ricoeur makes a similar point in his essay 'Theonomy and/or Autonomy' which was one of the papers offered at the *Festschrift* for Moltmann's seventieth birthday. For Ricoeur, God is love and the primary command God gives to human beings is nothing other than the call to enter into a relationship of love with God, which finds its proper expression, given our creaturely nature, in our loving obedience.[332] These observations made by Charry and Ricoeur would be strengthened by integration with Aquinas's reflections on the life of virtue, which will be considered in the fourth chapter of this thesis. For Aquinas, the Holy Spirit is love and our submission to God and to God's righteousness is not experienced as oppressive exterior domination but liberating interior fulfilment precisely because it is the work of the Holy Spirit within us.

---

[328] Rasmussen, *The Church as Polis*, 106.
[329] E.T. Charry, 'The Crisis of Modernity and the Christian Self' in M. Volf, ed., *A Passion for God's Reign* (Grand Rapids: Eerdmans, 1998) 93.
[330] Charry, 'The Crisis of Modernity', 98.
[331] Charry, 'The Crisis of Modernity', 108.
[332] P. Ricoeur, 'Theonomy and/or Autonomy' in M. Volf, et al., eds., *The Future of Theology: Essays in Honor of Jürgen Moltmann* (Grand Rapids: Eerdmans, 1996) 288-90.

It is also interesting to speculate on the directions Moltmann's thought might take if influenced by O'Donovan's assertion that authority is the correlate of freedom.[333] This would lead to an understanding of order, not as stifling but as liberating. Moltmann seems to contemplate such a possibility, at least in his conception of Church order. In *CPS*, he says: 'The order of Christ's church must therefore be an *order of freedom*, already showing man's redemption from sin, law and death. In the fellowship of Christ, people are freed from the oppression which separates them from others – freed for free fellowship with one another.'[334] This idea is not, however, developed further.

It may be that in organisations such as the Church, authority and obedience can be replaced by dialogue, consensus and harmony.[335] But what would it mean for 'the principle of concord' to displace the 'principle of power' in collectives with a much looser sense of commonality? At most it could mean that laws are promulgated and enforced by institutions having democratic or other communally-accepted forms of legitimacy, and which were administering laws which represented communal values. The customary legal systems across Europe, which Jacques Ellul regarded as classical,[336] and which continue to exist in the Anglo-American common law traditions would be exemplary of this approach to law.

Human Rights and Christian Ethics

It has been said of Moltmann's political theology that he uses human rights in the same way as liberation theologians use Marxist social analysis.[337] In fact, there is surprisingly little stress on human rights within Moltmann's two main cycles of work. Instead, Moltmann tends to talk in general terms in those works of 'liberation'. Reading these works alone, therefore, it might appear that Moltmann uses 'human rights' as a middle axiom, a way of mediating the Christian convictions about the dignity of human beings and the Christian hope of liberation, in a secular world.[338] On this interpretation, Moltmann is using a Christian account of human rights in order to enable Christians to use the same language as the humanists.[339]

However, Moltmann's vision of human rights is difficult to evaluate,

---

[333] Hauerwas thinks along similar lines with regard to the church: see Hauerwas, *A Community of Character*, 53-71, 85, 92; Rasmussen, *The Church as Polis*, 287-88.

[334] Moltmann, *CPS*, 292.

[335] Moltmann, *TKG*, 202; Müller-Fahrenholz, *The Kingdom and the Power*, 148.

[336] Ellul, *The Theological Foundations of Law*, 18-19, 28-36.

[337] Bauckham, *The Theology of Jürgen Moltmann*, 19.

[338] Moltmann, *On Human Dignity*, 7; Bauckham, *The Theology of Jürgen Moltmann*, 19; Rasmussen, *The Church as Polis*, 117.

[339] For another attempt to do so, see J.W. Montgomery, *Human Rights and Human Dignity* (Edmonton, Alberta: Canadian Institute for Law, Theology and Public Policy, 1986, 1995).

because he places it on two foundations, one of which is a distinctively Christian account of human rights and the other of which seems to adopt the prevailing understanding of them in secular thought and their use in interfaith dialogue.

Moltmann grounds his Christian understanding of human rights via the concept of dignity, which is manifested in the actions and attitude of God towards human beings.[340] Because God has given this dignity to all rather than power to one, authority must be justified from below rather than claiming an imprimatur from above. Respect for personal dignity is therefore essential for the legitimation of institutions of law, government and economy.[341] Moltmann also emphasises that the rest of creation has its own dignity too.[342] It too can be the image of God and it too will be deified.[343]

Moltmann's contention is that Christianity can by its faith makes its own contribution to the understanding of our humanity and our rights as human being. In *CPS* 179-181, this is set out in a series of theses. The first thesis insists on the priority of human beings over the state. Political rule must serve human dignity, freedom and responsibility. The second thesis insists on the identification of the rulers with the ruled.[344] The third thesis demands the economic rights to life, work and social security. The fourth thesis prioritises action for human rights 'among and for those who are oppressed and robbed of these rights.' The fifth thesis identifies human duties as important alongside human rights. However, the two duties which Moltmann specifically identifies are 'the right and duty to resist illegitimate and illegal rule' and 'the duty to liberate those to whom these rights are denied.'[345] Moltmann's sixth thesis is that our common humanity and the worldwide nature of the challenges which face us demand a transition towards 'a common organized humanity' and a 'world-wide home policy', which Moltmann seeks, in his later work, through a federal worldwide community of states,[346] which in *Experiences* at least, are related to one another through a series of covenants (*Experiences* 123). The seventh thesis expresses Moltmann's vision of the openness of human rights 'as a process, which is unfinished and, historically speaking, unfinishable.'[347]

Moltman then treats human rights as fundamental for his political thought. He argues that 'We can make human rights the guide-line for the political action and the political resistance of Christians, thanks both to their Christian

---

[340] Moltmann, *CPS*, 187; *On Human Dignity* 4, 9; *GSS* 55, 80-4, 119-23, 223.
[341] Moltmann, *GSS*, 122; *EH* 149-150.
[342] Moltmann, *GSS*, 110, 120, 132; *WJC* 307.
[343] Moltmann, *Coming*, 92, 273; *GIC* 150.
[344] See also Moltmann, *GSS*, 123; *On Human Dignity* 23-25.
[345] See also Moltmann, *EH*, 128-131.
[346] Moltmann, *Coming*, 191; *SL* 247, 252.
[347] Moltmann, *CPS*, 181.

foundation and to their orientation towards humanity as a whole.'[348] It is
'[t]hrough its relationship to human rights the church becomes the church for
the world.'[349]

Moltmann sees human rights as essential in moving away from the bestial
empires envisioned in Daniel towards the humane kingdom of the Son of
Man.[350] He argues:

> Without the enforcement of fundamental human rights to life, freedom and
> security, the lordship of man over man cannot be "human". Without the
> declaration and enforcement of economic human rights, little opportunity is left
> for political human rights. Without the orientation of particular national groupings
> towards world peace and the unification of mankind, there are no "human" states.
> It is in these three directions that Christians will proceed in their political
> professions ... Human rights and the rights of humanity are to be viewed as
> answering to and anticipating the kingdom of the Son of man in the power
> struggles of history.[351]

The programmatic results of this are: first, the desacralisation of political rule.
The emperor's claims to divinity are unmasked as assertions of power and
overreaching.[352] Second, an approach to political orders which sees them as
having a vocation to work towards the welfare of all but not to minister to
salvation. This distinction between welfare and salvation secularises political
rule.[353] To these elements, Moltmann adds democratization.[354]

One of the reasons why Moltmann finds it so easy, so 'natural' (?) to talk of
human rights is that, as he recognises, 'Human rights and personal liberties,
freedom of religion, freedom of belief and of conscience, democratic forms of
government and liberal views of life: all these things grew up together with
Protestantism.'[355] In *HIG*, he attributes the recognition of human rights and
human dignity and their protection by civil law to 'the trinitarian concept of
person'.[356]

However, in 'Human Rights – Rights of Humanity – Rights of the Earth', an
essay first published in 1990, he contends that human rights now make 'a
directly convincing appeal to those who accept that they are not just Americans
or Russians, black or white, men or women, Christians or Jews, but that they

---

[348] Moltmann, *CPS*, 181.
[349] Moltmann, *On Human Dignity*, 7; *EH* 147-148.
[350] Moltmann, *Coming*, 94; *EH* 149; *WJC* 128.
[351] Moltmann, *CPS*, 182.
[352] Moltmann, *CPS*, 178.
[353] Moltmann, *CPS*, 178.
[354] Moltmann, *CPS*, 178-79; *Jesus Christ for Today's World* 26.
[355] Moltmann, *GSS*, 91; *SL* 116.
[356] Moltmann, *History and the Triune God*, 104.

are first and foremost human beings.'[357] Human rights have therefore outgrown their particular origins and acquired the status of self-evident truths.[358] The agent for this universalising must be, on Moltmann's conception of God, the Spirit.

In that essay, Moltmann declares that the situation of the present world crisis is so severe that Christians, like all others, must make human rights their primary goal.[359] On this basis human rights take the place occupied by the principle of justice in the early work of the liberal philosopher John Rawls. They are the primary good to which all must assent, whatever else they are committed to. The danger in Moltmann's approach at this point is that the specifically Christian understanding of the concept fades into the background and is replaced by a mere baptism of the secular conception.[360]

The severity of the dichotomy in Moltmann's thought is illustrated by the decision he makes to choose a commitment to human rights over obedience to the Sermon on the Mount. In the essay, 'Political Theology and the Theology of Liberation', Moltmann identifies the Sermon on the Mount as the basic law (*Grundnorm*) or constitution of God's kingdom in this world.[361] He insists on its imperative in the creation of peace (*WJC* 127) through the demonstration of the divine alternative to violent and unjust societies[362] by the disciples of Jesus (*SL* 121, 153-54, 163; *Source* 62). Given these strong assertions, the following passage from 'Human Rights – Rights of Humanity – Rights of the Earth' is astonishing:

> Today the religions will really only become "world" religions when they begin to integrate themselves into the living conditions and the developing *community under law* of this *one world* and are prepared to surrender their particularist claims to truth in favour of the universalism of truth. ... That also means subordinating their legal codes – the Torah and the Sermon on the Mount, canon law and the Sharia, Hindu and Confucian ethics, and so forth – to the minimum demands of human rights, the rights of humanity and the rights of nature. To cling to the divergencies and contradictions between the religious groups would make them enemies of the human race.[363]

At this point, there are really three possibilities: either Moltmann is abandoning his previous position which emphasised the importance of the Sermon on the Mount, or he is totally confused, or there is a degree of lack of integration in his

---

[357] Moltmann, *GSS*, 117.
[358] Moltmann, 'Human Rights', 120; Rasmussen, *The Church as Polis*, 117. Yet compare Moltmann's own critique of natural rights in *Man* 71-75.
[359] Moltmann, *GSS*, 17, 118, 125; *Coming* 206.
[360] Rasmussen, *The Church as Polis*, 118.
[361] Moltmann, *GSS*, 58; *Jesus Christ for Today's World* 10.
[362] Moltmann, *GSS*, 197; *The Power of the Powerless* 59; *SL* 175.
[363] Moltmann, *GSS*, 133; *CJF* 46.

thought caused by a conceptual muddle. Of those three options, the last one seems to be the most likely. Whichever conclusion is reached on this point, there is an irreconcilable tension between Moltmann's wish to stress the importance of following Jesus' teaching on the one hand and his insistence on the absolute priority of human rights.

The reason for Moltmann's problem is clear in relation to his discussion of the rights of nature.[364] Moltmann's reasoning is purely survivalist, based on his belief that because God is so committed to God's creation, the devastation of this world would be catastrophic for God.[365]

There would be nothing in principle to stop Moltmann from identifying the nature of the global challenge facing humanity, and then plumbing the depths of his own religious tradition for the resources with which to meet that challenge. He could, and does, give good Christian reasons for believing certain actions and laws to be necessary to confront the crisis which faces humanity. He could then insist that the gravity of the challenge makes it imperative that thinkers in other religions either find similar resources from within their own traditions or modify them. None of this surrenders the Christian claim to normative truth nor relativises the uniqueness of Jesus and of His teaching.

The nature of Moltmann's difficulties merely establishes that human rights are the modern form of natural law.[366] The problem is how to balance an adequate Christian account of human rights or natural law with an account which establishes the universally binding nature of human rights or natural law.[367] Over-emphasis on universal relevance always risks the erection of a non-Christian or sub-Christian morality as normative. Moltmann's stress on human rights would be met by as emphatic a *Nein* from Barth as Brunner's views were!

There are also internal tensions within Moltmann's support for human rights. Such rights are not self-evident, at least not in their application nor where they conflict with one another. The Western liberal atomistic conception of human rights is one with which Moltmann is unhappy. He argues that

> [t]he person does not "take precedence" over the community, nor does the community "take precedence" over the person. ... The rights of persons can be implemented only in a just society, and a just society can be attained only on the

---

[364] Moltmann, *On Human Dignity*, 33-35.

[365] Moltmann, *CJF*, 34-36.

[366] J. Lockwood O'Donovan, 'The Concept of Rights in Christian Moral Discourse' in M. Cromartie, ed., *A Preserving Grace: Protestants, Catholics and Natural Law* (Grand Rapids: Eerdmans, 1997) 143.

[367] I have argued elsewhere that Aquinas was seeking to articulate just such a balance, and has been misunderstood by subsequent generations of thinkers: D.H. McIlroy, 'What's at stake in natural law?', *New Blackfriars* 89 (2008) 508-21. It is unclear whether the later Moltmann would continue to hold that natural law does not extend over time, as he did in an early essay: *Hope and Planning* 112-18.

foundation of personal rights. The liberty of persons can develop only in a free society, and a free society grows only out of the liberty of persons.[368]

In fact, as has been seen, Moltmann does have a specifically theological account of certain human rights.[369] However, he does not give a developed account of how his preference for solidarity and social justice ought to be integrated into theory and praxis. There are exceptions to this is in relation to the right to work and to private property. In both cases, Moltmann's critique is radical.[370] If Moltmann's general propositions were equally radical, the distinctive nature of his contribution to the debate about human rights would be clear, but the claim to self-evidence would have to be given up.[371] It is precisely as a Christian theologian that Moltmann makes his most important contributions to the debate about the shape of human rights and responsibilities. Yet with the singular exception noted above, Moltmann tends to speak in general terms of human rights.

In his adoption of human rights and the idea of liberation, Moltmann has been guilty of what Milbank would regard as the sin of allowing Christian theology to be overcome by pagan categories. Paeth reads Rasmussen's critique of Moltmann's theology in *The Church as Polis* as proceeding along Milbankian lines.[372] For Rasmussen, Moltmann is framed within Enlightenment categories such as 'freedom', 'self-realization', and 'rights' which are beholden to individualistic conceptions of autonomy and therefore contrary to a Christian understanding of society and of the nature of the good.[373] However, Paeth argues that this criticism is an excessive one, if Moltmann's emphasis on the Church as a contrast society which 'through its existence ... calls into question the systems of violence and injustice' is given due weight.[374]

Ellen Charry also sees the Christian gospel being supplanted in Moltmann's theology by the invocation of the hopes of modernity. With regard to our present crisis, the solution Moltmann proposes is not a re-appropriation of Christian themes, but rather the reinterpretation of Christian teachings 'so that they follow after secular movements, like environmentalism and feminism, that seem to point modern society in a salutary direction.'[375]

---

[368] Moltmann, *GSS*, 124.
[369] Rasmussen, *The Church as Polis*, 116-17.
[370] Moltmann, *On Human Dignity*, 37-60; *CJF* 13-14; *GSS* 164; Müller-Fahrenholz, *The Kingdom and the Power*, 113.
[371] Rasmussen, *The Church as Polis*, 118-19, 169.
[372] S.R. Paeth, 'Jürgen Moltmann's Public Theology', *Political Theology* 6 (2005) 220.
[373] Rasmussen, *The Church as Polis*, 89.
[374] Paeth, 'Jürgen Moltmann's Public Theology'; citing *WJC* 122.
[375] Charry, 'The Crisis of Modernity', 92.

The Spiritual Nature of Justice

In *Man* at 75, Moltmann seeks to define justice in dynamic terms.

... it is not the invocation of a supposedly objective moral law, but the unavoidable task of altering the world, of healing it, of bettering it, of making it more worthy of man and more worth living in, that can be regarded as the norm of justice. One then moves from the mythology of an abstract moral law to the concrete Utopia of the rights of man and to a legal system which is intended for citizens of the world. ... If in place of the natural rights of man we were to speak of man's "future rights", we would do more justice to the actual relationships of men.

The ideas of ordering implicit in *shalom* and Moltmann's own holistic pneumatology, and the use of justice as an eschatological concept,[376] lead to an understanding of justice as Spiritual, and the mission to bring justice as part of the mission of the Spirit of God. In 'Peace the Fruit of Justice', Moltmann makes the point, which is palpable in its absence in other parts of his thought, that 'Peace is not the absence of power, but the presence of justice.'[377] He goes on in the article to discuss the importance of the biblical concept *zedaka* (*tsedeqah*) for people's relations with God, with one another, and with the rest of creation.

In 'Peace the Fruit of Justice', Moltmann proposes the same epistemological approach to justice as that put forward by O'Donovan. The pursuit of justice begins by the recognition of injustice. In Moltmann's view, this primarily assumes 'the form of siding with the powerless and with victims of violence.'[378]

For Moltmann, the Spirit of God is the justice-making Spirit.[379] It is justice which frees law from domination. In *SL*, Moltmann speaks of the 'justice of compassion' as the highest form of justice and as the 'creative source of justice for every rule of law'. This creative justice, through which 'people receive the rights of which they have been deprived, and ... the unjust are converted to justice' is, Moltmann argues, 'not something outside the human rule of law ... [but] is itself the creative source of justice for every rule of law which leads to lasting peace.'[380] However, as Müller-Fahrenholz notes 'unfortunately he does not discuss what this must mean in detail.'[381] In particular, Müller-Fahrenholz laments the 'absence of an explicit discussion of the theme of forgiveness' in

---

[376] In 'What Has Happened to our Utopias?', at 120-21 Moltmann identifies 'the utopias we live from, and to which we are prepared to commit ourselves' as 'the utopia of justice', 'the social utopias of human equality' and 'a new love for life.'
[377] Moltmann, 'Peace the Fruit of Justice', 113.
[378] Moltmann, 'Peace the Fruit of Justice', 115-6.
[379] Moltmann, *Source*, 110.
[380] All quotations in this paragraph are from Moltmann, *SL*, 142. See also *CJF* 38-40.
[381] Müller-Fahrenholz, *The Kingdom and the Power*, 191.

human affairs,[382] which seems to be a consequence of Moltmann's emphasis on the fact that God alone can atone for sins.

Moreover, one of the major deficiencies in Moltmann's thought about law is that instead of seeing the possibility of the Spirit working righteousness beyond law, his primary reference is to the Spirit of justice working justice through the vindication of rights. This leaves out of account the dimensions of justice beyond rights and, even more pertinently, a positive vision for the contours of justice beyond law as people are conformed by the power of the Spirit to the image of the One who was Justice-Incarnate.

Müller-Fahrenholz sees law as a central, but limited, instrument in creating justice. It is limited because it can only deal with the grossest abuses and harms.[383] He rightly identifies the need for forgiveness and compassion beyond the law. Again this suggests the work of the Holy Spirit as the Spirit of redemption and of the resurrection working through law and beyond law.

It will be argued in the fourth chapter of this thesis that Aquinas affirms law within an eschatologically oriented account of sanctification. There is only one place in Moltmann's writings where he comes close to espousing a similar view. This is a sermon on Jeremiah 31:31-34 which he preached in the 1970's.[384] In that sermon, Moltmann reflects on the promise that God will write God's law in the hearts of God's people and describes it in terms of a vision of a renewed people for whom

> Doing good is no longer a task or a duty. It is a delight and a matter of course. A person does what is good just because it is good, not because it has been commanded, not out of fear and not out of hope. The law is no longer law for anyone for whom God's law is "written in the heart". He has become a new person. He no longer lives "under" the law, threatened and impelled by it. He lives "in" the law. He is righteous. "Love and do what you like", as Augustine rightly put it. (*The Power of the Powerless* 42).

The concept of living 'in' and not 'under' the law is a beautiful one, and approximates to Aquinas's understanding of Christians' relationship to the Holy Spirit, who is the new law. Regrettably Moltmann does not develop such a vision further in his major works.

Criticisms of Moltmann's Trinitarianism

Moltmann set himself the task of proving that belief in the Trinity makes all the difference to political theology. Having reviewed the pertinent dimensions of his thought, it is now possible to evaluate his success in that task.

---

[382] Müller-Fahrenholz, *The Kingdom and the Power*, 191; there is the briefest hint of it in *GSS* 189. See N.G. Wright, *Disavowing Constantine*, 167.

[383] Müller-Fahrenholz, *The Kingdom and the Power*, 192.

[384] Moltmann, *The Power of the Powerless*, chapter 5.

Unfortunately, the conclusion must be that he has failed, for the following reason. It seems as if Moltmann has considered the violent history of (European) humanity, has reflected on the challenges facing humanity and has projected into the future a vision of the sort of society he believes it is (self-evidently) necessary must come into existence in order to ensure human survival and flourishing. He then reads that vision of society up into the Godhead. To put it another way, the criterion of *praxis* becomes, for Moltmann, the criterion of truth. What kind of vision of God is most conducive to the social vision which is necessary for survival?

Rasmussen therefore sees not the Trinity but the worldview of the knowledge class to which Moltmann belongs as the operative force behind his theology.[385] Tanner finds it surprising that Moltmann can emphasise perichoresis so strongly without giving any theological weight at all to the *taxis* within the Trinity, and in particular to the evidence in the biblical economy of Jesus 'acting in a non-mutual relation of subordination to the Father.'[386] Otto's thesis is that it is German Idealism and Marxist revisionism which provide the foundations for Moltmann's thought and that his trinitarianism is merely a superstructure (in Marxist terms) which needs to be stripped away to reveal the anthropocentrism of his theology.[387] Molnar would categorise Moltmann as one of those contemporary trinitarian theologians whose conception of the Trinity is designed to give dogmatic status to relationality, which concept can then be used 'in order to create a society of persons existing in freedom and equality'.[388] Kilby is especially critical of the way in which this outcome is achieved, and would support Otto's assertion that in fact it is Moltmann's convictions about the desirable shape of human relations which dictate his account of the triune God.[389] The doctrine of the inner life of God is simply hijacked to justify a particular view of the just social order.

Without going as far as Otto, the best that can be said is that Moltmann's utopia of the *polis* – his vision of a non-authoritarian, liberating community of solidarity and respect for human rights – causes him to flatten out the biblical evidence regarding the Trinity. Elements of economic subordination (or at least submission) between God the Father and Jesus are ignored; the testimony to the divine *monarchia* of the Father is rejected on *a priori* grounds; and the way in which the prophets spoke of the promise of the Spirit is neglected. If Moltmann's trinitarianism fails to do anything other than reflect back theologically convictions already held on other grounds, it is ultimately because he has failed to engage sufficiently with the biblical texts upon which orthodox trinitarianism was built.

---

[385] Rasmussen, *The Church as Polis*, 150.

[386] Tanner, 'Trinity', 324.

[387] Otto, *The God of Hope*, 199, 211, 227-33.

[388] Molnar, *Divine Freedom*, 163.

[389] Kilby, 'Perichoresis and Projection', 433, 440-41.

Richard Bauckham is a much more sympathetic interpreter and critic of Moltmann, but even he recognises that the idea of the Trinity as 'an interpersonal fellowship in which we, by grace, participate'[390] is underdeveloped in Moltmann's thought. Bauckham points out:

> we enjoy highly differentiated relationship to the three divine persons. ... The point of Christian talk of the Trinity is to ground precisely this highly differentiated threefold relationship in which Christians come to know God and to participate in the divine life. ... The way in which this enables freedom needs developing in a different way ... from Moltmann's argument.[391]

It will be argued in the fourth chapter of this thesis that Aquinas can be read as offering an account of the differentiated threefold relationship between Christians and God which is richer in possibilities for conceptualising the role of human law than the way in which Moltmann seeks to draw analogies from the inner life of God to the model for human communities.

Towards a Synthesis of Moltmann's View of Law

As has already been seen, in the struggle between the oppressors and the oppressed, Moltmann has not one answer but two to the question: on which side of the battle lines is law to be found? There is an almost unequivocally negative aspect in much of his work, but at other points he is alive to the positive potentialities of good law.

Law as a Negative Power

In his early work, and most poignantly in *The Crucified God*, law appears to be equated with domination. Law finds itself arraigned alongside the other rulers of this age who are coming to nothing (1 Cor. 2:6).

The theme of law as a negative power evident in Moltmann's early work returns in *Coming*. The Christian understanding of human law is obviously heavily dependent on our view of God's righteousness and his laws, and of the relationship between divine righteousness and human justice. In *Coming*, Moltmann sets out his considered vision of God's righteousness. It is a vision in which although all people are accountable for sin,[392] hell is not eternal,[393] and there will be universal salvation of each and every thing, even the devil will

---

[390] Bauckham, 'Jürgen Moltmann and the Question of Pluralism', 160.
[391] Bauckham, 'Jürgen Moltmann and the Question of Pluralism', 161.
[392] This accountability is preserved, although God Himself has already atoned for sins: Moltmann, *SL*, 134.
[393] Moltmann, *Coming*, 250.

be redeemed.[394] All of this appears to be pneumatologically driven. Through the Holistic Spirit, God has invested too much (of Godself) in God's creation and God's creatures to let any part of it perish.[395]

At this point, it becomes clear that the cross and the resurrection have ceased to be the operative poles in Moltmann's thought. Because the salvation of all of creation is necessary pneumatologically, in the end it turns out that the resurrection and the new creation are consequent upon, not the cross, but the original creation.[396]

The question which such an understanding of Moltmann's theological schema leaves hanging is: why was the cross therefore necessary? The primary answer Moltmann gives to that question is that the cross is God's expression of suffering solidarity with God's creation.[397] But since such solidarity is also, and in *GIC* and *SL*, from before Christ expressed in terms of the Spirit's indwelling of the creation,[398] the cross is the result of the Spirit's outpouring and not vice versa. It is true that Moltmann does not exclude sin as part of the reason for the cross, but he conceives of such sin as having its origins in violence.[399] The result is that God overcomes sin by identifying with and consoling the victims of violence[400] so this necessitates no new dimension of the cross over and above its symbolic effect as a declaration of divine solidarity with creation (*In the End* 69).

As against human law and human justice, this eschatological demonstration of divine justice is Wholly Other.[401] It transcends any attempts to foreshadow it

---

[394] Moltmann, *Coming*, 254, 110, 240-41. It is not clear how this relates to Moltmann's comment in *WJC* at 286 that 'the powers of death which are hostile to God and life are not going to be reconciled and will not be integrated even into Christ's rule of peace. His rule means that they will be eliminated from creation.'

[395] Moltmann, *SL*, 50; *CJF* 67; *Coming* 255, 132; *In the End* 148. This is also a result of Moltmann's kenotic doctrine of creation: *GIC* 86-88, as is pointed out by Gunton, *The Triune Creator*, 140-41. Yet as Gunton points out, a trinitarian doctrine of creation ought to have quite the opposite effect: *The Triune Creator* 9. Another indication of this underlying theme in Moltmann's thought can be seen at *CJF* 32; Rasmussen, *The Church as Polis*, 326.

[396] Moltmann insists that the contrary is the case at *Coming* 251.

[397] Moltmann, *Future*, 22; *TKG* 4, 99; *WJC* 168; *Jesus Christ for Today's World* 38-40; Bauckham, *The Theology of Jürgen Moltmann*, 11, 15; Clarke, *A Cry in the Darkness*, 74; Letham, *The Holy Trinity*, 299-300.

[398] Moltmann, *GSS*, 104; *TKG* 111; *GIC* 68-69, 102; *SL* 34-35, 47-51, 62, 64; *Experiences* 288. Molnar, *Divine Freedom*, 221.

[399] Moltmann, *SL*, 132-38; see also *Coming* 255 where talking about 'sins' in the context of the Last Judgment he describes them as 'every act of violence, the whole injustice of this murderous and suffering world'.

[400] Bauckham, *The Theology of Jürgen Moltmann*, 11.

[401] Moltmann, *CG*, 142.

through human legal systems on earth.[402] Human law is then back to being a power over against people, at worst associated with violence and domination, at best belonging to the world order that is passing away.[403]

All of the above would be a coherent position, with its two-term interpretation of the world, of its depressing realities and God's glorious possibilities, but for the fact that it is undercut by Moltmann himself in another part of his thinking. As creation becomes more important for Moltmann, he increasingly recognises the necessity of law to protect human rights and the rights of nature.

Law as an Ordering Power

Moltmann challenges the discontinuities of creation and redemption (he should more accurately speak of nature (i.e. nature as it now is) and redemption) and in his second cycle of writings proposes instead a threefold categorisation of *creatio originalis – creatio continua – creatio nova.*[404]

Adopting this triad enables him to achieve three things. With regard to *creatio originalis*, it enables him to argue that this was good, but open for perfection from the beginning, a perfection which it will only attain in the *eschaton*.[405] With regard to the *creatio nova*, he can avoid thinking about salvation as redemption from this world doomed to destruction and think instead of salvation for the sake of this world destined to be re-created for recreation, worship and sabbath rest in God.[406] With regard to *creatio continua*, Moltmann places the idea of preparation side by side with that of preservation. God's actions in sustaining the world not only preserve it from destruction by the powers of evil but also prepare it for its re-creation.[407] In this way, Moltmann is able to emphasise the continuity and coherence between the Spirit's action in the creation and His work in bringing about the new creation.[408]

This analysis opens the door to a much more positive view of law as not only preserving and sustaining but also contributing to the new creation. The move is similar to that from the orders of preservation to the divine

---

[402] Moltmann, *Coming*, 250: '… the eschatological Last Judgment is not a prototype for the courts of kingdoms or empires. This Judgment has to do with God and his creative justice, and is quite different from the forms our earthly justice takes.' See also *CG* 142.

[403] Moltmann, *WJC*, 154; *Coming* 318-19.

[404] Moltmann, *TKG*, 209; *GIC* 55; *WJC* 286-7; *Jesus Christ for Today's World* 94-99; *SL* 8-9.

[405] Moltmann, *Coming*, 91.

[406] Moltmann, *GIC*, 189; *WJC* 283, 302. See also Gunton, *The Triune Creator*, 171.

[407] Moltmann, *TKG*, 209; *GIC* 209; *WJC* 291, 287.

[408] See also Moltmann, *WJC*, 281. Gunton observes in a footnote in *The Triune Creator* 89, that the same impetus can be achieved by simply twinning conservation with providence.

mandates.[409] This conception of law is capable of being both forward- as well as backward-looking. Law is no longer just about preserving the *status quo;* it has a calling. It can participate in the actions of the God who 'creates justice for those who have never known justice' and who 'fulfils his promises in historical experiences.'[410] It opens the way for Moltmann to escape from what has often been a Lutheran failing, a lack of reflection on the coordinating possibilities of power.[411]

In *WJC*, Moltmann seeks to give his pneumatological doctrine of creation christological foundations. In *WJC* 306-12, Moltmann develops what is, in substance, an ecological doctrine of reconciliation. The specific creation of human beings in the image of God is downplayed in favour of a greater emphasis on the continuities between human beings and the rest of creation. He argues:

> What is needed if there is to be collaboration based on life together [between human beings and nature] is the recognition of the particular and the common dignity of all God's creatures. This dignity is conferred on them by God's love *towards* them, Christ's giving of himself *for* them, and the indwelling of the Holy Spirit *in* them. A recognition of this dignity leads to the perception of the *rights* of every individual creature in the all-comprehensive community of creation, a community which is based on law.[412]

Moltmann argues that 'Reconciliation through Christ is the foundation for a community based on law, in the cosmos as well as among God's people.'[413] The parallel here seems to be between the work of Christ and the Exodus of Israel, both of which are followed by the giving of a new law. [414] Moltmann chooses the idea of the sabbath as the biblical proof that '[t]he community of creation is a community based on law'.[415] From the sabbath laws, he deduces that 'God's people and his land belong within a common order of law. The land is not only given to *God's people*; the people is also given to *God's land.*'[416] The people therefore not only have rights over the land, they also have responsibilities towards it.

The reason for this change of emphasis is that Moltmann's assessment is that

---

[409] In Moltmann's first programmatic theological work *The Community against the Horizon of the Rule of Christ* (1959), Moltmann refers to Bonhoeffer's divine mandates, at 25. For the significance of this work, see Müller-Fahrenholz, *The Kingdom and the Power*, chapter 2.

[410] Moltmann, *WJC*, 291.

[411] N.G. Wright, *Disavowing Constantine*, 47.

[412] Moltmann, *WJC*, 307; *SL* 10; *CJF* 68.

[413] Moltmann, *WJC*, 307.

[414] Moltmann, *SL*, 114.

[415] Moltmann, *WJC*, 309-10; *CJF* 66-71.

[416] Moltmann *WJC* 310; *CJF* 61-65.

the present ecological crisis is so grave that law, rather than spontaneous liberating action, is the only viable solution (*Experiences* 314). The link to other aspects of Moltmann's thought is via human rights. Moltmann sees the legal basis for the community of creation in the universalisation of human rights, or to be more exact, the recognition that 'the earth system and all animal and plant species have their own rights, and that these must be observed.'[417] Law and legal systems become forces capable of good, provided that their primary function is to uphold and enforce these rights, especially, presumably, those which only the poor, the oppressed, the dumb and the silenced have as their entitlement.

Although this conception of law is pregnant with possibilities, it is not thought through by Moltmann. There seem to be two reasons for this which are caused by structural deficiencies in his theology. One is that Moltmann does not conceptualise, alongside his triad of creations, a triad of graces.

The idea of saving grace (*gratia salvifica*), which correlates to the *creatio nova* is classical in Christian thought. Neo-Calvinism partnered this with common grace (*gratia communa*), which correlates with *creation continua*. Common grace is the idea that God's grace is at work in the many blessings which God showers on human beings irrespective of their righteousness or their response to God. Moltmann speaks of 'the grace which is already shown in the preserving and sustaining of creation, human sin and cosmic disorder notwithstanding' which manifests God's patience and gives us time.[418]

It is grace which resolves the theological conundrum of why God created the world. The *creatio originalis* is an act of divine grace, freely willed and congruent with God's nature. The *creatio continua*, God's perseverance with the world, is another act of grace on his part, freely willed and flowing from God's nature of love.[419] The *creatio nova* is a further act of divine grace, established in the free choice of God the Son and God the Father united by God the Holy Spirit that Jesus should surrender Himself to death in order to break the powers of death and sin which had enslaved the world. All is grace. Original grace joins saving grace and common grace to complete the triad of graces.

If Moltmann's three-fold scheme of *creationes* is understood in the light of grace, and to this is added his ideas about human dignity and reconciling justice, then Moltmann begins to offer a positive vision of the possibilities for human law to anticipate the new creation and to be a parable of the kingdom of God.

The great strength of grace as a mediating concept in this regard is that if it is viewed as a dynamic, not as a thing, as an action of the Holy Spirit, rather than a *stasis*, then it can be understood as an eschatological concept, even if the

---

[417] Moltmann, *WJC*, 308.
[418] Moltmann, *WJC*, 290.
[419] Moltmann, *GIC*, 163.

Church has often failed to do so. On such an understanding, grace captures precisely the essence of the inbreaking of something new, the *advent* of new possibilities which Moltmann insists is at the heart of Christian hope.[420] Common grace, understood in this way as an activity of the Holy Spirit, then brings the orders of creation to life, giving them eschatological direction as well as ontological justification, and providing the solution to the problem of the conservatism of Protestant station-ethics.[421]

Seeing law as a provision of God's grace therefore makes it possible to understand liberating justice as having a place in human legal systems. Understanding it to be a provision of God's common grace means that this can be done without mistaking it as having saving value in itself.

In trinitarian terms, this common grace would seem to be *per appropriationem* the work of God the Holy Spirit, creating time and space for the work of God the Son whose liberating justice leads human beings and creation back to the perfect rule of God the Father. God's common grace is then, like God's special grace, understood as being God's power and forbearance at the disposal of God's glory and for the sake of God's kingdom.

However, Moltmann cannot conceive of *gratia originalia* because he never manages to escape from a position in which creation itself is necessary for God.[422] This has profound ramifications in *Coming*. His eschatological universalism is the consequence of the fact that he does not conceive sufficiently of creation as being God's free and gracious choice. Without original grace, common grace and saving grace cease to be acts of the God who loves in freedom and become necessary actions on the part of God.

The second reason is that a whole dimension of the importance of morality and law is ignored by Moltmann, and in particular the messianic hopes associated with morality and law. This blindspot is the result of the fact that the Third Person in the Trinity is, for Moltmann, the Holistic rather than the Holy Spirit. Moltmann grounds Christ in Israel's hope but he fails to do the same with the Holy Spirit. Whatever the controversies about the gospel saying to the same effect, when Paul says in 2 Corinthians 3:6 that 'the letter kills, but the Spirit gives life' it is expressly in the context of a comparison between the Law of the Old Covenant and the Spirit of the New Covenant. In this passage and its parallel in Romans 7 to 8, Paul is undoubtedly drawing on his personal experience. But it seems likely that he is also drawing on the corporate experience of Israel recorded in Jeremiah and Ezekiel to the effect that the Torah is unable to give life and that what is required to make human beings

---

[420] Moltmann, *TOH*, 92; *GIC* 133; *Coming* 114-116.

[421] Moltmann, *TOH*, 332.

[422] Bauckham, *The Theology of Jürgen Moltmann*, 24-25 records this criticism although without explicitly endorsing it himself. Other than an early essay in which he articulates the classical understanding of creation: *Theology & Joy* 40-41, the closest Moltmann comes to the idea suggested here is in *TKG* 59.

righteous (Rom. 8:4) and into the image of God (2 Cor. 3:18) is a new spirit.

Notwithstanding these deficiencies, there is in *WJC* and *SL*, a basis for conceiving of the positive possibilities of law in creating justice. It is (self-) evident that the human rights and rights of nature which Moltmann emphasises, require legal protection. They demand a corresponding theory of liberating justice. There is ample biblical material upon which to base such a theory.[423] The law may have, under certain circumstances, negative consequences, but this is not necessarily the whole story. Retributive justice is not the only face of the law.

Integrating Solidarity, Liberation and Human Rights into a Theology of Law:
Law as Creative Justice

The importance of the ideas of liberation, solidarity and human rights in relation to a theology of law is that their implementation in society necessitates a commitment to justice.[424] If Moltmann does not have a developed theology of law, he has the building blocks for a theology of justice, and therefore a potential contribution to make to a theology of law.

As Moltmann recognises in *WJC* and in *God for a Secular Society*, human rights and even more the rights of nature can only be secured by law.[425] Just as the legal abolition of slavery was necessary to effect liberation (*GSS* 111), so too, 'a community of life shared with all other living things on earth remains no more than an illusion and a dream unless it is realized in the form of a community of all the living which has *a legal basis.*'[426]

What develops then is an account of law in which those who hold legal authority do so not 'in their own right' but rather 'on behalf of the community.' Political authority and its concomitant 'monopolization of the legitimate use of physical force in the enforcement of its authority' is derived from the people and 'can only be legitimated if it is exercised for the benefit of those involved.'[427] The legal authorities are nothing more than that, they are authorities under law, accountable to the people, bound by the constitution and subject to a separation of powers.[428] Moltmann denies that Christianity provides a justification for authority 'from above' and insists that political authority must be justified 'from below' on the basis of a contract between the people and their rulers.[429] Just as God has bound Godself to God's people through the covenant,

---

[423] See, for example, my exploration of this material in chapter 5 of my *A Biblical View of Law and Justice.*

[424] Moltmann, *SL*, 271.

[425] Moltmann, *GSS*, 110-1

[426] Moltmann, *GSS*, 130, italics original.

[427] Moltmann, *CPS*, 176.

[428] Moltmann, *GSS*, 123.

[429] Moltmann, *On Human Dignity*, 23-25.

so human rulers are called to do likewise.[430] Power is therefore not *malum per se*, but it is dubious, and therefore in need of perpetual justification. Its principal source of justification is its role in creating justice. Ordering is also necessary, but Moltmann is continually fearful that law and order will turn into security for the oppressors.[431]

It is thus possible to derive from Moltmann's thinking the recognition that wielding coercive power involves the temptation and tendency to domination[432] but is subject to the calling and possibility of effecting liberation.

Even though law can be used preferentially in this way, to protect the rights of the poor, given the corrupting nature of power, law-making and law-enforcing power must be used responsibly. Moltmann seeks to provide a framework for this through the idea of covenant.[433] The power of rulers is not to be used arbitrarily, in assertion of the tyranny of free choice. On the contrary, Moltmann would want to model it after his conception of God's exercise of free choice; rulers should commit themselves to keep faith with the people.[434] In *WJC*, Moltmann sees the problem as being one of transforming power relationships from relationships of straightforward lordship and subjugation into relationships of reciprocity.[435] Power is justified in the interests of the people it serves, not on the basis of a divine imprimatur.[436]

The 'health warning' which Moltmann would immediately wish to attach to any such view of law, however, is that

> even service can make people dependent and be a concealed form of the love of domination. In Christendom titles like *servus servorum* and "the first servant of the state" were claimed by spiritual and secular potentates. It is therefore important to grasp that acknowledgment of Jesus as Lord leads not to domination through service but to service for freedom. ... What is meant is selfless service, which is solely out for the human rights and dignity of the other.[437]

Moltmann would wish to prevent the development of the omnicompetent state, which through its civil service and its social services, deprives people of the responsibility for and the opportunity to live their own lives. He does not advocate paternalism, but liberation. Power is therefore legitimate if it is used for the benefit of others, to attain a good which they could not secure for

---

[430] Moltmann, *EH*, 127-129.
[431] Moltmann, *History and the Triune God*, 63; *GSS* 155.
[432] Moltmann, *RPS*, 39.
[433] Moltmann, *SL*, 252.
[434] Moltmann 'Covenant or Leviathan?'. This is also the implication from Moltmann's account of the liberty of persons at *GSS* 87.
[435] Moltmann, *WJC*, 246.
[436] Moltmann, *RPS*, 40.
[437] Moltmann, *CPS*, 103; N.G. Wright, *The Radical Kingdom* (Eastbourne: Kingsway, 1986) 93; Rasmussen, *The Church as Polis*, 289.

themselves. Law is called to intervene in the service of justice to effect liberation for people which they cannot achieve for themselves.

Synthesising Moltmann's Visions of Law

Is any reconciliation possible between the two different approaches to law present within Moltmann's work: a predominantly negative one and one alive to the positive possibilities of good law? If the issue was that Moltmann speaks with two different voices depending on whether he is talking about christology and eschatology on the one hand, and pneumatology, on the other, reconciling what he says would be difficult enough. Matters are not so straightforward, however, because when Moltmann returns to the theme of christology in *WJC*, he is far more positive about power than he was in *CG*. In *WJC*, Moltmann moves beyond a vision of law as retributive justice, and envisages the use of power to create justice. In this regard the theology of *WJC* is much more in tune with that of *SL*, to which it is closest in time, than with either Moltmann's earlier *CG* or his later *Coming*.[438]

To what extent can, should, and must human legal systems reflect the fatherly rule of God, the grace of Jesus Christ and the solidarity of the Holy Spirit? An exasperated critic might conclude, as Moltmann himself does in his considerations of some aspects of biblical teaching,[439] that there are two different visions which cannot be harmonised. Producing a complete synthesis does appear to be unachievable.

However, attempts might be made in that direction in thinking about the distinction between:

1) what law is called to do: preserve order and create justice; and
2) what law is tempted to do: protect the powerful and legitimate injustice.

In that case, Moltmann's views in *WJC* and *SL* represent an appreciation of law's calling, and his criticisms in *CG* and *Coming* an understanding of the extent to which it in fact falls short of that calling.

Another way of putting it might be to think about the difference between:

a) the standard against which human laws will be held accountable; and
b) what we may *realistically* expect from them.

This latter distinction would chime more clearly with Reformation theology's views of all human beings as under God's judgment. It opens the way to think

---

[438] There is an isolated reference in *Coming* at 301 to the importance of legal systems for securing the free spaces in social life in which individual freedom can be realised.
[439] Moltmann, *WJC*, 286.

about human legal systems as sustained by God's grace,[440] provided that it is immediately qualified by the assertion that Moltmann is not a Christian Realist but rather would see God's grace as constantly breaking in from his future into the situations of despair today.[441] What seems impossible to human beings may be possible with God.

Perhaps the clearest explanation of Moltmann's mature understanding of the potential of human law as an anticipation comes in the essay 'The Liberation of the Future' published in 1999. In that essay, Moltmann makes reference to the 'creative justice of God' which 'gives human laws their legitimation and at the same time relativises them. Faithful observance of the established law and the demand for better justice then make of the prevailing legal system a process that points towards the future.'[442]

A legal system may be anticipation of the kingdom, if it encourages 'acts of human justice on the foundation of the approaching justice of God' and so in this way 'earthly justice' may '*prepare the way* for God's coming kingdom.'[443] However, using the example of international trade, Moltmann maintains the eschatological proviso by pointing out that:

> juster prices in international trade are [not] already the kingdom of God itself; but, for all that, they correspond to the kingdom more closely than unjust prices. There is no identity between the divine justice of the coming kingdom and the human justice of conditions in our world.[444]

Conclusion

A Critique of the Powers-That-Be

The decisive implication of Moltmann's trinitarianism is that God is not to be understood as the Almighty, legitimising the tyranny of the powerful over the weak. God is instead the loving God who has identified Godself through the Son and in the Spirit with the suffering creation.

Moltmann's critique of the powers-that-be in the name of the lordship of Christ calls the use of law into question. His views about the kingdom of God as freedom tend to suggest that authority in general, and therefore legal authority in particular, ought to be suppressed and restricted as much as possible.

If the law is conceived of as essentially conservative, as having as its function to preserve order and to stabilise society against chaos and collapse,

---

[440] Moltmann, *SL*, 143.
[441] Rasmussen, *The Church as Polis*, 96.
[442] Moltmann, 'The Liberation of the Future', 285.
[443] Moltmann, 'The Liberation of the Future', 289, italics in the original.
[444] Moltmann, 'The Liberation of the Future', 288.

then it is by its nature resistant to and possibly even antithetical to Moltmann's social vision.

What is, on the face of it, inescapable is that law belongs to the age which is passing away.[445] As a secular ordinance all human laws are destined to be transcended by the rule of God. That this is the inherent nature of law appears to make it antithetical to Moltmann's ideas of the eschatological hope and to raise questions about whether it is possible to expect 'anticipations' of the future within human legal systems, in the same way that Moltmann expects anticipations in other spheres of human life.

Moltmann understands the Church as having a vocation, not to support authority, law and order in society, but rather to 'criticize and stand back from the partial historical realities and movements which [people] have idolized and made absolute.'[446] Because Christianity is a religion of promise and hope, Christians can never be resigned to, nor even satisfied with, the *status quo*.'[447]

However, when governing authorities intervene on behalf of the lost, the rejected and the oppressed, then they are acting in line with the mission of the Church, and the Church can therefore offer them critical support.[448] The Church is therefore affirmative of good laws and legal systems which minister to life whilst being alert never to accord to these provisional, fallible and fragile systems of order either ultimacy or uncritical support. Christians seek to love their neighbours, which usually includes obedience to the law but may, as the old Calvinist Scottish Confession of 1560 recognises require us to resist unjust laws '… to save the lives of innocents, to represse tyrannie, to defend the oppressed.'[449] Moltmann invokes a natural law logic here, arguing that if power is exercised in a way which is contrary to human rights, it is illegitimate and must therefore be resisted as an act of obedience to God.[450]

Justice as the Calling of Human Law

It is through a conception of the spiritual nature of justice that law as an institution in theory, as a structure ordering human societies, is justified. The strong emphasis on justice in Moltmann's theology, understood in terms of solidarity (i.e. social justice), liberation (i.e. freedom from oppression and for autonomy) and human rights, constantly places the legal powers-that-be in the position of being answerable to the poor for their use of their authority. This is

---

[445] Moltmann, *CPS*, 63, 350.
[446] Moltmann, *CG*, 12.
[447] Moltmann, *TOH*, 102.
[448] Moltmann, *CPS*, 352.
[449] Article 14 of the Scottish Confession of 1560, cited by Moltmann in *CPS* 385, footnote 81 to chapter 4; 'Covenant or Leviathan?', 20-23; *On Human Dignity* 24-25; *EH* 129, 140.
[450] Moltmann, 'Covenant or Leviathan?', 26.

the message which Moltmann draws from the life of Jesus.

It is justice which frees law from domination. Although Moltmann seeks to ground solidarity and liberation in the incarnation of Jesus, the difficulty is that Moltmann's own account of solidarity, liberation and human rights seems too close to the current debates within humanist liberalism to offer a distinctive Christian perspective.

The danger with Moltmann's political theology is that the openendedness he envisages with regard to liberation leads us to deify *our* visions of justice.[451] Moltmann paints the ideal future in such broad terms as to render concrete criticism of it from a Christian perspective almost impossible: who, after all, is against the idea of a just and peaceful society?[452] The counterbalance is Moltmann's eschatology, which argues for God's justice, although it is far from clear whether and how such justice could be reflected in human institutions.

Another danger of putting Moltmann's approach into practice, is that he too blithely assumes that it is possible to tell, in advance, and in the here and now, which side is right and which is wrong.[453] Also, there is perhaps insufficient space in Moltmann's theology for what may be one of the most humble analytical tools: the doctrine of the lesser of two evils. Again the doctrine of the Holy Spirit serves to identify that there are some evils for which God alone has the cure.

Nonetheless, it is possible to develop from Moltmann's thinking the insights that human laws and legal systems are subject to the temptation of domination,[454] but have the calling of liberation. To put it another way, the temptation of law is to support the powerful; the calling of law is to defend the weak. It is justice which delivers law from the temptation of domination.

The fact that political authority has a given function means that there is a calling upon it, a calling which it can live up to or repudiate. As with all human beings and all human enterprises and institutions, government and each particular example of it fails to live up to their calling. The continuing existence of particular governments is therefore a matter of grace. This should not be a surprising conclusion, because God's continued toleration of the human race at all is a matter of grace.

Righteousness beyond Justice

However, having said all this, Moltmann's theology of law is skewed, because

---

[451] Rasmussen, *The Church as Polis*, 131-2.

[452] Rasmussen, *The Church as Polis*, 350-51; J.H. Yoder, *The Priestly Kingdom: Social Ethics as Gospel* (Notre Dame, 1984) 144.

[453] Müller-Fahrenholz, *The Kingdom and the Power*, 181; Rasmussen, *The Church as Polis*, 225.

[454] Moltmann, *CPS*, 90; Müller-Fahrenholz, *The Kingdom and the Power*, 86; N.G. Wright, *Disavowing Constantine*, 173.

it places primary emphasis on politics (of which law is seen as part) as the locus for justice. Moltmann says far less about justice in private relations. Given his emphasis on eschatology and on God coming from the future, Moltmann's account poses the question of the extent to which law can and should have a forward direction to it. It is the Holy Spirit whom one would expect to provide this direction. In Moltmann's thought it does so as the Spirit of freedom and the Spirit of justice. As Moltmann himself notes in *SL*, 'Unjust and evil structures compel people to do evil, ... But just structures and beneficial conditions do not automatically make people good.'[455]

In the New Testament, there is a far greater emphasis on internal righteousness which then expresses itself in external actions rather than a primary focus on external behaviour alone. In this framework, human law is exposed as limited in its scope. Whereas the Law governing external behaviour came through Moses, grace and truth came through Jesus Christ (John 1). If such is the comparison to be drawn between the revelation of Christ and the Spirit-given Law of Moses, *a fortiori* human laws are incomplete and inadequate when compared with Spirit-empowered living. The way forward to the new creation of all things is not through constrained conformity to the wills of human legislators but through joyful, spontaneous obedience to the loving direction of God.[456] On this analysis, law is given forward direction not *in se* but in being transcended through righteous living in the Spirit.[457] This is what one would expect to find from the power of the resurrection.[458] While Moltmann sees that obedience to law cannot justify,[459] he fails to explore the idea of righteousness in the Spirit because his pneumatology is one-sidedly holistic and lacks a messianic or salvation-historical dimension. The hints which do emerge in his thought are consequent upon his christology, which is seen in this light.[460]

Ironically, were Moltmann to incorporate the 'messianic' references to the Spirit in the Old Testament into his theology, it might enable him to give full weight to his negative comments about authority. If the Old Testament is read as demonstrating the fallenness and inadequacies of human legal systems, even if their laws *are* God-given (as opposed merely to being seen as such), then the prophecies about the Holy Spirit in Jeremiah and Ezekiel are seen as promising a change of heart through the giving of the Spirit which will make justice,

---

[455] Moltmann, *SL*, 140; *Experiences in Theology* 247.
[456] Moltmann, *Future*, 95; *The Open Church* 38; *SL* 123; Rasmussen explores in *The Church as Polis* at 99-108 the reasons why Moltmann is not able to develop his thought in this direction, which are in large part due to Moltmann's failure to appreciate how and why self-control is a fruit of the Spirit.
[457] There are hints in this direction in Moltmann *Future* at 54-55.
[458] Moltmann, *TKG*, 89; *Coming* 71.
[459] Moltmann, *Future*, 160-62; *RPS* 34.
[460] Moltmann, *GIC*, 292.

righteousness, holiness and social virtue possible. The Holy Spirit then becomes the means by which the community of virtue[461] becomes conceivable.

This line of thought also challenges those tendencies in Moltmann's work, especially in his early work, which are overoptimistic about what can be achieved through political change. If this is so, then we are freed from precisely the dangers of excessive deference to legal authorities which Moltmann is worried about. Political change and political orders can no longer be the bearers of the divine future, because they are incapable of effecting the internal changes which are at the heart, literally, of the new life which the Spirit of God comes to bring.

This aspect of the work and person of the Holy Spirit presupposes the inability of law alone to create a just society and reveals that in terms of law/morality it is through the agency of the Spirit that justice/righteousness is promoted. It is not primarily legal systems and power structures but rather human beings who are indwelt by the Holy Spirit and given future orientation through the Spirit's presence.

---

[461] This is the description Rasmussen gives in chapter 10 of *The Church as Polis* to a key aspect of Hauerwas' ethics, as set out in *A Community of Character* and elsewhere.

Chapter 3

Oliver O'Donovan: Political Authority in the Light of the Ascended Christ

Introduction

Whereas Moltmann aims for breadth, what is particularly impressive about O'Donovan is the depth of his immersion in the classical tradition of Christian political thought. However, if Gunton is right that there is a trinitarian deficiency in that tradition, the risk O'Donovan runs in building on that tradition is of incorporating its trinitarian deficiency into his own thought.

O'Donovan is acclaimed for his work in the fields of moral and political theology. He offers an account of political authority which seeks to affirm the important but limited role of such authority. In particular, he emphasises that political authority is limited by law and that the practice of judgment is the central function of political authority in the Christian era. In this chapter, O'Donovan's account of political authority will be examined in the light of the Trinity. It will be argued that for all its emphasis on the kingship of God and the centrality of Christ, there is a pneumatological deficit which has not yet been adequately remedied. It will then be suggested, in the second half of this chapter, that addressing this deficit might strengthen O'Donovan's arguments regarding the practice of judgment whilst calling for a re-consideration of his position regarding the appropriate relationship between political authority and the Church.

Trinitarian Considerations in O'Donovan's Account of Political Theology

The Kingship of God

O'Donovan's account of political authority begins with an account of the reign of God over God's people, Israel.[1] His political theology could be summarised as a sustained reflection on the political implications of the First Temple refrain *YHWH malak* (*DON* 32).

O'Donovan's argument regarding political authority proceeds in three

---

[1] O'Donovan, *DON*, 19.

stages. The first stage is an account of the reign of God. The second is to identify the Davidic monarchy as the unitary representation of that divine rule within Israel. The third is to treat that representation as paradigmatic of political authority generally, subject to its re-orientation in the light of the Ascension.

At the first stage, O'Donovan argues that YHWH's kingship over Israel is manifest in YHWH's provision of salvation, judgment and possession.[2] God's actions in these regards call forth the praise of God's people. O'Donovan argues that the three notions of salvation, judgment and possession

> shape Israel's sense of political identity and define what is meant by saying that YHWH rules as king: he gives Israel victory; he gives judgment; he gives Israel its possession. ... [E]ach of these affirmations can be tilted towards either of the others: the notions of victory and judgment come together in the idea of YHWH's "vindication"; the notions of judgment and possession meet in the conception of YHWH's law; and the notions of possession and victory are associated in the role played by Mount Zion as the focus of Israel's security. (*DON* 45).[3]

The kingship of YHWH meant that the natural order was stable, that the international political order and the future of Israel were under God's control, and that YHWH was concerned for justice and law within Israel, especially in favour of the oppressed and the vulnerable (*DON* 32). It also meant that there was a fulfilment of the goods of creation to be expected (*DON* 19) and this fulfilment was consonant with and an outworking of God's reign over God's people. O'Donovan argues that 'Israel's knowledge of God's blessings was, from beginning to end, a political knowledge, and it was out of that knowledge that the evangelists and apostles spoke about Jesus.' Precisely because of this, Jesus was the one around whom were centred hopes for 'a new national life for Israel' and 'the hope of a restored world order. The future of the one nation was a prism through which the faithful looked to see the future of all nations.' (*DON* 23)

Secondly, O'Donovan understands the kingship of YHWH was conferring authority on 'the political act' (*DON* 20). In *DON* O'Donovan claims that such acts and consequently political authority are personal, and 'The assimilation of the idea of authority to office and structure was a cardinal mistake which arose as Western politics turned its back on its theological horizons.'[4] However, *WOJ* displays much more enthusiasm for 'institutions', that is to say, for differentiated arrangements for the deployment of various sorts of power and

---

[2] O'Donovan, *DON*, 36; C. Bartholomew, 'Introduction' in Bartholomew et al., eds., *A Royal Priesthood?* (Carlisle: Paternoster, 2002) 29.

[3] S. Hauerwas, and J. Fodor, 'Remaining in Babylon: Oliver O'Donovan's Defense of Christendom', *Studies in Christian Ethics* 11 (1998) 37.

[4] O'Donovan, *DON*, 20, 16.

the execution of different forms of judgment.[5] Those who are called to exercise judgment typically do so within the context of roles, each of which has its own responsibilities, and those responsibilities bind the actor (*WOJ* 53). O'Donovan's point is that the act is prior to the institution (*WOJ* 128, 234), so that where the institutions have failed, whoever finds themselves in the position to carry out the act should do so (*WOJ* 208). Nonetheless, institutionalised authority is the normal case and is valuable because it provides 'a series of common practices in which the exercise of political authority has a regular position.' (*WOJ* 135). Operating within regular human institutions is therefore an important part of the normal practice of political authority, but O'Donovan argues, is not essential.

A third key characteristic of the reign of God which O'Donovan identifies is that it has been uniquely expressed through the history of Israel.[6] Attention to the history of Israel is important because it purports to take seriously the whole history of divine action as it has been *revealed*.

Thus at the first stage of the argument, O'Donovan identifies the three dimensions of his reflection on the reign of God: it is a reign which purposes the redemption and fulfilment of the goods of creation, which gives authority to human political acts, and which is to be understood in the history of Israel as paradigmatic for all other nations. However, following the resurrection-ascension, the kingship of God must be understood as 'the authority of the exalted Christ',[7] and it is O'Donovan's understanding of that authority which must be explored once the other two stages in his argument have been sketched.

At the second stage of the argument, in *39 Articles*, O'Donovan considers sympathetically the approach the English Reformers took to the Old Testament monarchy. Faced with the exaggerated claims of the pope, and in the absence of a readily available biblical model of monarchy shorn of the special features of the Davidic covenant,[8] 'the patterns of authority established in the Davidic monarchy in ancient Israel' were an obvious place to turn.[9]

O'Donovan recognises that in the Davidic monarchy there is a messianic and typological element to this rule which cannot properly be translated into political authority after the coming of Christ. However, he argues that the Old

---

[5] Allocation of authority among different institutional bearers does not, for O'Donovan, imply that political authority is intrinsically plural. On the contrary, in 'What Can Ethics Know about God?' in A.J. Torrance and Michael Banner, eds., *The Doctrine of God and Theological Ethics* (Edinburgh: T&T Clark, 2006) at 43, O'Donovan insists that 'The very possibility of political community rests on the fact that a unitary authority may underlie a multitude of bearers. … The source of authority unifies the field, however distributed and diversified its exercise may be.'

[6] O'Donovan, *DON*, 21.

[7] O'Donovan, *RMO*, 141.

[8] O'Donovan, *On The Thirty Nine Articles: A Conversation with Tudor Christianity* (Carlisle: Paternoster, 1986) 103.

[9] O'Donovan, *39 Articles*, 102-103.

Testament is short on non-theocratic models of kingship and of exemplars of natural political rule shorn of additional claims (in the case of the Egyptians, Assyrians and Babylonians) or calling (in the case of the Davidic monarchy). Nonetheless, ultimately his judgment is that the use made of Josiah at the coronation of Edward VI illustrates precisely the same mistake as is made by those who defend Christian sacerdotalism on the basis of continuity with the Levitical priesthood, in that it fails to take into account the decisive changes wrought by the Incarnation.

It is, however, regrettable that O'Donovan does not spend more time reflecting on the Old Testament material which speaks about the relationship of God to the kings of the nations. Whatever the questions about the dating and the historical accuracy of the stories of Joseph, Moses before Pharaoh and Daniel, they contain clear theological messages.[10] In particular, and whatever its date, Daniel spells out an understanding of Nebuchadnezzar's power as held from the Lord (Dan. 2:31-35) and subject to a duty is to do what is right and to be kind to the oppressed (Dan. 4:27).[11]

O'Donovan identifies similar obligations as incumbent on the Israelite kings. The king's role was to safeguard the relationship between the people and YHWH through protection of the land and enforcement of the law, but he was not free to re-define that relationship. The kings were always answerable to God's law.[12] Their role was to offer security and judgment which the judges had failed to provide (*DON* 56). However, although the king was under law, it was legitimate for him to provide 'unitary representation of YHWH's rule' (*DON* 61).

Whilst O'Donovan recognises 'the unique meaning of the monarchy in Judah as an expression of the covenant of election between God and his chosen people',[13] he insists on its value as a paradigm of the virtues of princely government. He makes the telling point that: 'When the prophets rebuke the kings about their failures to give judgment for the poor, or when the king solemnly swears to walk with integrity of heart within his house, we ... immediately suppose that all rulers are meant to hear and imitate. There is, then, in the Davidic monarchy ... a model of what kings as such should rightly be.'[14] In O'Donovan's view, to deny this is almost to annul the ability of the Old Testament to instruct us in matters of social justice. Given the example of Nebuchadnezzar quoted above, this may be to overstate the case.

O'Donovan's approach to his Old Testament material has the considerable

---

[10] O'Donovan accepts a Seleucid dating for Daniel, but discusses its message only briefly, at *DON* 83, 87-88.

[11] D. Hughes with M. Bennett, *God of the Poor: A Biblical Vision of God's Present Rule* (Carlisle: OM Publishing, 1998) 27-28.

[12] O'Donovan, *DON*, 62.

[13] O'Donovan, *39 Articles*, 103.

[14] O'Donovan, *39 Articles*, 103-104.

merit of consistency with the findings of modern scholars about the probable dates at which the books in the Hebrew canon reached their final form.[15] However, as McConville points out, canonically speaking, both the Torah and the critique of the monarchy stand as prior facts before the narrative of Judges-2 Kings is presented.[16] What O'Donovan risks losing by adopting such an approach is hearing the 'story' which those books, in their canonical form, seek to tell.[17] It is doubtful, by way of prime example, whether O'Donovan's understanding of the Judaic kings as the unitary mediator of YHWH's judgments to YHWH's people (*DON* 60-61) can be said to be the message which the editors of the Old Testament books as they stand intended us to hear. His use of the historical-critical method also means that he is reading the Old Testament in a way which was not open to the thinkers of Christendom whose thought he is also attempting to interpret.

Whenever the Torah was reduced to written form, its basic themes and some of its material reflect a pre-monarchical consensus as to the distinctive nature of the Israelite polity. The prophetic rebukes to the kings were predicated on the basis of that understanding of what God required. It is the Torah rather than the kingship which provides the fundamental model of social justice, and the interaction between prophets and kings is merely a vivid demonstration of its outworking.

Instead of the Torah, O'Donovan's account of the Old Testament is dominated by a vision of the king at the centre of things and by the exile. The former point is dependent upon his re-construction of the sequence in which the Old Testament texts were written, which is radically different from the canonical presentation of the texts.[18] The latter idea, of exile, as a separation of political and religious power is critical for his conclusion that in Christ those branches of power are reunited.

The third stage of O'Donovan's argument, which treats the Israelite understanding of kingship as paradigmatic is, as Wolterstorff points out, asserted by O'Donovan rather than argued by him.[19] O'Donovan outlines its

---

[15] O'Donovan, 'Response to Respondents: Behold the Lamb!', *Studies in Christian Ethics* 11 (1998) 96; Bartholomew, 'Introduction', 37.

[16] G. McConville, 'Law and Monarchy in the Old Testament' in Bartholomew et al., eds., *A Royal Priesthood?* (Carlisle: Paternoster, 2002) 73.

[17] R.W.L. Moberly, 'The Use of Scripture in *The Desire of the Nations*' in Bartholomew et al., eds., *A Royal Priesthood?* (Carlisle: Paternoster, 2002) 50-53, 63; McConville, 'Law and Monarchy', 72-73. A.T. Lincoln makes a similar point with regard to the treatment of the Gospels: 'Power, Judgement and Possession: John's Gospel in Political Perspective' in Bartholomew et al., eds., *A Royal Priesthood?* (Carlisle: Paternoster, 2002) 149.

[18] N. Wolterstorff, 'A Discussion of Oliver O'Donovan's *The Desire of the Nations*', *Scottish Journal of Theology* 54 (2001) 90.

[19] Wolterstoff, 'Discussion', 100-101; Hauerwas and Fodor, 'Remaining in Babylon', 46.

paradigmatic nature through six theorems:[20]

1) Political authority arises where power, the execution of right and the perpetuation of tradition are assured together in one co-ordinated agency (*WOJ* 142);

2) That any regime should actually come to hold authority, and should continue to hold it, is a work of divine providence in history, not a mere accomplishment of the human task of political service (*WOJ* 189);

3) In acknowledging political authority, society proves its political identity;

4) The authority of a human regime mediates divine authority in a unitary structure, but is subject to the authority of law within the community, which bears independent witness to the divine command;

5) The appropriate unifying element in international order is law rather than government (*WOJ* 211);

6) The conscience of the individual members of a community is a repository of the moral understanding which shaped it, and may serve to perpetuate it in a crisis of collapsing morale or institutions.

These theorems will be considered in more detail in subsequent sections of this chapter. Before doing so, however, it is necessary to explore the difference O'Donovan believes the coming of Christ has made to the practice of political authority.

The Centrality of Christ

O'Donovan's *Resurrection and Moral Order* addresses a fundamental challenge for Christianity: how does one give full value to the affirmation that something decisive took place in and because of the life, death and resurrection of the incarnate Son of God, whilst at the same time acknowledging its continuity with the created order, as a new act of the same God who created the universe within which the incarnation took place.

For O'Donovan, 'God makes himself known supremely in the historical event of Easter'.[21] O'Donovan places the accent on the resurrection because it is this moment which is the manifestation of Jesus as the Christ and the Son of God, rather than just a tragic, self-sacrificing hero.

O'Donovan insists that something new happened at the resurrection, of

---

[20] The theorems emerge in O'Donovan, *DON*, on pages 46-47, 65, 72, and 80 and are conveniently collected together by Bartholomew in *RP* 29-30 and by Hauerwas and Fodor in a footnote in 'Remaining in Babylon', 39.

[21] O'Donovan, *39 Articles*, 60.

which the ascension is best understood as a part.[22] The resurrection has meaning *in itself*, and is not merely revelatory of what has already happened on the cross. The meaning of the resurrection-ascension is, for O'Donovan, decisive both for ethics and politics.

O'Donovan affirms creation, preservation and redemption as distinct activities of the triune God.[23] Apart from the works of creation and redemption, God rules over history through providence.[24] He distinguishes the relationship of Christ to the moral order on the one hand and political authority on the other on the basis that the moral order is founded in creation whereas political authority is located exclusively in providence.

O'Donovan is in agreement with Moltmann's statement that 'In the New Testament the raising of Christ from the dead is always bound up with his enthronement as Lord of the divine rule.'[25] However, O'Donovan understands the link between resurrection and ascension to have very different implications in terms of what the lordship of Christ means in the here and now.

For O'Donovan, the resurrection is both Easter *and* Ascension (*DON* 142, *RMO* 14). 'The resurrection of Christ, upon which Christian ethics is founded, vindicates the created order in this double sense: it redeems it and it transforms it. For the resurrection appears in the Gospels under a double aspect, as the restoration of Jesus from the dead and as his glorification at God's right hand.'[26] The transformation of the created order is a distinct act of divine freedom, 'in keeping with the creation, but in no way dictated by it.'[27] Thus O'Donovan prevents Christian eschatology from collapsing into teleology. 'The eschatological transformation of the world is neither the mere repetition of the created world nor its negation. It is its fulfilment, its *telos* or end.'[28] Seeing creation in the light of the resurrection, enables human beings to discern the natural meaning of things and the natural purpose of things.[29]

However, despite the resurrection vindicating creation order, O'Donovan insists that creation and redemption are distinct works of God. He rejects the idea of 'continuous creation' as a Manichean idea constituting 'a denial of the decisiveness implied in the term "creation" and [being] really only concerned to assert continuousness. (*DON* 143).[30]

For O'Donovan, the resurrection was a decisive and complete victory. Although there is a balance to be kept 'between what has been accomplished

---

[22] O'Donovan, *39 Articles*, 35.
[23] O'Donovan, *JWR*, 2.
[24] O'Donovan, *Begotten or Made?* (Oxford: OUP, 1984) 13.
[25] Moltmann, *GIC*, 172.
[26] O'Donovan, *RMO*, 56.
[27] O'Donovan, *RMO*, 64; 'The Natural Ethic' in D.F. Wright, ed., *Essays in Evangelical Social Ethics* (Paternoster, 1981) 27.
[28] O'Donovan, *RMO*, 55.
[29] O'Donovan, 'The Natural Ethic', 23.
[30] Hauerwas and Fodor, 'Remaining in Babylon', 32.

and what remains to be accomplished', in O'Donovan's view it is 'only from within the perspective of our time-frame [that] anything remain[s] to be accomplished at all. Christ's triumph is complete, and in that event mankind has been brought into the presence of God's glory. Nothing remains to be added to what has been done; we wait only for a fuller sight of it.' (*DON* 143). Nonetheless, 'the present hiddenness of God's new creation demands its fulfilment in public manifestation, the *parousia* or "presence" of the Son of man to the cosmos in which God is to be all in all.'[31] Our personal redemption awaits 'the public redemption of the cosmos.'[32]

It is easy to misunderstand O'Donovan as thinking in terms of a straight line from Jesus' resurrection-ascension to his *parousia*; from the inauguration of the new eschatological era to the final display of His glorious reign. The danger of this misunderstanding is compounded because, as Carroll complains, O'Donovan 'offers no sustained exposition of the "not yet" of eschatology'.[33]

Moltmann's approach to this time between times in which we live is to think in dialectical terms of two opposite movements: one of victory over the powers which enslave the world and the other of identification with the poor and the godforsaken. These two movements: of humiliation and of exaltation, stand side by side in the present age.[34] For O'Donovan, while the note of martyrdom is not absent from his theology, it is a *possibility* rather than integral to the life of the Church.[35] Furnish argues that there is, in O'Donovan's political theology, a feeling at times that the cross has dropped out of sight, and that O'Donovan is proclaiming an exalted and enthroned Christ rather than the resurrected-Crucified One.[36]

THE CENTRALITY OF CHRIST TO THE MORAL ORDER

Taking his cue from Augustine,[37] in *Resurrection and Moral Order*, O'Donovan argues that the moral reality in nature can only be truly understood and interpreted on the basis of the realised eschatology of the resurrection-ascension, albeit that even then some things remained veiled until the *parousia*.

---

[31] O'Donovan, *RMO*, 249.

[32] Bartholomew, 'Introduction', 32.

[33] M.D. Carroll, 'The Power of the Future in the Present: Eschatology and Ethics in O'Donovan and Beyond' in Bartholomew et al., eds., *A Royal Priesthood?* (Carlisle: Paternoster, 2002) 123; Hauerwas and Fodor, 'Remaining in Babylon', 42 footnote 6; *DON* 91ff; R.J. Neuhaus, 'Commentary on *The Desire of the Nations*', *Studies in Christian Ethics* 11 (1998) 58.

[34] Moltmann, *TOH*, 83.

[35] O'Donovan, *DON*, 178-79, 215, 217, 269; Hauerwas and Fodor, 'Remaining in Babylon', 42 footnote 6.

[36] V.P. Furnish, 'How Firm A Foundation? Some Questions about Scripture in *The Desire of the Nations*', *Studies in Christian Ethics* 11 (1998) 23.

[37] O'Donovan, *The Problem of Self-Love in St. Augustine* (New York: Yale University Press, 1980) 79.

It is in *Problem* that he first argues that

> Between that which is and that which will be there must be a line of connection, the redemptive purpose of God. ... However dramatic a transformation redemption may involve, however opaque to man's mind the continuity may be, we know, and whenever we repeat the Trinitarian creed with Saint Augustine we confess that our being-as-we-are and our being-as-we-shall-be are held together as works of the One God who is both our Creator and Redeemer. (*Problem* 159).

O'Donovan is a moral realist, that is to say, he believes that there really is an objective moral order given in creation.[38] Central to O'Donovan's account of the objective moral structure of creation are teleology and ordering.[39] The things which constitute human goods have been given to us by God.[40] 'There is given in creation an order of kinds and ends, within which our actions ... attain their intelligibility. Our task as moral agents is to participate in this order, understanding it and conforming to it in what we think and do.'[41] Human beings, both as individuals and as societies, confronted with this objective moral order, seek to make sense of it in order to enable themselves to live within it.[42] It is the correspondence of Christian ethics to the true nature of reality, as revealed and affirmed in the resurrection, which grounds their universal force.[43] The problem is that, because of the Fall, human beings misinterpret this objective moral order because in failing to recognise Christ, they fail to acknowledge their true place within it.[44]

O'Donovan seeks to relate both creation and history to God. Creation is, however, primary; because it is the framework within which history takes place.[45] Only a recognition of the created order, apart from history, argues

---

[38] O'Donovan, *RMO*, 191; 'What Can Ethics Know about God?', 39; R. Black, *Christian Moral Realism: Natural Law, Narrative, Virtue and the Gospel* (Oxford: OUP, 2000) 8.

[39] O'Donovan, *The Christian and the Unborn Child*, 2nd edn. (Nottingham: Grove Books, 1975) 9; *RMO* 143; Carroll, 'The Power of the Future in the Present', 120.

[40] Black provides a list of the goods identified by O'Donovan in tabulated form at *Christian Moral Realism* 53.

[41] O'Donovan, *RMO*, 127, 250; J. Chaplin, 'Political Eschatology and Responsible Government: Oliver O'Donovan's "Christian Liberalism"' in Bartholomew et al., eds., *A Royal Priesthood?* (Carlisle: Paternoster, 2002) 296.

[42] O'Donovan, *BOI*, 318.

[43] O'Donovan, *RMO*, 16. Milbank, another contemporary theologian heavily influenced by Augustine, has advanced a similar line of argument, most famously in *Theology & Social Theory*, though his clearest appeal to the resurrection as the point which determines that the Christian worldview is the only one which sees the world as it really is, comes in *The Word Made Strange* at 250. Where O'Donovan's account is superior, however, is that it is more firmly grounded in the actual biblical narratives.

[44] Black, *Christian Moral Realism*, 117.

[45] O'Donovan, *RMO*, 188-90.

O'Donovan, provides us with a definite criterion against which to judge sin and evil.[46] Our discernment of the moral order is not the invention of a moral framework in a vacuum, it is a response to the moral structure which is *already there* in creation.

Rules such as do not murder and do not commit adultery are universally binding because they are operative in the context of the 'reality of a divinely-given order of things in which human nature itself is located.'[47] The basis for moral action is 'a public and publishable understanding that claims all mankind, whether or not it comprehends it.'[48] However, and this is where O'Donovan departs from Brunner and joins with Barth, this ontological reality may only be apprehended in the light of the resurrection of the Christ in whom it finds its coherence.[49]

'[I]n Jesus we meet the moral order itself revealed as incarnate.'[50] In the resurrection of the incarnate Christ, the one in whom creation finds its coherence is made manifest. What is unique about Jesus is not the 'moral authority' of His teaching, but His authority as the divine Word demonstrated 'in his resurrection [in which] the moral order was publicly and cosmically vindicated by God.[51]

With regard to O'Donovan's theory of epistemology, a note of qualification must be sounded. We live in the era between Christ's resurrection and our own. Paul in 1 Corinthians 13 famously pointed out that our knowledge in this world is still partial and incomplete. Jesus taught that our love of Him, our obedience to Him and our knowledge of Him grow together. In this world they will all be incomplete. Therefore our appropriation of His resurrection vision is incomplete.

For O'Donovan, with the resurrection-ascension of Christ the moment of vindication of creation *has* occurred. The peace of God (*shalom*) which is the ontological truth of creation and the goal of history has broken into creation through the death and resurrection of the incarnate Son of God.[52] In his essay 'The Political Thought of the Book of Revelation' O'Donovan argues at length how the message of the Apocalypse is that '[t]he sacrificial death of God's

---

[46] O'Donovan, *RMO*, 63.

[47] O'Donovan, *RMO*, 16.

[48] O'Donovan, *Begotten or Made?*, 12-13.

[49] O'Donovan, *RMO*, 85-86, 249; Bartholomew, 'Introduction', 22-23, 38; 'A Time for War', 101-104; L. Bretherton, *Hospitality as Holiness: Christian Witness Amid Moral Diversity* (Aldershot: Ashgate, 2006) 4; G. de Kruijf, 'The Function of Romans 13 in Christian Ethics' in Bartholomew et al., eds., *A Royal Priesthood?* (Carlisle: Paternoster, 2002) 226.

[50] O'Donovan, *RMO*, 147.

[51] O'Donovan, *RMO*, 148.

[52] O'Donovan, *JWR*, 2. Milbank similarly lays stress on the fact that Christianity holds to an ontology of peace: *Theology & Social Theory* 363, 409; *Being Reconciled: Ontology and Pardon* (London: Routledge, 2003) 42; *Word Made Strange* 225.

Messiah is the event to interpret all events. It alone can offer human existence the assurance of cosmic meaning which is required. It justifies creation within history, and justifies history within creation.'[53] O'Donovan argues strongly that the Bible should be interpreted as the unfolding of God's self-revelation through historical process.[54] O'Donovan contends that the Hegelian presuppositions about the nature of history *in general* are only illuminating when applied to the Bible because the Bible itself claims to reveal a sacred history.[55] O'Donovan would deny such a sacral character to extra-biblical history, although without abandoning it to chaos.[56] History is neither meaningless nor overwhelmed by meaning. The work of the Holy Spirit within history may be discerned, but only with the eyes of faith and only interpretatively rather than 'objectively'.[57] Such is the mystery of divine providence.

However, although it is the resurrection which gives meaning to history, human societies are constantly tempted to find alternative keys. For O'Donovan, human politics faces the constant temptation to ascribe ultimate value to itself: the Party, the *Volk*, the Empire, the cause of international socialism, free trade or other ideologies can all lay claim to be the bearers of history, the future or ultimacy.[58] In one of his strongest uses of the Trinity, O'Donovan opposes nuclear deterrence on the basis that it seeks to place the future of the world *entirely* in our own hands.[59] Against this, O'Donovan says:

> *Our objection ... takes on a trinitarian shape.* The deterrence-idea tells the truth neither about the Creator, nor about the Messiah, nor about the Spirit. The Creator did not make total disorder and set it abroad in war; the Messiah is not revealed in war; and the Spirit does not direct history simply through irrational outbreaks of mass violence.[60]

Nonetheless, although the resurrection-ascension is the vantage point from which the meaning of history and the shape of the ethical landscape may be truly discerned, it is not the sole moment of ethical importance. O'Donovan argues that in discerning the moral order Christians have to reflect on all the

---

[53] O'Donovan, *BOI*, 30; 'The Natural Ethic', 25-27; *DON* 153.
[54] O'Donovan, *39 Articles*, 58-64.
[55] O'Donovan, *39 Articles*, 58-59.
[56] O'Donovan, *39 Articles*, 61.
[57] O'Donovan, 'Behold, the Lamb!', 104.
[58] O'Donovan, *Peace and Certainty: A Theological Essay on Deterrence* (Oxford: Clarendon, 1989) 28, 86; *BOI* 36-37; W. Schweiker, 'Freedom and Authority in Political Theology: A Response to Oliver O'Donovan's *The Desire of the Nations*', *Scottish Journal of Theology* 54 (2001) 121.
[59] O'Donovan, *Peace and Certainty*, 46-47, 59-62.
[60] O'Donovan, *Peace and Certainty*, 47, 102, emphasis mine.

moments of the Christ-event: on His advent, passion, restoration, exaltation.[61]

Christian ethics is not static, because God's vindication of creation points forwards towards its renewal, 'towards a life which goes beyond this order without negating it.' (*RMO* 15). The history of God's actions does give rise to developing ethical demands. Putting it in trinitarian terms, the moral order in creation owes its origin to the Father, finds its coherence and redemption in the Son, and is directed and perfected by the Spirit. The resurrection-ascension looks both back over the created order and forwards to the eschatological horizon.[62] O'Donovan argues that in 1 Peter 1:13, 2:13ff., is to be found such a structure of ethics elaborated with regard to the institutions of human life, especially the institutions of government, labour and marriage.[63] It is this which O'Donovan seeks to develop programmatically in relation to politics in *The Desire of the Nations*.

CHRIST'S KINGSHIP AND THE *ESSE* OF POLITICAL AUTHORITY

What O'Donovan grasps and reasserts is the transcendental nature of political authority; it must find its legitimation outside itself, whether in popular sovereignty, in nature or in its God-givenness.[64] He argues that Christian political thought must begin from the conviction that "there is no authority but from God" (Rom. 13:1).'[65]

O'Donovan wants to rehabilitate the concept of 'authority', which he sees as an elementary structure of reality,[66] against the outright scepticism of much of contemporary political theology and its omission in liberation theology.[67] He argues that the notions of authority and of political activity as kingly become intelligible if we reflect upon the reign of God.[68] In doing so, the primary sources of instruction about the nature of political authority are to be found in the Old Testament model of kingship (already considered) and in Romans 13.

Understanding authority is essential for O'Donovan because our commitment to the goals of justice, peace and human dignity, 'must take place within a context of political institutions supposedly serving those very ends...'[69] This context is one of political authority expressed fundamentally in

---

[61] O'Donovan, *RMO*, prologue to the second edition xvii-xviii.
[62] Black, *Christian Moral Realism*, 115.
[63] O'Donovan, *RMO*, 58.
[64] D. Novak, 'Response to *The Desire of the Nations*', *Studies in Christian Ethics* 11 (1998) 66.
[65] O'Donovan, *39 Articles*, 98.
[66] O'Donovan, *DON*, 15.
[67] O'Donovan, *DON*, 16.
[68] Bartholomew, 'Introduction', 27; C.J.D. Greene, 'Revisiting Christendom: A Crisis of Legitimization' in Bartholomew et al., eds., *A Royal Priesthood?* (Carlisle: Paternoster, 2002) 314.
[69] O'Donovan, *DON*, 17.

terms of 'structures of command and obedience.'[70]

For O'Donovan, political authority is not given in creation in the way that family life is. It is postlapsarian and derives solely from God's providence.[71] Following Augustine, O'Donovan understands secular government as a product of the Fall. This locates it within the order of preservation and emphasises its responsibility for maintaining order and restraining evil.

O'Donovan sees 'Authority [as] the objective correlate of freedom. That is to say, it evokes free action, and makes free action intelligible.'[72] Human freedom takes shape in correlation to authority and social identity (*WOJ* 132). For O'Donovan, 'Political representation is not a zero-sum operation. As Hannah Arendt understood ... to found a structure of political representation is to multiply freedom and authority, leaving everyone with more.' But, he argues, this understanding is only possible if we understand 'the eschatological transformation of politics by the Christ-event. It is not clear how we can see political authority as conferring freedom, rather than taking it away, unless we have first learned to think in terms of a rule that is salvific.' (*DON* 126-127). But this noetic gain may be made without transferring politics into the order of redemption. If, as O'Donovan insists in *RMO*, Christ illuminates the order of creation, His coming must also illuminate the order of providence. It is He who discloses the triune God who is at the heart of the work of God in creation, providence, and redemption.

O'Donovan's correlation of authority and freedom recognises that there is potential for political authority to be liberating, and that means, therefore, that there is potential for human law to be liberating, if understood as limited in scope, obedient to the Son and directed by the Spirit. It is also open to further development in a trinitarian direction if O'Donovan's account of Christ-centred ethics is complemented by an emphasis on the transformation of Christians into Christ-likeness through the power and the presence of the Spirit.

Because political authority is postlapsarian and providential, political authority is consequently not a universal, and there may be areas and times when its necessary pre-conditions are not met. 'Political authority requires (1) sufficient might to govern, (2) sufficient identification with the tradition of the community to govern legitimately, and (3) sufficient commitment to righting wrong to govern justly.' (*RMO* 129, *WOJ* 227). In *DON* this becomes O'Donovan's first theorem. What O'Donovan offers, therefore, is not a description of all human communities but only of those which pass sufficient threshold criteria to be described as 'political orders' which give rise to genuine moral obligations of obedience to their commands. Only where might, tradition

---

[70] O'Donovan, *DON*, 18.

[71] O'Donovan, *RP*, 239; *BOI* 35; C. Rowland, 'Response to *The Desire of the Nations*', *Studies in Christian Ethics* 11 (1998) 81; Lockwood O'Donovan 239-40.

[72] O'Donovan, *DON*, 30, *RMO* 120; 'Behold, the Lamb!', 99; *WOJ* 68, 128; 'What Can Ethics Know about God?', 40.

and right are united can 'justice, in the relative sense in which it is appropriate to speak of it in human communities ... be realized'.[73]

O'Donovan wants to get away from talk of 'the State', as being unbiblical and anachronistic when applied to classical Christian thought, and as obscuring what is at stake when reflecting on questions of rule and authority.[74] He argues that 'political structures are historically fluid, not, as some other structures are, given in nature.'[75] The *need* for political authority is a constant in this fallen world; its *form* is not.

In O'Donovan's account, political authority is held by those who, providentially, unite in a single agency of effective public judgment, the claims of power, right and tradition. These claims correlate to those of salvation, judgment and possession which characterise YHWH's kingship. The combination of the three claims is the indispensable *esse* of political authority.

By locating political authority within the order of providence, O'Donovan is able to offer a realistic account of political authority which recognises it as preferable to the lawless chaos currently experienced by places such as Somalia (*DON* 94). Political authority is therefore necessary for human flourishing (*WOJ* 134). The correlation of the characteristics of power, representative status and judgment which are necessary for political authority to be effective is a provision of common grace, given in order that power and representative status should be harnessed in the service of judgment and law in order that human societies might be relatively peaceable.[76]

Whilst O'Donovan acknowledges that the holding of power may give rise to certain temptations and be susceptible to abuse, in his view, it is not, as such, illegitimate or suspect. He criticises Karl Barth for abnormalising not just the conduct of war but also the exercise of power itself.[77]

In *RMO*, O'Donovan argues that the Ascension is the demonstration of the elements of divine kingship which he finds reflected in human kingship. Through the raising of Christ, God demonstrates His power, His vindication of Christ, the One in whom humanity is truly represented.[78] It is the resurrection-ascension therefore, which is paradigmatic for political authority. However, in *DON*, O'Donovan argues that, since the coming of Christ, it is only the execution of judgment that constitutes the *bene esse* of political authority. Between the Ascension and the Last Judgment, 'the political structures of worldly society depend upon the representation of divine judgment in the form

---

[73] O'Donovan, *RMO*, 129.
[74] O'Donovan in O. O'Donovan and R. Sider, *Peace and War: A Debate About Pacifism* (Grove Booklets on Ethics No. 56, 1985) 13; *WOJ* 149.
[75] O'Donovan, *DON*, 14.
[76] O'Donovan, *JWR*, 32.
[77] O'Donovan, *BOI*, 251.
[78] O'Donovan, *RMO*, 143-44.

of coercive rule'.[79]

Moreover, in *DON*, O'Donovan advances a second, more controversial thesis. He presents an idealistic vision of what government could be like if it responded positively and appropriately to the mission of the Church which others have seen as a defence of the idea of Christendom. In O'Donovan's thought, there are two chords which the Church must sound to rulers: the first chord is subjection; the second chord is calling.

The first chord is to be found in Jesus' challenge to Pilate to identify the source of his own authority. The point of this exchange is that, whether they like it or not, political authorities are only mandated by Christ who gives them their justification, to fulfil the tasks which He has ordained (*DON* 140-141). It is He, and not constitutional regularity, which is the fundamental pre-condition for their authority (*BOI* 216).

Like the neo-orthodox and the neo-Calvinists, O'Donovan asserts the claim of God over the whole of life. 'God's demand is not one among others. ... God's claim embraces the whole of our duty, ordering the other claims before us as they ought to be ordered.'[80] O'Donovan argues that whilst the early English Reformers' Erastianism meant that aspects of the life of the Church fell under the jurisdiction of the monarch, the corollary, understood by the Tudors but lost by Anglicanism in the seventeenth century, was that the authority of God's word extended over the whole of society and obliged, above all, the godly prince.[81]

O'Donovan argues from the fact that Israel was 'a political community by virtue of being a worshipping community' (*DON* 47), that 'within every political society there occurs, implicitly, an act of worship of divine rule' and that state-authority is what is left when the sacred origin of that authority is forgotten.[82] Late-modern liberal polities have abandoned 'the Pauline tradition of understanding all acts of government as "judgment", i.e. as applying divine law (natural and revealed) to the "infinite possibilities of human wrongdoing."'[83] The result is that political authority is either deemed to be self-standing or to derive from the will of the people. It is now self-legislating rather than referable to the given moral order and excessive emphasis is given to its representative functions over against its obligation to give judgment.[84] It is the

---

[79] O'Donovan, *RMO*, 173. For a critique of O'Donovan's model, particularly with regard to the question of pacifism, see J. Neufeld, 'Just War Theory, the Authorization of the State, and the Hermeneutics of Peoplehood: How John Howard Yoder can save Oliver O'Donovan from himself', *International Journal of Systematic Theology* 8 (2006) 410-32.

[80] O'Donovan, *RMO*, 233; Moberley, 'The Use of Scripture', 58.

[81] O'Donovan, *39 Articles*, 100.

[82] Hauerwas and Fodor, 'Remaining in Babylon', 35-36.

[83] O'Donovan, *BOI*, 14.

[84] O'Donovan, *Common Objects of Love: Moral Reflection and the Shaping of Community* (Grand Rapids: Eerdmans, 2002) 69.

naked will to which late-modern liberalism bows down.

In contrast, the thinkers of Christendom taught rulers that 'government is responsible. Rulers, overcome by Christ's victory, exist provisionally and on sufferance for specific purposes. In the Church they have to confront a society which witnesses to the Kingdom under which they stand and before which they must disappear.'[85] Government's function is to execute judgment, and in doing so derives its law from the laws given by God. It is always accountable to God's law for the way in which it exercises its authority.[86] This is expressed in O'Donovan's third theorem: 'The authority of a human regime mediates divine authority in a unitary structure, but is subject to the authority of law within the community, which bears independent witness to the divine command.' (*DON* 65).

Thus O'Donovan seeks to recognise both sides of the biblical witness that human governments have authority from God to give judgments but may transgress the boundaries of that authority by claiming for themselves an ultimacy which belongs to God alone.[87]

In the era after Christ, political authorities are now called to put the might which they possess in accordance with the established order of a society at the service of righting wrongs within that society. Because of original sin, evil and violence must be restrained. However, also because of original sin, political authorities mandated to restrain evil, lay claims to omnipotence and to divine honours (*Peace and Certainty*, 26). 'The best Christian political thought ... emphasises the need to set up restraints in both directions, against evil and against the evil implicit in the restraint of evil'[88] by seeking to constrain the use of force 'to the service of the common good'. Political authorities present two faces to us. O'Donovan insists that they do represent the rule of God, as opposed to merely 'rule as such'. However, they also represent humanity's rebellion against the rule of God, and express the particular forms which it takes in our societies.

O'Donovan seeks to recognise that both Paul and John of Patmos were right about the nature of political authority in the present age. Insofar as such authority conscientiously renders judgments on right and wrong, it acts in accordance with God's will; insofar as it erects itself as the ultimate arbiter of right and wrong or as ultimate claim on the loyalty of its subjects, it is Antichrist (*DON* 274) and subject to God's wrath and judgment.

However, although O'Donovan accepts that 'Holding sovereigns accountable may be an excellent thing to do', there seems to be little space

---

[85] O'Donovan, *DON*, 231.

[86] Wolterstorff, 'Discussion', 99; Schweiker, 'Freedom and Authority', 120.

[87] O'Donovan, *Measure for Measure: Justice in Punishment and the Sentence of Death* (Nottingham: Grove Books, 1977) 6.

[88] O'Donovan, *Peace and Certainty*, 26-27.

within his theory for institutionalising and regularising this accountability.[89] O'Donovan's fourth theorem understands the king as the supreme ruler, but as one who 'is subject to the authority of law within the community, which bears independent witness to the divine command. ... it is a *political* reality in society to which government is answerable.'[90] His preferred model of accountability seems to be that of the Israelite kings to the prophets, or of Henry II after the murder of Thomas à Becket.

Although O'Donovan has concerns about the temptation of totalitarianism which political authorities always face, in his theology there is a heavy presumption of obedience to the lawful commands of such authorities.[91] For O'Donovan, authority is entitled to presumptions of regularity and good faith. The conscientious soldier or citizen is not obliged to second-guess the decisions of the generals and politicians. He can simply do *his* duty, unless and until there are compelling reasons to do otherwise.[92] Reform is usually far preferable to revolution. [93]

However, O'Donovan recognises that there may be exceptional cases (*WOJ* 142). On the one hand, '[w]ithin any civil community a situation may arise in which civil order is confronted with defiance too great to overcome by normal judicial processes.'[94] *In extremis,* a government is justified in making war on its own citizens, if that is what is *necessary* to restore order. On the other hand, a political authority may so depart from its mandate to do justice that revolution is justifiable. For O'Donovan, this can only ever be a last resort because settled government is what 'God has given us as a severe blessing for our mediocre world.'[95]

O'Donovan's preference for political quietism stands in some tension with what Lockwood O'Donovan sees as distinctive in proto-modern Christian political thought, namely '[the] novel level of concern with the right of political society to protect itself against the lawlessness of rulers (against their insupportable violations of divine, natural, and positive laws)' which she discerns 'was a concern with *the right of political society to be governed,* the intention of which was to reinforce rather than undermine the theo-political tradition of rule.'[96]

---

[89] Chaplin, 'Political Eschatology and Responsible Government', 294-95.
[90] O'Donovan, *DON*, 64-65.
[91] O'Donovan, *JWR*, 27.
[92] O'Donovan, *JWR*, 110, 113.
[93] O'Donovan, *JWR*, 70.
[94] O'Donovan, *JWR*, 69.
[95] O'Donovan, *In Pursuit of a Christian View of War* (Nottingham: Grove Booklet on Ethics No. 15, 1977) 12.
[96] Lockwood O'Donovan, *BOI*, 165.

CHRIST'S KINGSHIP AND THE *BENE ESSE* OF POLITICAL AUTHORITY

O'Donovan seeks to demonstrate, in *DON*, the impossibility of a value-neutral secular state, through reflections on the kingship of YHWH as revealed in the Old Testament, the four moments of the Christ-event: advent, passion, restoration and exaltation, and the witness of the Church to that history. In particular, however, O'Donovan argues that Christ's ascension is decisive for politics in the Christian era because: 'The *Exaltation* ... is clothed in the imagery of royal coronation. ... The Son of Man is presented before the Ancient of Days and receives the Kingdom.'[97] O'Donovan argues that Western theology has lost sight of the political implications of the kingship of Christ because of its persistent tendency to interpret the death of Christ apart from the resurrection of Christ (*DON* 128).

In O'Donovan's view, notwithstanding the heavenly nature of Christ's kingdom, there is

> an analogy ... between the acts of God and human acts, both of them taking place within the one public history which is the theatre of God's saving purposes and mankind's social undertakings. The Kingdom of God is not a mere kingdom, but it is a real kingdom. The point is ... to push back the horizon of commonplace politics and open it up to the activity of God.[98]

For O'Donovan the analogy to be drawn is the following: Jesus is King: Political Authorities are kings.[99] They are, however, kings under His authority and subject to the limits which He has placed on their powers.

O'Donovan's central thesis put forward in *DON* and defended in *WOJ* is that in the era after the resurrection-ascension, the continuing role of government is justified on the basis of the need for provisional judgment, pending the return of Christ. However, the essential judgment has already been rendered, in the cross and resurrection.

Given his earlier work, what one would expect to find in *DON* is an account of human government which places it in primary reference to creation and to the moral order inherent in creation which is disclosed in its fullness by the resurrection. In short, one would expect to find some account of the relationship between human laws and the moral laws given in nature as a prominent feature of O'Donovan's political theology. While this is present, it is muted, because of the emphasis O'Donovan gives to the need for laws to take account of the condition of the society which is being governed and because O'Donovan says comparatively little about the Torah.

Moreover there was a key development in O'Donovan's political thought between *RMO* and *DON*. In 1977, O'Donovan wrote:

---

[97] O'Donovan, *DON*, 144.
[98] O'Donovan, *DON*, 2.
[99] O'Donovan, *DON*, 19.

In the Old and New Testaments alike the paradigm of political activity is "giving judgment": defending the rights of the weak plaintiff against the oppression of the strong. Government exists not to serve *every* interest of its people, but the specific interest that they all have in just arbitration.' ... 'Justice was the concern of the king in any and all of his activities. All government is concerned with "giving judgment", for all government is concerned with reconciling conflicting claims of different parties ... it touches on legislative and executive, as well as on judicial acts ...[100]

In *RMO*, he holds to the same view. At *RMO* 129, O'Donovan argues that might, tradition and right all contribute to the idea of justice as 'public right action' but that it is 'right' which is primary. Wherever government is effective, it is primarily concerned with enacting right.[101]

In *DON*, however, O'Donovan's central claim is that the centrality of judgment (vindication of right) over the claims of representation (tradition) and might (power) is a result of the new situation resulting from the Ascension. Up till then 'Government was given to safeguard Israel's existence in relation to the land and the law' or to guarantee the protection of the polis (*DON* 148).

In the Christian era, however, all political authority, is 'subject to the discipline of enacting right against wrong.' (*WOJ* 5). What is left to rulers is the 'judicial service' of witnessing to 'the coming reality of God's own act of judgment.' (*WOJ* 5). O'Donovan defines judgment as 'an act of moral discrimination that pronounces upon a preceding act or existing state of affairs to establish a new public context.' (*WOJ* 7). As a political act, it is subject to the criteria of truth and effectiveness, and must hold a balance between the two (*WOJ* 9), recognising not only the moral order but also the realities of the society it is regulating.

However, this exclusive justification, which is the *bene esse* of political authority, exists in dialectical relationship with the *esse* of political authority, which remains the broader 'union of power, the execution of right and the perpetuation of tradition in one centre of action.' (*DON* 233). A government's capacity to execute judgment depends on its ability to use force and the general acceptance of those who are governed.[102]

The use of force is essential to the practice of government because the task God has given to governments is that of controlling violent men. However, the use of force without acceptance of the right to govern from those who are governed is unstable. 'For true political authority to flourish, there must be a stronger motive of obedience than is furnished by fear of sanction and habitual conformity. People obey political authority because they think they ought.'[103]

---

[100] O'Donovan, *In Pursuit of a Christian View of War*, 9.

[101] O'Donovan uses this description in *WOJ* at 142-43 in preference to 'injured right' which is the terminology he adopts in *RMO*.

[102] O'Donovan, *In Pursuit of a Christian View of War*, 11-12.

[103] O'Donovan, *RMO*, 128.

On O'Donovan's account, political authority is exercised when the community feels that the judgments of its rulers are representative of its judgments.[104] O'Donovan sees 'tradition', the common values, the common assumptions, and the 'common objects of love' of a political society as shaping and constraining the actions of its leaders.

Although they remain *conditiones sine qua non* of political authority, what has changed in the light of the resurrection-ascension is that 'The accumulation of power and the maintenance of community identity cease to be self-evident goods; they have to be justified at every point by their contribution to the judicial function. The responsible state is therefore minimally coercive and minimally representative.' (*DON* 233). Because of its threefold basis, however, political authority is subject to the endemic temptation to forget its primary obligation and to concentrate on the exercise of power or its representative role.

In *DON*, O'Donovan argues that the paradigm of political activity as giving judgment is an unprecedented feature in Paul's thought, specific to the Christian era. *DON* therefore, is not consistent with the ethical project set out in *RMO* because in relation to political authority, the resurrection of Christ does *not* on O'Donovan's account, vindicate the political order given in creation but re-founds it on a new and more limited basis. The change is all the more significant for the fact that O'Donovan was unaware of it until Jonathan Chaplin drew it to his attention.[105] Once the inconsistency has been revealed, it becomes obvious why O'Donovan has to place political authority exclusively within the order of providence. Only by removing politics from the moral order of creation can O'Donovan maintain both the general thesis of *RMO* and the specific thesis of *DON*.

The overriding question for O'Donovan's political theology is how to understand politics in the light of the kingship of Christ established in heaven.[106] He insists that 'We cannot discuss the question of "secular" government ... unless we approach it historically, from a Christology that has been displayed in narrative form as Gospel.' (*DON* 133). The key implications of Christology for political theology are its interpretation of Christ's roles as (1) the mediator of God's rule and (2) the representative individual *(DON* 123; *WOJ* 185).

For O'Donovan, all human actions are overshadowed by the fact that the Ascended Christ is Lord. In political terms, the primary eschatological assertion is that 'the authorities, political and demonic, which govern the world ... have been made subject to God's sovereignty in the Exaltation of Christ.' But 'this awaits a final universal presence of Christ to become fully apparent.' (*DON* 146). God's judgment has already been definitively given in Christ; only its

---

[104] O'Donovan, *JWR*, 21.
[105] O'Donovan, *WOJ*, 143; Chaplin 'Political Eschatology and Responsible Government' in *RP* at 300, and O'Donovan's, 'Response', at 309.
[106] O'Donovan, *DON*, ix.

disclosure is awaited.

That Christ *has ascended*, means that He needs no earthly ruler to establish or to confirm His rights. To claim such a vocation is to blaspheme.[107] Equally, the 'security [of the church] is guaranteed by the ascended Christ and needs no further underwriting.'[108]

Like N.T. Wright, O'Donovan sees Christ as bringing to an end the exile with its separation of secular and religious authority. However, Christ is the only worthy priest-king.[109] He has united all authority within Himself. O'Donovan is clear that it is in Christ that true peace and true justice are to be found.[110] O'Donovan re-founds political authority on the lordship of Christ over all creation and all history. There is no sphere of secular right to which he does not lay claim.[111] O'Donovan identifies the political rulers of this age among the powers whom Christ has defeated.[112] 'The coming of Christ the King first displaces all other authorities, and then subordinates and justifies their claims within limits he sets.'[113] 'The moment of divine irruption is more than an irruption: it is the foundation of a renewed order. ... As the divine conqueror he triumphs over the false authorities of the fallen world; as the Son of man he exercises authority over the redeemed world.'[114] There is no 'permanently twofold locus of authority ... only a transitory duality which belong[s] to the climax of Israel's history, a duality between the coming and the passing order.' (*DON* 93).

Following the triumphal Ascension of Christ, the subdued '"authorities" of this age, '[t]he secular princes of this earth, shorn of pretensions to our loyalty and worship, are left with the sole function of judging between innocent and guilty.' (*BOI* 209). Henceforth, political authorities can either obediently accept their limited function of judgment or idolatrously reject their rightful place and assert themselves against God. There is no other choice.[115]

---

[107] O'Donovan, *In Pursuit of a Christian View of War*, 9-10.

[108] O'Donovan, *DON*, 218.

[109] O'Donovan, *DON*, 214-215, 273-274.

[110] O'Donovan, *Peace and Certainty*, 115-116.

[111] O'Donovan, *DON*, 91; Neuhaus 'Commentary on *The Desire of the Nations*', 56-57. In this regard, O'Donovan's thought is in line with that of John Milbank, another contemporary theologian indebted to Augustine: 'The Programme of Radical Orthodoxy' in L.P. Hemming, ed., *Radical Orthodoxy? – A Catholic Enquiry* (Aldershot: Ashgate, 2000) 34.

[112] De Kruijf, 'The Function of Romans 13', 226-228.

[113] O'Donovan, *DON*, 253; J.W. Skillen, 'Acting Politically in Biblical Obedience?' in Bartholomew et al., eds., *A Royal Priesthood?* (Carlisle: Paternoster, 2002) 400.

[114] O'Donovan, *RMO*, 143.

[115] O'Donovan, *Peace and Certainty*, 116-117, *DON* 147, 156-57; Hauerwas and Fodor, 'Remaining in Babylon', 31.

Secular institutions have a role confined to this passing age (*saeculum*). They do not represent the arrival of the new age and the rule of God. ... [T]hey are not agents of Christ, but are marked for displacement when the rule of God in Christ is finally disclosed. They are Christ's conquered enemies; yet they have an indirect testimony to give, bearing the marks of his sovereignty imposed upon them, negating their pretensions and evoking their acknowledgment.[116]

What the triumph of Christ does to secular authority in O'Donovan's view is to de-authorise it by de-sacralising it.[117] But to what polity, apart from Old Testament Israel, was it ever given to be sacral?[118] The ancient empires of the Near East were idolatrous precisely because it was not given to the rulers of Egypt or Babylon either, even under the Old Covenant Era, to claim divine honours.

On either view, however, with regard to the present day, because the correlation of power, representative status and judgment is indispensable to political authority, political rulers are always tempted to overemphasise the other two characteristics to the detriment of their overriding duty to execute judgment.

In *RP* at 239, O'Donovan explains that he does not want to give the state a direct christological status. Instead, he argues that 'The state ... remains under the direction of the First Person of the Trinity; it is not filled with the Holy Spirit at Pentecost; but it attests, negatively and by the yielding up of its powers, the fulfilment of the Father's purpose in the Son.'

As in some comments made by Lockwood O'Donovan,[119] this can be read as divorcing both the Second and the Third Persons of the Trinity from the providential work of God. However, in *WOJ*, O'Donovan offers a counter-balance to such statements through the assertion that 'As ecclesiology belongs within the doctrine of the Holy Spirit, so does political theology'.[120] There is therefore some space at least in O'Donovan's theology for the work of the Father acting through His Spirit to preserve sinful human community in preparation for the acceptance of the revelation of His Son. A more complete

---

[116] O'Donovan, *DON*, 211-12; Carroll, 'The Power of the Future in the Present', 124.

[117] O'Donovan, *RP*, 239.

[118] The Old Testament is clear that kingship is limited and accountable. Even the visible identity between the religious community and the national community is called into question by Jeroboam's revolt. Jeroboam is condemned for his attempt to divert the worship of YHWH in order to maintain this identity; the implication being that God intended the northern tribes to be loyal subjects of Jeroboam whilst continuing to worship God at the temple in Jerusalem. If Jeroboam had no such right, how much less do secular rulers after the time of Christ.

[119] J. Lockwood O'Donovan, *BOI*, 136, 286; 'A Timely Conversation on Civil Society, Nation and State' in Bartholomew et al., eds., *A Royal Priesthood?* (Carlisle: Paternoster, 2002) 386.

[120] O'Donovan, *WOJ*, 239.

trinitarian analysis would see governments directed by the unseen hand of the Spirit, authorised by the Son and bearing witness, however indirectly, to both the call and the wrath of the Father.

Human political authority stands outside Christ's kingdom but is not unaffected by its establishment. 'The limited and deficient judgment that is the content of "the political" belongs to the messianic era, but not in the way that the corporate action of the Church belongs to it: for the Church's action participates in the victory of the resurrected Lord, while political judgment only points to it.'[121]

However, '[t]he ultimate is not merely a negation of the penultimate. Certainly, the fact that God's will is declared only in the face of Christ *limits* the significance of our actions and negates their pretensions to ultimacy. Yet at the same time it *shapes* their significance, giving them an importance precisely as a penultimate reflection of the final peace-giving.' (*DON* 116).

Although Christ in his two natures is the unique mediator between God and humankind, and He is the only one in whom all authority is united,[122] O'Donovan also argues that Christ is paradigmatic, and that 'As it is *God's* rule over the people that the ruler represents, and for that very reason the *people's* rule under God, we cannot avoid a sense in which the ruler speaks both with God's authority and the people's.'[123]

Hauerwas and Fodor point out that the drawing of analogies is highly problematic, precisely because 'the reign of God among the people of Israel and in the person of Jesus is markedly unlike the kingly rule of monarchies of the nations ... The anointed one (Jesus) is, after all, both servant and messiah, victim as well as priest, sufferer as well as liberator, afflicted as well as physician.'[124] If those paradoxes are suppressed in a vision of the Exalted Christ as Pantocrator, then it is no longer the biblical Messiah of whom we are thinking.

Moreover, is there a messianic secret to the lordship of Christ which persists, even now? Although there is a place in his theology for martyrdom, there is a tendency at times in O'Donovan to expect not only the claims of Jesus to be made public by the Church in the here and now, but also for those claims to be vindicated in public here and now.

That messianic secret can be better appreciated if the work of the Holy Spirit is to establish the kingship of Christ which is manifested in the present age in the hearts of human beings.[125] This internal change of heart may have

---

[121] O'Donovan, *BOI*, 22.
[122] O'Donovan, *WOJ*, 239.
[123] O'Donovan, *RP*, 224.
[124] Hauerwas and Fodor, 'Remaining in Babylon', 47; Rowland, 'Response to *The Desire of the Nations*', 80.
[125] *DON* 246, where O'Donovan comments on the Puritan emphasis on the private conscience.

considerable public consequences but those are the outworkings of the establishment of the kingdom in the hearts of human beings.

There are hints in O'Donovan's thought which could be developed in this direction. O'Donovan's conception of freedom is pneumatologically-based. The Holy Spirit gives us freedom because the Spirit enables and empowers us. 'Freedom is "potency" rather than "possibility".'[126] Therefore, '[w]hen the Holy Spirit makes a person free, that freedom is immediately demonstrated in self-binding to the service of others'.[127] The freedom which counts is 'the realization of individual powers within social forms'.[128] O'Donovan defines freedom as 'the character of one who participates in the order of creation by knowledge and action.'[129] The one who, guided by the Spirit, recognises their own position within the moral order and the relationships which have been given to them, is the one who is truly enabled to act responsibly as a free agent.

The Place of the Spirit in O'Donovan's Thought

Whereas Moltmann leaves too little space to the distinctive work of the Holy Spirit at Pentecost, O'Donovan offers insufficient account of the work of the Holy Spirit *apart from* Pentecost. This emerges most starkly in his account of the moral order but also to a less extent in his political theology.

THE ROLE OF THE SPIRIT IN O'DONOVAN'S ACCOUNT OF THE MORAL ORDER

The closest one gets to an exposition of O'Donovan's views on questions of systematic theology is in his work entitled *On the 39 Articles*, in which his own ideas emerge as one of the partners in what O'Donovan describes as a conversation with Tudor Christianity.

In that work, O'Donovan endorses St Basil's reflections on the baptism of Christ which understands the Father as the one who anoints, the Son as the anointed one, and the Spirit as the anointing.[130] The strength of this image is that while it makes the Trinity a sufficient and complete community, it is also one which is potentially open to our participation. This image makes sense of Pentecost as *our* anointing, and therefore the confirmation of *our* adoption as sons of God, in virtue of *our* relationship to the eternal Son of God.

Also in *On the 39 Articles*, O'Donovan expresses the view that 'Predestination … is a formal way of expressing the truth that the reality behind mankind's salvation is the eternal relation of the Father, the Son and the Holy Spirit within the Godhead' and ought to remind us that the 'economy of

---

[126] O'Donovan, *RMO*, 107.

[127] O'Donovan, *RMO*, 108.

[128] O'Donovan, *WOJ*, 68.

[129] O'Donovan, *RMO*, 107.

[130] O'Donovan, *39 Articles*, 47. The same image is found in Irenaeus, *Against Heresies*, 3.18.2-3.

creation and redemption' is an expression of the relationship between the Father, Son and Spirit, through which 'we, created through the Son, are drawn by the Spirit to be the community of the Son's glorious Kingdom.'[131]

However, O'Donovan does not draw any implications for his political theology from this conception of the Trinity, as a communion into which Christians are drawn into relationship, whereas it will be argued in the following chapters that it is in fact of decisive importance.

O'Donovan's dominant image for the Trinity seems to be the Augustinian description of the Spirit as the bond of love between God the Father and God the Son, which O'Donovan values because it safeguards the truth that 'it is in the Father's relation to the *Son* that the Spirit has his source of being – from the Father!'[132] The fact that O'Donovan is able to combine this Augustinian understanding of the Trinity with an obvious emphasis on mission in his own thought, illustrates that *some* of Moltmann's criticism of Augustine's trinitarianism is misplaced. However, it does raise the question mark about whether O'Donovan's own theology suffers from the same tendency to de-personalise the Spirit which some theologians have discerned in Augustine.

O'Donovan also follows Augustine in linking the Ascension with Pentecost.[133] It is Christ who gives the Spirit for the mission of the Church as a fruit of His ascension.[134] 'This is of very great importance; it means that the presence of the Spirit in the Church does not in any way go *beyond* the triumph of Christ.'[135] In understanding the resurrection-ascension in connection with the session of the Son at the right hand of the Father and the sending of the Spirit, O'Donovan's exploration of the doctrine is thoroughly trinitarian. However, the danger in O'Donovan's conception is that it restricts the activity of the Spirit to the Church. As Carroll points out, glimpses of signs of the kingdom of God outside the Church are rare indeed in O'Donovan's writings.[136]

This view is confirmed by O'Donovan's description of the Holy Spirit as 'the gift of God for the time of Christ's absence.'[137] Notwithstanding some indications to the contrary, O'Donovan tends to think of the work of the Holy Spirit as *only consequent* upon the work of the Son (see *WOJ* 266). In much of O'Donovan's thought, the work of the Holy Spirit is reduced to the Spirit's activity in the life of believers and in the Church.[138] O'Donovan, following traditional Protestant explanations, identifies the Spirit as applying to the believer subjectively what the Son has already done for the believer

---

[131] O'Donovan, *39 Articles*, 83-84; Bretherton, *Hospitality as Holiness*, 83.

[132] O'Donovan, *39 Articles*, 47-48; *RMO* 236.

[133] O'Donovan, *DON*, 161-162; *39 Articles* 42, 45.

[134] O'Donovan, *39 Articles*, 42.

[135] O'Donovan, *39 Articles*, 45.

[136] Carroll, 'The Power of the Future in the Present', 124-25.

[137] O'Donovan, *39 Articles*, 43.

[138] O'Donovan, *DON*, 129.

objectively.[139] The Holy Spirit's field of operations is conceived as a subjective one, in marked contrast with the objectivity of both the finished work of Christ and the created order in O'Donovan's thought.[140]

It is the Son who has, by His work on earth, renewed the world order. What the Holy Spirit does is to renew the moral agent to respond to the renewed world order in free obedience and recognition of their *telos*.[141] '[T]he individual believer, filled with the Holy Spirit, participates directly and subjectively in the life of God' (*WOJ* 296). In political terms, the government of the Spirit in the life of each believer and the rule of God through the Spirit in the Church constitutes an alternative community, which challenges existing notions of political good and necessity (*DON* 122-123).

With respect to O'Donovan, whilst this is true, all this is also reductionist. It is not necessarily clear that the Spirit only works subjectively. Certainly, the Spirit participated in the creation of an objective reality. It may be that O'Donovan is driven by proper concerns not to detach the Spirit from the Son. If that is so, what is necessary in order to keep the Spirit of God distinct from the cosmic-Spirit or the *Zeitgeist* is not an assertion of the subjective nature of the operations of the Holy Spirit but rather a recognition that the Spirit's work in creation is resisted by the forces of evil, so that fallen human beings only perceive partially the truth the Spirit reveals, unless they come to a decisive new relationship with God the Father, through the acknowledgement of the Son and the re-birth in the Spirit.

Moreover, even if it is accepted that the Spirit only works subjectively, why, given that O'Donovan can speak of the Spirit 'mak[ing] the reality of Christ's triumph present to us, and us to it',[142] should he not write in equivalent terms about the Spirit's role in making the reality of the created order *partially clearer* to us, and us to it, even before we come to acknowledge Christ in whom that reality is vindicated?

The Spirit's work in preparing for Christ seems to be missing from O'Donovan's thought, only finding a belated and limited place in *WOJ*, and the reason for that is the domination of O'Donovan's view of the objectivity of the created order. In chapter 3 of his book *Hospitality as Holiness*, Luke Bretherton sets out the way in which O'Donovan develops Christian ethics by reference to the Son and the Spirit. The Spirit is, however, given no place in O'Donovan's account of the apprehension of the moral order available to non-Christians.

In *RMO*, O'Donovan writes:

---

[139] O'Donovan, *39 Articles*, 44, 79.

[140] O'Donovan, *RMO*, 17.

[141] O'Donovan, *RMO*, 25, 183, 236; Carroll, 'The Power of the Future in the Present', 121.

[142] O'Donovan, *39 Articles*, 43.

Christians need have no problem understanding how there can be, in societies and cultures untouched by Christian influence, a recognition of moral principles which are true, simply because they know that such cultures stand within a created order of things and may be expected to demonstrate this fact in many ways.[143]

With respect to O'Donovan, this appears to attribute too much self-evidence to creation and not enough activity to the Holy Spirit. What O'Donovan does not, but should, say is that such recognition is given by God to individuals and communities through the unseen operations of the Spirit. The distinction between general and special revelation would fill in the gaps in his ethical theory better than what he seems to do, which is to make the created moral order partially self-revealing.[144]

THE WORK OF THE SPIRIT AND POLITICAL AUTHORITY

In *DON*, the sense of trinitarian balance is equally missing from O'Donovan's political theology. The references to the Holy Spirit in *DON* are concentrated in chapter 5 entitled 'The church' and in the section of chapter 6 headed 'Mission or coercion?'. Isolated references elsewhere are also to the work of the Holy Spirit in the Church or in individual Christians.[145] Whilst this is undoubtedly the most decisive and dramatic work of the Holy Spirit in the era after Pentecost, O'Donovan's approach in his writings has tended to reduce the Holy Spirit to the possession of the Church, contrary to Moltmann's insistence that their correct relationship is the other way around.

This reduction of the realm of the Spirit's activity to the Church seems to be the result of the influence of Augustine on O'Donovan's thought.[146] Augustine's political theology is driven by his eschatology. He is quite clear that there are two cities: an earthly city, which loves itself and earthly goods instead of God, and a heavenly city, which loves God more than it loves itself and earthly goods. The earthly city is destined for eternal destruction and the heavenly city for eternal bliss. Whatever the confusions of the present age, that is, for Augustine, the underlying reality. For Augustine, only one of those cities, the heavenly one, possesses the Holy Spirit, and for Augustine, because of the Donatist schism the Holy Spirit's sphere of operations is defined very tightly as the Catholic Church. While O'Donovan does not follow Augustine in his narrow denominational understanding of the work of the Spirit in the Church, he does follow Augustine in his general tendency to identify the Church as the sphere of the Spirit's operations. But this confuses the noetic

---

[143] O'Donovan, *RMO*, 17.
[144] O'Donovan, *RMO*, 19-20.
[145] O'Donovan, *DON*, 122.
[146] It should be noted, however, that Milbank is far more positive about the gracing of the world, because at this point the dominant influence in his thought is de Lubac and de Lubac's reading of Aquinas: see J. Milbank, *The Suspended Middle: Henri de Lubac and the Debate concerning the Supernatural* (London: SCM, 2005) 2, 5-6, 39, 41-42.

with the real. To say that the Church is the only place where the Holy Spirit is recognised, even to say that the Church is the only place where the Holy Spirit is manifest, is not the same as saying that the Church is the only place where the Holy Spirit is at work. Human institutions and acts of judgment may be providentially used by the Spirit in the work of 'convicting the world of sin, justice and judgment.'[147]

This line in O'Donovan's thought has the potential to reduce God's action in history beyond the confines of the Church to deistic providence. O'Donovan is thus presented with a similar problem to that which he identifies in Barth. The juxtaposition in Barth of the universal claims of the Barmen Declaration with his later assertion that the State is constitutionally pagan, leaves Barth unable to account for how the state can be 'reminded' of what it never knew.[148] How, apart from the operations of the Spirit, can rulers be led to realise the limitations of their role and their responsibilities?

John Colwell contends that O'Donovan's argument breaks down because of the lack of reference to the Spirit or of explanation of 'the dynamic by which this kingdom authority of the risen Christ might be known "generally" among the "nations".'[149] He argues that in order to avoid the alternatives of independent rational foundationalism or sectarian dualism in knowledge, O'Donovan needs to offer a pneumatological epistemology in which 'the being-givenness by which we come to know the gospel is the work of that same Spirit as the being-givenness by which we come to know anything at all.'[150]

On the basis of the resurrection, the Church indwelt by the Spirit has the epistemological privilege of discerning the true moral order of creation.[151] But on what basis does it resonate in wider society? May the Spirit not be at work, revealing aspects of that moral order even when the truth about Jesus Christ is not acknowledged or is rejected? For O'Donovan, 'The redemptive work of the Holy Spirit involves the restoration of our access to reality.'[152] But if Christian epistemological insight is the work of the Holy Spirit, why should the response

---

[147] Rowland, 'Response', 84.

[148] O'Donovan, *DON*, 214.

[149] Colwell, *Living the Christian Story*, 243. In a similar vein, David Fergusson has argued that the possibility of true ethical insights beyond the church 'is not merely to be thought of as the result of an occasional action of the Holy Spirit or the reconciled status of all people in Christ. The possibility of ethical perception and action beyond the church is recognised not only under the second and third articles of faith, but also under the first. The doctrine of creation provides a context in which the sharing of convictions and insights can be recognised': *Community, Liberalism and Christian Ethics* (Cambridge: CUP, 1998) 29, 165-67.

[150] Colwell, *Living the Christian Story*, 243.

[151] B. Wannenwetsch, '"Members of One Another": *Charis*, Ministry and Representation: A Politico-Ecclesial Reading of Romans 12' in Bartholomew et al., eds., *A Royal Priesthood?* (Carlisle: Paternoster, 2002) 197.

[152] O'Donovan, *RMO*, 112.

to the given moral order invoked in those who are not(-yet) Christians not also be the work of the Holy Spirit?

To put the matter more simply, O'Donovan needs to say that the Spirit is not only at work in the Church, although the knowledge of the Spirit's presence is peculiarly revealed to the Church, but also that the Spirit of the resurrection and of Jesus who was raised and of the Father who raised Jesus from the dead, is at work in the world bearing witness to the crucified and risen One.

To say this is not to render the Spirit independent of the Son, but rather to insist that just as the Spirit witnesses to the centrality of the Son with regard to redemption, so the Spirit also witnesses to the centrality of the Son with regard to creation.[153]

Despite the absence of this kind of language in *RMO* or *DON*, there are hints that O'Donovan's thought could be developed in this direction, to be found in *On the 39 Articles*. In that early book, O'Donovan regrets the omission from the *39 Articles* of article 10 of Cranmer's original 42.[154] This article, entitled 'Of Grace' states 'The grace of Christ, *or the Holy Spirit by him given,* doth take away the stony heart and giveth an heart of flesh. ...' O'Donovan in his commentary, goes on to point out the usefulness of associating the Holy Spirit with grace because, by doing so 'we are delivered from the anxiety that divine grace may become some kind of usurpation of our agency' and from 'the tendency for divine grace to be understood in terms of the providential direction of the world by the First Person of the Trinity'.[155]

O'Donovan has not been wholly deaf to these criticisms of his work. The companion volume to *DON*, *WOJ* is divided into three parts: Part I: The Political Act: Judgment; Part II: Political Institutions: Representation; Part III: Life Beyond Judgment: Communication. The reason for this triadic structure O'Donovan advances at *WOJ* 239 is that 'political theology ... properly has a trinitarian shape'. Judgment speaks of the 'God-given right of judgment within the world' and is presumably appropriated to the Father. Under representation one is to think of 'the God-given representative of mankind, and of the church's challenge to all other political representations.' Here Christ is clearly in view. Under communication (which is O'Donovan's translation of *koinonia*), O'Donovan writes of 'the eschatological summons to social communication, and of the church's modeling of communication as life beyond judgment.' The Church is therefore 'the model of the communication of the Spirit in the world' (*WOJ* 240).

There are problems with this claim, however. First, it is obscurely buried well into the book rather than given programmatic status, and that fact alone may alert one to its questionability. Secondly, the first two parts relate to the political act and to political institutions but the third, precisely because

---

[153] Colwell, *Living the Christian Story*, 247.
[154] O'Donovan, *39 Articles*, 44.
[155] O'Donovan, *39 Articles*, 44, emphasis mine.

O'Donovan makes judgment definitive of the political, refers not to politics but to society beyond politics and to the Church in particular. This leads to the third problem with the claim. In the triadic division of his work, the Holy Spirit appears again associated with society beyond the political, and in particular with the Church, and hence apart from the political.

If O'Donovan does make a significant theoretical gain in *WOJ*, it is in offering the much-needed assertion that political theology belongs within the doctrine of the Holy Spirit, who is not limited to the Church but 'runs ahead' of it and prepares for its mission.[156] In *WOJ* at least, this action of the Spirit is accounted for in the doctrine of providence, but the point is not developed.

In *DON*, O'Donovan's second theorem of political authority is 'That any regime should actually come to hold authority, and should continue to hold it, is a work of divine providence in history'.[157] He insists that political authority is given providentially and not in creation.[158] In *WOJ*, O'Donovan situates political theology within the doctrine of the Holy Spirit who providentially directs history towards its God-given goal. It therefore seems possible to piece together from O'Donovan's writings an account of the Spirit's providential works in sustaining political authority in human communities.

In O'Donovan's thought, although references to common grace are rare,[159] it seems to be equivalent to providence. In *JWR*, O'Donovan makes explicit, foundational even to his argument, that common grace operates 'through governments and their institutionalised judgment' (*JWR* 8). Governments are recipients of God's grace for the sake of the societies which they govern, providing the judgment which such societies need in order to be sustainable. O'Donovan defines providence as 'God's work in history which is not directly purposive- or saving-history, the work of preserving and sustaining the created universe.'[160] In a violent world,

> God has provided us with a *saeculum*, a time to live, to believe and to hope under a regime of provisional judgment; here, too, it is possible to practise reconciliation, since God's patience waits, and preserves the world against its own self-destruction. The practical content of this interim common grace is the *political act*, ... government-as-judgment.[161]

It is this which God graciously gives to us while we wait for the Second

---

[156] O'Donovan, *WOJ*, 239.

[157] O'Donovan, *DON*, 46, 236; *WOJ* 53.

[158] O'Donovan, 'Deliberation, History and Reading: A Response to Schweiker and Wolterstorff', *Scottish Journal of Theology* 54 (2001) 137; *WOJ* 239; Chaplin, 'Political Eschatology and Responsible Government', 297; Skillen, 'Acting Politically in Biblical Obedience?', 407.

[159] Wolterstorff, 'Discussion', 97 footnote 1, 105.

[160] O'Donovan, 'The Natural Ethic', 32.

[161] O'Donovan, *JWR*, 6.

Coming.[162]

On O'Donovan's account, the political act does not fall within the order of redemption. He denies that the ruler's role can be an office in the Church because, as he points out, 'it belongs to the old aeon that is passing away.'[163] In O'Donovan's terms, the State's facilitation of the mission of the Church is not part of saving grace but comes within God's providence. O'Donovan sees the New Testament as 'recognizing that political authority, though not the final answer of a God who adopts men as his sons, nevertheless has divine authorization as a provisional arrangement for a world not yet redeemed.'[164] The providential ordering of government points forward to the final judgment,[165] to 'the day when Christ assumes [the] office [of the magistrate] into his own.'[166]

What will be explored in the following section is whether O'Donovan's providentialist understanding of the Spirit's work in sustaining political authority is sufficiently complemented by an account of the Spirit's operations in relation to the political task of judgment. Although O'Donovan has now gone some way towards clarifying the Spirit's role in the establishment and sustaining of political authority, he has not articulated the Spirit's involvement in the exercise of political authority.

Law and the Trinity in O'Donovan's Thought

In *DON* at 217, O'Donovan sets out his vision of the role of political authority:

> The service rendered by the state to the church is to facilitate its mission. The state itself cannot pursue the mission of the church, for it is not consecrated to that task and its weapons of coercion are not fitted for it. But it may facilitate the mission of the church, or impede it. It may facilitate it, first, simply by performing its own business responsibly and with modest pretensions. In the Christian era there is no neutral performance on the part of rulers; either they accommodate to the energy of the divine mission, or they hurl themselves into defiance ... Beyond that, however, there may be a conscious facilitation, based on the recognition of the church and acknowledgment of its mission.

O'Donovan's account of political authority after the Ascension of Christ identifies it as still resting on the three bases of power, tradition and judgment but as having only two tasks. The first task is the necessary task of delivering judgment. The second task is the possible task of consciously facilitating the Church's mission. The two will be considered separately, although O'Donovan

---

[162] O'Donovan, *JWR*, 136.
[163] O'Donovan, *DON*, 218.
[164] O'Donovan, *In Pursuit of a Christian View of War*, 8.
[165] O'Donovan, *RMO*, 177.
[166] O'Donovan, *In Pursuit of a Christian View of War*, 8.

might argue that the facilitation of the Church's mission is, in truth, part and parcel of the task of delivering judgment and is, in certain circumstances necessary for that primary task to be carried out appropriately. In considering each of these tasks in the light of the Trinity, it will be contended that O'Donovan has not yet sufficiently integrated the Holy Spirit into his argument. Before addressing these tasks, however, they have to be understood in terms of O'Donovan's framework for political authority, which gives priority to the mission of the Church.

The Priority of the Church's Mission

In the Christian era, human political authority is bounded by the work of God on two sides. On the one hand, it is bounded by the laws of God, given in creation, which human authorities are constrained to take account of when forming their judgments. On the other hand, it is bounded by the Church as the community of God's people, which reveals the provisionality of secular society.

In the New Covenant era, O'Donovan insists that the theological account of worldly rule 'must proceed from and through an account of the church.' (*DON* 159). O'Donovan contends that the Church itself is a political society, that is to say, 'It is ruled and authorised by the ascended Christ alone and supremely; it therefore has its own authority; and it is not answerable to any other authority that may attempt to subsume it.'[167]

O'Donovan sees the Church as having theological priority over political authority. If Pentecost is the direct consequence of the Ascension, then it is the primary manifestation of the lordship of the Ascended Christ. The decisive work of God in the era of the Ascended Christ is the gathering to Godself of a people through the work of the Holy Spirit. The obedience of rulers can be no more than a derivative response to that work of God.

The Church is the body of the people of God, shaped by the Spirit, and 'giving social form to the triumph of Christ'. 'The catholic identity of the church derives from the progress of the Spirit's own mission. It is therefore always larger than its ordered structures, taking its shape from the new ground that the Spirit is possessing.'[168] O'Donovan therefore seeks to hold to a charismatic, non-sectarian account of the Church.[169]

Liberal pluralism with regard to religions is historically attributable to the Reformation and to the Wars of Religion which accompanied and followed

---

[167] O'Donovan, *DON*, 159.

[168] O'Donovan, *DON*, 169.

[169] Bretherton identifies O'Donovan as having a threefold definition of the church, distinguishing the invisible, universal body of Christ; the pre-structural, visible, catholic church; and the particular congregations and institutional arrangements and orders that are expressions of this pre-structural, visible reality: *Hospitality as Holiness*, 102.

it.[170] O'Donovan denies that such pluralism is healthy when it degenerates to a claimed indifferentism to religious questions.[171] He side-steps the question of how or on what grounds a ruler is to prefer one church to another by asserting the unity of the Church (*RP* 418-419). His favoured model of establishment is that of Finland, where Orthodox, Catholic and Lutheran churches are recognised.[172] But the existence of groups claiming to be Christian such as the Unitarians, the Mormons, the Jehovah's Witnesses, and of exclusive or millennarist sects, means that such a manoeuvre is not as complete an answer as might first appear to be the case. Whatever the God-given reality of the unity of the Church, it does not present itself to government as a unity save in contexts where the national-church identity remains very strong (e.g. Greece) and in some contexts, such as Northern Ireland, remains highly polarised. The opposing sides in Northern Ireland may misrepresent the underlying reality, but government has to deal with what is presented to it.[173]

Secular rulers have to govern societies in which the Church is present, and are called by the proclamation of the Church to acknowledge their submission to the lordship of Christ.[174] This submission means the subordination of their power to the service of the Church's mission. O'Donovan's positive vision for political authority, often seen as a defence of Christendom, is at heart an attempt to answer the question: what would government look like if it responded positively to the Church's mission?[175] His answer is that human government is not called upon to play a direct role in the drama of salvation but is instead charged with the mission of creating the stable social conditions in which the gospel may be freely proclaimed and received. To reformulate the point in trinitarian terms, O'Donovan is asserting the priority of the missions of the Son and the Spirit over the role of human politics.

Therefore,

> [t]he most truly Christian state understands itself most thoroughly as "secular". It makes the confession of Christ's victory and accepts the relegation of its own authority. ... Like [John] the Baptist, it has a place on the threshold of the Kingdom, not within it. The only corresponding service that the church can render to this authority of the passing world is to help it make that act of self-denying recognition.[176]

Correspondingly, a society which has lost sight of eternity will inevitably

---

[170] O'Donovan, *DON*, 91; Neuhaus, 'Commentary on *The Desire of the Nations*', 58; Greene, 'Revisiting Christendom', 335-37.
[171] Lockwood O'Donovan, 'A Timely Conversation', 383-84.
[172] O'Donovan, *DON*, 244.
[173] Schweiker, 'Freedom and Authority', 124-25.
[174] Skillen, 'Acting Politically in Biblical Obedience?', 410.
[175] O'Donovan, *DON*, 195; Colwell, *Living the Christian Story*, 241.
[176] O'Donovan, *DON*, 219, 243.

overload the present age with meaning and significance, and so will cease to be secular.[177]

O'Donovan is correct that political order is only rightly understood if it is recognised (1) that it is secular, i.e. concerned only with matters of this age, (2) that it is subject to God. The question is: whose understanding is it which counts? Is it the understanding of the Church, of the society as a whole, or of the rulers which counts? Can a humble ruler resist the social pressures, in a society which no longer believes in the afterlife, to create the *societas perfecta* and *utopia* here and now? Can the Church, other than through martyrdom, witness to the true *bene esse* of government in such a society?

O'Donovan's contentions regarding the two tasks of government will now be considered in turn.

The Trinity and the Necessary Task of Delivering Judgment

As has been seen in the first part of this chapter, O'Donovan offers a christologically centred vision of natural law. One would therefore expect him to make the constraints which natural law imposes on human government a major theme in his work. While this is present to some degree, the emphasis is far more on the conventional nature of human law, formed as it is by a community's reflections on itself and on its relation to the created order. Collective identity therefore has the predominant role in law-making.

THE IMPERATIVE OF JUSTICE

For O'Donovan, the provision of justice as judgment is the fundamental political task in the present era.[178] O'Donovan's theology has a place for God's wrath as the underside of God's love.[179] The communal effects of human sinfulness create the need for justice, which governments fulfil by executing 'God's wrath on the wrongdoer.'[180] In doing so, they manifest both 'God's wrathful judgment on sinful humanity and his providential mercy toward it ... by providing a limited judgment and punishment of human wrongdoing, in lieu of the limitlessness of both God's eschatological judgment and the unrestrained human passion for vengeance.'[181] It is tempting to put this in terms which Aquinas might have used, to speak of human judgment as a fallible, limited, temporal participation in divine judgment, but O'Donovan's Augustinianism

---

[177] O'Donovan, *Common Objects of Love*, 42, 69; *WOJ* 76-77.

[178] O'Donovan, *Common Objects of Love*, 67; A. Rasmussen, 'Not All Justifications of Christendom Are Equal: A Response to Oliver O'Donovan', *Studies in Christian Ethics* 11 (1998) 72; Lockwood O'Donovan, 'A Timely Conversation', 387.

[179] O'Donovan, *39 Articles*, 31.

[180] O'Donovan, *In Pursuit of a Christian View of War*, 8-9; *DON* 148.

[181] O'Donovan, *BOI*, 289, Lockwood O'Donovan, *BOI*, 227, 'A Timely Conversation', 389.

may cause him to baulk at such language.[182]

The task of judgment is orientated towards justice, and it is wisdom which enables the ruler to do justice.[183] By stressing the fundamental task of political authority as 'judgment', O'Donovan is able to render plausible his account of 'political authority as an expression of God's providential *will*, of which political institutions are merely the contingent, historically variable, channels.'[184]

In the biblical witness as a whole it is law and righteousness-justice not politics which are the primary categories. In chapter 11 of *WOJ* O'Donovan makes clear the priority of law over the institutions which give effect to it, thus correcting a possible misapprehension arising from a reading of *DON* in isolation from *RMO*. In doing so, he relativises the disagreement between Augustinian and Thomist thought over whether human government is a pre- or post-lapsarian institution.[185]

In one of his most elegant definitions, O'Donovan describes 'Legitimacy [as] the subjection of representation to law.' (*WOJ* 165). He argues that Christian political thought has insisted on legitimacy, not as a substitute for representation, but in order to prevent representation descending into idolatry (*WOJ* 165-66, 184).

O'Donovan defines 'Law' as 'the reality that determines how we conduct ourselves ... the order within the world that is given to us.' (*WOJ* 189). This law is the prior reality behind any act of human law-giving (*WOJ* 190). Human government is therefore placed within the context of prior divine law-giving. However, human government both arises, on an Augustinan view, as a providential ordering required because of humankind's disobedience to divine law, and is constrained both by the criterion of the true reality of divine law on the one hand and the reality of the fallen society which it must administer on the other. Human law-making and law-enforcement must therefore plot a graph between the axes of truth and effectiveness (*WOJ* 9).

What the idea of government as judgment brings to the forefront is the idea of rulers arbitrating the claims of their subjects. For O'Donovan, '[j]udgment has two aspects to it: the separation made between innocence and guilt, ... and the affirmation of the innocent against the guilty in an act of vindication and condemnation.' (*DON* 136). Justice is therefore a matter of rights and wrongs, not merely a matter of procedural fairness. '... [A]cting justly *gives apt*

---

[182] Milbank, whose Augustinianism is not mediated by English Reformed expressions, but rather by neo-Platonism, would be happier with such language precisely because of its metaphysical content.

[183] O'Donovan, *Common Objects of Love*, 49.

[184] Chaplin, 'Political Eschatology and Responsible Government', 291.

[185] O'Donovan, 'Christianity and Territorial Right' in Buchanan and Moore, eds., *States, Nations and Borders: The Ethics of Making Boundaries* (Cambridge: CUP, 2003) 127; *WOJ* 60.

expression to the moral quality of the situation. ... It is the nature of an act of judgment to express the moral truth of a situation effectively in a new action.'[186]

However, whilst O'Donovan uses the language of rights and wrongs (*WOJ* 138-40), he and Lockwood O'Donovan offer a penetrating critique of human rights liberalism.[187] O'Donovan argues that thinking of secular society in this way dissolves the unity and coherence of the idea of justice into 'a plurality of "rights".'[188] 'Our concrete obligations are not divided between the negative duty of not flouting obligations, on the one hand, and the mere enactment of moral *faits accomplis* on the other. We have a duty of responsibility which outruns subjective rights.'[189]

Key to O'Donovan's view of judgment is that while a human judge is incompetent to declare comprehensively what it is right to do, such a judge is obliged to determine when a wrong has occurred of such a nature that it demands public remedy. In the practice of judgment by political authorities, therefore, 'wrong has epistemological priority over right' (*WOJ* 58). The view that governmental action is only justified in response to wrong might be called the "wrong principle".

Greene[190] and Wolterstorff[191] have argued against O'Donovan that there is more to governing rightly than merely righting injustices. O'Donovan's response has been to insist that, in his usage, the terms 'judgment' and 'justice' include both corrective and attributive justice,[192] and therefore governments can engage in welfare-promoting tasks, provided it can be demonstrated that 'without the state's use of its powers in these spheres, *wrong* would be done'.[193] A *'prima facie* threat to the common good' is sufficient justification for governmental intervention (*WOJ* 66). This widening of the scope of judgment is not made without cost, however. O'Donovan's "wrong principle" is, like Mill's "harm principle" an anti-totalitarian principle. The insistence that governmental action must be in response to wrong is intended to guard against tyranny. If the definition of wrong is widened, it becomes necessary to recognise that the "wrong principle" cannot, by itself, circumscribe the field of governmental action sufficiently to provide a principled basis for objection to tyranny.

The execution of justice is necessary in order to preserve the peace of the

---

[186] O'Donovan, *BOI*, 194; *WOJ* 7.

[187] O'Donovan, *BOI*, 77; Lockwood O'Donovan, 'The Concept of Rights in Christian Moral Discourse'.

[188] O'Donovan, *DON*, 247-248, 276.

[189] O'Donovan, *BOI*, 203; *WOJ* 221.

[190] Greene, 'Revisiting Christendom', 324.

[191] Wolterstorff, 'Discussion', 105-108; *Until Justice and Peace Embrace* 63.

[192] O'Donovan, 'Deliberation', 133-135; *BOI* 167-203; *WOJ* 61-66.

[193] O'Donovan, 'Deliberation', 135.

political community.[194] '[I]t must achieve *peace*, understanding that term properly to include all that is comprised in a stable and settled political order, including the justice and law-governed character of relations established within it.'[195] However, '[a]ny quest for peace that is not linked to a quest for justice will be illusory.'[196]

But that immediately raises the question of the criteria for judgment. If rulers are to determine when the common good is threatened and are to choose between the innocent and the guilty, how is this to be determined; *in relation to what?* O'Donovan's answer is that our judgments are not given 'in a vacuum, but in responsibility to the generic judgments of God known to us through divine law, natural and revealed, and through salvation history. God's judgments illumine the categorical structure of all events, and so teach us how to appraise particular events' (*WOJ* 17). What the Christ-event makes primary is 'authoritative judgment and communal law, that together constitute the tradition of legal justice.'[197]

As has been seen, whereas Moltmann stresses social justice and human rights, O'Donovan prefers to speak of judgment. By judgment he means that responsible choices have to be made by those who govern. Faced with wrongs, they have to take action. He prefers the term judgment to that of justice because the cry for justice can all too easily become distorted into a claim for 'my rights'. As Howard Marshall points out, justice is in danger of becoming a 'hooray' word – universally acknowledged to be a positive thing, but with either an uncertain or a partisan content.[198] Yet it is precisely the elusive and open-ended nature of justice which constitutes its conceptual appeal for Moltmann.

O'Donovan would regard Moltmann's approach to justice and human rights as insufficiently rigorous, and open to the very risk which he seeks to avoid, that of elevating *our* particular vision of justice into universal or divine status. In contrast, O'Donovan is constantly aware that seeking ultimate peace and or ultimate justice in the present age is what leads to Antichrist.[199]

Human law is made under, administered and accountable to the divine law, both natural and revealed. But this divine law can only be truly discerned in the light of the resurrection because it is nothing other than the natural and evangelical moral orders which find their coherence in Christ. Therefore it

---

[194] O'Donovan, *BOI*, 272.

[195] O'Donovan, *JWR*, 59.

[196] O'Donovan, *Peace and Certainty*, 116.

[197] Lockwood O'Donovan, *BOI*, 286.

[198] I.H. Marshall, 'The Biblical Concept of Justice', *Shaftesbury Project Working Paper* (Nottingham: Shaftesbury Project, 1977) 3; O'Donovan, *RMO*, 60.

[199] O'Donovan, *Peace and Certainty*, 115; N.T. Wright, 'Paul and Caesar: A New Reading of Romans' in Bartholomew et al., eds., *A Royal Priesthood?* (Carlisle: Paternoster, 2002) 176, 178.

seems that it is the Church which must enlighten rulers as to the nature of their moral duty. What is missing in O'Donovan's answer is an account of the work of the Spirit of God to complement his description of the word of God.

NATURAL LAW AND HUMAN LAW

For O'Donovan the moral order given in creation gives rise to 'natural right', that is to say an objective ordering which must be respected. Although he is chary of using the term 'Natural Law' as this undercuts his claim that apart from Christ, human beings do not understand the moral order of creation,[200] Novak is right to describe him as presenting 'the most theological view possible of the doctrine of natural law.'[201]

Human institutions do not create the right or rights, they respond to the fact that there exist pre-political relations of right given in creation.[202] O'Donovan, following Augustine and Aquinas, argues that the role of the political ruler is to interpret these divine, i.e. God-given relations of right, and also those human rules, both customary and statute, which embody the common judgment of the whole community which they are called to serve.[203]

In O'Donovan's view, the thinkers of Christendom always understood that 'The legislative activity of princes, then, was not a beginning in itself; it was an answer to the prior lawmaking of God in Christ, under which it must be judged.'[204] O'Donovan's fifth theorem is that God's lordship over the nations is reflected in a universally binding law, which Christendom ultimately succeeded in formulating as international law.[205] While political entities require representation by a monarch, humanity itself is unified only by its common obligations to God's law, as revealed in the moral order of creation (*DON* 72). God has already provided for representation of all the people of the world through the man Jesus Christ. Nonetheless, the international order is not a world without judgment because it is bounded by law, by the law of God, natural and revealed, as well as by customary *ius gentium*, treaties and conventions (*WOJ* 211). It is that prior law which gives force to the judgments of the international community (*WOJ* 218-219).

The kingship of God grounds the existence of an objective moral order *given* in creation, from which human societies depart at their peril. Political authorities therefore have to reckon with the objectivity of that moral order. They also have to reckon with the prevailing interpretation or denial of that moral order within human societies and devise a set of rules which render

---

[200] O'Donovan, *RMO*, 85-87; Black, *Christian Moral Realism*, 118.

[201] O'Donovan, 'Response', 63.

[202] O'Donovan, *JWR*, 22.

[203] O'Donovan, *BOI*, 209-11; Lockwood O'Donovan, *BOI*, 227, 242-43.

[204] O'Donovan, *DON*, 234, 236; Rasmussen, 'Not All Justifications of Christendom Are Equal', 70.

[205] O'Donovan, *DON*, 236, 267.

human existence in that society within the given moral order bearable. Because they are faced with the objective moral order, the contours of well-made human law bear an indirect witness to that divine law.[206] Conversely, *in extremis*, a human law may so violate 'divine or natural right' that it is illegitimate.[207]

However, for O'Donovan, political authority in general, of which law-making and law-enforcement is a major aspect, stands at one remove from justice.[208]

> [E]ven at its best, public right action can bear only an indirect relation to the demands of truth and goodness considered absolutely. Justice in human communities is only relatively just. It is not mistaken to think of political authority, by positive law or by other means, as "applying" the principles of natural law to social life; for "applying" is a sufficiently broad term to cover any kind of conscientious attempt to make action correspond to the demands of right. But this "application" is something rather different from what is involved in individual moral decision.[209]

O'Donovan does not believe in justice as a specifically political virtue. Political authority is a witness to the truth but compromised by the circumstances of governing fallen men. In his response to Jonathan Chaplin's perceptive critique of *DON*, he identifies 'general justice' (or 'righteousness') as 'simply the sum of all that is good to do', our responsiveness to the universal law which is given in the reality of creation. This righteousness 'belongs to the original createdness of humankind' and does not presuppose the Fall. He contrasts this idea of righteousness as obedience to the moral law with the task of 'judgment', which is 'the response to actual wrong'. This is a specifically postlapsarian activity, which is limited and subject to constraints, and which is therefore informed by 'principles of justice', that is to say by 'political virtues and especially the virtue of "special" justice. But these special principles and special virtues are not known directly from creation order; they are derived inductively, as heuristic descriptions, from the practice of judgment itself.'[210]

O'Donovan denies the existence of any 'special virtue of justice' which is not 'either the law of the universe or the political principles by which judgment must be rendered.'[211] The reason for this is that 'Political authority or kingly rule, including God's own, belongs to the category of *act*. ... The question about the political act, as about every act, is whether it is well, or wisely,

---

[206] Lockwood O'Donovan, 'A Timely Conversation', 389.

[207] O'Donovan, *BOI*, 223.

[208] O'Donovan, 'John Finnis on Moral Absolutes', *Studies in Christian Ethics* 6 (1993) 58.

[209] O'Donovan, *RMO*, 130.

[210] O'Donovan, *RP*, 310; *WOJ* 32.

[211] O'Donovan, *RP*, 310-11.

done.'[212] Judgment is an art not a science, and in O'Donovan's view it is a tragic art practised only of necessity.

Nonetheless, because 'Justice is a train of corrective reasoning about all the goods of human existence, from God to land allotments, and ... can be nothing else',[213] it can only be understood correctly if the goods of human existence are understood correctly, i.e. as goods created by the triune God and as redeemed and transformed by God. O'Donovan's general ethical thesis seems to result in the conclusion that, in doing judgment, as in all other human activities, a ruler will not correctly understand how to obey the Second Great Commandment unless he has made a prior commitment to obey the First. Whilst asserting the importance of biblical revelation, John Warwick Montgomery has argued that, given that we live in God's world, it ought to be possible to argue for Christian moral principles, drawn from the Second Table of the Ten Commandments, on empirical grounds. In other words, even agnostics, pagans and followers of non-Christian religions should be able to see the justice of legislation based on the Christian understanding of morality and reality.[214] The two positions are not wholly antithetical. Montgomery is considering individual ethical and legislative choices, whereas O'Donovan is making the point that such choices are only coherent if understood in the light of a total commitment to following Christ. O'Donovan's political theology needs to allow for the possibility of a ruler, such as Cyrus, making wise choices on some matters even without an explicit commitment to Christ.

THE TORAH AS A POTENTIAL SOURCE OF ILLUMINATION FOR HUMAN LAW

O'Donovan does not believe in any form of autonomous Natural Law, which is somehow distinct from the general flow of the commands of God.[215] However, he does recognise that divine law precedes human law, and that this law may be either given in creation or revealed in Scripture. The problem is that there is little exploration in *RMO* or *DON* of the illuminating possibilities of the Torah with regard to natural law.[216]

O'Donovan constructs his account of the reign of God historically. God's rule over Israel, rather than over the creation as a whole, is the focus of O'Donovan's attention.[217] However, even on this approach one might expect a significant place to be given to the Torah. Furnish suggests that Israel found her

---

[212] O'Donovan, *RP*, 115.

[213] O'Donovan, *RP*, 313.

[214] J.W. Montgomery, 'Law and Morality: Friends or Foes?', *Law & Justice* 122 (1994) 105-106.

[215] O'Donovan, *DON*, 65-66; Novak, 'Response to *The Desire of the Nations*', 63.

[216] Novak, 'Response', 64.

[217] C. Bartholomew, 'A Time for War, and a Time for Peace: Old Testament Wisdom, Creation and O'Donovan's Theological Ethics' in Bartholomew et al., eds., *A Royal Priesthood?* (Carlisle: Paternoster, 2002) 106.

identity in the fact that she was God's covenant people and therefore the recipient of God's grace and faithfulness.[218] On such a reading of the Old Testament, the Torah then becomes the primary locus of Israel's understanding of her obligations to God under the covenant.

O'Donovan's relative silence regarding the Torah led McConville to accuse him of prioritising the kingship-judgment motif over the righteousness-law motif in the Old Testament.[219] If *DON* is re-read in the light of *WOJ*, it is doubtful that this was O'Donovan's intention. However, O'Donovan's relative silence regarding the Torah leaves his stress on the importance of the prophetic witness to the law, to 'the moral content of the tradition to which the kings were answerable' (*DON* 62), somewhat disembodied and thus lays him open to such a criticism.

O'Donovan acknowledges that the Torah is a useful source of revelation of the moral law given in the created order, but argues that this revelation has to be distilled in the light of the fact that the Torah stands on the other side of the climax of salvation-history from where we stand. [220] Furthermore, the revelation of the universal good within it has to be distinguished from that which is related to its contingent character as a society.[221] In distinguishing the universal from the contingent within the Torah, O'Donovan endorses the traditional distinction between the judicial, ceremonial and moral aspects of the Torah. As he points out, such a distinction 'purports to be a Christian hermeneutic of Old Testament law',[222] of validity precisely because Christians are reading the Torah after Christ. It seeks to distinguish between what in the Torah was proper to Israel and what in the Torah was representative of the universal moral order.[223]

In O'Donovan's view, Jesus was a serious interpreter of the Mosaic Law, who challenged the Pharisees' interpretation of it. '[His] central accusation against the Pharisees was that they attempted to construct holiness from outside in. But the holiness acceptable to God was God's own new work, in which, as the prophets had predicted, he would write the law upon the people's hearts.' (*DON* 102). In Jesus' interpretation, obedience to God was not only something to be demonstrated publicly but something to be lived out 'within the hidden sphere of attitudes and actions that are open to God's eyes alone.'[224] It is this insight which is decisive for Aquinas and is, it will be argued in chapter 5, an essential feature of a trinitarian theology of law.

O'Donovan grasps that in the New Covenant era, the promises that God

---

[218] Furnish, 'How Firm a Foundation', 21.

[219] McConville, 'Law and Monarchy', 70.

[220] O'Donovan, *39 Articles*, 64.

[221] O'Donovan, *39 Articles*, 63-64.

[222] O'Donovan, *RMO*, 159.

[223] O'Donovan, *RMO*, 160.

[224] O'Donovan, *DON*, 109.

would write the law on the hearts of God's people have been fulfilled.[225] Although O'Donovan points out that, because of the giving of the Holy Spirit, all the Church, rather than Moses alone, stands at the summit of Mount Sinai in the immediate presence of God,[226] is it not still the case that we have much to gain by reflecting on what was vouchsafed to Moses, albeit understood as subordinate to the Son in whom God was well-pleased? If the Spirit inspired the Torah, may it not have much to teach us about the organisation of a society which is waiting to discover the truth about Christ?

It is difficult to discern any tangible links in O'Donovan's thought between the fact that God gave the Torah to Israel and the political obligations placed on secular rulers today. As the Hebrew Scriptures are presented in canonical form, the Torah comes before the kingship. It is the Torah not the Davidic kingship which was the constant. There are strong grounds for arguing that the Torah, whether in written or oral form, served as a baseline for the Israelites in a wide variety of political orders: from the nomadic wanderings in the desert, through the period of the judges, the united and the divided kingdoms, and then beyond as a rule of life for the diaspora, before being taken up again by Ezra and Nehemiah. It is obedience to the law which defines possession of the land, and not the other way around.[227] The point can be made symbolically by reference to the Transfiguration. This pre-figuring of the Ascension sees Jesus in conversation not with David, the representative of the kingly tradition, but with Moses and Elijah, representing the law and the prophets respectively.

If that view is correct, then the Torah rather than in the particular circumstances of Israelite kingship, is a more promising starting point for considering what God requires in terms of social justice in each and every age. Torah is the means by which the sovereign authority of YHWH over Israel is given practical embodiment, and Moberly criticises O'Donovan for paying little attention to the actual content of Israel's law and for not drawing out how its emphases and priorities demonstrate the nature of God's rule.[228] Chaplin complains that O'Donovan does not take sufficient account of the biblical 'affirmation of a perdurable order of social justice, of which the Old Testament covenantal law codes may be seen as uniquely authoritative historical instantiations.'[229] McConville highlights the proliferation of *tsedeqah* vocabulary in Deuteronomy, and suggests that this 'is about established orders of relationship. More than this, it is an attribute of God, which is reflected in his creation.'[230] The lack of sustained attention to the Torah means that O'Donovan

---

[225] O'Donovan, *DON*, 234; N.T. Wright, 'Paul and Caesar', 187.

[226] O'Donovan, *RMO*, 153.

[227] B.K. Blount, 'Response to *The Desire of the Nations*', *Studies in Christian Ethics* 11 (1998) 8.

[228] Moberly, 'The Use of Scripture', 53-54.

[229] Chaplin, 'Political Eschatology and Responsible Government', 291.

[230] McConville, 'Law and Monarchy', 80.

misses a potentially useful source of illumination of the contours of the moral order given in creation.

To be fair to O'Donovan, faced with McConville's criticism, he pleaded guilty to not having read Deuteronomy closely enough when he wrote *DON* and to saying too little in that book about covenant, a feature which Chaplin rightly points out Calvinist and Puritan writers found fundamental to their reflections on kingship.[231] He also insisted that he regards the law as a much larger feature of the mediation of God's kingship in the Old Testament than was the Davidic monarchy, and that that he does remark on the law, albeit more in connection with the New Testament than with the Old Testament.[232] O'Donovan wishes, therefore, to be read as someone who has always promoted the priority of law over political authority, a point which emerges clearly in his fourth theorem of political authority.

To assert that the Torah is relevant is not to revert to what O'Donovan calls 'a celebrated thesis of the Reformation that the political judgments we enact are *Mosaic* and not *evangelical*' (*WOJ* 84). It is instead to insist that the Torah has not merely been abolished by the coming of Christ but rather, as O'Donovan himself discusses briefly, has been fulfilled in various ways and its inner logic exposed.

COLLECTIVE IDENTITY AND SOCIAL ORDER

'Government as Judgment' not as identity is what O'Donovan proclaims the political task to be about. O'Donovan is not a Roman Catholic, but a member of an established church with Erastian origins. His thought with regard to nationhood is nuanced. On the one hand, he acknowledges that to be human is to participate in a number of collective identities. Each of these collective groups is susceptible of being influenced by the Holy Spirit.[233] However, O'Donovan does not wish to fall into the trap of treating the Holy Spirit as the church-spirit or the community-spirit. Instead, he argues that 'If communities can be agents and subjects (though without being persons, or possessing personality), then they are human agents, just as much as individual agents are. The Spirit enables this agency in the case of the church and its dependent communities just as he does in the case of believing individuals.'[234]

These collective identities are important because the moral order given in creation is not self-interpreting. On O'Donovan's account, in order to function a political society must arrive at an interpretation of the given moral order which is reflected in its laws. It must decide what it holds to be true about marriage and sexuality, about possessions, about work and rest, and, on

---

[231] Chaplin, 'Political Eschatology and Responsible Government', 272; Hauerwas and Fodor, 'Remaining in Babylon', 38.
[232] McConville, 'Law and Monarchy', 89.
[233] O'Donovan, *RMO*, 106.
[234] O'Donovan, *RMO*, 107.

O'Donovan's account, about the relationship of all these things to the divine (*DON* 247). Its culture 'draws upon, and is shaped by, natural forces',[235] and its law will be an expression of its culture.

On the other hand, O'Donovan denies that nations or governments have any absolute rights.[236] In rejecting the nation/ State as the focus for identity, O'Donovan is, of course, asserting that Christians find their identity in Christ and no longer in the contingent relationships of political society, kinship, language or geography. Of the plenitude of reasons for politics in the ancient world, judgment is the only one which is licit in the era of the Ascended Christ.

In O'Donovan's account, the wise ruler does not make law *ex nihilo*, but mediates the judgments about right and wrong inherent in the natural order as discerned by the society over which they govern. Thus Justinian, who was revered in the Middle Ages as the 'model for the Christian lawmaker',[237] was not lauded as an innovator but as a codifier of the moral and legal judgments of classical Roman civilization, as tempered and informed by its adoption of Christianity.

In Western patristic political thought, 'the ruler's authoritative acts interpreted not only divine law (in an admittedly imperfect and incomplete way) but also human law, customary and statute, that embodied the common judgment of the whole community.'[238] For O'Donovan, this common judgment is exercised in relation to the objective moral order. What the political community does is to 'interpret' creation.

However, on O'Donovan's account, the ruler is not limited to recognition of the norms embedded in the natural moral order, obliged to ensure that, as Wyclif urged,[239] their judgments do not go beyond what natural law requires. There is a space for the ruler to create norms for the community they govern, ideally through the enactment of rules which embody the community's particular understanding of what justice requires.

The tradition of a society is formed by its identification of 'common objects of love' including 'representative objects, representative persons, representative histories, and representative ideas'. These 'express what the society is, and they express what it is good for; ... They constitute the central core of the society's common way of seeing the world and living in it.' [240] In them is to be found the society's interpretation of 'the order and rhythm of the cosmos and the nature and destiny of humankind.'[241]

---

[235] O'Donovan, *RMO*, 125.

[236] O'Donovan, *DON*, 151.

[237] O'Donovan, *BOI*, 211.

[238] O'Donovan, *BOI*, 227.

[239] Wyclif, *De Civili Domino*, 1:188-190; Lockwood O'Donovan, *Theology of Law and Authority*, 38.

[240] O'Donovan, *Common Objects of Love*, 32.

[241] O'Donovan, *Common Objects of Love*, 31.

O'Donovan sees a society's history, culture and community expressing themselves in 'law'. Therefore,

> to speak of "law" is to speak not only of eternal realities, but of orders that are tied to particular societies at particular times; ... The law of any society has two aspects. On the one hand, it is that which establishes and maintains order, and as such mediates the order of creation and establishes a relation between the life of society and the good for which mankind was created. On the other, it is not simply identical to the social good, but is in various respects arbitrary: societies are different from each other, and live under different pressures, with different capacities for organization and communication, different educational levels, different motivations. The law (even assuming that in every case it is wise and good law) will differ in accordance with differing social needs.[242]

By reflecting on divine law, natural and revealed, as mediated through traditions of right innate in a society, wise judgment can be given, as is done paradigmatically, for O'Donovan, through the development of the English common law, although subject to correction where necessary, by the legislator.[243]

The central case of political authority is, therefore, not arbitrary command, but an authoritative judgment which 'appeals to the confirmation of objective reality ... The authoritative command is the one which, even as it is uttered, strikes people as right. Not that they themselves would have been able to see it, or act in that way *apart* from the command; rather, the command itself brings the right course to light and enables people to see what should be done.'[244] Whilst this is paradigmatically true of Jesus, who is the sum of all authority, O'Donovan is arguing that this is also true of the central case of political authority. Rulers, at their best, are most perfectly exercising their authority to command when their legislation is in line with reality and illuminates the perceptions of the community with regards to that reality. What O'Donovan's account seems to demand, however, is something like the full-blown theology of Spirit-inspired justice which is advanced by Jonathan Burnside.[245]

For O'Donovan, Christian thought leads to a law-governed society, which is sustained and informed by 'the missionary presence of the church within its midst' and 'the law of the Spirit of life in Christ Jesus.'[246] The sympathetic ruler does not aim to implement the Kingdom of God by force or to make their whole populace good Christians, but instead to maintain a relatively peaceful and just social space within which the Church's mission can flourish. They acknowledge that their rule is subject to the rule of law, which it is their

---

[242] O'Donovan, *39 Articles*, 63.

[243] O'Donovan, *BOI*, 217.

[244] O'Donovan, *39 Articles*, 113.

[245] J. Burnside, 'Inspired Justice', *Justice Reflections* 1 (2002), JR-1.

[246] O'Donovan, *DON*, 249.

responsibility to promote and uphold (*BOI* 217).

O'Donovan regards the apogee of Christian political thought as what he calls 'early modern liberalism' which under the impact of the gospel arrived at the principles of freedom, mercy in judgment, natural right and openness to speech,[247] which O'Donovan might be persuaded to call political virtues, and which give rise to certain features of a liberal political order which O'Donovan discusses in chapter 10 of *WOJ*. Without ascribing ultimate value to these principles, O'Donovan wishes to preserve them whilst unmasking the dangerous claims to religious neutrality and the exaltation of individual wills present in late-modern liberalism.[248] Chaplin calls O'Donovan's position one of 'Christian liberalism', or better, 'Christian constitutionalism'.[249] Rowland describes *DON* as 'in many ways an apology for a consciously theological, though much chastened, liberal polity.'[250]

COLLECTIVE IDENTITY, SOLIDARITY AND THE COMMON GOOD

The first political lesson which the obedient political authority should learn from the Church is that the *polis* is not the ultimate society. Because of Christ, the Church is the primary society, and secular society cannot approximate to a *societas perfecta*.[251] As Lockwood O'Donovan writes 'The perennial truth of [Wyclif's] ecclesiology is that the community of faith is bound to a more exact and complete conformity to Christ's evangelical law of love than the civil community; that the Church polity, ruled immediately by the Spirit of Christ, constitutes a more perfect common good and fabric of relationships than the civil polity.'[252]

The justification for secular government in the era of the gospel is the provision of a social space out of which 'men and women of every nation' may 'be drawn into the governed community of God's Kingdom'.[253]

O'Donovan is critical of the Reformation's tendency to see human beings as atomised individuals rather than 'in Adam' and participating in corporate human solidarity.[254] Our common humanity takes shape through the recognition of a number of factors: our natural equality with one another, simply by virtue of being human beings (see also *WOJ* 40-41); the acknowledgment of structures of affinity in which we find ourselves at home; the reciprocal exchange which is possible between different communities of

---

[247] Bartholomew, 'Introduction', 34; Chaplin, 'Political Eschatology and Responsible Government', 272.

[248] O'Donovan, *Peace and Certainty*, 94; Lockwood O'Donovan, *BOI*, 139-141.

[249] Chaplin, 'Political Eschatology and Responsible Government', 269, 283 footnote 74.

[250] Rowland, 'Response to *The Desire of the Nations*', 77.

[251] O'Donovan, *WOJ*, 241; Lockwood O'Donovan, 'A Timely Conversation', 393.

[252] Lockwood O'Donovan, *BOI*, 95.

[253] O'Donovan, *DON*, 146; Chaplin, 'Political Eschatology and Responsible Government', 278.

[254] O'Donovan, *39 Articles*, 72.

affinity and finally, our inhabitation of a common world with non-human species (*DON* 262). Language, tradition, culture and law are all important elements of the affinities which create political communities.

Human community is, in O'Donovan's view, a fundamental part of human identity which cannot be abstracted from. Our lives are shaped and given *penultimate* meaning by the communities in which we undertake non-reciprocal roles and in which we are at home.[255] As part of these communities we express solidarity in the ways in which we allow ourselves 'to be restricted in our freedom of action by others' necessities' (*WOJ* 54). However, recognising our common humanity means both acknowledging our obligation to love our neighbour (*RMO* 229, 226) and not seeking to take responsibility for their welfare entirely away from them.

Moreover, not only are we formed by the communities to which we belong, we may ourselves sustain them, even as a lone voice (*DON* 80). This insight, which forms O'Donovan's sixth theorem, is developed in the final chapter of *WOJ* where he describes the conscientious individual, not as a pre-political reality, but rather as one who has reflected on their own place in society, and thereby discerned the service which they truly owe to that society and to its political institutions.

O'Donovan has strong notions of corporate identity and personality, which tend in the direction of a correspondingly thick conception of the common good. He certainly believes that there is more to society than the mere satisfaction of individuals' private purposes.[256] Equally, he is sympathetic to the argument that private property is not sacrosanct because it is accumulated 'by virtue of the conditions the state has maintained.'[257]

O'Donovan and Lockwood O'Donovan frame the Christian debate about the task of politics in terms of a debate between Augustine and the Aristotelians. Lockwood O'Donovan sees Aquinas as influenced by both Aristotle and Augustine, and as holding the two social visions in tension.[258] She contrasts the Aristotelian idea that the ruler should direct a society towards its common good with the Augustinian view in which 'political rule was established by God for the purpose of restraining human evildoing and encouraging virtuous conduct'.[259] Whereas the Christian-Aristotelians tend to see politics as originating before the Fall, the Augustinians regard it as postlapsarian. The danger O'Donovan, following Augustine, sees in the Aristotelian agenda is that it demands too much of government, overloading it with aspirations to create the *societas perfecta* which it is not called to establish.[260] The common good is

---

[255] O'Donovan, *DON*, 266.
[256] O'Donovan, *DON*, 275.
[257] O'Donovan, *Peace and Certainty*, 104.
[258] Lockwood O'Donovan, *BOI*, 227-228.
[259] Lockwood O'Donovan, *BOI*, 227.
[260] O'Donovan, *BOI*, 243; *WOJ* 172.

not something created by the ruler (*WOJ* 57), and social harmony is 'not a design conceived in a ruler's head, but a nexus of social communications that exist and flourish antecedently.' (*WOJ* 61). It is the proclaimed commitment to righting wrongs, rather than the embodiment of communal values or the pursuit of communal goods, which is the fundamental basis for political authority and law.[261] Government's task is merely 'to respond to *threats* to the common good, repelling whatever obstructs our acting freely together.' (*WOJ* 57).

O'Donovan combines his third and fourth theorems in the assertion that a political community's identity is to be found not in its 'subscription to a practical creed and plan of action', but in 'its collective recognition of a governing authority and consent to a body of laws'.[262] The derivation of these laws, however, seems to demand a substantive measure of agreement amongst the members of the community upon the values which they hold in common. Therefore, O'Donovan implicitly acknowledges a measure of truth in the Aristotelian vision. It is difficult to see that his account differs substantially from the attenuated Thomism of John Finnis, who defines the common good as 'a set of conditions which enables the members of a community to attain for themselves reasonable objectives, or to realize reasonably for themselves the value(s), for the sake of which they have reason to collaborate with each other (positively and/ or negatively) in a community.'[263]

For O'Donovan, the Church's unity with Christ means that 'Through the Spirit the church recapitulates the whole saving event, Advent, Passion, Restoration and Exaltation. In Christ it is represented in that event; in the Spirit it participates in it. These two aspects of the one relation to the representative act confer the church's political identity upon it.'[264] '[T]he four moments of Advent, Passion, Restoration and Exaltation shape the Church as a community which continually gathers, suffers, rejoices and speaks.'[265]

As Chaplin summarises it, the fundamental shape of O'Donovan's political thought is that 'what God has done in Jesus Christ is focused in the life and mission of the church, which is called to bear witness to the triumph of Christ before the world and its rulers, and to summon them to obedience to him.'[266]

Although it is only the Church which recapitulates the narrative of the Christ-event,[267] O'Donovan argues that a society 'shaped by the presence of the church forms a kind of penumbra to the church',[268] and should be characterised

---

[261] O'Donovan, *RMO*, 128; 'Payback', 19; *WOJ* 159.

[262] O'Donovan, *BOI*, 294.

[263] Finnis, *Natural Law and Natural Rights*, 155.

[264] O'Donovan, *DON*, 161; Greene, 'Revisiting Christendom', 318.

[265] O'Donovan, *DON*, 171.

[266] Chaplin, 'Political Eschatology and Responsible Government', 269.

[267] O'Donovan, *DON*, 174.

[268] O'Donovan, *DON*, 251.

by freedom,[269] merciful judgment,[270] natural order/right,[271] and freedom of speech.[272] As Hauerwas and Fodor note: 'What most captures O'Donovan about Augustine's political theology ... is the way in which, in Augustine's account, the progressive transformation of the social order is accomplished only through Israel and the church.'[273]

The analogy between the Church and Christ holds, of course, because the Church is the body and the bride of Christ. However it is more questionable whether the analogy holds between the Church and society in which the Church is present.[274] Chaplin inquires why Advent, Passion, Restoration and Exaltation are selected as the core of the gospel in this theoretical reconstruction rather than creation-fall-redemption-salvation, for example.[275]

The problematic nature of the analogy becomes acute if it is extended from society to government. The Church is properly analogous to Christ because it falls within the order of redemption. Government, on the other hand, falls, O'Donovan argues explicitly, within the order of providence.[276] To characterise the order of providence in terms of the moments of advent, passion, restoration, exaltation seems highly dubious. In Chaplin's view of O'Donovan, 'salvation *restores and vindicates* the created orders of *society*, but *restrains and disciplines* the providential order of *government.*'[277]

O'Donovan's political theology calls upon government to facilitate the mission of the Church, thus indicating that, in his view, the orders of providence and redemption are not impermeable. The difficulty is, if this concession is made, then O'Donovan has problems explaining why it is not the role of government to do more to promote the mission of the Church, to the point of discouraging, and perhaps even forbidding, error.

The Trinity and the Limits of Human Justice

O'Donovan argues that it is ideological to seek to base the social order on a

---

[269] O'Donovan, *DON*, 252-55.

[270] O'Donovan, *DON*, 256-61.

[271] O'Donovan, *DON*, 262-68.

[272] O'Donovan, *DON*, 268-71.

[273] Hauerwas and Fodor, 'Remaining in Babylon', 40 footnote 5. This is a point which features largely in Milbank's work too, and forms the main theme of chapter 12 of *Theology & Social Theory*.

[274] Hauerwas and Fodor, 'Remaining in Babylon', 51 footnote 12.

[275] Chaplin, 'Political Eschatology and Responsible Government', 272-73.

[276] In his critique of O'Donovan, in 'Just War Theory, the Authorization of the State, and the Hermeneutics of Peoplehood', at 428, Neufeld goes so far as to suggest that in O'Donovan's political theology, 'we find that the providence of God has become identified with the very structure of government.'

[277] Chaplin, 'Political Eschatology and Responsible Government', 296.

single principle.[278] O'Donovan agrees with Enda McDonagh that 'political theology needs to be organised ... around four "Kingdom values" ... [which] need to coexist ... in "perichoresis", since the social order that God has willed is one, but is determined by more than one factor.' In O'Donovan's list, the four principles are freedom, merciful judgment, natural order and freedom of speech. It is illuminating that his natural order equates to McDonagh's 'peace' and that O'Donovan concedes Wolterstorff's complaint that *DON* talks very little about *shalom*.[279] The ordered peace of *shalom* may be more relational than O'Donovan grants.

In O'Donovan's thought, these four principles stand under the primary assertion that secular political authority is limited. Over and above the limitations imposed by human finitude and sinfulness, it is limited compared with the work of the Son and the Spirit. The Son has reserved to Himself the ultimate judgment and the Spirit has reserved to Himself the power to appropriate the redemption achieved by the Son. Each of these limitations will be considered in turn.

THE LIMITATIONS OF HUMAN FINITUDE AND SINFULNESS

Lockwood O'Donovan provides a compact summary of the inadequacies of the judgment exercised by political authorities: it expresses itself as coercive power, it suffers from a lack of vision and insight, it can only provoke external obedience.[280] To that O'Donovan would add that political authority is both necessitated by and thwarted by the fact of limited resources.[281]

Human justice is necessarily fallible because of lack of information and insight.[282] Nonetheless, when judgment is necessary, 'Under God we must act on what we can know, use the best discretion, the best judgment, that we can bring to the situation, and do it in faith.'[283] This judgment may, in O'Donovan's view, be guided by culturally adopted rules such as the presumption of innocence.

O'Donovan argues that the justice meted out by political authorities must cause us to shudder, because of the violence and pain it inflicts, even on the guilty.[284] For O'Donovan, human legal institutions are always an ambivalent reality. On the one hand, they are necessary. Force is the only available weapon with which to do earthly justice.[285] On the other hand, the doing of justice itself is fraught with guilt. 'Society's justice will never be true justice, but always

---

[278] O'Donovan, *DON*, 250.
[279] O'Donovan, 'Discussion', 106.
[280] Lockwood O'Donovan, 'A Timely Conversation', 386.
[281] O'Donovan, *In Pursuit of a Christian View of War*, 8.
[282] O'Donovan, *Peace and War*, 24; *WOJ* 144.
[283] O'Donovan, *Peace and War*, 25.
[284] O'Donovan, *In Pursuit of a Christian View of War*, 10.
[285] O'Donovan, *RMO*, 72.

justice and guilt intertwined in a self-renewing cycle of injury and restitution. ... We cannot look to civilization to satisfy nature's claim; for always in doing justice it does injustice as well.'[286] However, notwithstanding its relativisation and limitations, publicly administered justice is a relative good when contrasted with untrammelled private vengeance.[287] Despite its ambiguities, and the fact that civil judgments cannot be redemptive, O'Donovan does hold that they can 'point beyond themselves to God's redemptive judgment',[288] although he never explores how this might be the case beyond saying that justice and mercy are in an ongoing dialectical relationship (*DON* 261; *WOJ* 100).

It is a workable justice, rather than an ultimate justice, for which we are to strive, whilst recognising fully that 'In life-situations our attempts at justice will be rough. ... We deal in approximations, and the deeper we examine situations the more we despair of knowing what justice demands. ... Justice is not to be measured by an absolute standard: in human dealing ... it is a relative matter, a question of more or less.'[289]

O'Donovan follows Augustine in thinking of 'acts of judicial authority in two lights: the same deed is at once inhuman and terrible, and it is an expression of love', refusing to regard it as either unproblematic demonstrations of love-of-God-and-neighbour or as so morally objectionable that Christians should have nothing to do with it.[290]

Whereas Moltmann tends to divide humankind too glibly into the guilty and the innocent, O'Donovan sees how all are guilty before God, and that in human society questions of guilt and innocent, of justice and injustice, are only ever relative. In Christ's death and resurrection we see the first and the complete demonstration of 'that justice [which] shall supersede all other justice.'[291]

Moreover, human judgments must reckon with the inveteracy of human sinfulness. Even though kingdom morality is continuous with creation morality, the moral order that the Church discerns within creation may be stricter than that which is susceptible of adjudication. In O'Donovan's view, political authority must be based on and in touch with reality, else it will collapse.[292] However, it must also be pragmatic, though not unprincipled.[293] Judgment 'is always relative to what is reasonably possible within that society.'[294] 'The truth of a law must also be a truth about the society in which the law will function.'

---

[286] O'Donovan, *RMO*, 74; *BOI* 262; 'Deliberation', 128. Hegel makes a similar point in *Philosophy of Mind* 529-31.

[287] O'Donovan, *RMO*, 129.

[288] O'Donovan, *DON*, 269.

[289] O'Donovan, *In Pursuit of a Christian View of War*, 17.

[290] O'Donovan, *In Pursuit of a Christian View of War*, 5.

[291] O'Donovan, *RMO*, 75.

[292] O'Donovan, *Peace and Certainty*, 76.

[293] O'Donovan, *Peace and Certainty*, 101.

[294] O'Donovan, *JWR*, 99.

(*WOJ* 19). The classic example is that of divorce,[295] but O'Donovan also explores the question of slavery.[296] As Aquinas also holds, the moral virtue of the citizens of a society is therefore essential to 'any good political community' (*WOJ* 138).

O'Donovan believes in practical politics. In relation to abortion, although he sets out the moral case against it from conception, he begins by observing that if the Christian Church wishes to act as guide to the legislature then it should 'be careful to frame [its] proposals in terms which realistically assess the legislative situation, considering that there are limits on what a community can be persuaded to accept, limits on what police can enforce, and that every society this side of Heaven tries to be content with controlling some evils that it cannot actually eradicate.'[297] Elsewhere he writes that 'Law is like a dyke built to contain the stream of human aspirations and ambitions: if we want to contain the floodwaters, we must leave a channel just large enough for them to find their way to the sea.'[298]

The wise ruler may, on O'Donovan's account, have to be content with not legislating fully in accordance with natural law because the community they have to adjudicate over is too hardhearted or the social evil so entrenched that it can only be controlled or removed by a series of carefully measured steps.[299] The ruler must therefore seek 'to squeeze out, as it were, the maximum yield of public truthfulness available within the practical constraints of the times',[300] seeking to enact enforceable laws which 'reflect the tradition of the community governed',[301] whilst perhaps attempting realistic reforms of society's mores. What O'Donovan does not say is anything about how the Spirit might guide a ruler towards wise choices in the execution of this task.

HUMAN JUDGMENT AND THE SON

O'Donovan's political theology emphasises that the Son is both the focus of representation and the focus of judgment.

With regard to the Son as the focus of representation, human political authority is fundamentally limited in its representative function in that humanity has already been definitively represented in Christ (*WOJ* 240). Furthermore, our identity as people before God is an eschatological reality, which can only be expressed indirectly on earth through the Church (*WOJ* 214- 15, 254). 'In the face of the church all previous identities are shown to be merely provisional, waiting to be brought under that final universal identity and

---

[295] O'Donovan, *DON*, 111.

[296] O'Donovan, *DON*, 184-85.

[297] O'Donovan, *The Christian and the Unborn Child*, 3.

[298] O'Donovan, *JWR*, 91.

[299] McConville, 'Law and Monarchy', 84.

[300] O'Donovan, *BOI*, 217; *WOJ* 97, 193.

[301] O'Donovan, *RMO*, 127.

subordinated to it.' (*WOJ* 240).

This observation of O'Donovan's is pregnant with possibilities, particularly when coupled with his reflections on *koinonia* in chapter 14 of *WOJ*. For O'Donovan, 'creation is a covenant, grounding a *coexistence* of God and his creatures', and the story of salvation looks forward to 'the eschatological community of the kingdom of heaven' (*WOJ* 245). Therefore, although the Church 'models the eschatological community ... it is not simply identical with the eschatological community' (*WOJ* 261). All it can do is to point 'to the future appearing of the one representative, and to the decisive judgment he will give.'[302]

The Son is the focus of judgment in two different respects. He is the one who was on the cross and in the resurrection the focus of God's judgment (*WOJ* 238). He is also the one who will render God's Last Judgment on humanity.

The prospect of divine judgment places limits on the practice of human judgment in a number of respects. There are some judgments which God alone can make. There are some judgments for which the time has not yet come. There are some judgments, such as the punishment of the sinfulness which afflicts us all, where an attempt to render that eschatological judgment now would be catastrophic (*WOJ* 66). Crucially, human judgments cannot be redemptive in the way that Christ's judgment is.

The recognition of these limits grounds human judgment by making it possible to accept its necessity and the limitations to its proper exercise in a world in which the final judgment has not yet been executed.'[303] This is a humility in authority which is analogous to the way in which Christ exercised His authority while on earth.[304] It is also born of the recognition of our own sinfulness (*WOJ* 98).

O'Donovan argues that:

> Final justice is not to be looked for, any more than final peace is to be looked for, until they are both shown to us in the face of Jesus Christ. Humane (*sic*) judgment is necessarily a more restricted affair than that divine judgment for which we hope. ... *Such peace as can be kept and such justice as is defended in keeping it define and limit each other.* ... The pursuit of this relative peace is always the

---

[302] By contrast, it is a criticism of Milbank that he appears, at times, to mistake the Church for the Kingdom: see *Theology & Social Theory* 403. Elsewhere he is more circumspect, e.g. 238, and *Being Reconciled* 204-205. The criticism is made by Lash, 'Not Exactly Politics or Power?', 362, while C. Insole argues that Milbank offers 'too smooth an identification of the visible with the invisible Church': *The Politics of Human Frailty: A Theological Defence of Political Liberalism* (London: SCM, 2004) 151.

[303] O'Donovan, *BOI*, 44; *JWR* 122; *DON* 150-51.

[304] T. Gorringe, 'Authority, Plebs and Patricians', *Studies in Christian Ethics* 11 (1998) 26.

character of well-judged political prudence, even when we practice the necessary ascetic discipline of postponing questions of peace to questions of justice. ...[305]

The fact that God has withheld the execution of the final judgment means that in the Christian era it is the necessity for human judgment, rather than the grounds for withholding it, which needs accounting for. As Chaplin notes,

> [O'Donovan] subscribes to the patristic notion, most fully articulated by Augustine and continued by Luther, of government as a post-lapsarian, remedial institution providentially established by God to curb human sinfulness and enforce a measure of "earthly" justice until the return of Christ, who will usher in a new, heavenly order of peace and harmony in which political authority will be redundant and so pass away.[306]

Rendering human judgment is a public action carried out by a representative of the community affected, given for the sake of peace and order within that community.[307] The need for human judgment is therefore triggered by the fact that the public interest is at stake.[308] O'Donovan distinguishes between three forms of error: (1) that which may not be discerned here and now; (2) that which may be discerned here and now, but which it does not fall to the ruler to sanction; and (3) that which may be discerned here and now and which it does fall to the ruler to sanction. In order for something to fall into the third category, 'The ruler has to establish a prima-facie interest in the implications for civil order before intervening between any man or woman and the God who commands. ... There can be no separation of law and morality; but what there can be, and is, is a sphere of individual responsibility before God in which the public good is not immediately at stake.'[309] The public good is not immediately at stake in questions of religious conviction and so it is not given to governments to regulate such questions.[310] As will be seen in the following chapter, this is a very similar account to that offered by Aquinas, but with the significant difference that O'Donovan recognises that a society can survive religious dissent on the part of some of its members.

HUMAN JUDGMENT AND THE POWER OF THE SPIRIT

Political authority is constrained by the realities with which it must deal and the limitation of the tools at its disposal for doing so.

Human authorities must reckon with the realities of human sin, and therefore

---

[305] O'Donovan, *Peace and Certainty*, 116, emphasis mine.
[306] Chaplin, 'Political Eschatology and Responsible Government', 276-77.
[307] O'Donovan, *JWR*, 31; *DON* 37.
[308] O'Donovan, *JWR*, 47.
[309] O'Donovan, *DON*, 255.
[310] O'Donovan, *DON*, 255; Chaplin, 'Political Eschatology and Responsible Government', 273.

this constrains them in terms of what is prohibited and what is enforced. 'The exercise of political authority is the search for a compromise which, while bearing the fullest witness to the truth that can in the circumstances be borne will, nevertheless, lie within the scope of possible public action in the particular community of fallen men which it has to serve.'[311] Although 'Law can be seen as the objectification of specified obligation',[312] not everything that is morally right can be legislated. What is left is a space for individual moral agents to go beyond what is required of them by the law (*RMO* 170).

For O'Donovan, therefore, human law is necessarily restricted in the ethical demands which it seeks to enforce. Beyond its strictures, the Church may call its members to distinctive evangelical obedience and beyond even that, individuals have their individual vocations. Indwelt by the Holy Spirit, Christians are uniquely able to discern for themselves what God requires of them in their relationships with their neighbours, and to resolve disputes when they arise (*DON* 112-113).

The most extraordinary feature of *WOJ* is its final chapter. In it, O'Donovan returns to a discussion of conscience, which formed a major theme in *RMO*, in order to reflect on what an individual does when they judge themselves.

> Here is the dialogue of "conscience" in its true form: "the Spirit of God joining with our own spirit" in a discovery of our powers of agency, as "sons of God." This dialogue "adopts" us into the family-relations of the godhead in the economy of salvation: we call on God as Father, as his Son calls on him; we share the wealth of his presence together with the glorified Christ. And the experience of our own lives takes on a shape like his, that of suffering that leads to glorification. (*WOJ* 316).

This passage in its explicit references to the Trinity re-opens a direction for O'Donovan's thought found earlier in *On The 39 Articles*; one which takes account of the participation in the Trinity into which Christians are invited, through the fellowship of the Spirit as those who are in Christ.[313] Such an understanding, it will be argued in the following chapters, buttresses O'Donovan's position against totalitarianism in ways which are superior to his present account.

In contrast to the expansive possibilities of Spirit-led self-judgment, human laws can only enforce condemnation, and though they may seek to encourage reconciliation and moral rehabilitation, they cannot compel it. Whereas 'God's redeeming judgment pours out the promised Holy Spirit upon all who believe and obey, human judgments convey no such power. The human judge may know the Holy Spirit's help in judging, but cannot shed the Holy Spirit abroad

---

[311] O'Donovan, *RMO*, 130.

[312] O'Donovan, *BOI*, 203.

[313] Bretherton, *Hospitality as Holiness* at 74 finds this understanding of participation to be part of O'Donovan's trinitarian account of Christian ethics.

on those who are judged.'[314] All that human judgments can do is to 'give concrete and effective condemnation'.[315] They address the wrongs of the past with 'the goal of establishing, or maintaining, a just social order.'[316] This is a task to be undertaken with the humble modesty of those who know their own sinfulness and who are influenced by God's grace.[317]

The Christian judge may therefore know the guidance of the Spirit as he or she carries out the task of judging, but can and must it be recognised that the Spirit can be at work in the conscientious judgments of those judges who have not (yet) acknowledged the Son, insofar as those judgments are wise ones, taking due account of the realities which they have to address? O'Donovan does not answer this question, and as has been discussed previously, the shape of his general ethical theory makes it unclear how he would do so.

The Trinity and the Possible Task of Consciously Facilitating the Church's Mission

The discussion so far in this section has considered only the first of the two tasks of government identified by O'Donovan. The second task, that of the government consciously facilitating the Church's mission, now falls to be explored. The description of O'Donovan's political theology as a defence of Christendom can be a shortcut to misunderstanding and misrepresentation.

O'Donovan argues that what he is doing is engaging seriously with the tradition of Christian political thought, seeking not to defend Christendom but to offer a sympathetic reading of Christendom, an account of what the *thinkers* about Christendom thought they were doing.[318] In *WOJ*, he says that he has in sight the even broader task of defending 'the coherence of political conceptions as such' (*WOJ* xiv), so as to render political institutions 'morally intelligible' (*WOJ* xi).

O'Donovan defines '"Christendom" ... [as] the idea of a confessionally Christian government, at once "secular" (in the proper sense of that word, confined to the present age) and obedient to Christ, a promise of the age of his unhindered rule.' (*DON* 195) O'Donovan insists that

> It is not ... that Christian political order is a *project* of the church's mission, either as an end in itself or as a means to the further missionary end. The church's one project is to witness to the Kingdom of God. Christendom is *response* to mission,

---

[314] O'Donovan, *WOJ*, 87, 99.
[315] O'Donovan, *WOJ*, 87.
[316] O'Donovan, *WOJ*, 93.
[317] O'Donovan, *WOJ*, 98.
[318] O'Donovan, 'Behold, the Lamb!', 103-105.

and as such a sign that God has blessed it. It is constituted not by the church's seizing alien power, but by alien power's becoming attentive to the church.[319]

O'Donovan acknowledges that this scenario created its own temptations, but points out that the thinkers of the Christendom era were far from unaware of them.[320]

O'Donovan is not seeking to defend enforced conversion or political enforcement of Christian attendance. He argues that the Church does not need the State to defend it because it has been vindicated by Christ.[321] Because it knows that judgment over it has already been given, the Church only has a limited need for secular government.[322] The Church can suffer persecution without despair because it can await its final vindication by the Just Judge.[323] The Church does not need to seek earthly retribution for the wrongs done to it, but can entrust 'the whole of judgment to the decisive act of God.'[324] Thus, in contrast with his mentor Augustine, O'Donovan does not believe that the Christian ruler is called to punish heretics or to protect the purity of the Church's truth. It is odd, however, that O'Donovan does not expressly advance another ground on which the roles of the State and the Church can be distinguished. As O'Donovan stresses so clearly, the resurrection-ascension both makes clear the shape of the moral order given in creation and points forward to the transformation of creation. While creation ethics and kingdom ethics are not, on this account, discontinuous, there is a distinct way of life to which Christians are called, and which is not susceptible of enforcement through secular law. Faith in Christ, and all that follows from it in terms of evangelical obedience, cannot be produced but only counterfeited by coercion, and such a counterfeit may bear the name 'AntiChrist'. What is missing is the affirmation that it is the unique role of the Spirit to draw us into the kingdom of the Son, as O'Donovan put it in *On the 39 Articles*.

Just as he is adamant that secular government should not use its powers to coerce people into the Church, O'Donovan is equally clear in his opposition to clerical dominance of secular government. Just as government does not purport to accomplish the Church's mission, so the Church should not attempt to arrogate to itself government's proper function (*WOJ* 240). The Church does not seek political authority but offers counsel, counsel which is, because it chimes with the realities of the created moral order 'authoritative without being

---

[319] O'Donovan, *DON*, 195; Rasmussen, 'Not All Justifications of Christendom Are Equal', 69; Colwell, *Living the Christian Story*, 241.

[320] O'Donovan, *DON*, 196.

[321] O'Donovan, *DON*, 150-51; 'Behold, the Lamb!', 105.

[322] O'Donovan might have said because it knows that its own ascension is guaranteed in the Ascension of Christ.

[323] O'Donovan, *DON*, 112.

[324] O'Donovan, *DON*, 149.

coercive.'[325] The epistemological authority of the Church is founded in the Paschal mystery. If the resurrection is key to perceiving the true moral order of creation, then the Church apprehends this because it is the recipient of the promises associated with the Ascension, namely Pentecost.[326]

From his earliest writings, O'Donovan has stressed the Western Christian tradition of distinguishing between secular and spiritual authority.[327] In discussing the duality of authority, he then says that against arguments from Plato onwards which would put political power in the hands of philosopher-kings, Christian political thought recognises only one, all-wise, all-powerful, sovereign, King Jesus.[328] O'Donovan believes that the positive achievement of Western Christendom was to maintain theological exclusivism whilst affirming political liberalism and pluralism.[329]

What O'Donovan is arguing for, however, is the legitimacy of a particular, positive response by secular government, as a sign of or after the 'success' of the Church's mission. *DON* sets out his vision for the State if the Church is successful in its mission, seen in the sense of bringing all things under the lordship of Christ. He is therefore prone to being misunderstood as understanding 'success' in straightforward, if not worldly, terms.[330] However, from the book of Daniel, O'Donovan draws the lesson that '[t]he co-operative relation between Israel and the empire is not a right, and to make a priority of preserving it can lead to fatal compromises.' (*DON* 87, 216). The co-operation is not a stable one because the empire itself is not stable. One of the reasons for their instability is that empires do not understand themselves; they are unaware of their own fragility (*DON* 88). Only by understanding the nuances of O'Donovan's qualifications that the mission of the Church is never complete and that the Church does not have the right to expect co-operation from government can premature triumphalism be avoided.

O'Donovan wants to rehabilitate the idea that it is legitimate for political authorities to 'offer deliberate assistance to the church's mission.'[331] He insists that he is only in favour of 'the theological *possibility* of the Christian state, but not its *necessity*'.[332] O'Donovan sees the First Amendment to the US Constitution as the paradigm denial of this possibility. He writes:

> The evangelical Christians who helped shape the new doctrine ... proposed to instruct princes that they were dispensable to the Holy Spirit's work, and to send them to the spectators' seats. ... [I]t ended up promoting a concept of the state's

---

[325] O'Donovan, *RMO*, 172.
[326] O'Donovan, *DON*, 161-62.
[327] O'Donovan, *39 Articles*, 98; *RMO* 174.
[328] O'Donovan, *39 Articles*, 98.
[329] O'Donovan, *39 Articles*, 76, 99.
[330] Hauerwas and Fodor, 'Remaining in Babylon', 34.
[331] O'Donovan, *DON*, 244.
[332] O'Donovan, *RP*, 239.

role from which Christology was excluded, that of a state freed from all responsibility to recognise God's self-disclosure in history.[333]

However, O'Donovan's argument in favour of governmental facilitation of the Church's mission assumes precisely the relationship between a society and its form of government which O'Donovan regards as problematic. Central to O'Donovan's 'defence of Christendom' is the claim that human societies have a need to express their shared moral and religious agency through their government, to have their government reflect their 'deep social agreements' (*DON* 222).[334] The political act 'can give moral form to a community by defining its commitment to the good in a representative performance' (*DON* 249). Because of this need, to exclude government from 'evangelical obedience' also undermines the capacity of society for such obedience.[335]

O'Donovan's argument at *DON* 246-50 is summarised by Chaplin as follows:

> ... given the need of society for government in order to express its shared moral and religious agency, excluding government from "evangelical obedience" also undermines the capacity of society for such obedience. ... [S]ince only government is able to define the unifying moral vision which every society needs, a vital part of the task of the church now is to proclaim anew the legitimate function of political authority as mediating the authority of God.[336]

O'Donovan's concern is that by asserting that religion is none of the government's business, the Church also concedes that government is none of God's business.[337] Whilst that is undeniably how the First Amendment has been wielded by some in the twentieth century, it is far from apparent that such a concession is logically implied.

O'Donovan's argument only works if the First Amendment is seen as an Aristotelian political project. His argument seems to run thus. Only when a society conceives itself as under the rule of God can it expect evangelical obedience of its rulers. Therefore if a society denies that its rulers are capable of or required to exhibit evangelical obedience, then it is denying that it is itself capable of or required to exhibit evangelical obedience. The problem with this is that it requires that the response from the ruler which is demanded be a representative response. O'Donovan has correctly ruled out the possibility of

---

[333] O'Donovan, *DON*, 245.

[334] Lockwood O'Donovan complains in 'A Timely Conversation' about the use of judicial interpretation of human rights legislation to 'undermine the legitimate representation of the moral and spiritual understandings within society' in *RP* 392.

[335] O'Donovan, *DON*, 246-50; Chaplin, 'Political Eschatology and Responsible Government', 287.

[336] Chaplin, 'Political Eschatology', 287.

[337] O'Donovan, *DON*, 213.

rulers' responding to the Church's mission as an act of their power, but his own theory seems to rule out the appropriateness of their response as a purely representative one. In the era after the Ascension, if the role of government is limited to determining questions of right and wrong, the ruler's response to the Church's mission can only be legitimate if it is required as an act of judgment, for that, according to O'Donovan, is the *bene esse* of politics. The First Amendment need not be read as a declaration that religious questions are non-justiciable. Instead it can be read as the assertion that secular government is not competent to or required to judge on such questions.[338]

For O'Donovan, 'the kingdoms of *this* age are not in the business of saving subjects' souls', that is what they are incompetent to do.[339] They may, however, lend assistance to the Church which is in that business. The way the account is put forward is reminiscent of old forms of argument that rulers act as fathers of their nations, who can commit on behalf of their nations to follow God.

The alternative view is that the declaration of an institutionalised commitment to a particular form of Christianity is a mistake of over-realised eschatology. On this account, eschatology is over-realised when the political authority purports, on behalf of an inevitably mixed society, to declare its commitment to a particular vision of Christianity. The obedience of the nations is an eschatological reality not to be pre-empted in our mixed polities, which exhibit neither pure nationhood nor pure obedience to Christ. For O'Donovan, eschatology is only over-realised when the political authority purports to enforce on all its citizens that commitment to a particular vision of Christianity which it has declared *pars pro toto*.

The institutional distinction between Church and State, and an insistence on their relative autonomy one from the other, can be defended on the following basis:

1)   Secular rulers are not competent to determine religious questions on behalf of the people.

2)   If wrong, their judgments lead the people away from the worship of the true God and must be rejected.

3)   Even if right, their judgments *presume* a change of heart in the people which only the Holy Spirit can effect.

4)   Even if directed towards the right worship of the right God, such decisions tend to become quickly corrupted into civil religion.

O'Donovan offers a vision of a liberal Christendom. He stresses that he has never argued 'that a tendency to coercion was not "endemic" [to historical Christendom], merely that it was not logically implied by the concept of a

---

[338] See Insole's argument that Edmund Burke opposed the use of state power to assert or promote religious truth, in *The Politics of Human Frailty* 42-43.

[339] O'Donovan, 'Behold, the Lamb!', 105.

Christian state.'[340] Even if this lesser claim is sustainable, it is still questionable whether in the face of the weight of evidence of the degeneration of the ideal into coercion it is a dream worth chasing. Gorringe argues that reflection on the hundreds of years of history of Christendom in mediaeval Europe and Latin America might reveal that 'the whole enterprise was ... a misunderstanding of mission, a mis-construal of what power and authority really look like in the light of Jesus of Nazareth.'[341] The danger with O'Donovan's vision of Christianising of the State is that history tends to suggest that the corruption of the Church rather than the sanctification of the secular power is more likely to be the result.[342]

The critical question to be asked of O'Donovan's liberal Christendom is whether he has sufficient reasons in his theology not to use coercion to enforce 'Christian truth'. There are two reasons O'Donovan can give for not following his mentor Augustine on this point. One is to do with over-realised eschatology, expecting now that division into the two cities which is their eternal destiny. O'Donovan regards coercion as offending against the Gospel, by 'violat[ing] the openness of unbelief to come to belief freely while God's patience waits on it'.[343]

The second reason can be given, and perhaps must be given, in trinitarian terms. The corollary of the argument that religious coercion is unavailing because true worship must be free worship, an argument that goes back to Tertullian[344] and Lactantius,[345] is the argument, made by Locke amongst others, that secular government ought not to compel religious observance because to do so is for rulers to presume to arrogate to themselves a work which the Holy Spirit has reserved to Himself.[346]

As Lockwood O'Donovan writes, in a jointly edited volume of essays by O'Donovan and her, 'The enlarging conceptions of gospel freedom that run from Ockham through Wyclif to Luther and Zwingli, Bucer and Calvin increasingly grasp free conformity to truth and righteousness as belonging to

---

[340] O'Donovan, *RP*, 343; A. Shanks, 'Response to *The Desire of the Nations*', *Studies in Christian Ethics* 11 (1998) 89-90.
[341] Gorringe, 'Authority, Plebs and Patricians', 27; Greene, 'Revisiting Christendom', 332.
[342] Bicknell, *Theological Introduction*, 400.
[343] O'Donovan, *DON*, 241.
[344] Tertullian, *To Scapula*, and *The Apology*, chapters XXIV to XXVIII, both in in A.C. Coxe, ed., *The Ante-Nicene Fathers vol. III: Latin Christianity: Its Founder, Tertullian* (Buffalo, NY: Christian Lit. Publ. Co, 1887).
[345] Lactantius, *The Divine Institutes*, book V, chapters XIX to XXI, in *Institutes* in A.C. Coxe, ed., *The Ante-Nicene Fathers vol. VII: Fathers of the Third and Fourth Centuries* (Buffalo, NY: Christian Lit. Publ. Co, 1887).
[346] Locke appeals in *An Essay Concerning Toleration* to the fact that men are to be brought to God not by any human compulsion but by 'the inward constraints of [God's] own spirit on their minds': *Political Writings* (London: Penguin Classics, 1993) 189.

Christ alone and to sinful human beings only through the power of the Holy Spirit of Christ.'[347] These thinkers realised, in a way that Augustine did not, that it is up to the Holy Spirit and not to secular rulers, to draw people to Christ. To be more precise, conversion is a distinct work of the Spirit of which the church and not government is the divinely appointed agent. Such a trinitarian qualification is required to avoid O'Donovan's political theology being misused to re-create an enforced pretence of Christian religious observance.

Historical experience demonstrates that the behaviour of governments ranges across a spectrum:

1)   a government which denies its accountability to God;
2)   a government which ignores its accountability to God;
3)   a government which acknowledges its accountability to God;
4)   a government which asserts its authority from God, e.g. the divine right of kings;
5)   a government which claims the worship due to God.

The third option of accountability without claiming divine honours has proven to be highly unstable historically. It may be that we have to choose between rulers who act as if there is no God and rulers who act as if they are God. Even if O'Donovan's critique is partially made out, the First Amendment may represent a justifiable preference for the second option as a result of bitter experience of the fourth and fifth. Whilst not ideal, it is hard to blame the founders of America for opening the door to what they might have regarded as the lesser evil.

The Grace of God and the Preservation of Political Authority

At *JWR* 121, O'Donovan argues that human legal regimes exist on borrowed time, balanced precariously on a combination of power, community recognition and the need for ordered justice for as long as God providentially ordains.[348] Governments exist by God's providence. Their judgments are providentially used by God to achieve God's purposes. The strength of O'Donovan's location of political authority in the order of providence is that it denies any sense of particular forms of political authority being either necessary or permanent, although the same gain could be made in other ways.

Those political authorities which do not place the task of doing judgment first in their list of priorities are, on O'Donovan's account, seriously defective. Nonetheless, their continued survival, for however long it may be, is an act of God's grace. As O'Donovan frames the matter this is a true grace because the alternative of the collapse of political authority is a greater evil.

---

[347] Lockwood O'Donovan, *BOI*, 163.
[348] Skillen, 'Acting Politically in Biblical Obedience?', 416.

Even wise rulers, informed by the Church, will not be able to render perfect judgment, because of the limits of the tools at their disposal for divining the truth and applying it. To the extent that their conscientious actions are acceptable to God and their political authority is preserved, this too occurs by the grace of God.

Even those political authorities which do place the task of doing judgment first, have to strike a balance between reflecting the moral order given in creation and taking cognisance of the practical possibilities within the society which they govern. Since that moral order can only be truly discerned in the light of Christ, it follows that the judgments of a conscientious pagan ruler will be defective. To the extent that they are not, and to the extent that the ruler's political authority is preserved, O'Donovan needs to say that this is by the grace of God and the work of the Spirit. On this basis one overcomes the difficulty, identified by Hauerwas and Fodor, that the consequence of O'Donovan's position is that 'The judgments required for legitimacy, that is, the kind of rule Paul justified in Romans 13, [are] morally impossible for societies that do not acknowledge God.'[349] Thus one can account for how the doing of judgment by the rulers of Egypt was the exercise of legitimate government but not their promotion of idol worship and the cult of the Pharaoh-god. Human authorities only have limited scope and may make improper demands on us (*WOJ* 136-37).

The merits of placing grace in the foreground like this are that the account of political authority is not reduced to an account which either ascribes legitimacy to or denies it to particular regimes but explains precisely what Paul seemed to think needed explaining – how it is that rulers who do not recognise Christ can nonetheless be used by God to minister to human beings as a whole and the Church in particular.

Conversely, grace being the free action of God must not be presumed upon. In particular, when a government is in manifest disobedience to God's purpose for it, then God's judgment is liable to fall.[350] On O'Donovan's account, such disobedience would be displayed when government claimed the worship due to God alone or when it abandoned any commitment to doing judgment, i.e. to righting wrongs.

In *WOJ*, the Holy Spirit is expressly recognised by O'Donovan as performing the key action of providentially sustaining human regimes, but in addition O'Donovan's arguments would be strengthened by the qualification that the Holy Spirit is the agent through whom the moral order may be discerned, wise judgment may be administered and the Church's mission may be appropriately responded to. Given his complaint against the development of a deistic account of providence which in the interests of underwriting liberal

---

[349] Hauerwas and Fodor, 'Remaining in Babylon', 51 footnote 12.
[350] O'Donovan, 'Behold, the Lamb!', 101.

regimes undermined the intelligibility of the doctrine of the Trinity,[351] his theory could be considerably strengthened by this amendment, which would secure the response of rulers as a work of the Holy Spirit who empowers the Church's mission.[352]

In his recent essay, 'What Can Ethics Know about God?', O'Donovan seems to be moving towards this position. Discussing political deliberation, he writes: "The possibilities for any common action we may devise depend not only on favourable objective circumstances but on a kind of illumination and disclosure which will shape the community's will to act with a common vision and resolution."[353] Such illumination and disclosure are surely works of the Spirit, whether the society thus addressed by God recognises it or not.

Conclusion

O'Donovan has gone part of the way towards offering a trinitarian account of natural law, by relating it to the Son. His theory would be strengthened, however, by reflections on the Spirit's role in the apprehension of the objective moral order and of natural law. The greater trinitarian emphasis in *WOJ* is also to be welcomed, but it must be recognised that O'Donovan has not yet given it a sustained exposition.

For O'Donovan, the kingship of the Ascended Christ restricts the function of political authorities to that of giving judgment. Secular rule stands outside the Church, which finds its identity in the Son and looks both back to the judgment of the Cross and forward to the Last Judgment. Rulers must perform their function in the light of the divine law, both natural and revealed, whilst taking full account of the particular conditions and sins which affect the societies which they govern. This task of giving judgment is the necessary service of secular rulers to the mission of the Church. Beyond that, O'Donovan offers a controversial account of the ways in which rulers may consciously facilitate the Church's mission.

O'Donovan acknowledges that the institutions of political authority through which human law is mediated in particular societies are not self-sustaining but are sustained by the Holy Spirit providentially. However, he has not yet given a developed account of how the conscientious ruler may be given wisdom by the Spirit to discern how to govern wisely.

Moreover, as will be argued in the following chapters, the anti-totalitarian elements in O'Donovan's theory would be strengthened by an account of the way in which the Spirit acts beyond human law in effecting the conversion of

---

[351] O'Donovan, *DON*, 246; Hauerwas and Fodor, 'Remaining in Babylon', 41.

[352] O'Donovan, 'Behold, the Lamb!', 104.

[353] O'Donovan, 'What Can Ethics Know About God?', 41. This quotation follows a reflection, at 40, on the limitations of individual moral decision-making which is similarly open to a recognition of the Spirit's work in partially revealing the moral order.

human hearts, transforming them into agents who are enabled to become truly free as they apprehend their God-given place within the moral orders of creation and God's kingdom.

Chapter 4

Thomas Aquinas's Theology of the Holy Spirit as the New Law

Introduction

What one makes of Aquinas depends on which of the three parts of the *Summa Theologiae*, if any, you regard as central to his thought. If it is the *Prima Pars*, then he is the worst example of a theologian who puts the unity of God first and then relegates the Trinity to an appendix at the end of his *Summa*. If, on the contrary, the Trinity is central to Thomas's understanding of the saving work of God which forms the capstone of his theology (*ST* III, prologue), then Aquinas's approach in the *Prima Pars* is driven by pedagogical concerns, and his intention at least, is to offer a reasoned account of the Christian doctrine of the triune God. The key question for the present study is: in Aquinas's thought, does human law relate solely to natural law given by a lumpen deity, or is it integrated into a trinitarian vision of salvation? The answer, it will be suggested, is the latter.

Aquinas is a subtle thinker, probably too subtle for those who came after him in mediaeval scholasticism. '[H]is ideas move more like knights than rooks and are no less difficult to corner.'[1] The consequence has been, as O'Connor notes, that Aquinas 'has been badly treated by his friends and his enemies alike.'[2] Faced with the ideas of that troublesome Augustininan monk, Martin Luther, the Council of Trent co-opted Aquinas in order to combat Protestantism. Thereafter, Protestants did not read Aquinas at all, and Catholics read him as interpreted by Cajetan. Both sides assumed that Cajetan's interpretation of Aquinas was correct.

The *Prima Pars* of the *Summa Theologiae* considers the question of the divine essence first (qq.1 to 26) before going on to explore the Divine Persons in qq. 27 to 43. Critics have argued that this results in Aquinas elaborating an autonomous natural theology, which deals with the being of God in general in abstraction from the God self-revealed historically in the Christian

---

[1] T. Gilby, *Principality and Polity* (London: Longman Green, 1958) xxv.
[2] D.J. O'Connor, *Aquinas and Natural Law* (London: Macmillan, 1967) 1.

dispensation.[3] Colin Gunton acquits Aquinas of setting out a natural theology, 'if by natural theology is meant a theological enterprise carried on in complete abstraction from the Christian faith.'[4] Nonetheless, the predominance of Greek metaphysical categories over the biblical attributes of God such as holiness and *hesed*, leads Gunton to conclude that Aquinas is, perhaps *contre coeur*, the prototype of the philosophically based 'classical theism'.[5]

However, although he has sometimes been written off as the pioneer of rationalistic theology,[6] there is currently a renewed engagement with and appreciation of Aquinas. During the twentieth century, it has been increasingly argued that Cajetan misrepresented Aquinas on a number of significant points.[7] A good case is being made that Aquinas did not believe in the static deity of Parmenides but sought to explore through both reason and faith the revelation of the living God.[8] Natural law is not the major note of Aquinas's doctrine of law but rather a minor theme. Aquinas did not swallow wholesale the thought of Aristotle but used it as a conceptual tool to illuminate aspects of biblical truth. Aquinas's thought, like that of Calvin's, finds its centre not in his systematic work but in his careful commentaries on the Bible.[9]

---

[3] See, for example, T.F. Torrance, *Karl Barth, Biblical and Evangelical Theologian* (Edinburgh: T & T Clark, 1990) 183-86.

[4] Gunton, *Act and Being*, 49.

[5] Gunton, *Becoming and Being: The Doctrine of God in Charles Hartshorne and Karl Barth* (Oxford: OUP, 1978) 1.

[6] Examples of this reading by evangelical theologians include G. Goldsworthy, *Gospel and Wisdom: Israel's Wisdom Literature in the Christian Life* (Carlisle: Paternoster, 1987, 1995) 138-39. F. Schaeffer is more sympathetic to Aquinas in *Trilogy: The God Who Is There, Escape From Reason, He Is There and He Is Not Silent* (Leicester: IVP, 1990) at 209-211, but ends up concluding, at 240, that 'Aquinas opened the door to an independent man downstairs, a natural theology and a philosophy which were both autonomous from the Scriptures.'

[7] Etienne Gilson in *Le Thomisme* 5th edn. (Paris: Vrin, 1947) took issue with Cajetan's account of Aquinas's ontology; Henri de Lubac in *Surnaturel: Etudes historiques* (Paris: Aubier, 1946) with the distinction drawn between nature and grace. Milbank in *The Suspended Middle* at 16-20, 24-30, makes a spirited defence of de Lubac's theology but expressly leaves open the question of whether de Lubac's interpretation of Aquinas is accurate.

[8] A. Malet, *Personne et amour dans la théologie trinitaire de saint Thomas d'Aquin* (Paris : Librairie Philosophique J. Vrin, 1956); Kerr, *After Aquinas*, viii, 198-99; J.P. Torrell, *Saint Thomas Aquinas*. Vol. II, *Spiritual Master* (Washington, DC: Catholic University of America Press, 2003) 47; contra Gunton, *The One, the Three and the Many: God, Creation and the Culture of Modernity* (Cambridge: CUP, 1993) 138-42.

[9] M.D. Chenu, *Toward Understanding St. Thomas* (Chicago: Henry Regnery, 1964) 322; Holmes, *Listening to the Past*, 56 footnote 12; M. Levering, *Christ's Fulfillment of Torah and Temple: Salvation according to Thomas Aquinas* (Notre Dame: University of Notre Dame Press, 2002 3; E.F. Rogers, 'The Narrative of Natural Law in Aquinas's Commentary on Romans 1', *Theological Studies* 59 (1998) 255-56; Torrell, *Aquinas*

In particular, building on the work of the French language writers Gilles Emery and Jean-Pierre Torrell, there is now a growing corpus of Anglo-American writing which seeks to rehabilitate Aquinas as a biblical and Trinitarian theologian. The principal representative of this school of thought whose work will be engaged with is Matthew Levering. Levering's two main works – *Christ's Fulfillment of Torah and Temple* and *Scripture and Metaphysics*, emphasise Aquinas's view of salvation and his trinitarianism respectively. Levering therefore offers a model for the interpretation of Aquinas which gives weight to his interpretation of Scripture, the metaphysics of his doctrine of the Trinity and the importance of God's actions in salvation as central aspects of his thought. In this chapter, this reading of Aquinas will be broadly, though not uncritically, followed.

It will also be contended that the same reassessment of the relationship between the influence of Aristotelian philosophy and Aquinas's biblical sources needs to be carried out with regard to Aquinas's teaching on law. Aquinas has too often been read simply as the theologian who baptised Aristotle's *Politics* without considering the important ways in which Aquinas's understanding of the biblical narrative of salvation altered the Aristotelian scheme. A major reason for this was the loss of Aquinas's doctrine of the Holy Spirit.

The Context and Contours of Aquinas's Thought

The Context of Aquinas's Thought

Aquinas lived in an intellectual and religious environment where there were major controversies.[10] His account of the virtues takes shape against the background of the Cathar heresy with its *parfaits*. His *Summa contra Gentiles* is directed not just against Christian heretics but also against Jews and Muslims. The imperative behind the *Summae* is to provide a convincing refutation of Averroism, the idea, which was creeping into Christian thought, that philosophical and religious truth could be in conflict (*ScG* I.7.2). However, the *Summa Theologiae*'s success in synthesising biblical truth and Aristotelian philosophy is also what leads to the permanent question mark against it: is it a demonstration that the Philosopher at his best had had natural insights into what had been revealed in the Bible, or is it in the end a constriction of biblical truth into an Aristotelian framework?[11]

Vol. II, 3; N.L. Geisler, *Thomas Aquinas: An Evangelical Appraisal* (Grand Rapids: Baker Book, 1991) 56, quoting Pius XII in support of the same view.

[10] A. Vos, *Aquinas, Calvin, and Contemporary Protestant Thought: A Critique of Protestant Views on the Thought of Thomas Aquinas* (Grand Rapids: Eerdmans, 1985) xv, 163-64.

[11] This description of Aquinas with primary reference to Aristotle does not foreclose the question about Platonic influences on his thought: see F. O'Rourke, 'Aquinas and Platonism' in F. Kerr, ed., *Contemplating Aquinas: On the Varieties of Interpretation*

There are also personal experiences which were to have a distinctive influence on Aquinas's thought. As a young man who abandoned wealth, defied his family and committed himself to chastity, Aquinas saw very clearly the distinction between natural goods and the eternal good.[12] He was also called upon to defend this distinction in responding to polemical attacks on the friars which accused them of ignoring their social responsibilities.[13] This is reflected in those moments when Aquinas is his most Augustinian, asserting that mortal sin is choosing transitory, natural goods over the eternal good (*ST* II-II.104.3; 118.1 ad.2; 118.5 ad.2; III.supp.97.1; *De Regno* I.10 [75]).

Aquinas the Biblical Theologian

Both before and during the composition of the *Summa Theologiae*, Aquinas was giving biblical commentaries as lectures.[14] He wrote commentaries on the Gospels of Matthew and John, all the Pauline letters (including, in his view, Hebrews), the Psalms, Job, Isaiah, Jeremiah and Lamentations. Aquinas's hermeneutic gives a privileged place to the literal sense of Scripture precisely because this maintains a focus on the history of salvation, whose proclamation was essential to the polemics of the friars.[15]

Amongst contemporary theologians there is a wide degree of consensus about the importance of the Bible to Aquinas's theology. The nature of Aquinas as a biblical theologian is defended by the American evangelical, Norman Geisler, who says: 'Except for the question of the extent of the canon, Aquinas's basic view of the nature and interpretation of Scripture is as orthodox and "Protestant" as that of any of the Reformers.'[16] The Radical Orthodox theologian, John Milbank similarly writes that, for Aquinas, 'as for Barth, all certainty regarding God derives from scripture.'[17] Matthew Levering,

---

(London: SCM, 2003) 247-79; D.C. Hall, *The Trinity: An Analysis of St Thomas Aquinas' Expositio of the* De Trinitate *of Boethius* (Leiden: E.J. Brill, 1992) 4. Milbank in particular reads Aquinas as 'adher[ing] to a neoplatonic sense of understanding as participation and an Augustinian understanding of illumination': *The Suspended Middle* 97.

[12] Torrell, *Aquinas Vol. II*, 348-51.

[13] Gilby, *Principality and Polity*, 244-47.

[14] Levering, *Christ's Fulfillment*, 8.

[15] N.M. Healy, 'Introduction' in Weinandy, Keating and Yocum, eds., *Aquinas on Scripture: An Introduction to his Biblical Commentaries* (London: T&T Clark, 2005) 9. For Aquinas's definition of the 'literal sense', see 16-17.

[16] Geisler, *Thomas Aquinas*, 56.

[17] J. Milbank in Milbank and Pickstock, *Truth in Aquinas* (London: Routledge, 2001) 25. What is questionable, however, is Milbank's assertion that 'for Aquinas, in an unBarthian fashion, scripture records the event of the augmentation of human intellect through a deepened participating in the divine simplicity'. This seems to bypass the mediating work of the Holy Spirit which, it will be contended in this chapter, is in fact

writing from a Catholic perspective, presents a view of Aquinas as a biblical theologian, whose Trinitarian metaphysics is a reflection on biblical truths rather than a substitute methodology.[18] While Aquinas has been criticised for describing the deity of metaphysical reason, Cavanaugh argues that in the opening questions of the *ST*, 'Aquinas thinks he is merely spelling out the implications of the scriptural revelation of God.'[19] The qualification is significant, because as Gunton points out: 'A work ... is to be judged not by what it sets out to do but by what it achieves'.[20]

Levering recognises that the structure of the *Summa Theologiae* is that of a 'scientific theology'[21] but he argues that its content is either expressly or implicitly supplied by biblical theology.[22] Healy similarly argues that the two *Summae* should be regarded as 'a kind of second-level exegesis.'[23] It is probably right to describe Aquinas as a canonical theologian, for he understood 'the whole biblical narrative, Old and New Testaments together, as proclaiming the one complete gospel'.[24] 'At the heart of ... Aquinas's scientific theology of salvation lies the narrative of Scripture – the fulfilment of Israel's Torah and Temple through the New Covenant in Christ Jesus.'[25] Yet Wilhelmus Valkenberg has pointed out that there has been no work done on Aquinas's use of Scripture in his systematic theology.[26] This is a serious lacuna, given that one might expect 'the mature fruit of Aquinas's biblical interpretation in his *systematic* works.'[27]

Levering argues that Aquinas works with a fulfilment model whereby the New Covenant fulfils rather than merely superseding the Old Covenant.[28] In

---

an important, but sadly neglected, aspect of Aquinas's thought..

[18] Levering, *Scripture and Metaphysics*, 169; Torrell, *Aquinas Vol. II*, 377-78. If this assessment is correct, then Aquinas differs significantly from John Milbank whose trinitarian metaphysics are not balanced by detailed engagement with Scripture in the way that Aquinas's reflections are. As R.R. Reno points out in 'The Radical Orthodoxy Project', *First Things* 100 (2000) 37-44, Milbank's approach to Scripture translates the Gospel stories themselves into 'allegories of a participatory metaphysics', and it is this neo-Platonic metaphysics which controls the narrative, rather than vice versa.

[19] W.T. Cavanaugh, 'A Joint Declaration?: Justification as Theosis in Aquinas and Luther', *Heythrop Journal* 41 (2000) 268.

[20] Gunton, *Act and Being*, 49.

[21] Levering, *Christ's Fulfillment*, 3.

[22] Emery makes a similar argument in relation to *ScG*: *Trinity in Aquinas* 81, 89.

[23] Healy, 'Introduction', to *Aquinas on Scripture* 13.

[24] T.G. Weinandy, 'The Supremacy of Christ: Aquinas' *Commentary on Hebrews*' in Weinandy, Keating and Yocum, eds., *Aquinas on Scripture* 224.

[25] Levering, *Christ's Fulfillment*, 3.

[26] W. Valkenberg, *Words of the Living God: Place and Function of Holy Scripture in the Theology of St. Thomas Aquinas* (Leuven: Peeters, 2000) 2; T.F. Ryan, *Thomas Aquinas as Reader of the Psalms* (Notre Dame, Ind: University of Notre Dame Press, 2000) 2.

[27] Levering, *Christ's Fulfillment*, 83.

[28] See also Ryan, *Thomas Aquinas as Reader of the Psalms*, 16.

this respect his position has strong echoes of that of N.T. Wright. This means that the God who has revealed Godself in the New Testament as Father, Son and Holy Spirit is the same as the God who revealed Godself to Moses as YHWH. It is this God whose nature Aquinas is interested in discussing. Therefore, 'Rather than bypassing God's eternal identity as YHWH, Aquinas integrates his metaphysical reflection on the name "I am who I am" into a complex account of YHWH, Moses, the Mosaic Law, and the relationship of Christians to the contemplative life enjoyed by Moses'.[29]

Aquinas the Trinitarian Theologian

The answer to the question: is Aquinas is a trinitarian theologian? depends on what one expects of a trinitarian theologian. Aquinas's trinitarianism is poles apart from the social trinitarianism of Moltmann. He would agree with Barth's concerns about the modern implications of the term 'person'.[30] Nor does Aquinas subscribe to the formulation and use of the Trinity as proposed by Gunton.[31] There is a significant measure of truth in Kerr's observation that 'Once the doctrines of divine immutability and impassibility have been jettisoned, it is no wonder that the only way to read Aquinas is as unbiblical and unchristian, or as offering only the Aristotelian or Parmenidean God.'[32]

If one expects an explicitly trinitarian structure to the whole of theology and a primary emphasis on the persons of the Trinity then Aquinas's theology is deficient, both in its methodology and its presuppositions. Aquinas is susceptible of being understood as seeing God's unity as prior to God's Trinity, because he places his treatment of *De Deo Uno* prior to his treatment of *De Deo Trino*. Levering's defence is that this is how God has revealed Godself: as One in the Old Testament and as triune in the New Testament. The *Summa Theologiae* is pedagogical and therefore follows the order of the divine revelation. The God and Father of our Lord Jesus Christ is none other than

---

[29] Levering, *Scripture and Metaphysics*, 71.

[30] The most vigorous argument that Aquinas has a personalist view of the Trinity is advanced by André Malet in *Personne et Amour*, but he points out at the outset that what Aquinas means by 'person' is something very different from its use in modern existential or personalist philosophies. For an extended discussion of Aquinas's conception of the Divine Persons, see Levering, *Scripture and Metaphysics*, 159-64 and 213-35.

[31] For Gunton, the personal attributes of God should take precedence over the metaphysical attributes, rather than vice versa: *Act and Being* 51. Most concerning in Aquinas's thought for a trinitarian theologian of Gunton's ilk is the extent to which the idea of divine simplicity threatens to overshadow the distinctions between the persons.

[32] F. Kerr, 'The Varieties of Interpreting Aquinas' in F. Kerr, ed., *Contemplating Aquinas: On the Varieties of Interpretation* (London: SCM, 2003) 39.

YHWH who revealed Godself at the burning bush to Moses.[33] In Aquinas's thought, 'the Mosaic revelation commands study of God in his essence, while the Gospel revelation will do the same for God in his Trinity.'[34] In this way, Aquinas integrates the message of the Old and New Covenants.

The expectations of those who assert that for Aquinas, 'the heart of the Christian teaching is the doctrine of the Trinity'[35] are different from those of his critics. For his defenders, the *sine qua non* of Christian theology is that it is a reflection on what God has done for us and for our salvation. In this regard, Fergus Kerr draws attention to Aquinas's affirmation in 1265 that 'The Christian faith consists above all in the confession of the Holy Trinity, and it glories especially in the cross of our Lord Jesus Christ'.[36] Such has been the scale of the re-discovery of the importance of the Trinity within Aquinas's thought that the present danger facing those who have paid close attention to it, is that of assuming that Aquinas has said all that needs to be and can be said about the Trinity.[37]

Aquinas's doctrine of God is not a matter of enquiry for the sake of enquiry. In *ST* I.2, he explains the division of the *ST* into three parts in terms of the aim which he ascribes to *sacra doctrina*. That aim 'is to teach the knowledge of God, not only as He is in Himself, but also as He is the beginning of all things and their last end, and especially of rational creatures ...'. In the body of the *Summa Theologiae* as elsewhere in his writings, Aquinas considers both the questions of creation and of the beatific vision in trinitarian terms. Already in his *Commentary on the Sentences*, in *I Sent.* d. 14 q. 2 a. 2, Aquinas speaks of both creation and redemption in trinitarian terms: 'Just as we have been created through the Son and through the Holy Spirit, just so is it through them that we are united to our final end.'[38] For Aquinas, creation was the act of the triune God, described in Irenaean terms.[39] The final end of human beings is the beatific vision, the completion of the divinity of the Blessed Trinity and the humanity of Christ.[40] In between times, the salvation of humankind is accomplished 'by the Son who became flesh and by the gift of the Holy Spirit.' (*ST* I.32.1 ad.3). For Aquinas it is always the triune God who acts in relation to

---

[33] Levering, *Scripture and Metaphysics*, chapter 2 'Yhwh and Being'; Kerr, *After Aquinas*, 183-4; Torrell, *Aquinas Vol. II*, 47.

[34] G. Lafont, *Structures et méthode dans la Somme théologique de saint Thomas d'Aquin* (Paris: Desclée, 1961) 473.

[35] B. Davies, *The Thought of Thomas Aquinas* (Oxford: Clarendon Press, 1992) 185.

[36] Aquinas, *De articulus fidei et ecclesiae sacramentis, ad Archiepiscopum Panormitanum* (Rome: Commissio Leonina, 1979) 42:207; Kerr *After Aquinas* 162.

[37] J.M. McCurry, 'Trinitarian Theology After and With – But Not Against – Aquinas', *Modern Theology* 21 (2005) 508-9.

[38] Aquinas, *ST* I.45.6; A.N. Williams, 'Deification in the *Summa Theologiae*', 245.

[39] Aquinas, *ST* I.45.6 ad.1; Levering, *Scripture and Metaphysics*, 228; Malet, *Personne et Amour*, 85-87; Torrell, *Aquinas Vol. II*, 25, 58-66, 162-63.

[40] Aquinas, *Comp. Theol.*, I.2; *ST* II-II.1.8; I-II.5.4.

human beings.[41] As Bailleux reads him, the economy of grace consists in the fact that 'le propre Fils de Dieu ... se fait homme, afin que les hommes, sauvés par lui et en lui, redeviennent des fils de Dieu. ... Devenus fils dans le Fils, les hommes divinisés, sous la conduite de l'Espirit, font retour vers le Père.'[42]

As Aquinas explains in *ST* I.32.1 ad.3, knowledge of the Persons of the Trinity is necessary to understand salvation properly, but is also imperative for a right understanding of creation.[43] Contrary to Moltmann's view, precisely because God is triune, we can see that God did not create the world out of necessity 'in virtue of any neediness on his part nor because of any alien cause extrinsic to him, but *on account of love of his own goodness*' (*ST* I.32.1). In short, God created the world because God is, in God's own eternal triune Being, love.[44]

Aquinas appropriates the eternal law, that is to say, providence, to the Son (*ST* I-II.93.1 ad.2; 93.4. resp., ad.2).[45] God's providence over the salvation of humankind (*ST* II-II.1.7) is therefore brought to its culmination through God's actions in Christ, who is 'the Word of the Father through whom all things were made and are preserved' (*In Ioan.* 5, 17, lect. 2, n. 740) However, in that God moves all things towards their proper end by God's Love, 'it is entirely appropriate to attribute government of the universe and propagation to the Holy Spirit.' (*ScG* IV, 20, n. 3572). Again, this reflects an Irenaean understanding of God's works, the Father accomplishes His purposes through the Son and the Spirit.[46]

With regard to salvation, Aquinas sees forgiveness and justification won by the Son, and the Spirit as indwelling the believer, working to sanctify them by conforming them to the image of the Son, making them fit for the beatific vision of the Father. The consummation of the believer is their glorification in union with God in Christ through the Spirit. Anna Williams finds this theme of deification present in both the *De Deo uno* and the *De Trinitate* sections of the *ST*. In her estimation, 'the *De Deo uno* and the *De Trinitate* are portraits of the same God viewed from different perspectives.'[47] As Brian Davies argues, for Aquinas, the Trinity matters because the triune God invites us to share in God's

---

[41] G. Emery, 'The Doctrine of the Trinity in St. Thomas Aquinas' in Weinandy, Keating and Yocum, eds., *Aquinas on Doctrine* 59.

[42] E. Bailleux, 'Le cycle des missions trinitaires, d'après Saint Thomas', *Revue Thomiste* 63 (1963) 165. 'God's own Son ... becomes a man, in order that men, saved by him and in him, may become the sons of God. ... Becoming sons in the Son, these deified men, under the guidance of the Spirit, make their return to the Father.' (translation mine).

[43] Emery, *Trinity in Aquinas*, 174, 285-86; Kerr, *After Aquinas*, 39.

[44] Cavanaugh, 'A Joint Declaration?', 269; D.B. Burrell, *Freedom and Creation in Three Traditions* (Notre Dame, Ind: University of Notre Dame Press, 1993) 165-66; Emery, *Trinity in Aquinas*, 23.

[45] Levering, *Scripture and Metaphysics*, 87.

[46] Torrell, *Aquinas Vol. II*, 75-76.

[47] A.N. Williams, 'Deification in the *Summa Theologiae*', 232.

life.[48] The present chapter centres round the exploration of how the invitation to participation in God's life is integral to Aquinas's theology of law.

In *Scripture and Metaphysics*, Levering concedes that Aquinas does not deploy the Trinity in a programmatic fashion. Instead, Aquinas seeks to contemplate God, and the practical outcomes are by-products of this contemplation rather than being the point of the contemplation.[49] The defence of Aquinas therefore proceeds by way of asserting that his systematic theology is the fruit of his contemplation of the God revealed in Scripture and that his metaphysics never lose sight of the drama of salvation.[50] Levering devotes an entire chapter to establishing that the Paschal Mystery is central to Aquinas's theology of the Trinity.[51] 'The doctrine of the Trinity informs the doctrine of salvation and vice-versa, as always in the *Summa Theologiae*.'[52] For Aquinas, the Trinity is not the structure of theology, it is the content of theology.

Aquinas did not intend his more philosophical arguments on the nature of God to be read apart from his more expressly theological reflections. At the outset of the *ST*, in I.1.1 he establishes not only that divine revelation 'was necessary for the salvation of man [in] that certain truths which exceed human reason should be made known to him by divine revelation' but also that divine revelation acts as a corrective to human reason even in regard to 'those truths about God which human reason could have discovered' because otherwise human sinfulness and finitude would mean that such truths 'would only be known by a few, and that after a long time, and with the admixture of many errors.' If Aquinas is faithful to his stated methodology in the discussion of the divine Essence which begins at *ST* I.2, then one would expect to find that his philosophical arguments in the opening questions of the *ST* are already conditioned by the biblical revelation and by the doctrine of the Trinity. This, argues Rowan Williams in his 2001 Aquinas Lecture, is in fact what one finds.[53]

Nonetheless, it has to be conceded that Aquinas's methodology in the *Summa Theologiae* left significant hostages to fortune.[54] As has already been discussed, his deferral of the discussion of the Trinity set several theological hares running. His powerful doctrine of divine simplicity continues to be controversial. Christopher Hughes has argued that it made it difficult for him to give full weight to the Trinity in his systematic thought,[55] whilst others have

---

[48] Davies, *Aquinas*, 207.

[49] Levering, *Scripture and Metaphysics*, 21-22.

[50] Levering, *Scripture and Metaphysics*, 8-12, 26, 46.

[51] Levering, *Scripture and Metaphysics*, chapter 4 pp.110-143.

[52] Levering, *Scripture and Metaphysics*, 195.

[53] R. Williams, 'What does love know? St Thomas on the Trinity', *New Blackfriars* 82 (2001) 260-72; see also Holmes, *Listening to the Past*, 55 footnote 12.

[54] Letham, *The Holy Trinity*, 235.

[55] C. Hughes, *On a Complex Theory of a Simple God: An Investigation in Aquinas' Philosophical Theology* (Ithaca: Cornell University Press, 1989).

argued that it is the Trinity which completes Aquinas's account of the divine simplicity.[56]

Finally, for Aquinas the persons are constituted by their relations.[57] For his defenders, this complex idea actually secures the identity of the divine Persons with the divine essence, giving Aquinas's theology a 'strongly personalist cast'.[58] Fiddes proposes a different reading of the idea that the Persons are their relations. He argues that Aquinas offers an account of the Persons in which they become dynamic, nothing other than their relations.[59] This risks dissolving the reality of the Persons of the Trinity and in Fiddes' own theology results in a mixture of a Moltmannian or process theology account of God's history with the world combined with an idiosyncratic but ultimately Augustinian model of God's inner life. The clue that Fiddes' reading may be a mis-reading is given by Fiddes himself, where he laments the fact that 'the potential here for developing a dynamic concept of being (an ontology) based on action and relationship is spoiled because Aquinas explains the self-existence or subsistence of the relationships by the fact that they are identical with the one essence of God.'[60] Fiddes' concern is that this gives credence to the Eastern Orthodox view that Aquinas is yet another Western theologian who gives priority to the divine essence over the divine Persons. Against this, however, Malet reads Aquinas's appeal to the divine essence as a means of Aquinas insisting that there is no divine essence apart from the Persons who are distinct subjects distinguished from one another by their relations.[61]

On voit que le mot relation a deux sens bien distincts. Il peut signifier la relation comme subsistante et c'est uniquement en ce sens que les personnes sont des

---

[56] In *Truth in Aquinas* at 53, Milbank argues that 'the essence and the persons are only distinct according to our modus significandi, in just the same fashion as being is only so distinct from goodness. This should indeed give pause to over-enthusiastic hypertrinitarians (Moltmann, Gunton, etc.) in our own day. For it suggests that when Aquinas speaks first of all of the divine unity and simplicity (following Dionysius, not Augustine), he is not simply speaking of the one essence, but rather (already as Eckhart), of a divine depth of unity beyond our perceived distinction of essence and relation ...'. While Milbank's dependence on the psychological analogy raises questions about the depth of his own trinitarianism, Aquinas is also ably defended by Stephen Holmes in *Listening to the Past* 55-58.

[57] Emery, *Trinity in Aquinas*, chapter 5, also 27, 116-17, 137-56, 280; Levering, *Scripture and Metaphysics*, 160-62; A. Nichols, *Discovering Aquinas: An Introduction to his Life, Work and Influence* (London: Darton Longman & Todd, 2002) 69; Kerr, *After Aquinas*, 198-9; Malet, *Personne et Amour*, 83-84, 92-94.

[58] Nichols, *Discovering Aquinas*, 67; R. Williams, 'What does love know?', 266-68; Malet, *Personne et Amour*, 151.

[59] P.S. Fiddes, *Participating in God: A Pastoral Doctrine of the Trinity* (London: Darton Longman & Todd, 2000) 12, 34-35, 50

[60] Fiddes, *Participating in God*, 35.

[61] Malet, *Personne et Amour*, 82, 85, 86.

relations : relation subsistante signifie *id quod, principium quod,* suppôt, personne. Il peut aussi signifier la relation au sens de *esse ad,* la relation qui se greffe sur une personne, ou qui n'est pas encore une personne, telle la relation d'origine. Cette distinction et cette conception de la personne comme relation *subsistante* et non pas simplement comme relation est tout à fait capitale.[62]

Fiddes' reading, and the more general tendency of Western theology to modalism may suggest that greater attention needs to be paid to the idea of God as 'persons in communion'. A moderate critic of Aquinas, such as Letham, would suggest that it is preferable to think of the unity of God's essence and the threefold nature of God's personhood as equally fundamental.[63] Rowan Williams claims that this is in fact the way Aquinas's trinitarianism works, describing it as 'a conceptual Moebius strip' in which each point in the argument from *ST* I.27 onwards, already presupposes what is being argued for.[64] However, he concedes that Aquinas's thought is muddled at points, so that, for example, Aquinas treats the Lord's Prayer as addressed to the Trinity as a whole (*ST* III.23.2). Aquinas makes this error, argues Rowan Williams, because he is trying to preserve the distance between God and creation and to establish the utter gratuity of creation and of our adoption as children of God.[65]

Without deciding on the adequacy of Aquinas's formulations of the immanent Trinity, it can be affirmed that Aquinas gives real weight to the persons of the Trinity in God's relations with us. Although Aquinas accepts the Augustinian maxim that *acta trinitatis ad extra indivisa sunt,* he qualifies it by

---

[62] Malet, *Personne et Amour,* 82: 'We see that the word relation has two distinct meanings. It can mean a relation as subsistent and it is solely in this sense that the persons are their relations: a subsistent relation signifies an *id quod,* a *principium quod,* a support, a being, a person. It can also signify a relation in the sense of *esse ad,* a relation which attaches itself to a person, or to something which is not yet a person, such as a relation of origin. This distinction and this conception of the person as a subsistent relation and not just as a mere relation is absolutely fundamental.' (translation mine – the one difficulty in translation is the word *suppôt* which is a translation of the Latin (*suppositus*) and which carries with it both the ideas of something being fundamental and it being personal.

[63] Letham, *The Holy Trinity,* 461, 493. This stands in direct contrast to the contention of Malet, who argued that Aquinas's understanding of the Trinity was even more personalist than that of the Greek Fathers!: *Personne et Amour* 104.

[64] R. Williams, 'What does love know?', 263-66; Hauerwas, 'The Truth about God: The Decalogue as Condition for Truthful Speech' in A.J. Torrance and M. Banner, eds., *The Doctrine of God and Theological Ethics* (Edinburgh: T&T Clark, 2006) 86; Kerr, 'Doctrine of God and Theological Ethics according to Thomas Aquinas', in the same volume at 77-78. Milbank's argument in *Truth in Aquinas* is similar. Milbank argues at xiii, 21, that 'contrary to usual readings, reason and faith in Aquinas represent only different degrees of intensity of participation in the divine light of illumination and different measures of absolute vision.'

[65] R. Williams, 'What does love know?', 269-70.

asserting that God the Father works through the Son and through the Spirit, and emphasises that '[t]he distinction of the Persons is not extrinsic to the acts of God *ad extra.*' (*ST* I.45.6, III.3.4)[66] Thus God's works can properly be appropriated to the different Persons, whilst always affirming that all the Godhead is involved in the Creation of the World, the Incarnation of the Son and the activities of the Spirit. The persons of the Trinity work in harmony rather than in unison.[67] Aquinas avoids modalism by defending the *filioque* on the grounds that the missions of the persons correspond to their eternal relations (*ST* I.43.1). The revelation of God in the economic Trinity can therefore be read back into the eternal relations of the immanent Trinity.

In the end, Levering's defence of Aquinas as a trinitarian theologian is just a little too neat. As Kilby observes, he over-systematises Aquinas's thought which is in fact more apophatic than affirmative at some points.[68] However, while significant criticisms of Aquinas can be made, Cavanaugh is right to claim that 'human participation in the Trinitarian life is written into the very structure of Aquinas's account of the Trinity.'[69] Aquinas's thought is profoundly teleological: our end is to return to the God who made us to be in communion with Godself.[70] So 'the first of all causes is the final cause' (*ST* I-II.1.2) and 'it belongs to the Divine goodness, as it brought all things into existence, so to lead them to their end (*ST* I.103.1).[71]

Despite some possible deficiencies, if the case can be made that in his intentions, Aquinas was doing theology in the light of the Trinity as revealed in the economy of salvation, then this has a significant effect on the reading of his account of law, resulting in a radically different theology of law from that which sees him as the first proponent of a rationalist, agnostic or even atheistic, natural law. The question marks over Aquinas's doctrine of the Trinity *in se* are of limited significance if the case can be made out that Aquinas has a pervasive and important emphasis on salvation history.

That such a reading is possible is revealed by Gilles Emery. He describes Aquinas's Trinitarian methodology as follows:

[Aquinas's] trinitarian theology consists of three steps: (1) the discovery of the mystery of the Trinity, by faith, through the action of the Trinity as taught by [the] Scriptures; (2) a speculative reflection on the being and properties of the divine persons; (3) a speculative reflection on the creative and salvific action of the

---

[66] Levering, *Christ's Fulfillment*, 34.

[67] Letham, *The Holy Trinity*, 404.

[68] K. Kilby, 'Aquinas, the Trinity and the Limits of Understanding', *International Journal of Systematic Theology* 7 (2005) 414; Emery, *Trinity in Aquinas*, 80; Hall, *The Trinity*, 120-23; Torrell, *Aquinas Vol. II*, 42.

[69] Cavanaugh, 'A Joint Declaration?', 265.

[70] Torrell, *Aquinas Vol. II*, 311; *ST* I-II.2.8 ad.2.

[71] M.L. Lamb, 'The Eschatology of St. Thomas Aquinas' in Weinandy, Keating and Yocum, eds., *Aquinas on Doctrine* 225; Torrell, *Aquinas Vol. II*, 80 footnote 1.

persons in the world (doctrine of the "economic Trinity") in the light of the properties and relations of the persons.[72]

Because, as has been argued above, Scripture is the controlling narrative in Aquinas's theology and because, it will be argued, Aquinas relates his account of law to the third step of his trinitarianism, the question marks and problems which arise in relation to his second step can be bracketed out. This is in contrast with Moltmann, for whom 'second step reflections' are at least, if not more, important in his political theology than are 'third step reflections'.

Aquinas's Account of the Role of Law in Salvation

The Eternal Law and God's Providence

The habit of taking extracts from the treatise on Law in isolation has led to a fundamental misunderstanding of its shape and purpose. In the prologue to the treatise, Aquinas explains that 'the extrinsic principle moving us to good is God, Who both instructs us by means of His Law, and assists us by His Grace'. The editions which regard the treatise as running to the end of q.114 are therefore correct.[73] The treatise is structured in a movement from Law to Grace, the aim of which is to demonstrate that notwithstanding the promulgation of God's Law, in creation and in the Mosaic Law, human beings have been unable to obey it and therefore need to be saved by God's grace. The treatise on Law is, therefore, soteriological in intention. It is concerned with the actions of God towards sinful human beings. As a result, what is said about human law is incidental to Aquinas's overall purpose.

Thomas begins his discussion of the category of law by defining law as rational (*aliquid rationis*), directed to the common good by a person or persons responsible for a community, and promulgated adequately (*ST* I-II.90.1-4). This category contains four species: eternal law, natural law, human law, and divine law, of which eternal law is clearly the core form, from which the others derive. Eternal law is the law 'ordered by God for the governance of things foreknown by him'.[74] It is therefore to be equated with God's providence, provided this is understood in the broadest terms as the entirety of God's good purposes for this world that He has created (*ST* I-II.91.1). God's providence is the ordering of things to their end, to the purpose for which they were created.[75] It therefore

---

[72] Emery, *Trinity in Aquinas*, 294.

[73] P. Delhaye, 'La Loi nouvelle comme dynamisme de l'Esprit-Saint' in Elders and Hedwig, eds., *Lex et libertas: Freedom and Law according to St Thomas Aquinas* (Rome: Liberia Editrice Vaticana, 1987) 268; Rogers, 'The Narrative of Natural Law', 261 footnote 38.

[74] Aquinas, *ST* I-II, 91, 1 ad.1, see also 93; Torrell, *Aquinas Vol. II*, 283.

[75] J.P. Yocum, 'Aquinas' Literal Exposition on Job' in Weinandy, Keating and Yocum, eds., *Aquinas on Scripture* 23.

encompasses both God's '*conservation* of things in the good and their *motion toward the good.*'[76]

For Thomas, the doctrine of divine simplicity means that 'the end or *telos* of divine government is God himself, and his law is nothing other than himself'.[77] The *telos* of the universe is to be found in the subsistent goodness of God (*ST* I.103.2). Thus natural law, Mosaic Law and the New Law of the Gospel are all only properly understood 'in the light of the eternal law which is nothing other than God himself, nothing other than the divine light in which the blessed see God.'[78]

At *ST* I-II.93.4-6, Aquinas presents his argument that God and the eternal law are identical in trinitarian terms. Thus, at *ST* I-II.93.4 ad.2 he says 'the Son of God is not subject to the eternal law: but rather is himself the eternal law by a kind of appropriation'. 'The eternal law embodies all that is true, just and good in relationship to God, that is, the law of love, and it is the Word himself who eternally embodies and so lives out this law.'[79] The eternal purposes of the God who has revealed Godself in Christ are Christ-centred. At q.93.6 ad.1, the Holy Spirit too is equated with, rather than regarded as subject to, the eternal law. It is the Spirit who leads created things to their appointed end. All of which suggests that a Christian doctrine of providence must be conceived in trinitarian terms – as overseen by the Father, ordered to the Son and accomplished in the Spirit.

Aquinas gives an extended account of God's providence in his commentary on Job, in which he argues that the Christian God preserves God's people through the traumas of the present life and promises them the reward of eternal life.[80] What Job teaches, according to Aquinas, is that the ways of God are not scrutable if viewed solely in terms of this life. God's justice will only be manifest at the end of time.[81] Thus temporal things are ordered to eternal things (*ST* I.113.2).

His particular account of how God's providence operates through political authorities is to be found not in the *ST* but in his commentary on Romans.[82] In his exegesis of Romans 13:1-7,[83] Aquinas wrestles with the issues of why Christians are commanded to obey even evil rulers and how such rulers can be regarded as God's servants.

The lynchpin of Aquinas's argument is *non est enim potestas nisi a Deo*. In

---

[76] Torrell, *Aquinas Vol. II*, 235, italics in the original.

[77] Kerr, *After Aquinas*, 106.

[78] Kerr, *After Aquinas*, 106.

[79] Weinandy, 'The Supremacy of Christ', 228.

[80] Yocum, 'Aquinas' Literal Exposition on Job', 21.

[81] Yocum, 'Aquinas' Literal Exposition on Job', 39; J. Finnis, *Aquinas: Moral, Political, and Legal Theory* (Oxford: OUP, 1999) 308.

[82] There is currently no published English translation of this commentary, although one is in the course of preparation.

[83] Aquinas, *In Rom.*, cap.13 l.1.

the hands of Aquinas, this idea is rendered a particular instance of his metaphysic of participation. He explicitly compares power with wisdom, of which he says *omnis sapientia a domino Deo est*. Just as all wisdom, all being, all truth (*ST* I-II.93.2), and as will be argued subsequently in this chapter, all justice, are derivative from God, so too is all power (*De Regno* II.1(=I.12) [93]).

But this move renders acute the conflict between the biblical assertions of Daniel 4:14 and John 19:11 that political power is God-given and the complaint of God in Hosea 8:4 that His people have been choosing their leaders without reference to Him. For Aquinas, the answer comes in stages. The first stage is to vindicate God from evil but to insist that God is the source of all goodness. Therefore, if the ruler acts *in bonum ordinetur, a Deo est*, while if he acts *ordinetur ad peccandum, est ex defectu creaturae, inquantum est ex nihilo*. The actions of rulers, insofar as they are rightly ordered to the good, are God-given; or to put it in metaphysical terms, participate in the goodness of God. However, the actions of rulers if they are disordered, that is to say sinful, are their own actions, and not attributable to God. Again, this is not a peculiarity of Aquinas's political theory but rather a particular instance of his general explanation of evil.[84] Nonetheless, God's providence brings good out of the evil choices which human beings make (*ST* I.109.4 ad.2; 114.1).

In particular, Aquinas recognises that the logic of Romans 13:4's claim that the authorities are God's servants is that *et malis principes ministri Dei sunt*,[85] in the same way that the Old Testament could describe Assyria and Babylon as such. The government of such evil princes is ordained by God, who in accordance with Romans 8:28, works all things for good.

In *De Regno* I.6 [52]; I.10 [83], Aquinas argues that evil princes are a divine punishment for the sins of the people. While there is some biblical support for this idea (he cites Hosea 13:11 and Job 34:30), on its own it is too simplistic an explanation, like that of the Pharisees who thought that sickness was always a punishment for sin. As with Jesus' answer to that school of thought, so Barth's response is superior. For Barth, God will be glorified, however secular power is used. If it is used rightly, the Church will be free to bring glory to God by preaching the gospel freely; if it is used wrongly, the Church will bring glory to God through its sufferings and martyrdom.[86] This Barthian argument is, however, entirely consonant with Aquinas's general doctrine of providence, according to which all things, including evil human actions, fall within God's providence (*ST* I.22.2 ad.4). '... nothing happens in the world save what is effected or permitted by Divine justice.' (*ST* I.113.7).

---

[84] As to which, see Aquinas, *ST* I.19.9; Levering, *Scripture and Metaphysics*, 93-5, 106-7; J. Saward, 'The Grace of Christ in his Principal Members: St Thomas Aquinas on the Pastoral Epistles' in Weinandy, Keating and Yocum, eds., *Aquinas on Scripture* 207.

[85] See also Aquinas, *De Regno*, I.8 [62].

[86] Barth, *Church and State*, 15-17, 54, 65.

Levering sums up Aquinas's doctrine of providence in the following way:

> Aquinas's understanding of divine providence means that history has an end that determines it as "history": the right ordering of everything to God, in accord with God's wise plan for history from eternity. This providential ordering of history is God's "eternal law". Human beings, in history, share in this law in two ways: by nature and grace. To all human beings, God gives (in the gift of creation) a participation in his "eternal law". By the exercise of rationality, human beings may understand what conduces to their right ordering. This rational sharing in God's eternal plan for creatures is called "natural law". The right ordering expressed in God's eternal law is, when put into action, justice. Justice means that human actions accord with the ends proper to human nature, that is, accord with God's eternal or wise plan for the attainment of human beings to their proper good.[87]

Long argues that with regard to the evil done by human beings, what Aquinas proposes is that God permits evil for the sake of a greater good, albeit that we will only understand how this can be so when we see God face-to-face. Hall sees the whole sweep of questions 49 to 114 of the *Prima Secundae*, with its treatment of virtues, sin, law and grace, as driven by Aquinas's need to account both 'for how human self-direction still falls under God's governance of the cosmos' and for how 'God's providence prevails even in men and women who turn away from it.'[88] It is the only teleological expectation of the beatific vision which will provide satisfactory answers.[89]

Aquinas and the Mosaic Law

Those editions of the *ST* that treat the treatises on law and on grace as a unity are right to do so. It is no accident that in the *Summa Theologiae*, there is only a single question about natural law (*ST* I-II. 94), in amongst 25 (90-114), of which three deal with human law, eight with the Mosaic Law ('the Old Law'), three with the New Law of the Gospel and six with grace. It is the Torah and not natural law which is the pivot of Aquinas's reflections on law, just as it forms the conclusion to his treatise on justice (*ST* II-II.122).[90] Cajetan missed this key point, as the brevity of his remarks about *ST* I-II.102-5 and III.35-45 reveals. It is the New Law, that is to say, the grace of the Holy Spirit, which is the apex of Aquinas's argument. Excising the Old Law and the Holy Spirit

---

[87] Levering, 'The Liturgy of the Eucharist', 185; *Christ's Fulfillment*, 129.

[88] P.M. Hall, *Narrative and Natural Law: An Interpretation of Thomistic Ethics* (Notre Dame: University of Notre Dame Press, 1994) 26.

[89] S.A. Long, 'Providence, Liberté et Loi Naturelle', *Revue Thomiste* 102 (2002) 371-76.

[90] T. Gilby, *Between Community and Society: A Philosophy and Theology of the State* (London: Longman Green, 1952) 324-25; Kerr, 'Doctrine of God and Theological Ethics according to Thomas Aquinas', 78; D.S. Long, *Divine Economy: Theology and the Market* (London: Routledge, 2000) 214.

from the treatise on law leaves a deformed rump. Contemporary extracts of Aquinas's work which customarily omit or abbreviate the questions on Old Law, by doing so, fundamentally misrepresent the shape of his thought.[91]

In this chapter, after some brief comments on why it is that the Torah and not the natural law is pivotal for Aquinas, it is proposed to consider Aquinas's analysis of the Mosaic Law, before re-locating natural law in the light of Aquinas's soteriology. This necessitates a discussion of Aquinas's account of the 'New Law', his virtue ethics, and his theology of glorification. Having done this, it will be clear that human law does not fit straightforwardly into Aquinas's category of law.

WHY THE TORAH?

For Aquinas, there are three fundamental problems with natural law. First, our knowledge of the natural goods towards which it directs us is obscured by sin.[92] Second, our natural ability to pursue those natural goods which we do discern is impaired by sin (*ST* I-II.93.6; I.113.1 ad.1). Third, these natural goods are not the end for which we are ultimately ordered. In order to direct us towards the end of eternal beatitude, it was therefore necessary for a divine law to be given (*ST* I-II.91.4).[93]

That divine law was the Old Law. In part its moral precepts reiterated the natural law (*ST* I-II.98.5; 100.1; II-II.122.1). It was, however, a law 'tailored (by God and by Moses, its mutual givers) to the needs of a specific community at a specific time.'[94] Some of its judicial provisions, such as those regarding divorce (*ST* I-II 105.4.8) and accepting usury from foreigners (*ST* I-II.105.3.3), therefore tolerate injustices from which it was intended that Israel would gradually be weaned.

For Aquinas, the moral precepts contained in the Old Law are binding for all, because they reiterate the natural law (*ST* I-II.98.5).[95] These moral precepts can be reduced to the Decalogue[96] (*ST* I-II.100.3), which can itself be reduced to the Two Great Commandments identified by Jesus (ad.1; II-II.122.5; *De decem preceptis* II-IV). The Old Law is therefore ordered to and around the love of God and the love of neighbour.

The Jews were, however, unable to keep the Old Law.

---

[91] E.g. R.W. Dyson, *Aquinas: Political Writings* (Cambridge: Cambridge University Press, 2002); R.J. Regan, *Thomas Aquinas: On Law, Morality, and Politics* 2nd edn. (Indianapolis: Hackett, 2002); R. McInerny, *Thomas Aquinas: Selected Writings* (Harmondsworth: Penguin, 1998).

[92] Aquinas, *ST* I-II.94.4, .6; 91.6; III.61.3 ad.2; Hall, *Narrative*, 34-35, 46.

[93] Hall, *Narrative*, 44.

[94] Hall, *Narrative*, 60; Aquinas *ST* II-II.122.1 ad.3.

[95] Hall, *Narrative*, 129, endnote 28; J. Finnis, 'Natural Inclinations and Natural Rights: Deriving "Ought" from "Is" according to Aquinas' in Elders and Hedwig, eds., *Lex et libertas* 52-53; *Aquinas* 125.

[96] Hall, *Narrative*, 56.

Thomas tells us that the Old Law could not in fact bring men and women into friendship with God. It could not by itself accomplish the reordering to God that it intended. ... Lacking the help of grace, those under the Old Law could not entirely fulfil its precepts (*ST* I-II.100.10 ad.3). Neither could the Old Law "justify" in the sense of conferring true justice, says Thomas, because true justice is also infused only through grace (*ST* I-II.100.12).[97]

Thus the Old Law reveals our need for grace (*ST* I-II.98.2 ad.3).[98]

For Aquinas, the Torah was given in the pre-existing context of the Abrahamic covenant.[99] Notwithstanding the limitations of the Torah, Aquinas places it firmly within the context of grace. In his commentary on John, Aquinas describes the Mosaic law as 'a great grace'.[100] However, it has this quality not in virtue of itself, but because it is ordered to Christ. In its promulgation, God already 'has in view the promulgation of the New Law, the grace of the Holy Spirit'.[101] Through the Torah, God withdraws men from idolatrous worship and includes them 'in the worship of one God, by Whom the human race was to be saved through Christ.' (*ST* I-II.98.2).

Israel was intended to be a just, that is to say, a beautifully ordered people (*ST* I-II.105.1 *s.c.*). For this reason, it was given a divine law so that its people might not just order their relations aright between themselves but might also be rightly ordered towards God. By this means, Aquinas explains those aspects of the Mosaic Law which seem impractical or inappropriate from an earthly point of view.[102] These provisions reveal especially, in Aquinas's view, the fact that divine law is ordered towards charity (*ST* I-II.107.obj.2).

Although the Mosaic Law does not *cause* grace, by obedience to it and participation in its sacraments the people of Israel participated in the New Law. That is to say, the grace of Christ given through the Holy Spirit was mediated to the people of Israel through the Mosaic Law.[103] Thomas makes this clear in *ST* I-II.98.1 ad.3 where he interprets verse 32 of the great Psalm in praise of the Torah, Psalm 119, as revealing the Psalmist's awareness that he has received an inner principle of grace which enables him to follow the way of God's commandments.[104]

However, as it looks forward to Christ, the Mosaic Law also serves as a pedagogue by demonstrating that sinful human beings are incapable of

---

[97] Hall, *Narrative*, 60.

[98] Hall, *Narrative*, 48, 52.

[99] J.P.M. van der Ploeg, 'Le traité de Saint Thomas de la Loi Ancienne' in Elders and Hedwig, eds., *Lex et libertas* 188.

[100] Aquinas, *In Ioan.*, paragraph 204.

[101] Levering, *Christ's Fulfillment*, 22.

[102] Levering, *Christ's Fulfillment*, 115-6.

[103] Aquinas, *ST* III.8.3 ad.3; I-II.98.2 ad.4; I-II.103.2; 106.1. ad.3.; Levering, *Christ's Fulfillment*, 23; Weinandy, 'The Supremacy of Christ', 239.

[104] Levering, *Christ's Fulfillment*, 157 endnote 33.

perfectly following even a God-given law, which is acknowledged to be righteous (*ST* I-II.91.5). Thus Israel was taught to hope for a Messiah 'who would fulfill the written law, both in its literal commands and in its figurative significance'.[105]

The Torah was given in order 'to make clear the elements of justice' and also to prefigure 'the way in which true justice would be perfectly fulfilled and elevated to the level of supernatural communion.'[106] The giving of the Torah thus looks both backwards and forwards. It looks backwards insofar as it is given because human beings do not discern the natural law as they ought.[107] It looks forwards insofar as it anticipates the coming of Christ and the restoration of full communion between God and humankind.[108] Thus, as Wawrykow puts it: 'Christ is the end of the Law. The Law was given to prepare people for the Christ who would save and as Romans 10 states, believing in the Christ who brings the Law to its term puts the individual into correct relationship – one of justice or righteousness – with God.'[109]

Levering sums up the position as follows:

> Israel ... is elevated above other peoples by its reception of divine law, which is ordered to charity. However, Aquinas never loses sight of the equally important reality that Israel could not, of itself, perfectly obey the law and that Israel awaited a Messiah who would bear Israel's sins and whose coming would be associated with the instilling of God's law in human hands.[110]

Aquinas understands Christ as the fulfilment of the Torah, and indeed, of all that is recorded in the Old Testament.[111] As Levering points out, this accords with N.T. Wright's insistence that Jesus' Incarnation is the fulfilment and restoration of Israel.[112] The fulcrum of this relationship is the Transfiguration, in which 'Christ shows that his glory and his upcoming passion, far from cutting him off from the law and the prophets, magnificently fulfill what they had foretold.'[113] Significantly, Aquinas also sees all of the Trinity revealed in this incident: 'the Father in the voice, the Son in the man, the Holy Ghost in the

---

[105] Levering, *Christ's Fulfillment*, 113.

[106] Levering, *Christ's Fulfillment*, 112.

[107] Nichols, *Discovering Aquinas*, 174.

[108] Hall, *Narrative*, 21; Levering, *Christ's Fulfillment*, 22.

[109] Wawrykow, 'Aquinas on Isaiah' in Weinandy, Keating and Yocum, eds., *Aquinas on Scripture* 47.

[110] Levering, *Christ's Fulfillment*, 116.

[111] Aquinas, *In Ioan.* paragraphs 576-577; *Catena Aurea*, Vol.1 *St. Matthew* (Turin: Marietti, 1953) 170.

[112] Levering, *Christ's Fulfillment*, 41; N.T. Wright, *Jesus and the Victory of God* (London: SPCK, 1996) 130.

[113] Levering, *Christ's Fulfillment*, 101; Aquinas *ST* III.45.3.

bright cloud.'[114]

The relationship between the Torah and the natural law in Aquinas's thought is the subject of close argument by Levering. 'God made human beings to be in communion with him, but the first human beings turned away from him, cutting off this integral communion.'[115] As a consequence, human beings became overwhelmed by disordered desires, and both their wills and their reasons became darkened (*ST* I-II.85.3). 'With reason obscured, human beings could no longer efficiently discern the natural law.'[116] The Torah operates at three levels. It contains a revelation of the moral precepts of the natural law. It is given in the context of a covenant by which God wishes to restore human beings to communion with God. Finally, it points towards God's will to enter into closer communion than would have been naturally possible. Nonetheless, for all that this is the role of the Torah, it remains, like any human law, concerned with exterior acts and is not 'an inner law which guides and perfects the movements of the soul.'[117] Aquinas recognises that although the judicial precepts of the Mosaic Law point towards 'the right order that should exist between man and his fellow men, ... in practice, like any human politics, they are unable to produce this right order.'[118] Precisely by virtue of these limitations, 'the Mosaic Law is dynamically ordered toward a new law (and new covenant) that will make explicit the communion that God has in store for us.'[119] The Old Law is therefore 'intrinsically ordered to Jesus Christ, the Messiah of Israel.'[120]

CHRIST'S FULFILMENT OF TORAH AND TEMPLE

'Christ fulfills Israel's Torah, which is the expression of the divine Wisdom.'[121] However, key to Aquinas's argument is his view that Christ fulfils the different aspects of the Torah in differing ways.

> Christ's Fulfillment of the law is not a merely literal accomplishment ... When Christ (divine Wisdom incarnate) fulfils the law, he reveals its divine meaning. Christ's passion explicitly reveals that the ultimate end of the law is found not in the ceremonial and judicial precepts themselves ... but in friendship with the divine Persons through the God-man Jesus Christ, who has fulfilled the precepts of the law for us.[122]

Aquinas distinguishes between the moral, ceremonial and judicial precepts of

---

[114] Aquinas, *ST* III.45.4.
[115] Aquinas, *ST* I-II, 91.6.
[116] Levering, *Christ's Fulfillment*, 20.
[117] Levering, *Christ's Fulfillment*, 21.
[118] Levering, *Christ's Fulfillment*, 61; Long, *Divine Economy*, 216.
[119] Levering, *Christ's Fulfillment*, 21.
[120] Levering, *Christ's Fulfillment*, 22.
[121] Levering, *Christ's Fulfillment*, 33.
[122] Levering, *Christ's Fulfillment*, 118.

the Mosaic law. Whereas the moral law remains of permanent validity, the 'ceremonial and judicial precepts come to an end in Christ.'[123] The moral precepts are built around the foundation of the love of God and the love of neighbour. The ceremonial precepts 'direct the particular way in which Israel is to express love of God.'[124] With regard to the judicial precepts, these 'are in conformity with the universal moral precepts, although in some cases, Aquinas thinks, God chose to tolerate (not to sanction) an injustice from which the people would gradually be weaned.'[125]

In accordance with the threefold division of the Mosaic Law, so Christ fulfils the Torah in three ways.

> Christ's passion not only fulfills but also perfects and elevates the Mosaic Law: Christ fulfills and transforms the moral precepts through his most perfect ... love of God and, in God, of all human beings; his perfectly free and loving self-sacrifice on the cross fulfills and transforms the animal sacrifices and purity laws; and his suffering and death ... fulfill and transform the judicial precepts by paying an interior "penalty" that is sufficient to rectify ... all the disorder caused by sin in human history.'[126] This action is not seen in isolation but as the culmination of Christ's life lived in obedience to the Mosaic Law.[127]

Levering interprets Christ's fulfilment of the law in the light of His embodiment and transformation of the threefold office of prophet, priest and king. He argues that 'Aquinas's treatment of Christ's threefold office ... provide[s] a model for uniting – in the light of the history of Israel – the Incarnation of divine Wisdom and the fulfillment of Israel's Torah.'[128] 'As Aquinas states, Christ came into the world for three purposes: to "publish the truth" (prophet), to "free men from sin" (messianic king), and "that by Him we might have access to God" (priest).'[129]

This seems to be the case, though Aquinas has to elide the roles of prophet and lawgiver in order to make his scheme work. In Aquinas's definition, a prophet 'teaches the people how to live according to God's law, awaiting the fulfillment of God's plan of salvation.'[130] Christ fulfils this office by giving a New Law 'which is the inner principle by which human beings are enabled to observe the moral precepts.' The priests were responsible for ensuring the right worship of God, Christ fulfils this office by offering the perfect, acceptable sacrifice. The kings were charged with the administration of justice. Christ

---

[123] Levering, *Christ's Fulfillment*, 17.

[124] Aquinas, *ST* I-II.99.3.

[125] Levering, *Christ's Fulfillment*, 26.

[126] Levering, *Christ's Fulfillment*, 28; Aquinas, *ST* III.47.2.1; *ST* I-II.103.3.2.

[127] Aquinas, *ST* III.40.4.

[128] Levering, *Christ's Fulfillment*, 67.

[129] Levering, *Christ's Fulfillment*, 42; Aquinas, *ST* III.40.1.

[130] Levering, *Christ's Fulfillment*, 69.

fulfils this office by 'establish[ing] justice between human beings by undergoing more than sufficient suffering for all sins.'[131] As Israel's king, when Christ fulfils the divine law, He does so *per pro* the people of Israel, as the embodiment of the community of Israel. Each of the three offices 'points to *one* reality: the engagement of Christ's salvific love in reconciliation.'[132]

What looks, on the face of it, to be the revocation of the Torah is, in fact, nothing other than its fulfilment. So, 'Christ does not abolish the commandments; rather, he shows how they can be truly obeyed in the light of the supernatural destiny that he reveals.'[133] After Christ, the Mosaic Law is not simply superseded. Instead, 'Aquinas holds that Christians continue to observe the Mosaic Law, but no longer in its old form.'[134] They continue to obey its moral precepts, which abide; but they celebrate the fulfilment of its ceremonial precepts in the sacrifice of Christ (*ST* I-II.103.3 ad.1). The Mosaic Law is ordered to faith, hope and charity. Through their union with Christ, Christians are enabled to fulfil its intentions.

Aquinas's view of the Mosaic Law is fundamentally, but not exclusively, positive. However, he does recognise that 'Christ, by fulfilling the Law in his passion, undergoes the fullness of the covenantal curses and thus pays the entire penalty of sin'.[135] Since divine law is ordered to charity, the Mosaic Law demonstrates that charity cannot be given by a written law. The consummation of the divine law requires the indwelling of God in the human heart (*ST* I-II.98.1).

For Aquinas, Israel's history reveals the inadequacies of an external written law and gave rise to the hope that with the coming of the Messiah, the written law would become an inner law so that it could be perfectly obeyed.[136] This inner law is the New Law, the grace of the Holy Spirit, given by Christ, who 'enables all people to participate interiorly, by living faith and the sacraments of faith, in Christ's righteous worship.'[137]

Levering also argues that the indwelling of the Spirit fulfils the Temple.[138] For Aquinas, the presence of God with God's people in God's Temple prefigures the presence of God with God's people through the indwelling Spirit.[139] For Aquinas, there is no division between worship and righteousness. '[F]ulfillment of the Temple in liturgy ... requires fulfillment of the Torah in

---

[131] Levering, *Christ's Fulfillment*, 69; *ST* III.46.5.

[132] Levering, *Christ's Fulfillment*, 79.

[133] Levering, *Christ's Fulfillment*, 76.

[134] Levering, *Christ's Fulfillment*, 88.

[135] Levering, *Christ's Fulfillment*, 52; *ST* III.46.6.

[136] Aquinas, *ST* I-II.106.1 *s.c.*; Levering, *Christ's Fulfillment*, 113.

[137] Levering, *Christ's Fulfillment*, 113.

[138] Levering, *Christ's Fulfillment*, 130.

[139] Levering, *Christ's Fulfillment*, 91; J. Hamilton, 'Were Old Covenant Believers Indwelt by the Spirit?', *Themelios* 30 (2004) 22.

justice. The two are ultimately one.'[140] 'Holiness is true worship of God, who is holy.'[141]

In Aquinas's commentary on Hebrews (*In Heb.* 2.1-4 [90]), he draws attention to another point. The commands of Christ are not burdensome (Mt. 11:30) whereas the Mosaic law became a yoke which the Jews were not able to bear (Act 15:10). As will be developed below, this is because Christians are empowered by the Holy Spirit to be obedient to Christ, are given wisdom by the Spirit to discern what it means to follow Christ, and have had revealed to them, in Christ, the end towards which virtuous action is ordained. In co-operation with the Holy Spirit, we are enabled to grow towards the end for which we were made, which is to reflect in a unique way the glory of God. Thus, Aquinas offers a trinitarian explanation of the paradoxes of the Christian faith that it is in becoming more Christ-like that we become more truly ourselves and that it is in obedience to Christ that we are free.

The Role of Natural Law in Aquinas's Thought

If the Mosaic Law is given its due prominence in Aquinas's thought, then natural law is seen in its proper light. That light is the same light which illuminates the Mosaic Law; it is a soteriological light, albeit that whereas divine law is situated in the history of salvation, natural law is grounded in creation.[142] It is key to the understanding the place of natural law in Aquinas's thought to realise that 'the natural law is linked time and again, within that section of the *Summa* designated as treating of laws, with eternal law, by which God governs the entire cosmos.'[143]

As Alasdair MacIntyre has pointed out, the *Summa Theologiae* follows Paul and Augustine in emphasising sin and the need for grace.[144] For Aquinas, the natural law is not meant to be a substitute for the teachings of Christ or the New Law. Only the New Law, not the natural law, is the bearer of salvation.[145] The primary role of the natural law is to point out to those who know nothing of Christ, what God requires of them. As he says in *De Regno* I.1 [4] 'the light of reason is placed by nature in every man, to guide him in his acts *towards his end*.' (emphasis mine). Aquinas repeatedly shows concern to establish the justice of God in God's dealings with those who know nothing of Christ,

---

[140] Levering, *Christ's Fulfillment*, 91, 128.

[141] Levering, *Christ's Fulfillment*, 113.

[142] J.M. Aubert, 'L'Analogie entre la Lex Nova et la Loi Naturelle' in Elders and Hedwig, eds., *Lex et libertas* 250; Rogers, 'The Narrative of Natural Law', 276.

[143] Hall, *Narrative*, 23.

[144] A. MacIntyre, *Whose Justice? Which Rationality?* (Notre Dame: Ind.: University of Notre Dame Press, 1988) 181; Rogers, 'The Narrative of Natural Law', 261, 264-5.

[145] Aubert, 'Lex Nova et la loi naturelle', 252; Rogers, 'The Narrative of Natural Law', 276.

without for one second denying that there is but one Mediator between God and humankind.[146]

In propounding a Christian doctrine of natural law, Aquinas is seeking to hold a theological balance between the Christian truths that the world is created by the triune God, that the world has fallen, and that the world has been redeemed by the triune God.

As Pamela Hall puts it:

> The world, to Aquinas, is a created world, and all things derive their being and goodness from God. Just so, the concupiscence to which men and women are prone after the Fall prompts neglect of God for the more immediately gratifying goods created by God. What Thomas suggests in his interpretation of the natural law is that attachment to such goods, without the anchor of a right relation to God, becomes itself distorting and inappropriate. In such inordinate attachments, we lose active knowledge of our own good; we lose the knowledge of how to value other goods as well.[147]

Therefore, although 'Thomas does not ... deny the goodness of natural goods; he ... argues that they cannot constitute the ultimate end for men and women. Indeed, he denies a constitutive place to all goods other than God in the ultimate end.'[148] (*ST* I-II.4.7-8).

For Aquinas, the primary sense of natural law is the fact that natural inclinations direct us to those things which we naturally apprehend are goods. The rules of natural law are a secondary sense of natural law, and consist of three sets of precepts which

> correspond to the hierarchy of the *inclinationes* themselves. The first set of precepts guides the preservation of human life, a good which we share with all living things. The second set pertains to the begetting and rearing of offspring, goods which we share with other animals. Third are precepts that govern the goods to which humans incline as specifically rational beings.; Thomas mentions in particular our desire "to know the truth about God and to live in society." (*ST* I-II.94.2).[149]

There are therefore a number of different activities which contribute to human flourishing in its different aspects. But there is also a hierarchy among human goods, they are ordered. The moral order of the universe is discernable from the discovery that God has made us for Godself.

Human action and human reasoning is the result of the complex interplay of the goodness in and for which we were created and the disorder consequent upon our fallenness. In this situation, God has not left us without guidance as to

---

[146] McIlroy, 'What's at stake in natural law?'.

[147] Hall, *Narrative*, 110; see also Cosden, *The Theology of Work*, 83.

[148] Hall, *Narrative*, 67; Torrell, *Aquinas Vol. II*, 244.

[149] Hall, *Narrative*, 32, 28.

right from wrong because we remain ordered towards God. What Aquinas affirms is that we *can* know what God requires of us.[150] That is what is meant by the famous self-evidence claim (*ST* I-II.94.2). We can know this because it is given to us to know the things which are human goods, and pre-eminent among those things is the knowledge and love of God. Hall argues that this 'directedness is in fact the primary sense of natural law for Aquinas.'[151]

Hall contends that the strength of Aquinas's theory of natural law is precisely the point identified as a weakness by critics such as Leo Strauss[152] and Harry Jaffa.[153] Natural law is viewed by Aquinas as a species of law, which must, as with all law, be an ordinance of reason for the common good, made by the appropriate legislator, which must be properly promulgated (*ST* I-II.90.1). Therefore, as Jaffa rightly points out, on this account 'for the natural law to be promulgated adequately to men and women, they must recognize the law as deriving from God as governor of the cosmos.'[154] This makes sense if Aquinas's discussion of natural law has a soteriological purpose. Whereas Levering emphasises the connection between natural law and belief in Divine Providence, amounting to implicit faith in Christ, Hall stresses that for Aquinas, 'The natural law is for educating people into the life of virtue.'[155] The two are complementary: right human action depends on discerning the revelation that God made us for Godself. The self-evidence of natural law does not establish that we do not need God in order to discern right and wrong, rather it establishes our guilt for failing to order our lives according to the revelation of right and wrong, and of Godself, which God has given us through the world God has made.[156]

It is therefore the goodness of God's creation and of God's saving purposes, not rationality narrowly construed, which dictates Aquinas's insistence that, however mistaken we may be on particular points, the natural law, in its most general (*communissima*) principles, is known to all and cannot be erased from the human heart (*ST* I-II.94.6).[157] When Aquinas insists that 'sin cannot destroy man's rationality altogether, for then he would no longer be capable of sin' (*ST* I-II. 85.2), he reveals that for him natural law means that humans are without excuse before God, not that human beings may be righteous before God by means of their own unaided perfect observance of the natural law.[158]

---

[150] Hall, *Narrative*, 2.
[151] Hall, *Narrative*, 96.
[152] L. Strauss, *Natural Right and History* (Chicago: University of Chicago Press, 1950) 163.
[153] H.V. Jaffa, *Thomism and Aristotelianism* (Chicago: University of Chicago Press, 1952).
[154] Hall, *Narrative*, 4.
[155] Hall, *Narrative*, 14.
[156] McIlroy, 'What's at stake in natural law?'.
[157] Hall, *Narrative*, 30-31.
[158] Rogers, 'The Narrative of Natural Law', 257-58.

Nonetheless, argues Hall, natural law is not merely an exterior law, it is a recognition of the way in which we are intrinsically ordered. It is only by understanding what constitutes the good for human beings that we able to grasp the reason for rules such as 'Do not murder'.[159]

This teleological and soteriological orientation in Aquinas's thinking about natural law means that Aquinas does not derive his account or principles of natural law as a result of proceeding straightforwardly from a description of what *is* to a prescription as to how human beings *ought* to act. For Aquinas, following Paul in Romans 3:23, it is the glory of God of which human beings have fallen short. We *ought* to live lives worthy of the glory of God; therefore we *ought* to behave in these ways.[160] It is our proper human response to God's action towards us, culminating in God's self-revelation and demonstration of perfect humanity in Christ, which definitively reveals our moral obligations.[161]

Aquinas's methodology has Christ at its heart. Humankind was made in the image of God. Because of sinfulness, that image is marred in each one of us. However, it is perfectly formed in Christ, and we are brought to our perfection through being conformed to His likeness. Natural law is that limited and partial participation in the created order of things in Christ which may be discerned by reflection upon the created world and our place within it. However, our ultimate end, our true beatitude, is not to be found in this world, but only when we see God face to face.[162]

As with the Mosaic Law, 'we cannot keep the natural law without grace',[163] and our discovery of our inability to do so reveals to us our need for the New Law, which is the grace of the Holy Spirit. G.K. Chesterton described Aquinas as the only optimist theologian. If Aquinas merits that description, his optimism is founded in Christ not in human beings' natural capacity to pull themselves up by their own boot straps.[164]

This reading of Aquinas brings him close to O'Donovan, both in his

---

[159] Hall, *Narrative*, 38.

[160] Finnis makes this point by reference to *de Caritate* a. 2c. in 'Natural Inclinations' at 48; *Aquinas* 127; *ST* I-II.99.1; II-II.66.1 sc. Geiger observes 'The end for which a being is created must ... be part of its definition, if the definition of that being is perfect. The end helps us understand the nature of a being ...': 'L'homme image de Dieu', 515; Torrell, *Aquinas Vol. II*, 343-44.

[161] For a discussion of the Christo-centric nature of morality and a critique of those views of natural law which treat nature as a separable source of moral obligations, see A.J. Torrance, 'On Deriving "Ought" from "Is": Christology, Covenant and *Koinonia*', 167-90.

[162] Aquinas, *ST* I-II.5.3 III.supp.92; *ScG* III. C.48; *Commentary on the Nicomachean Ethics* (Chicago: Regnery, 1964) I.10 n.12 [129]; *IV Sent.* d.43 a.1 sol. 1; *De Regno* I.9; Finnis, *Aquinas*, 105-07.

[163] Hall, *Narrative*, 104.

[164] Although his optimism is also partially explicable by the fact that he lived in relatively settled times: Gilby, *Principality and Polity*, 102.

recognition that human beings do not discern the moral order within creation as they should and also in his stress that Christ is central to a right understanding of the moral order. The crucial difference is that O'Donovan is chary of the term 'law' because he sees that it implies the possibility of universal knowledge of the moral order.[165] That, for Aquinas, is precisely the point: if God is to judge us justly for our rejection of God and of God's call among our lives, then God can only do so if we had the opportunity to discern that God existed and what God required of us.

It is because God has given creation a life of its own that it is possible and proper to speak of 'natural law'. However, this is not to be understood as a machine created by the Deist God of the Enlightenment. Nor is it to be understood as given once and for all and then operating as a realm of nature upon which grace is merely superimposed, as in Tridentine Catholicism. For sound metaphysical reasons, Aquinas understands that our very being and such goodness as we have are derived from God and constantly dependent on God.[166]

The other claim Aquinas is making by speaking of natural law is a claim that the Fall is not absolute. Despite the Fall, we still retain, as Milbank puts it, 'our capacities to eat, build houses, cultivate fields, deploy *techne*, have friends, marry and so forth. These capacities survive the Fall and the loss of sanctifying grace.'[167] From this it could be concluded that these capacities are independent of our supernatural orientation.[168] Were this conclusion to be reached then, amongst other things, marriage would be a purely secular affair divorced from our supernatural end.[169] However, for Thomas, marriage was a sacrament (*ST* III.65.1; supp. 42-68). Even those theologians and churches who have denied the name of sacrament to marriage,[170] have always understood the significance of marriage as a witness to important parts of the Christian message.

Fergus Kerr argues that Henri de Lubac interpreted Aquinas rightly, and that what Aquinas actually thought was that 'nature is predisposed for grace, the world is naturally waiting for the gospel – though it is only after the fact that

---

[165] O'Donovan, *RMO*, 85-87; Black, *Christian Moral Realism*, 118.

[166] Aquinas, *ST* I.45.3; I-II.62.1; 109.2; Lamb, 'Eschatology', 226; A.N. Williams, 'Deification in the *Summa Theologiae*', 241; Vos, *Aquinas, Calvin, and Contemporary Protestant Thought*, 142; Milbank, *The Suspended Middle*, 35.

[167] Milbank, *Being Reconciled*, 224 endnote 6 to chapter 6.

[168] The burden of Milbank's argument in *The Suspended Middle* is precisely to argue against this conclusion. Also, in *Truth in Aquinas* at 23, Milbank argues that finite realities cannot be comprehended in themselves but only in relation to God. Even things which are 'natural' can only be made sense of in the light of the fact that they have been created by God.

[169] In *Theology & Social Theory* 166-67, Milbank expressly criticises Hegel for reaching this conclusion.

[170] For a recent Baptist example to the contrary, see Colwell, *Promise & Presence*, chapter 11.

this becomes clear. Far from coming only as an unwelcome and disorientating shock, the Christian dispensation turns out to offer the beginnings of a fulfilment of dimly apprehended longings.'[171]

But even this formulation tends to suggest that the openness to grace is intrinsic to the creature, whereas it may be better to place the emphasis on the fact that such goodness and openness to perfection as is proper to creation and to human creatures is itself caused by divine grace, coming at the initiative of the Father, through the Son and by the Spirit. That human goods continue to be good, though impaired by the Fall, is the result of God's grace. That these goods can be transformed through an understanding of their place in relation to God's work in Christ is also the result of God's grace.

For O'Donovan, the lynchpin is the acknowledgment of God in Christ. If He is not known, then the teleology of the world is missed, and if the teleology of the world is missed, then its ordering will not be recognised.[172] If the world is not known to be ordered to God in Christ, then it is not known at all. On the reading set out above, Aquinas would have agreed, but subject to the following qualifications. Where Christ has been proclaimed, God has revealed that the world is ordered to God in Christ. Where Christ has not yet been proclaimed but the Mosaic law has been given, God has revealed through the declaration of its moral, judicial and ceremonial precepts that the world is ordered to God. Where neither Christ nor the Mosaic Law has been proclaimed, God has revealed through creation that the world is ordered to God. In all three cases it is the same ordering that is revealed. It is no accident that Aquinas appropriated natural law to the Second Person of the Trinity.[173] Where only creation points to the ordering of the world to God, both the discernment of God's nature and of God's requirements is inevitably unclear, but this merely confirms that, for Aquinas, salvation is by grace not a human achievement. Where the Mosaic Law has been given, God's nature and requirements have been more clearly revealed, but the totality of God's demands and the limitations of our fallenness are correspondingly more obviously exposed, and so again it is clear that, for Aquinas, salvation is by grace and not by works.

Grace is key to Aquinas's account of how natural law meets the criterion of promulgation which he has posited is essential for all law (*ST* I-II.90.1). Natural law is effectively promulgated because, [Aquinas] says, '*God puts it into men's minds* to be known naturally.' (*ST* I.II.90.4 ad.1, emphasis mine). What Aquinas needed to go on and say was that the triune God puts the natural law into human minds by means of the Spirit. To have done so would have stressed

---

[171] Kerr, *After Aquinas*, 134-35, commenting on de Lubac's *Surnaturel*. See also Milbank's *The Suspended Middle*, endorsing and developing de Lubac's theology, while remaining somewhat agnostic as to whether it is an accurate reading of Aquinas.

[172] O'Donovan, *RMO*, 81-88; Black, *Christian Moral Realism*, 118-22.

[173] Aquinas, *ST* I-II.93.1 ad.2 ; *In Rom* 1:20a no. 122, and 1:19 no.115; Rogers, 'The Narrative of Natural Law', 270, 272.

the personal agency of the Spirit and therefore guarded against rationalist distortions of the idea of natural law.

In Aquinas's thought, the difference between what we can do 'naturally' and what we can only do 'supernaturally' is not a distinction between what we can do without the aid of God and what we can only do with the aid of God.[174] Aquinas's theory of causality is not a theory of mechanistic causes but a theory of personal agency (*ST* I.44.4; 105.5),[175] although again it would have been preferable if he had been clearer on this point. Instead, the distinction is between what, by the grace of God, we can do without acknowledging that we are only enabled to act and to act rightly by the grace of God, on the one hand; and what, by the grace of God, we are enabled to do as we acknowledge that we are enabled to act and act rightly by the grace of God. What is 'natural' for Aquinas pertains to what has been given and continues to be given in God's work of creating, sustaining and providence, which God graciously gives for us to enjoy even if we reject God.

Aquinas on the New Law

God made all things good. For Aquinas, it follows from this that God created Adam and Eve in a state of justice or right order in relation to God and to each other (*ST* I.95). This just state was lost when the first human beings chose finite goods over God. The consequence was that the human race became unjust and disordered not only in relation to God but also to each other and internally. The result was that human beings no longer knew nor chose the good.

Unlike Moltmann, Aquinas is quite clear that the original sin was an act of disobedience (*ST* II-II.105.2 ad.3). Salvation must therefore be an act of obedience.[176] Humankind fell through the disobedience of Adam and Eve and is saved through the obedience of Christ, whose passion fulfills the Old Law.[177] Levering devotes a chapter to explaining how this is so.[178] He argues that Aquinas unites an Anselmian emphasis on the satisfaction achieved by Christ's death with the Abelardian stress on its exemplary nature. In Christ's death we are shown the extent of God's love, a love God wants us to imitate; and also in Christ's obedience we are shown the holiness which God desires us to exhibit. Both the crucifixion and resurrection have salvific effect, the cross delivering us from evil and the resurrection advancing us towards good (*ST* III.53.1). A

---

[174] Long, 'Providence, liberté et loi naturelle', 358-59, 361.

[175] Torrell, *Aquinas Vol. II*, 237-42; G. Grisez, 'The Doctrine of God and the Ultimate Meaning of Human Life' in A.J. Torrance and M. Banner, eds., *The Doctrine of God and Theological Ethics* (Edinburgh: T&T Clark, 2006) 127.

[176] Aquinas, *In Heb.* 5:8-14; Weinandy, 'The Supremacy of Christ', 235; R. Cessario, 'Christian Salvation' in Weinandy, Keating and Yocum, eds., *Aquinas on Doctrine* 124.

[177] Aquinas, *ST* III.47.2; Levering, *Christ's Fulfillment*, 53.

[178] Levering, *Christ's Fulfillment*, 51-82; Kerr, *After Aquinas*, 172-77.

similar point may be made by saying that the cross deals with the penalty of death, while the resurrection restores us to new life. Salvation is therefore unequivocally the work of Christ.

> Christ's pre-eminence ... is ... twofold. First, it resides ... in his unique origin as the eternally begotten Son of the Father ... Secondly, ... it resides also in his relationship to other sons in that they are sons only to the extent that they too share in and are so conformed by the word of the Son ... taking on the very likeness and image of the God of truth, that is, the Father.[179]

The terminus of this conformity, is the 'glorification of the saints ... brought about through Christ's instrumental headship'.[180]

The new life offered by Jesus is expressed in the form of a 'New Law'. Aquinas's understanding of this New Law is drawn from texts such as Rom. 8:2, 2 Cor. 3:3, and finds its centre in Jer. 31:33 as cited in Heb. 8:10.[181] The New Law is '[t]he law of the Holy Spirit [which] is superior to every human law.' (*ST* I-II.96.5 ad.2)[182] For Thomas, 'the New Law (of the Gospel) is already nothing less than "the grace of the Holy Spirit given inwardly to Christ's faithful".'[183] Thus the gift of the Holy Spirit is the chief mark of the New Covenant in Christ (*In 2 Cor.* 3.6-11 [90]). Salvation, for Thomas, is expressly conceived in trinitarian terms. Christians are saved by the work of Christ, and are given grace to accept that salvation through the Holy Spirit, who transforms the faithful through grace into Christ-likeness to make them fit for perfect communion with the Father (*ST* I-II.108.1).

The Holy Spirit is the capstone for Aquinas's theology both of law and of virtue in the *Prima Secundae*. The Spirit is the agent through which human beings participate fully in the eternal law and by whom they are enabled to live virtuous lives; to put it in other terms the Spirit is the agent through whom we are incorporated into Christ and conformed to Christ.[184]

Thomas uses the expression *gratia Spiritus Sancti* 158 times in his works.

---

[179] Weinandy, 'The Supremacy of Christ', 227.

[180] F.A. Murphy, 'Thomas' Commentaries on Philemon, 1 and 2 Thessalonians and Philippians' in Weinandy, Keating and Yocum, eds., *Aquinas on Scripture* 185; Aquinas, *ST* I-II.114-6; 62.1.

[181] Delhaye, 'La Loi Nouvelle', 267; P. Rodriguez, 'Spontanéité et caractère légal de la loi nouvelle' in Elders and Hedwig, eds., *Lex et libertas* 254.

[182] U. Kühn, 'Nova lex. Die Eigenart der christlichen Ethik nach Thomas von Aquin' in Elders and Hedwig, eds., *Lex et Libertas* 243-47.

[183] Aquinas, *In Rom.* VIII, 2, lect.1, n.602-605 ; Torrell, *Aquinas Vol. II*, 205-6 ; Kerr, *After Aquinas*, 6; Long, *Divine Economy*, endnote 106 to chapter 12; Delhaye, 'La Loi Nouvelle', 268.

[184] Aquinas, *De potentia* q.10 a.4; *ScG* IV, 21, n.3580; Kerr, *After Aquinas*, 132, 112, 6; Kühn, 'Nova lex', 245; Torrell, *Aquinas Vol. II*, 145, 361, 372.

However, Aquinas's formulation is pregnant with ambiguity[185] and consequently in need of qualification, clarification and elaboration. Matters are further complicated by, as McGrath has pointed out, the fact that Aquinas's account of grace altered significantly as his thought developed.[186]

In following Augustine's location of the Spirit as the bond of love and as gift, Aquinas is subject to the Western tendency to depersonalise the Spirit.[187] This tendency becomes especially problematic if Aquinas's references to grace are treated as supplanting the Holy Spirit rather than being regarded as the action of the Holy Spirit, and the consequences dire if grace is then reified and rendered captive to human logic. However, this need not be the case. Aquinas teaches that God is pure act (*ST* I.3.2; 9.1; 12.1; 14.2; 25.1; 54.1; Supp.92.1), which means, amongst other things, that God expresses Godself fully in God's actions. When Aquinas links grace with the Holy Spirit, he ought therefore to be understood as placing grace in the category of action, of dynamic, rather than in the category of things.[188] The distinction which Aquinas draws between uncreated grace and created grace, which can appear to be one of the prime examples of reification, is in fact drawn by Aquinas precisely because he thinks of grace as act. The Holy Spirit is uncreated Grace, in the same way that the Spirit is uncreated Love. What the Spirit works in us by His indwelling presence is created Grace (*ST* I-II.110.2 ad.2, ad.3) and created Love (*ST* II-II.24.3), because it brings about a real change in us.[189]

The grace of the Holy Spirit has two effects in the life of the believer. First, it operates to unite us to Christ. Second, it co-operates with our will to conform us through obedience to Christ. Aquinas, however, does not separate these two effects but insists on their inherent unity. It is through Christ that we are adopted as the sons of God but this adoption necessarily entails a conformity to the image of the Son of God, which is imperfect in this life, and perfect in glory (*ST* III.45.4; 3.4. ad.3; *De Regno* II.3 (=I.14) [109]).[190] This adoption, Aquinas describes in trinitarian terms: 'adoption, though common to the whole Trinity, is appropriated to the Father as its author; to the Son, as its exemplar; to the Holy Ghost, as imprinting on us the likeness of this exemplar.' (*ST* III.23.3

---

[185] It could mean either 'the grace that is the Holy Spirit or the grace given by the Holy Spirit': Torrell, *Aquinas: Vol. II*, 155.

[186] A.E. McGrath, *Iustitia Dei: A History of the Christian Doctrine of Justification* 2nd edn. (Cambridge: CUP, 1998) 103-109.

[187] Colwell, *Promise and Presence*, 8-9, 21. Emery argues that this is not Aquinas's primary model for the Spirit: *Trinity in Aquinas* 102. See also Torrell, *Aquinas Vol. II*, 184-88.

[188] Colwell, *Promise and Presence*, 29, 171; B.D. Marshall, 'Action and Person: Do Palamas and Aquinas Agree About the Spirit?', *St Vladimir's Theological Quarterly* 39 (1995) 388.

[189] Torrell, *Aquinas Vol. II*, 177-81.

[190] Torrell, *Aquinas Vol. II*, chapter 6; Marshall, 'Do Palamas and Aquinas Agree About The Spirit?', 398.

ad.3).

For the purposes of the present thesis, it is not necessary to examine closely the operating grace of the Holy Spirit which unites us to Christ. However, where Moltmann's heavy emphasis on the immanence of the Spirit throughout creation seems to leave little space for Pentecost, Aquinas is careful to distinguish between the ways in which God is present to God's creation in the natural world, by grace through the indwelling of the Spirit, and in the fullness of glory.[191]

What needs to be explored in more detail, however, is Aquinas's understanding of the relationship between grace, obedience, virtues and deification. The natural law was beset by the problems of human sinfulness affecting our ability to discern it and to obey it. The Old Law dealt with the problem of discernment through its explicit declaration of its moral precepts. However, the problem of obedience remained unresolved. The New Law transcends the Old Law in that its moral precepts are given internally as is the strength to obey. These gifts are the grace of the Holy Spirit, who is associated so intimately with the New Law that Aquinas can say that the Law of the Gospel is 'principally the grace of the Holy Spirit, which is given to believers in Christ.' (*ST* I-II.106.1), which sanctifies us through faith and charity and, on Aquinas's view, through the sacraments of the Church.[192] By these means, we are conformed to Christ.[193]

Just as Christ was circumcised in order to fulfil the requirements of the Jewish law, so His followers are to fulfil 'those things which are of obligation in our own time' (*ST* III.37.1 ad.2). Christ's obedience is the pattern for Christian obedience.[194] '[Christian] obedience is ultimately the conforming of one's human will to the will of God, who is love.'[195] This conformity of will takes place through the indwelling of the Spirit.

Thus 'Christ's followers, those who obey him, do so ultimately not because of their own goodness, but because of the grace of God.'[196] They are empowered to obey Him through the Holy Spirit, who gives not only interior knowledge of God's laws, but also 'inclines the will to act as well' (*In Heb.* 8.6-10b n.404; *ScG* IV.22 n.3588).

The relationship between the Holy Spirit and grace is so close that the Spirit

---

[191] Aquinas, *ST* I.8.3 ad.4; I.43.3; *ScG* IV.21 n.3575; *In Ioan* XV, 26, lect. 7, n.2061; Torrell, *Aquinas Vol. II*, 61, 71, 92-94, 164-65, 177, 193.

[192] Levering, *Christ's Fulfillment*, 93; Delhaye, 'La Loi Nouvelle', 270-71.

[193] Aquinas, *In Ioan.* 3, lect. 1

[194] Aquinas, *In Ioan.* 15, lect.2, [2003]; M.J. Dodds, 'The Teaching of Thomas Aquinas on the Mysteries of the Life of Christ' in Weinandy, Keating and Yocum, eds., *Aquinas on Doctrine* 108-9.

[195] Levering, *Scripture and Metaphysics*, 135; Torrell, *Aquinas Vol. II*, 171, 181-83.

[196] Levering, 'Reading John with St Thomas Aquinas' in Weinandy, Keating and Yocum, eds., *Aquinas on Scripture* 109; Torrell, *Aquinas Vol. II*, 215.

can be identified with the gift of sanctifying grace.[197] When this is given full weight, then grace ceases to be mechanistic and causal, and becomes instead a question of the personal agency of the Spirit. As Ulrich Kühn has demonstrated, Aquinas's realisation that the 'New Law' *is* the grace of the Holy Spirit goes beyond the Augustinian model, whilst at the same time being thoroughly Pauline in inspiration.[198]

For Aquinas, there is a fundamental difference between the Old Law and the New Law. The Old Law was exterior, the New Law is interior. Christians are to take Jesus' words to heart, not merely to assent to them intellectually.[199] They are enabled to do this by the indwelling of the Spirit.[200] As Keating explains Aquinas's teaching on this point: 'the indwelling of God [in his saints] as in a temple causes us to act in faith and love, enabling us to know and love God *because* he dwells within us.'[201]

> The New Law ... is not a set of laws governing external behaviour but instead an internal prompting to God directly. ... In fact, the New Law enables believers to achieve the highest end: union with God. It is of the nature of the New Law, understood as grace, to justify, says Aquinas, it makes possible the salvation of those who possess it. (*ST* I-II.106.2, s.c. and resp.)[202]

The essence of the New Law is this 'new relatedness to God, the fruit of which is an ease and joy in doing what is good.'[203]

This understanding of the New Law is not antinomian, for the moral precepts of the Old Law remain valid. 'The moral precepts necessarily retained their force under the New Law, because they are of themselves essential to virtue' (*ST* I-II.108.3 ad.3). Christians fulfil the moral precepts of the Old Law, which remain binding upon them, through the power of the Holy Spirit. However, the written precepts attached to the New Law are secondary to the grace of the Spirit; they are ordered to the instruction of the faithful as to the 'use of this grace' (*ST* I-II.106.1 ad.1).[204] 'Rather than informing a life through a multitude of specific outward observances, the New Law is a way of life marked by the indwelling of grace given varied expression. Just so Thomas

---

[197] Aquinas, *ST* I.43.3; A.N. Williams, 'Deification', 236.

[198] Kühn, 'Nova lex', 244.

[199] Aquinas, *ST* III.42.4 ; Levering, *Christ's Fulfillment*, 48.

[200] Aquinas, *In 1 Cor.* 3.16-23 n.173; *The Sermon-Conferences of St Thomas Aquinas on the Apostles' Creed* (Notre Dame: University of Notre Dame, 1998) 119.

[201] D.A. Keating, '1 and 2 Cor.: The Sacraments and their Ministers' in Weinandy, Keating and Yocum, eds., *Aquinas on Scripture* 140.

[202] Hall, *Narrative*, 69.

[203] Hall, *Narrative*, 72.

[204] Hall, *Narrative*, 70; Rodriguez, 'Spontanéité de la loi nouvelle', 256-59, 264; Delhaye, 'La Loi Nouvelle', 271-73; H. McCabe, *Law, Love & Language* (Sheed and Ward, 1968; London: Continuum, 2003) 22 ; Torrell, *Aquinas Vol. II*, 203.

takes the Sermon on the Mount as his representation of the Christian life, in which the life of grace is described and exalted in forms requiring interpretation and amplification.'[205]

The above reading has neatly glossed over the question which split the Western Church at the Reformation of whether justification and sanctification can be divided or are indistinguishable. As a Catholic interpreter of Aquinas, Levering argues that 'Aquinas's account of salvation is built around the idea that Christians, as members of the Mystical Body of Christ, share in the redemptive acts of their Head (Christ).'[206] By this he means, however, not a participation in atonement in Milbank's terms[207] but rather that all Christians share in the merits and benefits of Christ's redemptive acts because of our union with Him. 'Christ is Saviour not only because he bears our sin, but ultimately because he purifies our hearts and draws us, by his Spirit, into the communion of the relational three-Personed God.'[208] There are obviously both Catholic and Protestant accounts which can be given of how this is so, but it is beyond the scope of the present study to trace those accounts or to seek to attribute one of them to Aquinas.[209]

Aquinas the Virtue Ethicist

If the *Secunda-Secundae* of the *Summa Theologiae* is anything to go by, Aquinas is an obvious candidate for identification as a virtue ethicist. Although he is aware of its importance, Levering has not yet had occasion to provide a treatment of Aquinas's understanding of the life of virtue.[210] What he does argue, however, is that Christians participate in Christ's threefold fulfillment of the Torah and Temple through the virtues and the sacraments.[211]

Similarly, in his study of Aquinas's commentary on the Psalms, Ryan concludes that Aquinas's method was calculated to produce 'wise, Christ-like students.'[212] The reason for this is that is being Christ-like is key to Aquinas's

---

[205] Hall, *Narrative*, 73; Aquinas *ST* I-II.108.1 ad.1.

[206] Levering, *Christ's Fulfillment*, 28.

[207] Milbank, *Word Made Strange*, 161; 'The Second Difference: For a Trinitarianism Without Reserve', *Modern Theology* 2 (1986) 226, 232; *Being Reconciled* 41,154. For a critique of Milbank on this point (and others), see S. Hewitt-Horsman, 'The Kingdom in Milbank: A Critique', *Theology* (2003) 259-66.

[208] Levering, *Scripture and Metaphysics*, 164.

[209] On any fair view, however, grace is primary in Aquinas' account: see Keating, 'Justification, Sanctification and Divinization in Thomas Aquinas' in Weinandy, Keating and Yocum, eds., *Aquinas on Doctrine* 142. Christians are saved by Christ's death and resurrection, and are enabled to believe in Him and to follow Him through the grace of the Holy Spirit.

[210] Levering, *Christ's Fulfillment*, 108-9, 144.

[211] Levering, *Christ's Fulfillment*, 118.

[212] Ryan, *Thomas Aquinas as Reader of the Psalms*, 9, 144.

doctrine of sanctification and wisdom is the means by which the New Law is translated into action. As Aquinas puts it in *Hic est liber*, 'the precepts of wisdom should concern nothing other than acts of virtue.'[213]

Maria Carl stresses that, in Aquinas's thought, 'while the natural law is ontologically prior to virtue in order of generation as cause to effect, virtue is teleologically prior to law as final cause to that which for the sake of the final cause.'[214] Far from being incompatible, the standards of prudence and the natural law prove to be interdependent.'[215] Human beings grow in virtue as they reflect upon the natural goods which God has given human beings to pursue.[216]

For Aquinas, 'love is the form, mover, and root of the virtues.' (*De caritate*, 3). Unlike the natural virtues, 'the object of charity is not the common good, but the highest good.' (*De caritate*, 5 ad.4). It is to charity that the other virtues are ordered. It is also the case that it is to charity that the Mosaic law is ordered. Through fulfilling of the divine law through charity, followers of Christ also fulfil and surpass the demands of the Mosaic law and of the natural law.[217] Love for God entails worship of God and obedience to God. These are the ways in which love for God is manifested. Yeago reads Luther as offering an Augustinian understanding of the commandments of God, in which

> we cannot rightly understand what is called for by any commandment of God except in terms of the first commandment. Thus it is in a certain sense a misunderstanding of the divine commands to say that they demand particular behaviours; it is more accurate to say that they *demand* a heart that fears, loves, and trusts God, and that they *offer* such a heart the concrete form of life appropriate to it.[218]

Such a sentiment is entirely in tune with the reading of Aquinas being advanced here (see *ScG* III.11-16).

'For Thomas, there is no ability to love God and no movement of the moral agent towards this promised face-to-face vision of God except by the continual inspiration of the Holy Spirit.' (*ST* I-II.68.2).[219] 'Human beings become what they are meant to be only in union with God; and the specifically human activities, the practice of the virtues, are a form of participation in divine

---

[213] Aquinas, *Hic est liber mandatorum Dei* (Turin: Marietti, 1954) 1.438; Ryan, *Thomas Aquinas as Reader of the Psalms*, 54-6.

[214] M. Carl, 'Law, Virtue, and Happiness in Aquinas's Moral Theory', *The Thomist* 61 (1997) 442; Hall, *Narrative*, 11; S. Pinckaers, 'Liberté et Préceptes dans la Morale de Saint Thomas' in Elders and Hedwig, eds., *Lex et libertas* 15, 18-19, 21-24.

[215] Hall, *Narrative*, 22.

[216] Hall, *Narrative*, 20.

[217] Aquinas, *ST* I-II.93.6 ad.1; Levering, *Christ's Fulfillment*, 144.

[218] D.S. Yeago, 'Martin Luther on Grace, Law and Moral Life: Prolegomena to an Ecumenical Discussion of *Veritatis Splendor*', *The Thomist* 62 (1998) 181.

[219] Kerr, *After Aquinas*, 133.

beatitude in this life.'[220] It is only because by the grace of the Holy Spirit they are ordered to the eternal good of knowing and loving God, that the justified are able to order their love of lesser goods, by disciplining themselves and if necessary denying themselves (*ST* I-II.65.3 ad.2 and 3).[221]

Although the *ST* refers expressly to the indwelling of the Spirit only twice, Daniel Keating and Anna Williams argue that the idea is in fact central to Aquinas's theology. For Williams, what Aquinas means by the term 'infusion' is nothing other than a reference to the indwelling of the Holy Spirit.[222] In Keating's view, for Aquinas, true growth in virtue is only possible by 'co-operating grace', which enables us to make progress with God's help (*ST* I-II.111.2; II-II.83.15 ad.1). 'When describing the relation of grace to infused virtue, Thomas says that "the light of grace ... is a participation in the divine nature" (*ST* I-II.110.3). And he emphasizes that the gift of grace is nothing short of a genuine participation in God himself'.[223] This is made plain in his biblical commentaries, which offer 'a rich account of the Christian as a temple of the living God and of the indwelling of the Spirit producing in us all the fruits of faith and love.'[224] In *In 1 Thes.*, cap.1, lect. 1, Thomas argues that good deeds are the result of free will but also and at the same time the result of grace.[225] 'There can be no doubt, then, that for Thomas, the Spirit is the direct and personal source of all grace within us, and that he remains the personal source of the working of the gifts of grace in our ongoing sanctification.'[226]

However, 'the New Law itself is a figure of future glory' (*ST* I.1.10). Our worship and obedience, though superior to that under the Old Covenant, are still incomplete. In the movement towards the completion of salvation, both the Old Law and the New Law will be swept up into the heavenly liturgy which they foreshadow.[227] Glorification is the completion of grace, 'whereby man will not merely be able to persevere but will be unable to sin.' (*ST* I-II.109.10 ad.3).

Aquinas on Glorification

Ryan understands Aquinas's account of God's works under a fourfold division of creation, governance, reparation, and glorification.[228] In his commentary on the Psalms, he divides them into three groups of fifty concerned with the

---

[220] Kerr, *After Aquinas*, 158.

[221] Hall, *Narrative*, 80; Levering, *Christ's Fulfillment*, 98. 100; Aquinas, *In Rom.* V, 2-5, lect. 1, n.388.

[222] A.N. Williams, *The Ground of Union: Deification in Aquinas and Palamas* (New York: OUP, 1999) 72-89.

[223] Keating, 'Justification, Sanctification and Divinization', 154.

[224] Keating, '1 and 2 Cor.', 141; 'Justification, Sanctification and Divinization' 148-51.

[225] Murphy, 'Philemon, 1 and 2 Thessalonians and Philippians', 179-81.

[226] Keating, 'Justification, Sanctification and Divinization', 151.

[227] Levering, *Christ's Fulfillment*, 127.

[228] Ryan, *Thomas Aquinas as Reader of the Psalms*, 14.

human journey to salvation: penitence, justice and eternal glory.[229] It is almost impossible to overstress the importance of the final category, that of glorification, for understanding the rest of Aquinas's thought.

Kerr argues that beatitude is the key to Aquinas's whole theological project (*ST* I-II.2.7; III. prologue), and that, correspondingly, the key to Aquinas's ethics is not law or reason, but the happiness of beatitude which may be anticipated, though not fully possessed, in the here and now.[230] He therefore argues that:

> Thomas's moral theology ... is founded not on God's law (biblically revealed or built into creaturely nature) but focused on God's promise of perfect beatitude (revealed by Christ but best understood as the divinely given fulfilment of an Aristotelian conception of human flourishing).[231]

However, for Aquinas, beatitude is understood in terms of deification. In the *Compendium Theologiae*, Aquinas repeats and makes his own the Patristic maxim: 'The Son of God became man in order to make men gods and sons of God.' (*Comp. Theol.* I.214).[232] Anna Williams has championed the reading of Aquinas as a theologian of deification. She identifies *ST* I-II.112.1 as the clearest example in the *ST* of Aquinas taking deification for granted.[233] That article occurs in the treatise of grace, that is to say, in the second half of the treatise on law!

Far from being anchored to that which was given once for all in creation so as to give his ethics and philosophy a static and rationalist character, Aquinas is constantly looking forward to the beatific vision. '[B]eatitude is the reward of virtue.' (*De Regno* I.9 [68]). His thought therefore has an ecstatic dynamic running through it. As one who turned his back on many earthly pleasures, Aquinas is clear not only that the purpose of human life is union with God, but also that this fulfilment is to be found not on earth but in another life.[234] This union with God 'is achieved through the sending of the Son and the Spirit.'[235]

This teaching is clearly expressed in his commentary on Titus:

> In the state of ruination (*perditionis*), man needed two things, which he attended through Christ, namely participation in the divine nature, and the laying aside of

---

[229] Ryan, *Thomas Aquinas as Reader of the Psalms*, 20-21.
[230] Kerr, *After Aquinas*, 130; 'Doctrine of God and Theological Ethics according to Thomas Aquinas', 83; Torrell, *Aquinas Vol. II*, 83, 333; Aquinas, *Comp. Theol.* II.9.
[231] Kerr, *After Aquinas*, 114.
[232] Torrell, *Aquinas Vol. II*, 373.
[233] A.N. Williams, 'Deification in the *Summa Theologiae*', 223. *ST* III.1.2 sc would be another candidate.
[234] Yocum, 'Aquinas' Literal Exposition on Job', 31.
[235] Emery, 'The Doctrine of the Trinity', 61; T.G. Weinandy, 'The Marvel of the Incarnation' in Weinandy, Keating and Yocum, eds., *Aquinas on Doctrine* 83.

oldness (*vestustatis*). ... Participation as a son of God is so generated that man [himself] is not destroyed. ... Through Christ man also laid aside the oldness of sin, being renewed for the making whole of nature, and this is called "renovation". (*In Tit.*, cap.3, lect. 1).

Renovation, for Aquinas, is understood in trinitarian terms, as the work of the Father, in the Holy Spirit, through Christ.[236] As Anna Williams notes, for Aquinas, human sanctification and glorification are grounded in the intratrinitarian processions.[237] 'Those who enjoy the beatific vision do so as adopted sons in the Son',[238] an adoption which is secured by the Spirit.[239] '[S]piritual generation means conformity to the Son ... [which] comes about ... by our having his Spirit.'[240] 'By the Father's sending of Son and Spirit, in their public missions in saving history at the Incarnation and Pentecost and then in their invisible missions in our souls, we are to be conjoined to the divine being itself.'[241] This does not constitute the dissolution of our human nature, but rather its perfection and fulfilment.[242] 'By grace, ... the creature does not *become* the Creator but rather becomes a "new creation", enabled to participate in the divine liturgy.'[243] Against the God of Moltmann, whose being is in His becoming; Aquinas's God is in relation with God's creatures, but the effect of God's relationship with them is not that God changes, but that they do.[244] As Levering puts it, 'By knowing and loving the one God *as three Persons* – Father, Son, and Holy Spirit – human beings are fully taken up into the dynamism that is grace and glory, the freely-given perfection of the *imago dei*.'[245]

The New Testament completes and perfects the Old because Christ mediates a better covenant by which 'we are made partakers of the divine nature'. (*In Heb.* 8.6-10b [392]). 'For Thomas, the ultimate beatitude for humans consists

---

[236] Saward, 'The Grace of Christ', 218.

[237] A.N. Williams, *The Ground of Union*, 59; Levering, 'Reading John', 118.

[238] Levering, *Christ's Fulfillment*, 139; Aquinas, *ST* III.23.1; II-II.121.1 ad.3; *III Sent.* d.19 q.1 a.4 sol.1; *In Ioan.* 1460, 2187.

[239] Aquinas, *Sermon-Conferences on the Apostles' Creed*, 119; Emery, *Trinity in Aquinas*, 213, 227, 232, 289.

[240] Levering, 'Reading John', 106; Aquinas, *ScG* IV ch.24; *De potentia* q.10 a.4; In *Ioan.* 442, 1957.

[241] Nichols, *Discovering Aquinas*, 74.

[242] Nichols, *Discovering Aquinas*, 94; Cavanaugh, 'A Joint Declaration?', 273. Kerr, *After Aquinas*, 125 traces in Aquinas' thought three states in which human beings are made in the image of God: naturally, in the conformity of grace, and in the fullness of glory.

[243] Levering, *Christ's Fulfillment*, 138. Cavanaugh contends that it is the doctrine of divine simplicity which is the lynchpin of the distinction between the finite and the infinite: 'A Joint Declaration?', 266.

[244] Geisler, *Thomas Aquinas*, 116.

[245] Levering, *Scripture and Metaphysics*, 44; Torrell, *Aquinas Vol. II*, 371.

in the promise of 1 John 3:2 that we shall see God "just as He is".[246] That is the end towards which our salvation tends. But to know God fully is to love God fully and to love God is to worship and to obey God. Therefore, the beatific vision in the state of glory 'does not negate either the Old or the New Covenant. Instead, both are fulfilled by the perfect holiness and perfect worship enjoyed by the glorified human beings and angels in harmony with the renewed cosmos.'[247]

For Aquinas, Christ's kingship is founded on His suffering and attains its fullness in the *eschaton* when, 'Christ, having passed just judgment upon all things, establishes for eternity the heavenly community of beatitude.'[248] This kingdom is not like an earthly kingdom 'in which people are united by rules, common interests, force, and tolerance. Rather, Christ's kingdom is the communion of the blessed with God (and with each other in God) through the *inner* bond of charity ... Christ the king reigns in us, interiorly and intimately, through the power of self-giving charity.'[249] Far from Christ's kingship resembling earthly dominion, it is consummated in a communication of the divine beatitude (*ST* III.58.4.2). Aquinas's view on Moltmann's favourite passage, 1 Corinthians 15:24ff., is that what is signified by Jesus' delivery up of the kingdom to God and the Father is the moment when Jesus has led the faithful to the enjoyment of God in Godself (*ST* I.108.7 ad.1). That is what the saints have to look forward to in heaven.

Aquinas's account of the missions of the Son and the Spirit could have the significant merit of making continuing sense of the missions of the Son and the Spirit in the *eschaton*. Bailleux argues that Aquinas seems to have moved from a stress on our deiformity as being simply the effect of the Divine Nature, without regard to the distinction of the Persons (*III Sent.*, d.4, 1, 2, q1a) to favour speaking of our conformity to the likeness of the Son (*ST* III.23.1 ad.2; *In Rom.* 8.28-30), although there remains a tension here in his thought.[250] Even in the state of glory, the Incarnate Son remains the one mediator between God and humankind (*ST* III.26). Even in the state of glory, human beings are conformed to the likeness of the Son by the indwelling of the Spirit.

It may be questionable whether Anna Williams is correct to equate Aquinas's thinking on deification with that of Gregory Palamas,[251] but she is

---

[246] Kerr, *After Aquinas*, 78.

[247] Levering, *Christ's Fulfillment*, 140.

[248] Levering, *Christ's Fulfillment*, 69-70; Aquinas *ST* III.59.4.

[249] Levering, *Christ's Fulfillment*, 72.

[250] Bailleux, 'Le cycle des missions trinitaires', 187-88. The idea of being made like Christ through the Spirit is to be found in Aquinas's sermons on the Apostles' Creed, which were delivered in 1273, the year before his death: *The Sermon-Conferences on the Apostles' Creed* 119.

[251] See N. V. Harrison's review, 'The Ground of Union', *St Vladimir's Theological Quarterly* 45 (2001) 418-21; J.T. Billings, 'John Calvin: United to God through Christ' in M.J. Christensen and J. Wittung, eds., *Partakers of the Divine Nature: The History*

right to identify the importance of the theme in Aquinas's theology.[252] In line with Williams' argument, Kerr's view is that although Aquinas rarely uses the word 'deification', 'he nevertheless had a rich conception of the transforming effect of divine grace on the individual believer which clearly amounts to the traditional patristic doctrine of deification.'[253] Glorification is, for Aquinas, the culmination of salvation. Our destination is to share in the beatific vision which is for Aquinas so important in his account of Christ's earthly communion with His Father.

The Place of Human Law after the Drama of Salvation

It has been argued above that Aquinas's comments on human law are incidental to his purpose and direction in the treatise on Law. In consequence, they are difficult to systematise, and this difficulty is compounded when those comments are put alongside his views expressed elsewhere in the *ST* and in his other writings. What is clear, however, is that his assessment of the proper role of human law looks very different if the work of Christ and of the Holy Spirit are excised from or overlooked in his thought.

Joan Lockwood O'Donovan argues that in Aquinas's thought the Aristotelian directive and administrative paradigm of political authority is held in tension with Pauline juridical paradigm.[254] After Aquinas, the Aristotelian conception came to dominate, with a corresponding increase in confidence in 'a "natural" political society with a solid and independent structure of its own, a society for which much more in the way of social virtue could be claimed' than on an Augustinian view.[255]

There is, therefore, a tension in Aquinas's thought between two different assessments of the purpose and possibilities of human law. Like Lockwood O'Donovan, Nichols argues that Aquinas blends two ideas regarding the purpose of government: the Aristotelian idea that human social needs require government to promote certain forms of human excellence, and the Augustinian idea that the corruption of original sin renders government necessary to control vice.[256] Aquinas distinguishes between 'two "dignities" – *sacerdotium* ("priesthood") and *regnum* or *imperium* ("kingdom" or "empire")', and by doing so is able to grant civil power a relative autonomy, subject to the constraints of natural and, in the case of Christian rulers, divine law, to

---

and Development of Deification in the Christian Traditions (Grand Rapids: Baker Books, 2008). Williams is supported, however, by B.D. Marshall, see 'Do Palamas and Aquinas Agree About the Spirit?', 383-94.

[252] A.N. Williams, *The Ground of Union*, 159-160.

[253] Kerr, *After Aquinas*, 149; Torrell, *Aquinas Vol. II*, 126-28.

[254] Lockwood O'Donovan, *BOI*, 227-228.

[255] O'Donovan, *DON*, 207.

[256] Nichols, *Discovering Aquinas*, 99.

'establish those objective conditions, principally matters of justice, that allow citizens to lead the good life.'[257]

Aristotelian Optimism

On the one hand, the Aristotelian influences lead Aquinas to define Law in expansive terms. Human law is swept up in a broader account of rational ordering. Aquinas defines justice as having the object of directing human beings in their relations with one another (*ST* II-II.57.1). He sees 'justice [as] the dynamic foundation of all community and friendship, including communion and friendship with God, who is infinite Goodness.'[258] This stands in stark contrast with the approach of Augustine, for whom the very fact that justice is properly predicated of our relationship to God means that it cannot be used to describe relationships which are disordered because of a rejection of God.[259] Aquinas agrees with Augustine that perfect justice is a virtue properly attributed only to those who are Christians, and that 'faith in Christ' is 'the source and cause of justice' (*ST* II-II.104.6). However, for Aquinas, there is also a proper analogical sense in which justice can be used to describe the human virtue of treating others rightly (*ST* I-II.113.1).[260]

'[P]ublic authority is committed to rulers in order that they may safeguard justice.' (*ST* II-II.66.8). Human rulers are given authority by God to execute legal justice. Following Aristotle, Aquinas defines legal justice as directing a man's acts 'by regulating them in their relation to the common good of society' (*ST* I-II.113.1; II-II.58.5; 58.6). It is central to Aquinas's definition of law that it must order things 'to the common good' (*ordinem ad bonum commune*)[261]. Alternative formulations suggest that it must 'conduce to the common welfare (*ut communi saluti proficiat*)',[262] or be established 'for the commonweal (*pro communi utilitate*)'.[263] The common good is not a declaration of collectivist sentiments in opposition to liberal individualism, though Aquinas swallows a dose of corporatism from Aristotle; for Aquinas, the primary opposition is between government for the common good or government for the private good of the ruler (*ST* II-II.42.2 ad.3; *II Sent.* d.44 q.1 a.3; *In Heb.* 1.4 ad v.8).[264] The former is right and just kingship; the latter mere tyranny (*De Regno* I.1 [10-11];

---

[257] Nichols, *Discovering Aquinas*, 100; quoting Gilby, *Principality and Polity*, xxiii.
[258] Levering, *Christ's Fulfillment*, 112.
[259] O'Donovan, *BOI*, 60-61.
[260] Gilby, *Principality and Polity*, 123; *Between Community and Society*, 208-11.
[261] Aquinas, *ST* I.105.4; I-II.90.3.; 91.5; 95.4; 96.1.; 100.2. obj.3; 100.8.; 100.11 ad.3; 105.1 ad.5; II-II.58.7; 66.8 ad.3; Torrell, *Aquinas Vol. II*, 287-88.
[262] Aquinas, *ST* I-II.98.1. obj.2; 105.1 obj.3.
[263] Aquinas, *ST* I-II.98.4 obj.1.
[264] J. Porter, 'The Common Good in Thomas Aquinas' in P.D. Miller and D.P. McCann, eds., *In Search of the Common Good* 100, 107.

VIII Ethics lect. 10).[265] It is beyond the scope of the present thesis to conduct an exhaustive enquiry into what Aquinas meant by the term 'the common good'.[266] Two salient observations may, however, be made. First, that in his thought '[t]he *multitudo ordinata* was peopled with persons striving for their proper ends rather than with individuals set in their proper places.'[267] Second, that the term *bonum publicum* used in his commentary on Romans 13 is perhaps his best name for the solicitude for interpersonal justice and peace which is the rightful concern of government.[268]

However, Aquinas's classification of the various types of justice is, as Finnis points out, unstable.[269] The term 'legal justice' is properly applied to actions by people ordered to the common good and in accordance with human and or divine laws (*ST* II-II.79.1; 79.3). It also seems to include actions of rulers in making wise laws and in enforcing such laws (*ST* II-II.57.2 ad.2; 60.1 ad.4). The virtue proper to the just ruler is to make just laws submission to which is just in that it is ordered to the common good. It is in this latter sense that the term 'legal justice' will be used in the following discussion.

Legal justice is not a simple matter of reading off the rules of natural law and of divine law. 'The obligation of observing justice is ... perpetual. But the determination of those things that are just, according to human or Divine institution, must needs be different, according to the different states of mankind.' (*ST* I-II.104.4 ad.1). The maintenance of legal justice is therefore a matter of kingly wisdom (*ST* II-II.50.1 obj.1), a virtue which involves the application of 'practical wisdom' to discern what is most conducive to the public good (ad.1; 57.1 ad.2).[270] The application of legal justice therefore requires rulers to perform the tasks O'Donovan calls judgment. Aquinas says that 'the common good of a political community can be rightly disposed only if its citizens, at least those to whom its ruling belongs, are virtuous. But it suffices as regards the good of the community that other citizens be virtuous enough to obey the commands of the law.' (*ST* I-II.92.1 ad.3). The Platonic ideal of the Philosopher-King is merged here into the biblical vision of Solomon the Wise.

The relationship between human laws, on the one hand, and natural and divine laws on the other, is illuminated by Aquinas's commentary on Romans 13. For Aquinas, human authority is derivative from God's authority (*In Rom.*

---

[265] Gilby, *Principality and Polity*, 129-30, 288, 294.

[266] As to which, see the discussions in Gilby, *Principality and Polity*, 239, 242-264; *Between Community and Society* 211-12; Finnis, *Aquinas*, 111-17; 222-39, 313; Porter 'The Common Good in Thomas Aquinas'; Aquinas *ST* I-II.21.4 ad.3; II-II.65.1.

[267] Gilby, *Principality and Polity*, 277.

[268] Finnis, *Aquinas*, 226-27; *De Regno* I.2 [20] identifies the fruit of good government as peace, justice and prosperity.

[269] Finnis, *Aquinas*, 215-17.

[270] Aquinas, *ST* I-II.91.1; 92.1; Finnis, *Aquinas*, 255-58.

cap.13 lect.1). As such, a human king can no more overrule God's commands than can a proconsul an emperor's. In consequence, human laws cannot overrule either natural law nor divine law (*ST* I-II.95.2; 96.4; II-II.57.2 ad.2; 60.5 ad.1; *II Sent.* d.44 q.2 a.2). Well-framed human laws are therefore shaped by natural law and divine law. Human laws which are not so shaped are defective and deformed and have no authority.[271] They have no authority because such authority as human laws properly have is derivative from God's authority. In such circumstances, obedience to them becomes a matter of submission either for conscience's sake or for prudential reasons. Thus, in *ST* II-II.104.6, Aquinas writes '... faith in Christ confirms rather than takes away the order of justice. But the order of justice requires that subjects obey their superiors, since stability in human affairs could not otherwise be maintained.' He follows this, however, by adding, in ad.3: 'Human beings are obliged to obey secular rulers insofar as the order of justice requires. And so if secular rulers ... command unjust things, subjects are not obliged to obey them, except, perhaps incidentally, in order to avoid scandal or danger.' (see also *ST* I-II.96.4; II-II.69.4).

To this account of authority is coupled Aquinas's general metaphysics of participation. Like authority, and being, human justice is a participation in God's justice (*ST* I.105.6 ad.2). Legal justice is that limited participation in divine justice which results from the application of practical wisdom and reflection on the natural and divine law, with the end of the common good of the political community in mind.

Another way of making the same point is to say that for Aquinas, all good is necessarily a participation in God, who defines and encompasses all that is good; while all evil is a privation,[272] a falling short. It follows, therefore, that things can only be defined by reference to their end, to their perfection. Human law, when it fulfils its true purpose, is human government participating in God's governance of the world. Thus Aquinas would, like O'Donovan, locate human government in the doctrine of providence.

As justice is the foundation of a true kingdom, earthly kingdoms all fall short of what they are meant to be insofar as they fail to exhibit legal justice.[273] The Kingdom of God therefore defines, for Aquinas, what earthly kingdoms are meant to be, rather than a description of earthly kingdoms pre-determining the nature of the Kingdom of God.

Aquinas's emphasis on the common good, and his obvious drawing from Aristotle make him susceptible of being read as being an enthusiast about the

---

[271] R. McInerny, 'The Basis and Purpose of Positive Law' in Elders and Hedwig, eds., *Lex et libertas* 142.

[272] Aquinas, *ST* I.19.9; I.103.7 ad.1; I-II.21.1; II-II.118.5; Levering, *Scripture and Metaphysics*, 107.

[273] '... it is of the essence of a nation that the mutual relations of citizens be ordered by just laws.' (*ST* I-II.105.2); Levering, 'Reading John with St. Thomas Aquinas', 105.

possibilities for government. Aquinas places clear emphasis on the moral precepts contained in the Mosaic Law. Because he places human law in the same category as the Mosaic Law and the natural law, he thinks of it in the same terms as being dominated by moral precepts. However, unlike the approach taken by Lord Devlin in *The Enforcement of Morals* where there are few barriers to legislating morality, for Aquinas, there are limits to what may properly be legislated because law is only concerned with enforcing those matters of morality which belong to justice, i.e. those which relate to right relations between persons (*ST* I-II.99.5 ad.1).

Subsequent theorists seized on Aquinas's emphasis on the common good as the *raison d'être* for political authority. The medieval Church asserted that it knew what was the common good, and sought to extend its jurisdiction and influence over vast areas of human life. The directive element in Aquinas's definition of law derives from his teleological focus. One might expect the same danger to emerge in any practical version of Moltmann's political theology.

Limitations on the Role of Human Law

On the other hand, Aquinas's understanding of salvation relegates human law to no more than the antechamber of God's purposes at best. Human law-making and law-enforcement is set within a broader, more ultimate framework. Human law is not responsible for ultimate judgment (*ST* II-II.67.2 ad.2; supp.88.3 ad.3; 89.1; 90.1); human law is not responsible for ultimate reconciliation; these belong to Christ. The work of human governments to maintain justice and peace serves the ultimate justice- and peace-making activity of Jesus: the supreme King to whom alone supreme honour is due (ST II-II.104.4). This means that Aquinas is not a Kantian retributivist, because earthly judgments do not have to extract the full penalty for sin (*ST* II-II.61.4; 64.2; 66.6 ad.2; 68.1; 85.1 ad.1; 108.3 ad.2).[274]

Nonetheless, human judgments are necessary because of the effects of the Fall on humans' ability to discern and obey the natural law. It is because of human beings' ability to misunderstand the natural law, that human law is necessary to make it 'efficacious on the political level.'[275] It is because human selfishness means that we fail to give to others what is due to them, that human rulers must direct us to the common good (*ST* I.105.4). In addition, 'the general principles of the natural law must be further articulated (and supplemented) according to the specific needs of individual communities.'[276] Thus human law is derived from natural law in two ways: one as conclusions from principles,

---

[274] Gilby, *Principality and Polity*, 184-85; Finnis, *Aquinas*, 210-15, 280-84.

[275] Hall, *Narrative*, 21.

[276] Hall, *Narrative*, 41.

the other as particulars from generalities (*ST* I-II.95.2).[277]

Like O'Donovan, Aquinas agrees that well-framed laws must tell the truth about the communities which they are to regulate (*ST* I-II.98.1 obj.3); 'laws should be possible both according to nature and according to the customs of the country' (*ST* I-II.96.2; 97.1; *V Ethics* lect.2) Precisely because 'human law is established for the collectivity of human beings, most of whom have imperfect virtue ... human law does not prohibit every kind of vice, from which the virtuous abstain. Rather, human law prohibits only the more serious kinds of vice, from which most persons can abstain, and especially those vices that inflict harm on others, without the prohibition of which human society could not be preserved.' (*ST* I-II.96.2; II-II.69.2 ad.1; 77.1 ad.1) This was true even of the Mosaic Law, which Aquinas comments permits divorce because of the Jews' hardness of heart (*ST* I-II.105.4 ad.8) and lending money at interest to foreigners because of 'the proneness of the Jews to avarice'! (*ST* I-II.105.3 ad.3).

Human law is derivative from the natural law in the sense that human law may not command what natural law forbids nor forbid what natural law commands (*ST* I-II.95.2). It also falls to human law to determine how to enforce principles of the natural law. However, human law may tolerate what natural law forbids (*ST* I-II.96.2) and indeed must do so (ad.3). Well-framed human laws must take into account the fact that they are designed to control the behaviour of those who do not have the indwelling power of the Spirit.

For Aquinas, human laws can only achieve limited good. The reasons for this are to do both with human limitations and with human sinfulness. The limitations on human knowledge have at least two effects on human law-enforcement. First, framing a law that will operate justly in all, as yet unforeseen, circumstances is a task beyond human capacity. The application of human laws therefore requires the exercise of that species of justice called *epieikeia* (*ST* II-II.120.1; 60.5 ad.2).[278] Second, the limitations on human knowledge make determining guilt and innocence a perilous and uncertain business (*ST* II-II.60.3-6; 67-71).

What can be achieved through human justice is also radically qualified by the persistence of human sinfulness. Attempting to prohibit all vices through human law would bring the law into contempt through the impossibility of adhering to it (*ST* I-II.96.2 ad.2). These two sets of limitations, arising from the state of human knowledge and the state of the human heart, combine to render law-making and government a matter of practical wisdom, in which 'Human laws leave some sins unpunished because of the conditions of imperfect human beings, regarding whom many benefits would be prevented if all sins were to be strictly prohibited, and punishments for the sins were to be applied.' (*ST* II-

---

[277] Finnis, *Aquinas*, 266.

[278] Gilby, *Principality and Polity*, 308-10; S. Theron, 'St Thomas Aquinas and Epieicheia' in Elders and Hedwig, eds., *Lex et libertas* 171-82; Finnis, *Aquinas*, 271-72.

II.78.1 ad.3).[279] '[I]t is enough for human law to prohibit things destructive of human society' (*ST* II-II.77.1 ad.1).

The foregoing qualifications raise an issue about whether it is accurate to say, as Levering does, that for Aquinas, 'Law is meant primarily to aid people in their quest to know and do the good, although certainly law also has the secondary role of restraining the wicked.'[280] The problem is that while the statement is accurate with regard to Aquinas's view of the natural law, the divine law, and the eternal law, Aquinas's category of law contains an odd one out: human law. Although Aquinas may have begun by drawing analogies from human law to natural law, divine law and eternal law,[281] where he ends up leaves human law looking strangely out of place. In the light of Aquinas's discussion, human law is the odd one out. It is not directly given by God. It is not directly ordered to the eternal good of loving God and loving one's neighbour (in God). Instead, it is directly ordered to the temporal tranquillity and only indirectly ordered to eternal goods.[282] Human law is powerless to effect true virtue. Unlike the natural law and the Mosaic law, human law is not directly fulfilled in Christ. It is not of eternal value in the same way. It is a temporal ordinance, ordered providentially by God, during the time of humanity's rebellion against him.

Aquinas's most significant departure from Aristotle is his denial that human rulers are competent to ensure the virtue of the communities which they govern.[283] Given the limits on their powers, all they can achieve is a form of justice and a protection of freedom in which true virtue may flourish.[284] For human law, the priorities are reversed, restraining the wicked is its primary function and promoting defined forms of the good only secondary.[285] As Aquinas says, in his commentary on 1 Timothy 'law is for the unjust, not the just.'[286]

Aquinas's clearest distinction between the role assigned to human law and the New Law which is the grace of the Holy Spirit comes in *ST* I-II.98.1, in the context of a discussion about the goodness of the Old Law, which stands between the two:

> ... it must be observed that the end of human law is different from the end of Divine law. For the end of human law is the temporal tranquillity of the state,

---

[279] Gilby, *Principality and Polity*, xxiv.

[280] Levering, *Christ's Fulfillment*, 20.

[281] McInerny, 'The Basis and Purpose of Positive Law', 137.

[282] Gilby, *Principality and Polity*, 182, 230.

[283] Finnis, *Aquinas*, 222-52.

[284] Gilby, *Principality and Polity*, 130; Finnis, *Aquinas*, 237-38.

[285] Gilby, *Principality and Polity*, 179-80, 306; *Between Community and Society* 327; Finnis, *Aquinas*, 228-31.

[286] Aquinas, *In 1 Tim.* 1.3 ad v.9 [23] in *Super Epistolas S. Pauli Lectura* 2 vols. 8th edn. (Rome: Marietti, 1953).

which end law effects by directing external actions, as regards those evils which might disturb the peaceful condition of the state. On the other hand, the end of the Divine law is to bring man to that end which is everlasting happiness; which end is hindered by any sin, not only of external, but also of internal action. Consequently that which suffices for the perfection of human law, viz., the prohibition and punishment of sin, does not suffice for the perfection of the Divine law: but it is requisite that it should make man altogether fit to partake of everlasting happiness. Now this cannot be done save by the grace of the Holy Ghost, whereby charity, which fulfilleth the law, ... is spread abroad in our hearts (Rom. 5:5): since the grace of God is life everlasting (Rom. 6:23). But the Old Law could not confer this grace, for this was reserved to Christ ...

The contrasts in this section are as follows:

	Human Law	Divine Law
End:	the temporal tranquillity of the state	everlasting happiness
Means:	direction of external actions	the grace of the Holy Ghost spread abroad in our hearts
Perfection:	prohibition and punishment of sin	charity

The three contrasts will be considered in reverse order. With regard to the third distinction, since true justice is a work of the indwelling Spirit, and this human law is powerless to effect, therefore the role of human law in prohibiting and controlling vice must be more fundamental than its role in promoting virtue.[287]

With regard to the second distinction, the scope of human law is inherently limited because 'human beings can judge only sensibly perceptible external acts, not hidden internal movements.' (*ST* I-II.91.4; 100.9; II-II.58.8; *IV Sent.* d.15 q.3 a.4 sol.1 ad.3).[288] During the mediaeval period, it was recognised that the competence of the secular rulers extended only to external actions; while the Church reserved to itself, through the sacrament of confession, the competence to judge in respect of internal actions.

Because it is only concerned with external acts, human law is only interested in intention in a negative sense. If a person acts lawfully, it is irrelevant to the law whether they have done so willingly or only grudgingly. It is only when there has been a *prima facie* breach of the law, that human law is concerned with whether it occurred inadvertently, negligently, or deliberately. Human law is therefore content with what might be termed 'shallow justice' while questions of 'deep justice' are matters for God alone.

---

[287] Hall, *Narrative*, 85.
[288] Finnis, *Aquinas*, 241-42.

With regard to the first distinction, precisely because the consummation of salvation must await the *eschaton*, a distinction has to be drawn between the perfect peace of the beatific vision and the imperfect peace, which is the best that can be hoped for in this world (*ST* II-II.29.2 ad.4).

Before considering this distinction in more detail it is necessary to point out that what Aquinas means by 'the state' (*civitas*) is the political or civil community, not 'the State' conceived as the government or its organs.[289]

Without emancipating a realm of natural goods from Christian critique, Aquinas nonetheless argues that human government should be concerned with peace between human beings and not with peace between human beings and God.[290] At *ST* I-II.99.1.ad.2, Aquinas says: 'every law aims at establishing friendship, either between man and man, or between man and God.' This is further clarified, at *ST* I-II.100.5, where Aquinas writes: 'just as the precepts of human law direct man in his relations to the human community, so the precepts of the divine law direct man in his relations to a community or commonwealth of men under God.'[291] By this means, Aquinas distinguishes between the people of Israel, to whom was given the divine law to bring them into communion with God, and all other peoples, whose laws have a more limited purpose: a purpose which can be described as expansively as aiming at friendship between man and man (*ST* I-II.99.1 ad.2; 99.2) or more circumspectly as the temporal tranquillity of the state.[292]

This focus upon temporal tranquillity does not, however, mean that Christian rulers have no role to play in combating heresy, but Aquinas's justification for this is that the temporal tranquillity of the state usually demanded the suppression of heresy (*ST* II-II.11.3; 10.11). Moreover, at this point he appears to be following Augustine (quoted at *ST* II.II.10.8. obj.3 and ad.1, 3, 4; 10.11); and Bernard of Clairvaux (*IV Sent.* d.37) rather than reflecting independently on the implications of the fact that it is the Holy Spirit and not the secular ruler who is agent by whom the saints are preserved. If his comments about compelling heretics to return to the true faith seem unacceptable, he at least makes the salutary point that those who have never yet believed are not to be coerced into the Church (*ST* II.II.10.8).[293]

The distinction between 'temporal tranquillity' on the one hand, and 'everlasting happiness' on the other appears also in Aquinas's commentary on Romans 13. There Aquinas draws a distinction between kings who have responsibility for the common good in worldly possessions (*de bono publico in bonis temporalibus*), whereas the servants of God have responsibility in

---

[289] Finnis, *Aquinas*, 219.
[290] Finnis, *Aquinas*, 324-25; Gilby, *Between Community and Society*, 254-56.
[291] Also Aquinas, *ST* I-II.99.3 resp. and II-II.59.1 ad.1 'Even as legal justice is referred to human common good, so Divine justice is referred to the Divine good'.
[292] Hall, *Narrative*, 85.
[293] Finnis, *Aquinas*, 292-93, 323.

spiritual things. The 'servants of God' owe tribute to the kings, however, because the king works for their peace.[294] Human law is therefore concerned with what is temporal, with the natural goods which must be adjudicated upon in order to ensure a tolerable peace.

Where the role of the Holy Spirit as the agent of the New Law is forgotten, then Aristotelian corporatism dominates the rump of Aquinas's thought which remains. Whereas, if Aquinas is understood as a virtue ethicist, or if natural law is reduced to its proper scope within his theology, then a different picture emerges. Aquinas argues against aiming too high with human law.[295]

It is, in the New Covenant Era, not the role of human law but of the Holy Spirit to infuse virtue. The Holy Spirit alone can move human beings towards the beatitude of eschatological participation in the divine law which is attainable only through union with Christ and is the *summum bonum* of human existence (*ST* I-II.68.2). What human law can do, is to conduce to virtue (*ST* I-II.92.1 ad.1) and to habituate its subjects to externally virtuous actions (*ST* I-II 92.2 ad.4). It may even, insofar as it reflects the natural law or the moral precepts of the Old Law, instruct in virtue those who are inclined to good (*ST* I-II.98.6; 101.3) The truly spiritual man, however, may be said to be not under the law 'because he fulfils the law willingly, through charity which is poured into his heart by the Holy Ghost.' (*ST* I-II.93.6 ad.1).

This aspect of Aquinas's thinking chimes with Augustinian concerns. On Aquinas's account, the stability of an economic and social order depends on human laws, but its content will depend upon the virtues possessed by the citizens.[296] At *ST* II-II.64.6, he says 'the just are the most important members of the community.' The New Law therefore buttresses the peace of human communities through its transformation of the lives of the justified.[297] There are echoes here of the Augustinian view, expressed by O'Donovan, that the relative goodness of a society depends on the common objects of love pursued by its members.

Thinking about Human Law with, and beyond, Aquinas

As has been argued above, Aquinas did not set out to provide a systematic account of human law. At least four aspects of Aquinas's account of the place

---

[294] The relevant paragraph in full is *Hoc autem ideo aequum est, quia sicut reges sollicitudinem habent de bono publico in bonis temporalibus, ita ministri Dei in spiritualibus, et sic per hoc quod Deo in spiritualibus ministrant, recompensant regi quod pro eorum pace laborat.* Pending the appearance of the first English translation of Aquinas' commentary on Romans, I am grateful to Dr Tony Rich for his assistance in the translation of this section.

[295] Hall, *Narrative*, 85.

[296] Levering, *Christ's Fulfillment*, 116; Finnis, *Aquinas*, 232.

[297] Hall, *Narrative*, 86.

of human law can be developed. The first is to regard Aquinas as giving an account of the possibilities for human law when submitted to Christ. The second is to make more explicit the workings of the Holy Spirit through human law and beyond human law. The third is to draw a sharp distinction between natural goods and the *summum bonum*. The fourth is to temper the Aristotelian influences on Aquinas's account of human law by reference to his soteriology and his theodicy. If his thought is developed in these directions, then Aquinas points the way towards a relatively liberal, relatively peaceful and relatively just legal order which is concerned with temporal goods whilst open to God's calling to the eternal good.

HUMAN LAW AS SUBMITTED TO CHRIST

At the time Aquinas was writing, the Catholic Church was close to being omnipresent in Western Europe. Perhaps one of the reasons why he does not say much about the Church is because it was so pervasive. The positive place he attributes to human law can therefore be read as an account of the way in which human law should co-operate, through the enforcement of natural law, with the mission of the Church in proclaiming the New Law.

In *De Regno* II.3 (=I.14) [105] Aquinas talks about the extrinsic good of man's mortal life, that is to say, of the eternal beatitude of the enjoyment of God. This beatitude has, he says, been purchased by the blood of Christ and the Spirit has been given as an earnest of it, and it is the 'ministers of the church of Christ' who direct Christian men towards it. Secular rulers, therefore, play no part in securing this eternal good. In the following paragraphs of *De Regno*, Aquinas makes this explicit. At [107-108] he argues as follows:

> … since society must have the same end as the individual man, it is not the ultimate end of an assembled multitude to live virtuously, but through virtuous living to attain to the possession of God.

> If this end could be attained by the power of human nature, then the duty of a king would have to include the direction of men to it. …

> But because a man does not attain his end, which is the possession of God, by human power but by divine – according to the words of the Apostle (Rom. 6:23) "By the grace of God life everlasting" – therefore the task of leading him to that last end does not pertain to human but to divine government.

Having said that, *De Regno* is not a prototype for the First Amendment to the American Constitution. Aquinas's point, made at [109] is that Jesus is the supreme King, precisely because His government is directed to the eternal good. The obvious corollary, for Aquinas, was that the Pope outranked secular rulers [110] (*ST* II-II.60.6 ad.3). The temporal realm of natural goods has its own director, the king, and a relative autonomy, but for Aquinas this is subordinated to the eternal realm.[298]

THE WORKINGS OF THE HOLY SPIRIT

As has been argued above, for Aquinas, grace is the Holy Spirit or the effect of the Holy Spirit. This insight illuminates both how the Holy Spirit works as the New Law in Christians guiding and empowering them to obey God and how the Holy Spirit works through human law to achieve God's providential purposes.

What Aquinas needed to make plain beyond peradventure in his theology was that God's actions towards God's creation are gracious from beginning to end. He is clear about this in relation to his doctrine of God. Any sense of God needing to create the world to realise Godself in Moltmannian terms is resolutely excluded (*ST* I.30.3; 32.1 ad.3).[299] Equally, he is clear that grace has a pre-eminent role in God's work of salvation. Where he was not so clear was the relationship between grace and nature. Although he would not have accepted the two storey nature and grace model of Tridentine Catholicism, it requires careful reading to realise that this is so.

Integrating glorification into Aquinas's thought expands the nature-grace duality into a nature-grace-glory trilogy,[300] but this still does not bring out the role of the Holy Spirit in grace sufficiently. In terms of humanity's final end, human glorification is not something we earn but is the result of divine grace,[301] even if it is right to say that this is grace with which we co-operate. Equally, human nature is not something which is given once and for all. Human existence is, as Aquinas acknowledges, something which God both creates and sustains. All that we have and are is dependent on God moment by moment.[302] There are therefore rather a number of moments in grace: creating grace, sustaining grace, providential grace, redeeming grace, sanctifying grace, and glorifying grace. However one distinguishes them conceptually, all these moments must be understood in triune fashion as actions ordained by the Father, ordered to the Son and accomplished by the Spirit.

The Spirit is the unseen Person of the Trinity, the wind who blows where He will (John 3:8). The Spirit's actions in sustaining and providing, as worked out through human laws and human rulers are necessarily even more mysterious than the Spirit's work in human hearts. It is necessarily an affirmation of faith

---

[298] Finnis, *Aquinas*, 322-27.

[299] Aquinas, *ST* I.19.10; 104.3; R. Williams, 'What does love know?', 270; Finnis, *Aquinas*, 310.

[300] Aquinas, *ScG* IV.1.5.

[301] Aquinas, *ST* I.105.8; I-II.113.10 obj.1; Wawrykow, 'Aquinas on Isaiah' in *Aquinas on Scripture* 46.

[302] Aquinas, *ST* I.22.3 ad.4; 104.1; *Politics*, *Lect.* I.2; Levering, *Scripture and Metaphysics*, 102; Gilby, *Principality and Polity*, 99; Long, 'Providence', 365; Finnis, *Aquinas*, 304-05; Torrell, *Aquinas Vol. II*, 68, 75.

that the Spirit is so at work. Such an affirmation is credible only if it is recognised that God is in control whether or not human rulers are obedient to God and that God will be glorified irrespective of the acknowledgment or defiance of human rulers.

A SHARP DISTINCTION BETWEEN NATURAL GOODS AND THE *SUMMUM BONUM*

Two contemporary thinkers influenced by Aquinas have given his account of human law a particular twist in their exploration of the question of what constitutes human goods. Germain Grisez and John Finnis both posit lists of incommensurable goods which human beings may rationally pursue.[303] The role of human laws is therefore to promote, or at least not to impede unduly, the pursuit of these goods. Religion, broadly defined, is merely one of those goods which human laws should leave people free to pursue.

However, Nichols sees a key difference between Aquinas on the one hand, and Grisez/ Finnis on the other, on this point: for Aquinas, 'the vision of God in heaven is the unique overarching end or goal of the human person to which all human action – all moral action – needs relating if it is to be accounted, in the last analysis, good for man' whereas for Grisez and Finnis 'moral decision-making has no single superordinate ultimate end.'[304] Grisez and Finnis now themselves recognise that what they are doing is not merely interpreting Aquinas, but going beyond his thought.

The direction in which Grisez and Finnis develop Aquinas is the direction taken by Cajetan, who, in the words of Fergus Kerr, 'opened the way for post-Reformation Catholicism to insist so much on the value of nature that [the Council of Trent] ended with a two-storey model of nature and grace, juxtaposing the two, as it were, treating grace in relation to nature as essentially extrinsic and adventitious.'[305]

Yet Aquinas, at his most Augustinian, stresses that 'an evil human being participates in his ... own corruption by abandoning the spiritual goods ... in favour of the earthly goods'.[306] Such comments are not surprising coming from a man who abandoned wealth, family and sexual fulfilment for the sake of following the call of Christ upon his life.

On the other hand, provided they are subordinated to the eternal good, a

---

[303] Grisez, Boyle and Finnis, 'Practical Principles, Moral Truth and Ultimate Ends', *American Journal of Jurisprudence* 32 (1987) 107-8; Black, *Christian Moral Realism*, 53.

[304] Nichols, *Discovering Aquinas*, 92. Hall also notes that Finnis and Grisez's theory differs from Aquinas in that whereas Aquinas has a teleological account, they offer an irreducible plurality of goods. In Hall's view, it is their commitment to the is/ought separation which causes them to believe themselves to be obliged 'to divorce themselves from teleological claims': Hall, *Narrative*, 18.

[305] Kerr, *After Aquinas*, 136.

[306] Yocum, 'Aquinas' Literal Exposition on Job' in *Aquinas on Scripture* 30; Aquinas, *On Job* 1.6, 380-90 (p.79).; *In Matt.* 5.3 [404-13]; *ST* I-II.99.6.

Christian may lawfully enjoy the natural goods (*ST* II-II.83.6 ad.1). In order to act in a virtuous manner, it is necessary to have 'a sufficiency of those bodily goods whose use is necessary for virtuous life' (*De Regno* II.3 (=I.14) [118]), and procuring such a supply of those goods is the responsibility of the ruler.

The eternal good is not *necessarily* incompatible with the natural goods and may shed light upon them. Thus not only does Christianity give an account of the natural goods for which marriage is given, but it also identifies its ideal form as the union of one man and one woman and its purpose as a sacrament, signifying the union of Christ and the Church.[307] Christianity has a distinct account of what is good for human beings which the secular rulers need to hear, because as Julian Rivers points out 'it is unrealistic to suppose that politics can avoid concerning itself with conceptions of human flourishing and well-being. One only needs to think of the moral judgments implicit in family law to see that.'[308]

Secular power is temporal power concerned with temporal goods. What Aquinas offers is a distinction between a human common good, to which legal justice is directed; and the Divine good, to which Divine justice is directed (*ST* II-II.59.1 ad.1), albeit that if the human common good is treated as the ultimate end this is idolatrous.

TEMPERING HUMAN LAW IN THE LIGHT OF SOTERIOLOGY AND THEODICY

For Aquinas, righteousness cannot be attained by observance of an exterior law. The Old Law demonstrated that. Similarly, human law can only be instrumental in bringing about limited peace. It can only constrain exterior acts. Only Christ can render the whole person peaceful.[309] Humans can only attain the good for which they were made, communion with God, through the saving work of Christ and the transforming work of the Holy Spirit. Human law is therefore powerless to effect salvation or sanctification. It is for good reason, therefore, that Aquinas warns against aiming too high with human law.

This observation on its own, however, leaves the door open for a wide variety of coercive measures to be implemented on the basis that they are conducive to the common good conceived in terms of purely natural goods. The brake on this in Aquinas's thought is his observation that 'human laws cannot punish or prohibit all evil deeds ... because in seeking to eliminate all evils, one would thereby take away many goods and not benefit the common good necessary for human companionship.' (*ST* I-II.91.4) This is, however, but a particular illustration of Aquinas's theodicy. Aquinas does not offer a complete theodicy but only the beginnings of one. Central to his explanation of evil is the

---

[307] Aquinas, *ST* III.suppl. 41-68; *In 1 Cor.* 7.1-9 [318]; Yocum, 'Sacraments in Aquinas', 176.

[308] A.J. Rivers, 'Public Reason' *Whitefield Briefing* 9(1) (2004).

[309] Levering, 'Reading John', 117-118; Aquinas, *In Ioan* 1964.

importance which God gives to human free choice.[310] It is because the destruction of evil would involve the abolition of human free choice that God stays God's hand. Precisely because, for Aquinas, human governance participates in divine governance, what should be enforced through law ought therefore to be limited because, on Aquinas's account, human free choice is of importance to God. Thus it becomes a factor to be weighed in the balance against the imperatives of pursuing collectively particular forms of the goods through the use of human law.[311]

Unlike Finnis and Grisez, this account acknowledges that human goods are ordered and affirms the priority of the Church's mission in bearing witness to the ultimate good for which God has made us. However, Aquinas tempers those observations with the recognition that human law sustains human communities in a different way from the Church's mission, but it is ordered towards that mission. In his commentary on Romans 13, Aquinas describes kings as labouring for peace, a peace which the servants of God can make use of. Unlike Finnis and Grisez, this leaves the door open for the understanding of human goods embodied by human laws to be permeated by explicitly Christian reflection rather than having constantly to disguise such reflection under the rubric of natural law.

It belongs to human law to direct and control human behaviour in respect of sensibly perceptible and earthly goods, and in this respect to be informed by the Church's proclamation of what the true nature of those goods is. However, 'it belongs to the divine law [that is to say the Holy Spirit] to direct human acts regarding the order of righteousness.' (*ST* I-II.91.5).

If Aquinas is read as a virtue ethicist who gave natural law and human law only a limited scope in his thought, then, on this reading, politics ought to be concerned and limited to similar questions to those addressed on a maximalist Augustinian vision such as the one which can be derived from O'Donovan's work.

Aquinas and O'Donovan

As has been suggested above, Aquinas can be read as endorsing limited government, concerned only with finite goods, whilst expecting virtue to be promoted primarily through the workings of the Holy Spirit rather than the machinations of government. As has been seen in O'Donovan's thought, if emphasis is placed on government's involvement in the selection, endorsement and promotion of a society's common objects of love, then this maximalist version of Augustinian political theory arrives at the same place as a trinitarian

---

[310] Geisler, *Thomas Aquinas*, 156.
[311] Such a theological line of argument would strengthen the philosophical arguments Finnis identifies in Aquinas as circumscribing the extent to which governments can direct the communities over which they rule: *Aquinas* 234-39.

Thomist vision. If a choice is to be made between the two theoretical underpinnings, then the version of trinitarian Thomism explored in this chapter is preferable.

Such a trinitarian reading of Aquinas recognises the God-given, inherent, goodness of finite goods, the pursuit of which may be regulated by a society's government. It does this whilst affirming the Augustinian truth that the pursuit of such goods *per se* is necessarily misguided because they only find their true place if subordinated to the love of God.

Aquinas's account of the New Law also has another advantage over O'Donovan's model of political theology. Amidst much admiration for O'Donovan's work, Gilbert Meilaender in his extended review of *DON* raises the concern that O'Donovan presents Christ primarily as the one who commands rather than the one who loves.[312] Significantly, he points out that alongside the metaphor of the heavenly City, Revelation offers that of the Bride of Christ, suggesting that the holy City is not primarily a transformed community under God's direct political rule but rather 'a communion in which each participant is loved personally and intimately.'[313] Aquinas's theology of law reflects this deeper reality more clearly than O'Donovan's, through offering an account in which the love of God and obedience to God are thoroughly infused.[314]

However, in its political implications, the trinitarian reading of Aquinas's thinking on law proposed in this chapter, needs to be carefully qualified in order to avoid the danger of ending up with a position reminiscent of some forms of Lutheran thinking, in which the Church is concerned with salvation conceived exclusively in spiritual terms, leaving the State free to control and organise *ad infinitum* the pursuit of material goods.[315] The resources are there to provide the necessary qualifications. The definition of the material, 'natural' goods, must constantly be supplied by Christian thought. Such thought must inform what counts as a meaningful relationship, what marriage is, what amounts to rewarding work, what is important about human life, dignity and liberty. Thomas's account of natural law must be seen as an account of a realm of given reality and rules which have stability and normativity precisely because they have been created by God. The good gifts of God to humankind in creation are ordered to the Son, through whom they were given, and who dignified them through His Incarnation.

Conclusion

Despite the merits of the account of Aquinas's thought being offered in this

---

[312] G. Meilaender, 'Recovering Christendom', *First Things* 77 (1997) 41.

[313] Meilaender, 'Recovering Christendom', 42.

[314] Gilby, *Between Community and Society*, 332.

[315] Gilby, *Between Community and Society*, 206.

chapter, it has to be recognised that this was not the way in which he was read by subsequent generations. Whatever may be made of Aquinas's own thought, the fact remains that after Aquinas's synthesis of Aristotelian and Augustinian elements in his political theology,[316] subsequent scholastics were overwhelmingly Aristotelian. Natural law was uprooted from its proper setting in the theological forest and planted as a monoculture. For later thinkers, Aquinas's God who is the living God, the source of Being, became merely the Supreme Being, a static, lumpen deity. The Holy Spirit, the one through whom we are made holy, virtuous, and Christ-like, was excised from Aquinas's political philosophy. Aquinas was not read by his successors as a virtue ethicist. Instead, it was the idea of the hierarchy of norms which came to dominate the later Middle Ages. The mediaeval theory of law was bedevilled by the problems of hierarchy, authority and legalism.

Evaluation of the role of the Trinity in Aquinas's thought must begin by acknowledging that it pervades his thinking to a far greater extent than has been recognised. Having said that, the problems and occasional inadequacies in his conceptualisation of the Trinity must not be ignored. Despite these deficiencies, Aquinas offers a highly significant account of law from a trinitarian perspective. That he is able to do so is testament to the fact that in theological terms, what ought to be of primary importance is the relation of the triune God to us. Key to Aquinas's account is his conception of the Spirit as the New Law, working in Christians to guide them and empower them to obey God. This work of the Spirit culminates in the eschatological glorification of human beings, when the need for external constraints is eliminated as human beings enjoy perfect communion with the Father, in the Son, by the Spirit.

Precisely because Aquinas's trinitarianism is focussed around a fully-orbed doctrine of salvation, he is able to say valuable things about the place of human law within the divine economy. Human law is recognised to be incompetent to effect true, inward, transformation but as performing the valuable function of executing 'shallow justice'. Aquinas points the way to a relatively liberal, relatively peaceful and relatively just legal order which is concerned with temporal goods whilst being open to God's calling to the eternal good.

---

[316] Lockwood O'Donovan, *BOI*, 227.

Chapter 5

Human Law in Relation to the Work of the Son and the Spirit

Methodology

It has been a central concern of the present thesis to argue that the deployment of the Trinity as a bare image is an inadequate and misplaced use of the doctrine. As was explored in the second chapter, Moltmann's social trinitarianism is problematic for the reasons Kilby and Tanner identify. *A priori* commitments to the desirable shape of human society, rather than the biblical narrative of God's self-revelation in Christ, are the driving force behind Moltmann's speculations regarding the Trinity.

Whilst Moltmann is right to insist on the necessity of a trinitarian understanding of the central events of the gospel, it is contended that the focus of such an understanding should be on the economic Trinity. This involves the adoption of a circular hermeneutic, seeking the mutual illumination which is provided by reflecting on who God is in the light of what God does.[1] The third chapter considered O'Donovan's careful reading of the biblical narrative, but argued that his theological conclusions would be both strengthened and modified by a sustained reflection on the triune God who is revealed through those narratives, in order to be buttressed against a possible collapse into authoritarianism. In the fourth chapter, a reading of Aquinas has been proposed in which it is argued that his theology of law can be understood as oriented around an understanding of the work of the Son and the Spirit.

If the approach being adopted in this thesis is fruitful, it ought to be possible to derive coherent conclusions by means of either canonical or systematic theology. My own previous attempt at doing so through a canonical theology was *A Biblical View of Law and Justice ('BVLJ')*.

The reading of law and justice which I offered in that book treated *tsedeq* as a foundational concept and understood it as both righteousness in the sense of personal holiness and justice in the sense of right relations to other human beings. I argued that the early chapters of Genesis sketch the rudiments of justice through the identification of the good gifts which God has given to

---

[1] Kilby, 'Perichoresis and Projection', 443.

human beings and tell an account of how humanity has rejected God and refused a relationship with God.

Part of God's gracious response to humanity's rejection of God was to institute human government as an agency through which some of the worst effects of human sinfulness could be curbed.[2] However, such government is an ambiguous blessing as it is itself caught up in the rejection of God which necessitated its institution.

I argued that the Torah represented God-given guidance as to how human laws were to be organised and how human beings ought to behave towards one another in a particular society at a particular time and space. The Israelite kings held limited power and were accountable for their observance and enforcement of the Torah, through a prophetic tradition which both pointed back towards the Torah and also forwards towards its transformation. I offered a reading of the Old Testament in which the inability of the Torah to render Israel a just society confirms that humanity's problem is not just that God's laws are not known and that there is uncertainty about what constitutes justice but that external laws are unable to make human beings just.

Chapter six of *BVLJ* then asserted that the kingship of Christ was rightly understood by his enemies as having important political implications. Nonetheless, the fact that Jesus did not take up political power but chose instead to die on the cross, to ascend to the right hand of the Father, and to send the Spirit, reveals that the transformation of the human condition requires more than the mere enactment of just laws. In chapter seven, I claimed that Paul recognised the inadequacy of the Torah as a remedy for human sinfulness, and that he taught instead that the Holy Spirit enabled people to become just by working within them to sanctify them and to guide them towards right relations with others.

Human law is therefore bounded by the work of the Son and of the Spirit. It is orientated in relation to the work of the Son on the cross and at the Last Judgment. It has been exposed as limited in its ability to produce justice through the narrative of the failures in the Old Testament and the importance of the work of the Holy Spirit. Having established those parameters I then argued in chapter 8 of *BVLJ* for an active Christian involvement in human law, one which does not 'seek to create heaven on earth, ... but rather to promote those Christian values, derived from God's revelation of himself, which can be demonstrated to have social utility.'[3]

Already, therefore, in that reading of the canon, I was arguing for the centrality of an understanding of the work of the Son and the Spirit for a Christian perspective on the role of human law. However, the present volume goes beyond my previous work in that the Spirit's action in relation to the New

---

[2] This leaves open the question of whether the co-ordinating function of human government would have been required apart from the Fall.
[3] McIlroy, *BVLJ*, 188.

Law is now understood to culminate in the glorification of human beings, in the completion of an inner transformation.

The present thesis began with the systematic assertion that the Trinity is foundational to Christian theology.[4] The Church came to the recognition of the Trinity because of the revelation of God in Christ and the events of Pentecost and afterwards. It understood the coming of Christ and the giving of the Spirit as not only the beginning of its own life but also as the culmination of God's plan of salvation, manifested throughout God's dealings with God's people, Israel. Thus the Trinity is revealed in the context of and as the context of the salvation-history of Israel's God.

Understanding the Trinity as a biblical doctrine means thinking about the Trinity in the light of the economy of salvation whose crux is the events of the incarnation, cross and resurrection. Stressing the biblical revelation of the Trinity means, however, affirming that what the Church has said subsequently about the Trinity in its creeds and confessions does not stand on its own authority but claims to be an authentic interpretation and witness to the God of Scripture. Only by understanding the Trinity as a biblical concept, can the temptations to reduce it to a Platonic reality or to project onto the internal relations of God our own desired views of human community be avoided.[5]

The first trap to be avoided is a reversal in the order of reasoning. Barth is right to insist that theology should be constructed *from above* not *from below*. A trinitarian theology *from below* might, for example, begin with Montesquieu's separation of powers and make the following identification: legislative (God the Father), executive (God the Son), judicial (God the Holy Spirit). However, as is the tendency with all attempts to take a 'given' human structure and to legitimate it by reference to theological concepts, rather than proceeding in reverse, the consequence is to create a procrustean bed. While the Father as the source of the Trinity's action can be readily identified with the legislature in the British constitutional system where Parliament is sovereign, this would not follow in other constitutional arrangements. The Son not only carries out the will of the Father but has also been entrusted with the function of judgment. God the Holy Spirit is closely identified with wisdom in the Eastern tradition, and there is therefore justification in linking the Spirit to the function of interpreting what God requires of us. There is also warrant for this in relation to the Old Testament law.[6] The Spirit's role expressed in John 16:8-11 as convicting the world of its sin, revealing the standards of God's righteousness and demonstrating Christ's judgment could be regarded as judicial, but the Spirit mediates and demonstrates not the Spirit's own judgment, but the judgment of Christ. Furthermore, although God the Son in Incarnation and

---

[4] Barth, *CD*, I/1, 358: 'the doctrine of the Trinity is the basic presupposition for the doctrine of God.'

[5] Molnar, *Divine Freedom*, 312.

[6] Burnside, 'Inspired Justice'; McIlroy, *BVLJ*, 143-47.

Passion executed the key moment of divine action on earth,[7] God acted before and since. The Holy Spirit is not just judicial; the Spirit is also, perhaps even primarily, executive, carrying out God's plan of salvation in, through and beyond the Church.

The normative importance of the Trinity can be derived from an interpretation of its inner life. On this view, the Trinity becomes a model to which human beings or human communities ought to conform. Such an approach might lead to a defence of hierarchy, if the Son's willing subordination to the Father is seen as paradigmatic. Alternatively, as Moltmann's theology is sometimes caricatured, God is presented as a commune or a committee of free, loving individuals, and this is what human communities ought to reflect.

In contrast, the approach adopted in the present thesis emphasises God's loving invitation to humankind to participate in intimate communion with God. The theology of law developed in this chapter emerges out of a theology which emphasises the human destiny to be conformed to the Son, by the indwelling of the Spirit, to be restored to right relationship with the Father.

The present chapter contains a more developed account of glorification than was offered in *BVLJ*.[8] As was explored in the reading of Aquinas proposed in the previous chapter, an exploration of the culmination of sanctification in Christ-likeness, through the work of the Spirit, issuing in perfect communion with the Father, is essential to the eschatological resolution of the present ambiguities surrounding law. In terms of contextual theology, it would also be imperative to offer a developed account of the atonement. However, although I have begun such a task elsewhere,[9] the Church has never included a precise theology of atonement within its Creeds and therefore in a work of primarily systematic rather than contextual theology, it is permissible merely to sketch an account of atonement. Moreover, although a theology of atonement is potentially highly material for a theology of penology and criminology, is of less importance with regard to the theology of law *per se*.

A trinitarian theology of law must pay close attention to three narratives. First, to the nature of God's disclosure of Godself and of God's acts in Scripture. The God of the Old Testament is shown to be the living God, exercising sovereignty over all the nations and acting in covenant faithfulness to God's people.[10] Jesus Christ reveals that living God to be Father and to have acted in person to reconcile the world to Godself. That revelation culminates in

---

[7] T. Smail, *Like Father, Like Son: The Trinity imaged in our Humanity* (Carlisle: Paternoster, 2005) 70.

[8] In the subsequent discussion, the term 'glorification' will be used as a description for the particular doctrine of deification/ *theosis* being advanced in this chapter.

[9] D.H. McIlroy, 'Towards a Relational and Trinitarian Theology of Atonement' *Evangelical Quarterly* 80 (2008) 13-32.

[10] McIlroy, *BVLJ*, 65-67, 105-112.

the trinitarian events of the crucifixion, resurrection, ascension and Pentecost in which the God-man offers Himself as the acceptable sacrifice of obedience to God, is raised to new life, ascends into the presence of the Father and releases the Spirit upon His Church, that is to say His Body.

The second narrative is the history of God's work among the nations. There is not space in this work to trace a history of that work to rival the accounts given by O'Donovan and Milbank, nor is the work of God in this regard perspicacious. That it is not is because the work of God among the nations is the work of the Holy Spirit, who is notoriously unseen and even self-effacing. Yet, in the midst of the mess of human history stand such moments as the abolition of slavery which bear all the hallmarks of the work of the liberating Spirit. Moltmann is right to identify the Spirit as the one who brings the power of the future into the present.[11] Wherever the Spirit is at work, the Spirit bears testimony to the kingship of Christ and the Fatherhood of God. The Spirit reveals too, the inescapable call and commands of God, which no human being can safely ignore.

That is why the third narrative to be attended to is God's work in reconciling people to Godself, by the Son, through the Spirit. The second narrative forms the background to this third story, the story of men and women wooed by the Spirit of God, reconciled to the Father through the Son of God, and transformed by the Spirit of the Father into the likeness of the Son. Human law is only the background to this story, bearing indirect witness to the law given in creation and pointing, through its own incompleteness, to the need for transformation which good legislation, policing and judgment alone are wholly insufficient to achieve. Only part of this third narrative can be sketched here. The significant role of the Church in this narrative falls outside the scope of the present study.

What is needed is a Christian political theology informed by a dynamic vision of the Trinity which recognises that the God who transcends time, has condescended to be involved in time and to act in time. Such a political theology would take its patristic inspiration not from Eusebius, nor even, with all due respect, from Augustine, but instead from Irenaeus whose 'theology is stamped throughout by an interest in the history of God's dealings with mankind, the "economy" of salvation, in which creation, incarnation and judgment form the key dramatic moments.'[12]

What will be considered therefore is what God has done in the world, in creation and redemption. The framework adopted here is one which takes into account the moments of creation, Fall, incarnation, crucifixion, resurrection, the giving of the Spirit and the *eschaton*.

---

[11] Moltmann, *SL*, 74.

[12] O'Donovan and Lockwood O'Donovan, *IG*, 15.

The Trinity and Law in the Doctrine of Creation

The first affirmation that the doctrine of the Trinity makes possible about creation is the assertion that God graciously created the world.[13] Moltmann's criticisms of Augustine's view of the Spirit as the bond of love between the Father and the Son miss their mark. Rather than the classical ideas, either Western or Eastern, of the Trinity turning God in on Godself; such conceptions of the tri-unity of God affirm that God does not *need* to create in order to be fulfilled in God's essence as love. On the other hand, the fact that God is love means that God is free to will to create a world which God will commit Godself to love.[14]

The second affirmation that the doctrine of the Trinity makes possible about creation is that it gives an account of the ordering of creation. The triune God has ordered creation in, for and to Godself. The created world has been planned by the Father, is ordered to the Son, and accomplished by the Spirit. Creation is not seen as a static mass but rather as a living organised realm which finds its origin in the will of the Father, its cohesion in Christ and its direction in the Spirit. The Spirit who breathes through all that the Father has created witnesses to the foundation of all reality in the Son.[15] There is something of the sense of this idea in that strand of Moltmann's thought to be found at *WJC* 306-12 and discussed in the section on 'Law as an Ordering Power' in chapter 2.

This affirmation makes possible a trinitarian understanding of natural law, of the kind offered by O'Donovan and Aquinas. To affirm natural law is to affirm that the world, as created by God, is ordered to Christ. In this ordered world, human beings have an ultimate purpose, an eternal end, as well as having created ends, which have been God-given and which form the framework within which a good life may be lived. Beyond O'Donovan and Aquinas, however, it has to be said expressly that the Spirit guides human beings towards those ends. How this is so, is one of the mysteries of the faith. The being-givenness of such guidance, and its nature as an activity of the Spirit rather than a purely static reality, is conserved by remembering that natural law is given in general revelation,[16] whereas the term 'natural law' stresses that human beings have ends which are given to them rather than constructed *ex nihilo* by them.

Like the Mosaic law, natural law is orientated around the calling of God to love God and to love our neighbours.[17] Adam was called to be obedient to God because that was what was expected of humankind in the relationship of love to God which God wanted Adam to enjoy.

Over and above the general revelation of the natural law, the Bible offers in

---

[13] Colwell, *Promise and Presence*, 43; Holmes, *Listening to the Past*, 8 n.15.

[14] T.J. Gorringe, *Karl Barth: Against Hegemony* (Oxford: OUP, 1999) 144.

[15] Colwell, *Living the Christian Story*, 247-49.

[16] Smail, *Like Father, Like Son*, 31.

[17] McIlroy, *BVLJ*, 28, 163-64; 'What's at Stake in Natural Law?'; 'The Relevance of Old Testament Law for Today: Part Two', *Law & Justice* 150 (2003) 22-28.

Genesis 1-3, a mythic account of a divine command, given before the Fall, to which human beings were called by God to be obedient. This anchors obedience to God, within a relational context, as an essential fact about human life. The call to love God incorporates a call to be obedient to God. An account of the relations between the triune God and humankind which is faithful to the biblical revelation regarding those relations must therefore explain how obedience to God is compatible with the fulfilment of human life and identity. Aquinas's doctrine of deification is such an explanation.

Law and the Fall

The narrative of the Fall reveals the existence of law, unmediated by human authority. The Bible begins with human beings confronted by the command of God calling them to live in *shalom* with God, with one another and with creation. Law, in the sense of the rule laid down for us by another, is given in creation. That it is mediated through human rulers and that we are alienated from it, is the consequence of our rejection of the laws given in creation and our rebellion against our Creator.

The most fundamental human laws take their contours from the created order given by the Father in Christ and through the Spirit.[18] They attempt to provide a structure within which human social life is tolerable, despite the Fall. It is because human laws cannot but, to some extent, echo (however faintly), the divine commands given to us as created beings, that they can point us towards Christ, however indirectly.[19]

Human politics as we now know it begins after the Fall, but it only makes sense because of the Fall, and because of the original disobedience to the divine command. Despite our rejection of the divine law, and for all our consequent fallenness, human political authority is given by the providence of God for the avoidance of the complete collapse of human society. Human politics therefore harks back to the original good order of creation and looks forward to the *shalom* of the eternal city. Both are out of its reach. It therefore stands like a signpost pointing at them.

The Trinity and the Doctrine of Providence

Just as the doctrine of creation must be conceived in a trinitarian fashion, so too must the doctrine of providence. That this must be so is easy to state. That the government of the world is purposed by the Father, ordered to the Son and

---

[18] A. Storkey, *Jesus and Politics: Confronting the Powers* (Grand Rapids: Baker Academic, 2005) 178-80; Torrell, *Aquinas Vol. II*, 286.

[19] This is subject to the possibility, which O'Donovan recognises, that a people may be without effective government for a time. The rule of law may be entirely abandoned and a legal system may cease to exist in a particular place at a particular time.

accomplished by the Spirit may be said plainly. The work of the Son is at the centre of all that God does in the sustaining, governing, preparation, and reparation of the world which God created as good but which has fallen. The Incarnation, Crucifixion, Resurrection and *parousia* of the Son are the points to which all the activity of God for, in and through the world is ordered. This much is obvious. Thus, providence is a work of God's grace, of the God who has chosen not to destroy the fallen world but to redeem it.

But as Colwell insists, grace is a dynamic not a thing.[20] It is an action. It is the action of the triune God whose being is perfectly expressed in God's actions. Grace is the action of the triune God in preserving and saving the world, and much of what is done in that regard is most helpfully appropriated to the Holy Spirit. This means recognising that the Holy Spirit has more of a role to play 'than [simply] the application of the work of Christ to believer, church and the rest'.[21] As Torrell says about Aquinas's pneumatology, 'The Spirit was already the one through whom and in whom all the gifts of God come to us, those of nature as well as those of grace.'[22] Such an approach means that common grace ceases to be reified and assumes its true form as a recognition that the Holy Spirit is at work in all places and at all times of human history.

This raises the intriguing possibility that justice has also been inappropriately reified because the definition has been too directly drawn from Roman law rather than by paying close attention to the biblical message. As a divine attribute in which humans participate, justice ought to be understood as a dynamic as in Amos' declaration that justice should roll on like rivers (Amos 5:24).

As was argued in chapter two, seeing law as a provision of God's grace makes it possible to understand liberating justice as having a place in human legal systems. Understanding it to be a provision of God's common grace, that is to say, as a work of the Holy Spirit, means that this can be done without mistaking it as having saving value in itself.

But with the turn from the work of the Son to the work of the Spirit one has moved from what has been plainly revealed to what is mysterious. It has not been given to human beings to comprehend how the Spirit is at work in sustaining, preserving and preparing the world for its appointed end. The fact of the Spirit's mission may be affirmed but the manner of its operation can only be hinted at.[23]

The first aspect of the Spirit's work which must be affirmed is the Spirit's work in ordering human societies. It is through the action of the Holy Spirit that

---

[20] Colwell, *Promise and Presence*, 29, 171.

[21] Gunton, *Promise*, 168, 134, 136.

[22] Torrell, *Aquinas Vol. II*, 223.

[23] E.F. Rogers, 'The Mystery of the Spirit in Three Traditions: Calvin, Rahner, Florensky or, You *Keep* Wondering Where The Spirit Went', *Modern Theology* 19 (2003) 244, 247.

human sinfulness does not lead to the annihilation of the human race. To affirm this as the work of the Holy Spirit is to highlight the fact that the search for a Christian theology of law in particular, or for a Christian political theology in broader terms, is not an exercise in seeking to uncover a self-sustaining basis upon which the millennial social order is to be constructed.

At *JWR* 121, O'Donovan argues that human legal regimes exist on borrowed time, balanced precariously on a combination of power, community recognition and the need for ordered justice for as long as God providentially ordains.[24] What is being argued for in the present thesis is just such a theology of law, which is dependent on the recognition of the role of the Spirit, both in relation to common grace and in relation to sanctifying grace. Those terms are preferable because they emphasise the gratuitous nature of God's actions towards God's creation.

Grace comes first and, against all attempts at self-righteousness, a Barthian emphasis on the inadequacy of human actions in this as all other regards, must be maintained. However, to affirm that human social orders are only sustained by God's grace is not to say that the Holy Spirit will conserve human societies come what may. Human agents have their part to play in co-operating with the preserving and preparing grace of the Holy Spirit. In the case of those who are tasked with law-making or law enforcement, that co-operation takes the form of making wise decisions which tend to promote order and justice.

Order may be prior to justice in the sense that there cannot be a just social order unless there is a social order to begin with, but no social order is sustainable without a commitment to justice (*BVLJ* 178-80). Aquinas's teleology reveals that law is ordered to justice. The justice to which law is ordered may only be 'shallow justice', it may only be concerned with the distribution and protection of earthly goods, and it may only be able to combat and commend a limited range of external actions, but this form of 'shallow justice' is nonetheless valuable because God has ordained it and God is able to work in and through it, despite the manifold ways in which the 'shallow justice' executed by human authorities falls short of the perfect justice which will be realised in the *eschaton*.

As is explored in the section 'Overcoming alienation through free obedience in the Spirit' below, the Spirit is the One who works 'deep justice' in human hearts. The Spirit is also the agent who enables 'shallow justice' to be done by earthly rulers.[25] The basis for doing so is to be found in the ordering of law to justice which was sketched in the opening chapter and re-visited in the chapter on Aquinas. Because human law is ordered to justice human rulers are

---

[24] Skillen, 'Acting Politically in Biblical Obedience?', 416.

[25] As John Saward explains the Thomist understanding on this point: 'God, the First Cause, is at work, by concurrence, in whatever is positive and good in the actions of His creatures, even in the natural ones ...': 'The Grace of Christ in his Principal Members', 207.

constrained to present their actions as right and just.[26] This is, however, double-edged. On the one hand, this requirement that human rulers appear to be acting justly means that justice is, to however limited and imperfect a degree, sometimes actually done. On the other hand, this requirement presents a temptation for human rulers to claim that what they are doing is actually providing perfect or the best possible justice. The constraint to do justice carries with it the temptation to claim ultimacy for that justice.

The Holy Spirit works in and through human legal institutions to achieve God's purposes. Somehow, out of the mess, the Spirit works for God's good purposes. The basis for this affirmation is the nature of the Spirit's work in the all-too human Church. Understanding the doctrine of common grace as an account of a particular aspect of the Holy Spirit's work could also lead to an understanding of how human governments retain their relative authority despite their failings. That actual manifestations of the state (using that term as convenient shorthand for human authorities) fail in their mission but are nonetheless sustained by the grace of God is no more surprising than that actual manifestations of the Church fail in their mission but are nonetheless sustained by the grace of God.[27] God is pleased, through the Spirit to sustain and give validity to such God-given institutions, however fallen their contemporary expressions may be. In addition, understanding this grace to be nothing other than the operation of the Spirit reveals why it is inappropriate to presume that particular human governments or configurations of human authority are permanent.

Law and the Work of Christ

Law and the Incarnation

Jesus, the God-Man, relates to the law in two different ways. On the one hand, as fully God, He is Righteousness-Incarnate.[28] On the other hand, as the Second Adam, He is fully obedient to God's law. This obedience, as genuine human obedience, is to be understood as Spirit-empowered obedience.

It is because the categories of law and righteousness-justice are primary that politics witnesses to them. It is because Jesus is righteousness-justice incarnate and because, as John's Gospel clearly presents the matter, in Him the divine call is definitively made within history that politics is confronted with Him and must acknowledge its imperfections and limitations.[29]

Jesus' relationship with law as a category has to be approached in three different ways. First, there is Jesus' relationship to what Aquinas calls the

---

[26] Moltmann, *The Power of the Powerless*, 35.
[27] The same is also true of the marriage relationship, which is unequivocally founded in the created order: Gorringe, *Karl Barth: Against Hegemony*, 204.
[28] McIlroy, *BVLJ*, 137.
[29] Storkey, *Jesus and Politics*, 117-29.

eternal law. Second, there is Jesus' relationship to human law. Third, there is Jesus' relationship to the Torah.

Jesus *is* the eternal law. He is the one who incarnates all of God's purposes in the world. Jesus submitted to human law, but did so in a way which asserted His lordship over it. His position in that regard was, therefore, complex, and is discussed in detail in chapters 6 and 8 of *BVLJ*.

Jesus claimed an authority over the Torah.[30] On Levering's reading of Aquinas, explored in the previous chapter, the New Testament offers a trinitarian account of the ways in which the Torah is fulfilled through the work of Christ and by the Spirit in the life of the Christian.[31] That account hinges on the perfect obedience of Christ to the moral precepts of the Torah and on His perfect sacrifice completing the ceremonial precepts of the Torah.

Aquinas's account of Christ's fulfilment of Torah and Temple has already been discussed at length in the previous chapter.[32] The important aspects of the relationship between Christ and the Torah, for the purposes of the present thesis, are that Christ is obedient to the Father where Israel has failed to be obedient to God, and Christ is the perfect sacrifice to end all the sacrifices prescribed by the Torah. Thus, the necessity of Christ's work is the concomitant of the inability of external law to make human beings just. Christ's incarnation, death and resurrection reveals that human laws are incapable of achieving deep justice. It lies beyond their reach.

Law and the Crucifixion

In the moment of the crucifixion we are called back to the origins of human political authority. Human political authority is necessitated by humanity's rejection of God, of God's law and of God's call upon our lives. That primordial choice is reiterated on the choice when God's Anointed King is put to death. Moltmann is right to see in that moment God's self-identification with the victims of human legal orders. The injustice of earthly regimes which purport to provide peace, justice and security is thereby called into question. From the perspective of the cross it ought to be inconceivable that any human political regime could be above scrutiny. The crucifixion exemplifies the fact that the injustices perpetrated by human rulers do not thwart the purposes of the triune God.

However, the crucifixion must also be understood as the moment at which God deals with our own injustice and sinfulness. The cross is the moment at which God overcomes the consequences of humankind's violations of the natural law and Israel's failure to keep the Torah. The book of Hebrews

---

[30] McIlroy, 'The Relevance of the Old Testament Law for Today: Part One', 25-34.

[31] See also McIlroy, *BVLJ*, chapters 6 and 7.

[32] See also McIlroy, *BVLJ*, 122-30.

understands the crucifixion in terms of the ultimate sacrifice for sins,[33] and this is rightly prominent in Aquinas's consideration of its meaning. The crucifixion and resurrection are, taken together, God's decisive action to deal with the consequence of humankind's rejection of a relationship with God and the failure of sinful human beings to keep God's laws, both those revealed in the created order and those given in the Torah.[34] The cross is the supreme moment at which the disorder caused by humanity's rejection of God's love and of God's authority is resolved through God's reconciling, just action, in Christ.

Law and the Resurrection

Moltmann is right that the theological impact of the crucifixion and the resurrection must not be softened by merging the two events into one. O'Donovan is correct to insist that a focus solely on the cross to the detriment of the resurrection is imbalanced. As is apparent from the previous section, a rounded understanding of the cross must already begin to speak about it in the light of the resurrection.

The resurrection points forwards in two directions. It points, through the Ascension to the *eschaton* and the Last Judgment. Here, as O'Donovan stresses, the implication for human law is that Christ is King, and therefore all human rulers are answerable to Him.[35] This, however, needs careful qualification by reference to the cross as exemplifying the manner in which Jesus exercised His Servant Kingship. Second, the resurrection is the inauguration of new life through the power of the Spirit of God who raised Jesus from the dead. Here the resurrection points to Pentecost. The implication for human law is that developed in the next section; human law is limited because of what only the Holy Spirit can do.

Law and the Work of the Holy Spirit

The Holy Spirit and the Torah

An account of the Torah in relation to the Holy Spirit sees the Torah as a gift of God's grace, set within the context of the promise to Abraham,[36] and making plain to a particular community what the holy God required of them. 'The Mosaic Law was given to God's people, chosen and saved by grace, as guidance for right living in relationship with God.' (*BVLJ* 41). Again, law is

---

[33] McIlroy, *BVLJ*, 124-25.

[34] I have begun to explore this in 'Toward a Relational and Trinitarian Theology of Atonement'.

[35] McIlroy, *BVLJ*, chapter 6 and 180-82.

[36] P.A. Barker, *The Triumph of Grace in Deuteronomy* (Carlisle: Paternoster, 2004) 16; McIlroy, *BVLJ*, 41; J.N.D. Anderson, *Freedom under Law* (Eastbourne: Kingsway, 1988) 105; C.J.H. Wright, *Living as the People of God*, 22, 113.

seen to be integral to God's relationship with God's people.

However, though the Torah is seen as good it is also understood to be incomplete. The biblical narrative from Joshua to 2 Kings tells a story about the repetitive rejection by God's people of God's lordship over them and of the inveteracy of human sinfulness. The problem is exemplified in the golden calf incident referred to in Deuteronomy 9, which makes clear that the giving of the law does not solve the problem of sin.[37]

The response of God, expressed through the prophets, reveals the depths of God's love, the unavoidability of God's judgment and the constancy of divine grace.[38] Barker argues that the themes of the inexorability of Israel's failure and the persistence of God's grace are evident in the chapters in Deuteronomy which form a frame around the law and that, in consequence, the law should be read 'in the light of Israel's expected failure.'[39] What Israel needs is a circumcised heart, something God alone can give, and which the New Testament associates with the death of Christ and the giving of the Spirit.[40]

The Mosaic law is the demonstration that the best of laws, even those mediated by angels and expressing God's will for God's people, are inadequate to bring about deep justice, if treated as an external written code of rules. In his doctoral thesis on Deuteronomy, Paul Barker argues that this is the theological perspective of this book, with its pivot at Deut. 30:6.[41] This process of failure culminates in the Exile. On a Christian understanding of the Old Testament, the giving of the Spirit is seen as the fulfilment of the prophecies of Jeremiah 31:33 and Ezekiel 36:26. The Spirit is the One through whom Christians are enabled to live in right relationship with God, loving God and obeying God.[42] The indwelling of the Holy Spirit means, as Moltmann identified in the sermon he preached on Jeremiah 31:33, that Christians no longer live 'under' the law but instead 'in' the law.[43]

As has already been mentioned, O'Donovan is critical of the Western doctrine of the atonement for the exclusive emphasis it places on Good Friday, thus rendering the resurrection a mere appendix to the work of Christ. An understanding of the Torah in the light of the Trinity is in agreement with O'Donovan about the integral nature of the new life of righteousness to the redemption won on the Cross. On the reading of the Old Testament proposed above, the failure of the Torah to make Israel a just people is the problem to which the death of Christ and the giving of the Holy Spirit are the solution.

---

[37] Barker, *The Triumph of Grace*, 89.

[38] McIlroy, *BVLJ*, chapter 5.

[39] Barker, *The Triumph of Grace*, 1, 71, 205.

[40] Barker, *The Triumph of Grace*, 178, 195; McIlroy, *BVLJ*, 148-151.

[41] Barker, *The Triumph of Grace*, 84, 157-68, 181, 220.

[42] C.J.H. Wright, *Knowing the Holy Spirit through the Old Testament* (Oxford: Monarch, 2006) 129-31.

[43] Moltmann, *The Power of the Powerless*, 42.

On the reading of Aquinas developed in the previous chapter, the Holy Spirit enables the righteous requirement of the Torah to be fulfilled, through working internally in Christians to make them holy/ just/ righteous.[44] It is by the grace of God, understood as the coming of the Spirit, that humans are enabled to be obedient to God. This obedience is not alienating but fulfilling because it is the expression of our love for God. The Spirit is thus understood to be the agent through whom there is deep justice. The Spirit is the One who inspires, indwells and empowers Christians to become more like the One who was Justice Incarnate.

Whatever the other deficiencies of his conception of the relationship between Christians and secular authority, Martin Luther saw that human laws would be redundant in a society of Christians who were wholly Spirit-led:

> If all the world were composed of real Christians, that is, true believers, there would be no need for or benefits from prince, king, lord, sword, or law. They would serve no purpose, since Christians have in their heart the Holy Spirit, who both teaches and makes them to do injustice to no one, to love everyone, and to suffer injustice and even death willingly and cheerfully at the hands of anyone.[45]

If they co-operate fully with the Holy Spirit, Christians are beyond the law, in the sense that they freely and fully obey all that human laws and divine laws require, and go freely beyond those laws in their love of God and of their neighbour. However, although a Christian who is fully submitted to the Spirit would not need the coercion of external human law in order to act justly, this does not mean that the category of law, as defined at the outset of this thesis, is no longer of relevance to such a person. Instead, such a person would be obedient to the leading of the Spirit and would thereby perfectly fulfil the righteous requirement of the divine and natural laws. However, such perfect attuning to the Spirit is not to be found this side of glory.

Overcoming Alienation through Free Obedience in the Spirit

After Pentecost, the Holy Spirit continues the work of sustaining the world and moving it towards the goal for which it was created. The Holy Spirit continues to be at work in human lives, leading people to faith in God, but now explicitly through faith in Christ. Furthermore, in a new way, the Holy Spirit is present in those who believe, sanctifying them and preparing them for their glorification, in the Son, in the *eschaton*. This work of sanctification and glorification is the solution to the problem of the alienation from authority and to the experience of law as an extrinsic burden. This is the 'deep justice' which is out of the reach of

---

[44] Rybarczyk, *Beyond Salvation*, 190; McIlroy, 'The Holy Spirit and the Law', *Justice Reflections* 3(14) (2003) JR14; *BVLJ* chapter 7.

[45] M. Luther, 'Temporal Authority: To What Extent it Should be Obeyed?', (1523) in vol. 45 *Luther's Works* (Philadelphia: Muhlenberg Press, 1955-75*)* 89.

human law. Through the Spirit, God's laws are known to be good for human beings, to accord with our true nature and to be conducive to the fulfilment of human needs. Freely chosen, internalised obedience is integral to the flourishing of our true humanity.

Such an understanding of the relationship of the Spirit to obedience is superior to the vision offered by Moltmann. As a child of Nazi Germany, Moltmann has good reasons to be fearful of authority. However, his theology evacuates the sovereignty of the Father of meaning. The result is that he is unable to offer an understanding of our relationship to God which integrates love and obedience.

In contrast, Bauckham points out that

> we know God in three dimensions: as God above us (the Father), alongside us (Jesus, the Son), and within us (the Spirit). The fact that this is the structure of God's *love* for us excludes the domination that eliminates freedom. But also the fact that God's love for us has *this* structure excludes the merely paternalistic care that inhibits freedom. The structure gives Christian freedom three poles between which it takes its shape: authority with belonging, solidarity, spontaneity. ... Each of the three would need careful exposition to explode the myth that God's lordship is incompatible with human freedom and to show how, on the contrary, it enables human freedom.[46]

O'Donovan is, like Barth, insistent on the lordship of God. His account of political authority is therefore much clearer than that of Moltmann's. However, although O'Donovan acknowledges the role of the Holy Spirit in providentially sustaining human regimes, he does not give enough attention to the Spirit's involvement in the discernment of the moral order and the administration of wise judgment. Moreover, O'Donovan's thought would be strengthened by an account of the way in which the Spirit works inwardly in people, transforming them to live lives in the light of the resurrection.

Aquinas's understanding of the work of the Spirit offers a way forward in terms of integrating human fulfilment, love for God and obedience to God. Although he wavers at times, at his best, he offers a description of the Christian life as culminating in conformity to the likeness of the Son, through the indwelling of the Spirit, thus placing us within the Son's relationship to the Father.

A particular understanding of human freedom is the concomitant of a teleologically focussed account of human nature and of human flourishing. It is because Aquinas believes that he knows where humanity is intended to be and what is good for human beings that he is able to integrate freedom and law. Freedom is not to be conceived in Enlightenment terms as the capacity for indeterminate choice. It is not the arbitrary exercise of the naked will. On the contrary, true freedom comes with the responsible exercise of choice in

---

[46] Bauckham, 'Jürgen Moltmann and the Question of Pluralism', 164.

accordance with what I know, have learnt or believe is good for me, that is to say is in accordance with who I have been created to be.[47] It is the work of the Holy Spirit to reveal these things to followers of Christ, who are empowered by the Spirit to choose freely to submit themselves to the will of the Father who they know to have their best interests at heart.

One of the benefits of recent Western attention to Eastern Orthodox theology has been the rediscovery of glorification as a catholic doctrine, that is to say, as a doctrine of the whole Church. The doctrine of glorification is a biblical doctrine. As well as the *locus classicus* of 2 Peter 1:3-4, the doctrine can also be discerned in John 14:16ff., in 1 John 3:1-2 and in the imagery of the Church as the Body and the Bride of Christ. Through Jesus we are brought into a relationship of sonship with God the Father (John 20:17; 16:10, 17, 28; 14:1-3). Although Richard Bauckham is cautious about whether 2 Peter 1:4 must be interpreted as referring to human participation in the very life and being of God, he recognises the doctrine of deification as a biblical one on the basis of the Pauline concept of the Christian's participation in God through the Holy Spirit (Rom. 8:11; 1 Cor. 15:42-53).[48] The advantage of approaching the doctrine from this direction is that it makes explicit that our participation in God is a communion with the Father, in the likeness of the Son to whom we are conformed by the Spirit. As Rybarczyk notes, *'our focus should not so much be upon becoming fully divine as it should be upon becoming fully human.'*[49]

The Fathers were therefore faithful to the biblical witness in reflecting on the idea. Although sometimes regarded as a typically Eastern doctrine, recent research has highlighted the fact that it is a doctrine also found in the great theologians of the West. Gerald Bonner has explored it in the thought of Augustine.[50] As has been discussed in the previous chapter A.N. Williams and others have argued for its presence in Aquinas.[51] Finnish scholarship has

---

[47] Colwell, *Promise and Presence*, 28; J.A. Kirk, *The Meaning of Freedom: A Study of Secular, Muslim and Christian Views* (Carlisle: Paternoster, 1998) 200-12.

[48] R. Bauckham, *Word Biblical Commentary vol. 50: Jude, 2 Peter* (Milton Keynes: Word, 1983) 180-82. See also R.W. Jenson, who argues that the very notion of eternal life requires the doctrine of deification: 'The Triunity of Common Good' in Miller and McCann, eds., *The Common Good* 340.

[49] Rybarczyk, *Beyond Salvation*, 170-71, italics original. In a similar vein, Milbank sees deification as 'a self-fulfillment, an offering that is at the same time our reception of the fullness of Being.': 'Postmodern Critical Augustinianism: A Short *Summa* in Forty-two Responses to Unasked Questions' in G. Ward, ed., *The Postmodern God: A Theological Reader* (Oxford: Blackwell, 1997) 271.

[50] G. Bonner, 'Augustine's Concept of Deification' *Journal of Theological Studies* (1986) 369-86; 'Deification, Divinization' in Fitzgerald, ed., *Augustine Through the Ages: An Encyclopedia* (Grand Rapids: Eerdmans, 1999) 265-66.

[51] A.N. Williams, *The Ground of Union*. See the chapter on Aquinas.

suggested its presence in the thought of Luther,[52] and the same direction has been pursued by Robert Jenson. As Kerr summarises Jenson's conclusions, 'According to Jenson, the "content" of patristic language about hope for participation in God's own nature is substantially the same as biblical eschatology.' The wrong turning came when 'Lutheranism followed Philip Melanchthon, ... rather than Luther, in understanding justification of the unrighteous in strictly forensic terms. By the participation in Christ which occurs as the believer accepts the word of the gospel, Luther takes it that the believer is "ontically righteous". For Luther, justification is "a mode of deification" ...'[53] Mosser and Billings make a compelling case for glorification as a theme in Calvin's writings.[54] Even the Westminster Larger Catechism speaks of salvation as 'union and communion with Christ in grace and glory.'[55]

Most recently, in his textbook on the Trinity, Robert Letham presents a careful account of the doctrine from a Reformed perspective. He argues, following Athanasius, that the basis for our union with God is God's union with humankind through the Incarnation.[56] It is the Incarnation which guarantees not only the possibility of our union with God, but also that fact that such a union will not destroy but fulfil our human nature.[57] Glorification is the completion of our sanctification. It is our perfect and complete union with Christ, assured through the Holy Spirit, which enables us to be fully ourselves in the presence of God.[58] 'Our salvation consists of union with Christ, and so our resurrection is a sharing in his human resurrection and is part of the same reality.'[59]

The Western Church is therefore teaching an impoverished doctrine of salvation if it restricts its focus exclusively to regeneration and justification (as in some forms of 'easy-believism'), or goes no further than an account of sanctification.[60] The goal of our salvation is our union with Christ, our

---

[52] T. Mannermaa, *Der im Glauben gegenwärtige Christus* (Hanover: Arbeiten zur Geschichte und Theologie des Luthertums, 1989); S. Peura, *Mehr als ein Mensch? Die Vergöttlichung als Thema der Theologie Martin Luthers von 1513 bis 1519* (Mainz: Verlag Philipp von Zabern, 1994).

[53] Kerr, *After Aquinas*, 152-53, citing R.W. Jenson, *Systematic Theology* vol.1 (Oxford, OUP, 1997) 71.

[54] C. Mosser, 'The Greatest Possible Blessing: Calvin and Deification', *Scottish Journal of Theology* 55 (2002) 36-57; J.T. Billings, 'John Milbank's Theology of the "Gift" and Calvin's Theology of Grace: A Critical Comparison', *Modern Theology* 21 (2005) 92, 97. See also E. Doumergue, *Jean Calvin* vol. IV: *La pensée religieuse de Jean Calvin* (Lausanne: Georges Bridel et Cie. Editeurs, 1910) 241-42.

[55] Westminster Larger Catechism QQ.65-90. By contrast, the theme of glorification is almost invisible in the Westminster Confession of Faith.

[56] Letham, *The Holy Trinity*, 394.

[57] Letham, *The Holy Trinity*, 467, 471.

[58] Gunton, *The One, the Three and the Many*, 182.

[59] Letham, *The Holy Trinity*, 394.

[60] Letham, *The Holy Trinity*, 464.

enjoyment of an uninterrupted relationship with the Father through the power of the Spirit. Union with Christ is therefore both the ground and, in a fuller sense, the goal of our salvation.[61]

The work of God in us is brought to completion by the power of the Spirit. It is the Spirit who gives us new birth, it is the Spirit who sanctifies us, it is the Spirit who glorifies us. By this is meant that in the *eschaton*, we who are children of God and the bride of Christ are swept up into the perfect fellowship of the Trinity. The importance of this doctrine for our understanding of the Trinity is that it demonstrates the Trinity is not just a reality which stands over against us but is the very life of God in which we will one day participate. Because our participation is through the Spirit, this does not mean the loss of our identity but its fulfilment. As we are made fully Christ-like so we become at last ourselves, the people God made us to be. The very fullness of God's Spirit indwells us.

A theology of glorification is preferable to Moltmann's panentheism. As was discussed in chapter 2, Richard Bauckham indicates how Moltmann's theology could be developed in this direction but this would require the corrective addition of a developed understanding of the sanctifying work of the Holy Spirit enabling us to become Christ-like in our wise obedience to the good commands of the Father.

Only such a doctrine enables us to make sense of the biblical teaching that, as man, Jesus Christ was obedient to God the Father,[62] and that His disciples are called to follow His example of obedience. This obedience is not stifling servitude, but rather life-giving liberty. The paradox is expressed in the 1662 Book of Common Prayer's description of the service of God as perfect freedom.[63]

Contrary to Moltmann's fears, obedience to God is not slavish, it is 'the fulfilment of being human.'[64] The reason for this is that it is not a matter of conformity to an external law, but of obedience to the guidance of the indwelling Spirit. It is the Spirit who works in us to conform us to the likeness of the Son. Obedience to God is not an end in itself; our perfect obedience in glory is ordered to our love for God. We will express our purified and perfected love for God through our purified and perfected worship of God and obedience to God. In doing so, we are drawn up into the life of the Trinity, whose members express perfect love for one another, who glorify one another and are in perfect communion with one another.

Because we are indwelt by the fullness of the Holy Spirit in the *eschaton* we become totally holy, that is to say our wills are wholly aligned with the will of

---

[61] Letham, *The Holy Trinity*, 466.
[62] Barth reads this obedience back into the life of the Godhead: *CD* IV/1:192-205; see also Letham, *The Holy Trinity*, 394-404.
[63] Letham, *The Holy Trinity*, 310.
[64] Letham, *The Holy Trinity*, 393.

the Father. As such, our Christ-likeness comes to its summation. Our obedience, empowered and mediated by the Spirit, it is integral to our transformed nature.[65]

The Last Judgment

The Christian doctrine of the Last Judgment relativises human judgment, affirms human judgment and has implications for human judgment. The Last Judgment relativises human judgment because it demonstrates that all human judgments are provisional and that the triune God has reserved the last word in judgment to Godself. This liberation from pretensions to ultimacy frees human rulers to exercise relative judgments about good and evil in the limited context and for the limited purposes for which they are asked to perform their task. Where the prospect of the Last Judgment is denied, the burden upon human organs of judgment is once again rendered intolerable.[66]

The Last Judgment affirms human judgment. The Judge on the last day will be Christ, who is not only divine but also human. To the extent that human governments are tasked now with judgment, even though it is fallible, finite and marred by human sinfulness and vindictiveness, they participate in an activity which is not sub-Christian because it is not inappropriate for the risen Christ to perform. However, Christ's judgment is preter-natural.

Moreover, the Last Judgment has implications for the content of human judgment. Human rulers ought to temper their judgments both in the light of the fact that they will be answerable for their actions and their lives before the Great Judge and in the light of the character of that Judge as it was revealed when He walked upon the earth.

Summary

Law is therefore given by God in creation. After the Fall, human beings are no longer just addressed by the call of God, which we have rejected, but through the gracious providence of God are given structures of political authority which restrain evil through the enforcement of human laws. What difference does the incarnation make? The call of God given in creation was a call to glorify God and to be fulfilled in God's image. Jesus came as the embodiment of that image, as the Man, made in the image of God, who became perfect in obedience even unto death. He is justice-incarnate. What difference does the crucifixion make? In the crucifixion, the just man was put to death by the

---

[65] Thus, as Milbank sees in *The Word Made Strange* at 229, the need for law backed by sanctions falls away, though I would want to insist, far more clearly than Milbank, that the reason for this is the nature of our participation in the Trinity rather than the mere fact that in the *eschaton* humanity 'consciously partakes of the creativity of God.'

[66] O'Donovan, *Measure for Measure*, 9-10.

unjust. The injustice of earthly regimes which purport to provide peace, justice and security are exposed and called into question. What difference does the resurrection make? God's verdict on human injustice and sinfulness is confirmed, and that Jesus was the one who has exhausted the curse of sin and stood in the place of sinful humanity is affirmed. What difference does the giving of the Spirit make? A new way forward is provided, so that people may be righteous-just not by mere obedience to an external code but through a radical change of heart. What difference does the *parousia* make? That there is a final judgment, and the merciful Judge who sees truly, will give it, is a source of enormous consolation to the victims of what masquerades as justice on earth.

The Limited Role of Human Law

If, as O'Donovan argues, government is to be minimally representative and minimally coercive, it must be because the ultimate locus for human representation and human judgment is to be found elsewhere: in Christ.

The Ambivalent Relationship between Human Government and Divine Government

As the biblical canon recounts the story, God gave the people of Israel the Torah before God permitted them the kingship. *Pace* Aquinas's speculations about human authority in Eden, Genesis records God giving humankind a command. Law as a category may precede the Fall, but human government, at least as we experience it today, is a consequence of human rejection of the authority of God over our lives.

An adequate account of political authority must therefore proceed via a doctrine of the Fall rather than drawing direct analogies between divine governance and human government. An account of political authority, such as that offered by O'Donovan, needs to be tempered by the more fundamental reality of the relationship between law, both human and divine, and divine grace. As has been argued in this thesis, to relate law to grace is to relate law to the triune God, whose actions perfectly express God's Being, and in line with Irenaeus, to relate law to the work of the Son and of the Spirit.

Earlier in this chapter it has been argued that the Son and the Spirit together accomplish what human law cannot; the salvation of human beings from the consequences of their own and other's injustice and their transformation towards conformity to God's perfect justice.

The Role of Human Law in the Light of Redemption

O'Donovan, who seeks to understand government post-Christ, argues that the only sense of political authority acknowledged within Christendom was the law of the ascended Christ, and that all political authority was the authority of that law. Those theologians who insisted, against Ambrosiaster, that the source of political authority was Christ, not God the Father alone, understood something important: however much political authority survives from the old aeon, it does so upon terms set by the new.[67]

Key among those terms is the new understanding of the limits of human law. As Aquinas acknowledged and as Barker points out,[68] even the Mosaic Law had to make significant concessions to the brute fact of human sinfulness. If humanity had simply needed a new lawgiver, Jesus would merely have given a new law.[69] On the contrary, because humanity needed a new justice beyond law, Jesus gave the Holy Spirit.

There is room for disagreement about whether the effect of the coming of Christ on the scope of human political authority was merely revelatory or in fact innovative. Either way, the coming of Christ spelt out the terms on which political authority could henceforth be exercised.

However, pending the Last Judgment, human communities still need ordering towards such peace as may be maintained and such justice as may be enforced, and in pursuing those goals, rulers facilitate the Church's mission of proclaiming the gospel, whether they know it or not. O'Donovan stresses that Jesus has left space for a limited but necessary function of human judgment. O'Donovan emphasises the prohibitory aspect to such judgment, arguing that where a wrong has been committed which requires a judicial response, human authorities are called upon to 'give concrete and effective condemnation.'[70] This is complemented by Alan Storkey's claim that '[Human law] is subordinately and fallibly instituted to uphold what is good.'[71] As will be developed in the section on 'Human Freedom and the Image of God' below, I am contending that, subject to proper constraints and recognition of people's liberty and dignity, an emphasis on what is good is an essential part of the function of human law.[72]

Moreover, as O'Donovan argues, the shape of the judgment meted out by rulers ought to be informed by mercy and enlightened by reflection upon the nature of God's actions in Christ, whilst recognising that salvation is not achieved through the tools of human judgment. Human law cannot be redemptive *in itself*, but it ought to be informed by the fact that God has acted

---

[67] O'Donovan, *DON*, 233.

[68] Barker, *The Triumph of Grace*, 107.

[69] On the relationship between Jesus' ethical teaching and the Mosaic law, see McIlroy, 'The Relevance of Old Testament Law for Today: Part One', 29-34.

[70] O'Donovan, *WOJ*, 87.

[71] Storkey, *Jesus and Politics*, 180.

[72] My argument for these values, and also for the goods of life, rewarding work and meaningful relationships is to be found in McIlroy, *BVLJ*, at 20-26.

to redeem humanity. No human legal system can guarantee the transformation of the criminal or the reconciliation of the parties to a lawsuit, but the way in which the legal system works ought to tend to promote such a possibility rather than being inimical or antithetical to it.

In seeking to find the right balance, Moltmann's double idea of God's providential actions in terms of preservation and preparation is a helpful one. Law must not only preserve social order but ought also to point beyond itself, creating space and opportunities for redemption, forgiveness and changed lives.

Human Freedom and the Image of God

It is beyond the scope of the present thesis to provide an exhaustive account of the goods which human law is or may be called to protect. Nonetheless, it has been suggested that as well as the primary function of restraining the wicked, human law has a secondary function of promoting defined forms of the good. As was explored in the section on 'The Trinity and the necessary task of delivering judgment' of chapter 3 of this thesis, O'Donovan is concerned that when human law is granted a role in promoting the common good, this may cause us to expect too much from it, with a consequent loss of freedom and even the potential for law or the state to become an idol. Despite these concerns, however, he acknowledges that political authority has a role to play in protecting the common good which exists in society as something prior to the political authority which serves it.[73] In relation to Aquinas, who is typically read as falling prey to the problems which O'Donovan identifies with a legal order focussed around the common good, it has been suggested that he may be understood as arguing that the role of the ruler is to enable their people to pursue their proper ends, rather than subordinating them to a single, grand project of society.[74]

In the present section it will be argued that the idea of the Trinity itself provides a theological reason why personal liberty should be protected and the role of political authority confined. Central to Western understandings of Christianity has been the idea of faith in Christ and of committed obedience to Him. Such an understanding can be grounded in the way in which human beings bear the image of God and is of decisive importance in delimiting the role of human law. In advancing this contention, it is not being suggested that this is the totality of the way in which human beings are made in the *imago Dei*, merely that this is an important aspect of this reflection of God's nature.

Molnar defends the conception of the immanent Trinity as necessary to establish God's freedom.[75] Colwell makes a similar point: it is only a proper conception of the doctrine of the Trinity which enables us to be assured that

---

[73] O'Donovan, *WOJ*, 57-61.

[74] See the section on 'The eternal law and God's providence' in chapter 4.

[75] Molnar, *Divine Freedom*, ix-xii, 8.

God is eternally loving, and free in love with regard to God's creation.[76] The doctrine of the Trinity makes the assertion 'God is Love' fundamental to the being of God. Notwithstanding the differences between Molnar's 'Western' and Colwell's more 'Eastern' account of the Trinity, both thinkers stress that the accounts which they offer secure God's freedom to love in God's eternal nature.

The analogy being proposed is an analogy which asserts that being free to love is essential to true humanity. Thus the call of God to human beings is a call made to free human beings, enjoining them to enter into freely chosen relationships of love with God and with other human beings.

From this perspective it is possible to understand the truth in Desmond Tutu's statement: 'God who alone has the perfect right to be totalitarian, has such a profound respect for our freedom that he would rather that we go freely to hell than to compel us to go to heaven.'[77] Human governments are not called upon by God to command people to belong to the Church or to have faith in Christ (if the two can be divided) because their weapon is coercion.[78] Human beings are called by God to worship God, not commanded by political authority to do so. God the Father makes His appeal in the person of the Son, through the agency of the Holy Spirit. The work of the Holy Spirit is the corollary of the arguments from free will that Lactantius and Tertullian offer against attempts to secure faith through coercion.[79] On Aquinas's account, the triune God is unequivocally the first mover in our salvation but does not violate our free will in achieving it (*ST* I.23.3 ad.3; 83.1 ad.3). The distinction between Church and State is rooted in the way in which God calls human beings into fellowship with Godself. That call, as presented in Jesus and by the apostles, was not in the form of coercion but rather an appeal of love.

Human law is ordained to provide a space for the proclamation of the gospel, not to replace it with an enforced, external conformity to Christian rituals. In addition to this mandate, and in order to fulfil it, human law is mandated to restrain evil. This restraint of evil is an inevitably compromised task but one which can, to the extent that it is carried out conscientiously, in some sense anticipate the justice which the triune God enacted through the cross and resurrection and will enact finally in the Last Judgment.

The Need to Restrain Evil

O'Donovan is right to assert the epistemological priority of injustice. His conclusion on this point is the same as that of Gary Haugen, the founder of

---

[76] Colwell, *Promise and Presence*, 24.

[77] D. Tutu, lecture at the London University Institute of Education, 4th March 2004.

[78] Storkey, *Jesus and Politics*, 166.

[79] Bretherton discusses these and other arguments for toleration in his *Hospitality as Holiness* at 123-26.

International Justice Mission.[80] O'Donovan reasons that human law is primarily concerned with restraining evil rather than promoting good for two reasons. One is the indeterminacy and the plurality of the human good. The other is an Augustinian or Barthian insistence on the absolute distance between the justice of God and human justice.

Both these reasons are valid, though the second one needs some qualification, as is discussed in the next section. However, the present study has argued that the main reason why human law is primarily concerned with restraining evil is because that is the task which is left to it given the transformation of the human condition effected by God in Christ and in Christians through the Holy Spirit. It is not just that God has given the decisive judgment and effected ultimate reconciliation in Christ; it is also that God is working towards making human beings truly just through the indwelling presence of the Holy Spirit.

Human legal orders are bounded by Christ. They are bounded by His cross and His judgment seat. In this sense, Barth is right to insist that they fall within the christological sphere.[81] The cross stands over human legal orders and emphasises that they cannot, and are not called to, reconcile us to God. The Last Judgment stands over human legal orders and affirms that the task of judgment is one which Godself will ultimately undertake. All human judgments are therefore temporary and provisional.

Nonetheless, the grace of the triune God is such that God has purposed that even amidst the mess which humans make of the inevitable task of judgment, God the Holy Spirit is pleased to work, using the experience of judgment to call to faith in God the Son those who are on the receiving end of judgment, those who witness its administration and its absence, and those who are involved in its pronouncement and execution.

On the Relationship between Human Justice and Divine Justice

Where Augustine and Aquinas divide is on the first note to be sounded with regard to the relationship between human justice and divine justice. Aquinas's metaphysics lead him to affirm the residual goodness of creation notwithstanding the Fall. He asserts that human governance participates in God's governance of the world, and that human justice participates in God's justice. That primary assertion is then heavily qualified by the recognition that what passes for human justice is beset by practical problems, is not straightforward in its execution, and may be subverted by the ruler's private agenda.

For Augustine, followed by O'Donovan, human attempts at justice are

---

[80] G.A. Haugen, *Good News About Injustice: A Witness of Courage in a Hurting World* (Leicester: Inter-Varsity Press, 1999) 69-74.

[81] Barth, *Church and State*, 120.

irretrievably compromised by the Fall. The task of governing a community is one of making the best of a bad job, stopping the worst excesses of evil and trying to preserve a tolerable peace.

There are dangers with both accounts. Unless Aquinas's qualifications are taken seriously, his primary emphasis could lead to absolutism, in which God is reduced to a rubber stamp of the outcomes of human justice. The danger in Augustine's account is that of despair, of acceptance of the status quo because any gains against injustice are ultimately immaterial. The result of such despair is again to eliminate Christian criticism of the present legal order. Once Roman justice has been denounced as not being true justice, it is possible to read Augustine as leaving the field open to *Realpolitik*.[82] Augustine is, however, too cognisant of Romans 13:1-7 for that to be an accurate description of his position. Nonetheless, the same motif resurfaces in the work of that influential Augustinian monk, Luther.

Neither Augustine nor Aquinas would have condoned such distortions of their thought. Both are agreed that human justice is a temporary expedient and that ultimate judgment is reserved to God alone. Aquinas's theory is intended to subordinate human justice to divine justice, and to remind Christian rulers of their obligations to decide in accordance with the laws, both natural and scriptural, which God has revealed. Equally Augustine was clear about the obligation on the Church to intercede with secular rulers to ask that judgment be tempered with mercy.

Perhaps the choice between the two conceptions is a matter of temperament, perhaps it is explicable by the different times in which Augustine and Aquinas were writing. It would require at least another thesis to arbitrate between the two. What needs to be reckoned with is the fact that God's governance of the world is mediated. The Angelic Doctor is, of course, famous for his lengthy discussion about how God's governance is mediated through angels (*ST* I.105-114). A trinitarian doctrine of providence would also, however, affirm the mediation of God's governance through human rulers. There is a mystery and a double-sidedness to this which Barth brings out clearly. When human rulers perform their appointed tasks conscientiously, God works through them by the Holy Spirit in sustaining human societies. When human rulers depart from their appointed task, the witness of the Church in the face of such injustice brings glory to God.[83]

I have suggested in section discussing 'The Trinity and the doctrine of providence' in this chapter that a distinction might be made between 'shallow justice' and 'deep justice'. 'Shallow justice' is what human rulers are called to administer. The biblical call to do justice is one of the clearest messages of the Hebrew Scriptures, explored at length in chapters three to six of *BVLJ* and in

---

[82] C. Kirwan, *Augustine* (London: Routledge, 1989) ch. 11.

[83] Barth, *Church and State*, 15-17, 54, 65; Moltmann hints at the same idea in *Experiences in Theology* 101.

Gary Haugen's *Good News About Injustice*. Moltmann's insistence on this is salutary.[84]

However, 'deep justice' is something which is out of reach for human rulers. They have neither the means to effect it, as they cannot give the Holy Spirit; nor do they have the means to police it, as the state of a man's heart is beyond human examination.

We were made to live in right relationship with God; we were made to live in right relationship with one another. Divine justice transcends earthly justice as the light of the Sun surpasses the flickering glow of a candle flame. As with human happiness, which is fragile and incomplete at the best of times in this life, so too with human justice. But to acknowledge the fragility and incompleteness of 'shallow justice' is not to deny its goodness, as something through which is God is pleased to work by the Spirit.

The notion of mediation is illuminated by the idea of grace, understood as the free action of God, ordained by the Father, ordered to the Son, and accomplished by the Spirit. It is the idea of grace which makes it possible to understand how God can graciously work through imperfect human law insofar as it tends towards truth, love and justice; and graciously preserves human societies insofar as their legal order falls short of truth, love and justice. It is by grace that, in the performance of its limited tasks, human law is used providentially by the Holy Spirit to witness indirectly to the justice of God in Christ and to prepare a space for the direct witness of the Church to Christ.

The present study has said little about the relationship between Church and State. But there is an analogy to be drawn between the two. Churches are human communities which witness to the love of God, both insofar as they reflect that love into the wider societies in which they are situated, and also insofar as they fall short of the glory of God, in that He nonetheless is pleased to work in and through them.

The Christian critique of government ought to be a humble attack on hypocrisy: condemning the difference between the claim of government to act justly and the actual practice of judgment with all its failings. However, it must be a humble critique, because the Church must necessarily recognise its own hypocrisy and the degree to which its own practices fall far short of the King whom it professes to serve.[85]

Conclusion

What is being contended for here is an account of human law as ordained as a means of shallow justice but incompetent to pursue deep justice and the conversion of hearts to Christ. Human law is ordained to pursue shallow justice

---

[84] Moltmann, *SL*, 53-54, 142-43; *Coming* 206, 211; *Experiences in Theology* 298; In *the End* 62-74.

[85] Moltmann, *Theology Today*, 20-21

because that is what the triune God wills to work through it by the Spirit. It is not ordained to pursue deep justice because the triune God who loves in freedom seeks to draw human beings into relationship with Godself through their own free decision to love God.

Understanding the Trinity as a reality we respond to and into which we are drawn, rather than an image we appropriate gives rise, when applied to a theology of law, to an affirmation of the positive but limited role which human law is called to play, in maintaining a relative justice and peace.

It is the Holy Spirit, not human law, which is the means through which God achieves deep justice, as the Father transforms human beings by the power of the Spirit, into the likeness of the Son. Such human beings are salt and light within the societies in which they find themselves, acting, as Aquinas recognised, as 'the most important members of the community' (*ST* II-II.64.6), in accordance with the Holy Spirit, to foster a level of social morality which law alone cannot maintain.[86]

Finally, however, it has been argued that the search for an account of human law which establishes the institution as self-sustaining, would be thoroughly misguided. All human legal systems fall short, even in pursuit of merely shallow justice.[87] All are therefore simultaneously under the judgment of God and, to the extent that they are not undone, sustained by the grace of God, both judgment and grace being understood as attitudes of the Father, mediated by the Son and the Spirit.

---

[86] Letham, *The Holy Trinity*, 11.
[87] Storkey, *Jesus and* Politics, 175.

Chapter 6

Conclusion

The Church formulated its understanding of the Trinity because of the revelation of God in Christ and the events of Pentecost and afterwards. It understood the coming of Christ and the giving of the Spirit as not only the beginning of its own life but also as the culmination of God's purpose of salvation, manifested throughout God's dealings with God's people, Israel. Thus the Trinity is revealed in the context of and as the context of the salvation-history of Israel's God.

The present study has argued for the indispensability of reflections on the Trinity in developing a Christian account of the role of human law. However, it has been contended that the mere symbolic invocation of the Trinity is insufficient and that the doctrine of the Trinity is properly deployed in conjunction with a presentation of the narrative of God's actions towards the world which demanded the emergence of the doctrine in the first place. This is an important reminder that whilst the Trinity is a fundamental doctrine which has often been ignored to the detriment of the development of a distinctively and authentically Christian doctrine of law and authority, neither is it able to bear the weight of such a doctrine on its own. It has been argued that the Trinity must inform a Christian view of human law and authority, but that it must be understood from a biblical perspective. Essentially this means that the Trinity must not be detached from the divine economy, or to put it another way, who God is must not be seen in isolation from what God does. Only by understanding the Trinity as a biblical concept, can the temptations to reduce it to a Platonic reality or to project onto the internal relations of God our own desired views of human community be avoided.[1]

It has therefore been suggested that the most fruitful approach to the Trinity is one which centres attention on the economic Trinity and regards God's trinitarian life as something into which human beings are invited to participate rather than a reality to be mastered and studied objectively.

Applying this approach to the three theologians whose work has been explored, it is submitted that Moltmann's social trinitarianism is unhelpful at the points where he abstracts from the narrative of God's actions towards the

---

[1] Molnar, *Divine Freedom*, 312.

world and engages in undisciplined speculation about God's inner life in order to draw conclusions about human social life. For Moltmann, the Trinity functions more as a symbol than a foundation for his thought.[2] With regard to O'Donovan, while there is much to commend in his attention to the narrative of God's actions towards the world, there is a pneumatological deficit in his thought which has not yet been sufficiently corrected. Aquinas, surprisingly, offers a participatory approach to the Trinity which, for all the questions which may be raised about the adequacy of his conceptualisation of the Persons, is closest to the type of understanding of the Trinity which is being commended.

Each of the three theologians has something of significance which needs to be integrated in a trinitarian theology of law. Moltmann's emphasis on the priority of the poor and the ordering of law to justice are central Christian themes. He offers an insight into the possibilities of law for both good and evil through the recognition that wielding coercive power involves the temptation and tendency to domination but is subject to the call and the possibility of effecting liberation. That strand in Moltmann's thought which sees the Spirit as 'an ordering power immanent in the world' (*SL* 46) opens up an understanding of law as an ordering force which may promote liberation and justice, whilst he stresses that the Church must never offer uncritical support to any particular political regime.

For O'Donovan, the work of Christ leaves judgment as the central activity which legitimates political authority. Rulers must give judgment in the light of the divine law, both natural and revealed, whilst taking full account of the particular conditions and sins which affect the societies they govern. Political authority is not only defined by Christ, and accountable to God but is dependent on God's gracious action in sustaining it providentially by the Holy Spirit.

Aquinas, read as a theologian of the Holy Spirit, offers a way of understanding human law as performing real but limited justice whilst recognising that true, inward, transformation is beyond its scope. Key to Aquinas' account is his conception of the Spirit as the New Law, working in Christians to guide them and empower them to obey God. This work of the Spirit culminates in the eschatological glorification of human beings, when the need for external constraints is eliminated as human beings enjoy perfect communion with the Father, in the Son, by the Spirit.

In the previous chapter, those insights have been drawn together and developed, and integrated with my earlier work in *A Biblical View of Law and Justice*. What has been sketched in that chapter is a particular trinitarian account of the doctrines of justification, sanctification and glorification by reference to natural law and the Torah. The Trinity is understood as a reality we respond to and into which we are drawn, rather than an image we appropriate. Such an understanding of the Trinity, which is grounded in salvation history

---

[2] Otto, *The God of Hope*, 224.

gives rise, when applied to a theology of law, to an affirmation of the positive but limited role which human law is called to play, in maintaining a relative justice and peace.

While human law belongs to the age which is passing away, it performs a stabilising function which enables the Church to pursue its mission. Furthermore, if such law is to be informed by the shape of the moral order which finds its coherence in Christ, and the work of Christ, it is possible to expect 'anticipations' of the future, or at least an openness to the work of the Spirit expressed within human legal systems.

Human law is recognised to be incompetent to effect true, inward, transformation but as performing the valuable function of executing 'shallow justice'. The recognition of the work of the Spirit both prevents the imposition of compulsory Christianity and provides a framework for understanding the value of 'shallow justice'. Aquinas points the way to a relatively liberal, relatively peaceful and relatively just legal order which is concerned with temporal goods whilst being open to God's calling to the eternal good. Such a legal system will focus on its primary task of restraining evil, whilst promoting certain forms of the good which are fundamental to human wellbeing.

All human legal systems are simultaneously under the judgment of God in so far as they fall short in their pursuit of 'shallow justice' and are sustained by the grace of God in so far as God uses them to preserve human societies. Human law is therefore overshadowed by the work of the Son, included in the purposes of the Father, and used as an instrument by the Holy Spirit.

However, the possibilities for further work in this field have not yet been exhausted. There are at least four different directions in which further work could usefully be done. First, taking the present thesis as established, its implications could be drawn out. What concrete consequences does the present thesis have in terms of penology and criminology?, in terms of forms of dispute resolution? What are its implications in terms of substantive law? How could the present thesis be widened to embrace other aspects of political theology?

Second, it has been strongly argued in this thesis that Aquinas has been widely mis-read and that Gunton's criticism of the Western tradition ought to be qualified as a criticism of what the Western tradition has made of Aquinas. Is the same also true of Luther and Calvin? Are there trinitarian elements in their thought which have been undervalued by subsequent generations and which, if developed, have the potential to re-orientate Lutheran and Calvinist reflections on law?

Third, the present thesis could be brought into dialogue with other recent theological currents. It could be tested against the insights of feminist and liberation theologies, both of which raise in their different ways the question of authority. There is also the possibility of fruitful dialogue with the neo-orthodoxy of Barth and the radical orthodoxy of Milbank and Cavanaugh. With regard to these two theologies, natural law, pneumatology and readings of Aquinas are all areas which could be explored further.

Finally, the understanding of law presented in this thesis resolves the questions of law and authority through a doctrine of glorification. Edmund Rybarczyk's ground-breaking study Beyond Salvation: Eastern Orthodoxy and Classical Pentecostalism on Becoming Like Christ similarly identifies the potential for a carefully nuanced understanding of theosis to inform and enrich Western understandings of God's work and purpose for human beings. However, as Rybarczyk points out, the Orthodox doctrine of theosis is typically presented within a framework which understands the significance of Christ in terms of the healing rather than the pardoning of humanity.[3] The importance of a doctrine of glorification in the present study suggests that the juridical and therapeutic understandings of the work of God in Christ and by the Spirit ought not to be understood as mutually exclusive alternatives but rather as complementary aspects of reality.[4] If this is right, then there is reason to continue ecumenical dialogue on this point.

Envoi

Having said all of the above, the importance of the present study must not be over-estimated. O'Donovan is right to identify questions relating to political authority as subsequent to the Church. In Zechariah's vision, the Lord declares that the *missio Dei* will be accomplished 'Not by might, nor by power, but by my Spirit, says the Lord of hosts' (Zech. 4:6). Richard Bauckham has argued that this theme is picked up in Revelation's vision of history, which begins with a trinitarian greeting from the eternal God on the throne, the sevenfold (i.e. perfect) Spirit, and Jesus Christ 'who is the faithful witness, the firstborn from the dead, and the ruler of the kings of the earth.' (Rev. 1:4).[5] The government of God is not of this world though, as Alan Storkey has pointed out in his recent book, it has profound implications for the ways in which human political authorities are regarded.[6]

A political theology is necessitated by the fact that the Church is called to serve and witness to the one who is the ruler of the kings of the earth. A political theology is inevitable given that the Church is a polis. But the mission of God in the world will not be solely or primarily accomplished through human politics or human law-making and enforcement. The righteousness of God will only be manifested on earth through a people who display the love of the Father, follow the example of the Son and are transformed by the Spirit.

---

[3] Rybarczyk, *Beyond Salvation*, 87, 77
[4] Malet, *Personne et Amour*, 151-52.
[5] R. Bauckham, *The Theology of the Book of Revelation* (Cambridge: CUP, 1993) 110.
[6] Storkey, *Jesus and Politics*, 115.

Bibliography

Books and Articles

Anderson, J.N.D., *Freedom under Law* (Eastbourne: Kingsway, 1988)

Aquinas, T., *Catena aurea in quatuor Evangelia* ed. A. Guarenti (Turin: Marietti, 1953)

—, *Commentary on the Gospel of John: Part I* tr. Weisheipl and Larcher (Albany, NY: Magi Books, 1980)

—, *Commentary on the Nicomachean Ethics* tr. C.I. Litzinger (Chicago: Regnery, 1964)

—, *Compendium Theologiae* (Rome: Commissio Leonina, 1979) vol. 42

—, *De articulus fidei et ecclesiae sacramentis, ad Archiepiscopum Panormitanum* (Rome: Commissio Leonina, 1979) vol. 42

—, *De decem preceptis* tr. J-P. Torrell as 'Les *Collationes in decem preceptis* de Saint Thomas d'Aquin. Edition critique avec introduction et notes', *Revue de Sciences Philosophiques et Théologiques* (1985) 5-40 and 227-63

—, *Hic est liber mandatorum Dei. Opuscula theologica* ed. R. Verardo (Turin: Marietti, 1954)

—, *The Literal Exposition on Job* tr. Anthony Damico (New York: Oxford University Press, 1989)

—, *On Kingship – to the King of Cyprus* tr. G.B. Phelan (Toronto: The Pontifical Institute of Mediaeval Studies, 1949)

—, *On Law, Morality, and Politics* tr. R.J. Regan 2nd edn. (Indianapolis: Hackett, 2002)

—, *Quaestiones disputatae de potentia* tr. English Dominican Fathers (Westminster, Maryland: The Newman Press, 1952)

—, *Quaestiones disputatae de veritate* tr. Mulligan, McGlynn and Schmidt (Chicago: Henry Regnery Company, 1954)

—, *Scriptum super libros sententiarum Magistri Petri Lombardi* ed. P. Mandonnet and F. Moos (4 vols.: Paris, 1929-47)

—, *Selected Writings* tr. R. McInerny (Harmondsworth: Penguin, 1998)

—, *The Sermon-Conferences of St. Thomas Aquinas on the Apostles' Creed* tr. N. Ayo (Notre Dame: University of Notre Dame, 1998)

—, *Summa contra Gentiles*, tr. by A.C. Pegis et al. *On the Truth of the Catholic Faith* (5 vols.: New York: Doubleday, 1955-57)

—, *Summa Theologica* tr. The Fathers of the English Dominican Province, 1911 (5 vols.: Allen, TX: Christian Classics, 2000)

—, *Super Epistolam ad Hebraeos* in *Super Epistolas S. Pauli Lectura* 2 vols, 8th edn., ed. R. Cai (Rome: Marietti, 1953)

—, *Super Evangelium S. Ioannis Lectura*, 5th edn., ed. R. Cai (Rome: Marietti, 1951)

—, *Super Evangelium S. Matthaei Lectura*, 5th edn,, ed. R. Cai (Rome: Marietti, 1951)

—, *Thomas Aquinas, The Literal Exposition on Job: A Scriptural Commentary Concerning Providence* tr. A. Damico (Atlanta: Scholars Press, 1989)

Atkins, E.M., and Dodaro, R.J. eds., *Augustine Political Writings* (Cambridge: CUP, 2001)

Aubert, J.M., 'L'Analogie entre la Lex Nova et la Loi Naturelle' in Elders and Hedwig eds., *Lex et libertas* 248-53

Augustine, *The City of God* tr. H. Bettenson (Harmondsworth: Penguin, 1955)

—, *The Trinity* tr. E. Hill (Brooklyn: New City Press, 1991)

Austin, V.L., 'Method in Oliver O'Donovan's political theology', *Anglican Theological Review* 79(4) (1997) 583-594

Badcock, G., 'Karl Rahner, the Trinity and Religious Pluralism' in K. Vanhoozer ed., *The Trinity in a Pluralism Age* (Grand Rapids: Eerdmans, 1997) 143-54

Bailleux, E., 'Le cycle des mission trinitaires, d'après Saint Thomas', *Revue Thomiste* 63 (1963) 163-92

Barker, P.A., *The Triumph of Grace in Deuteronomy* (Carlisle: Paternoster, 2004)

Barth, K., *Church Dogmatics* tr. G.W. Bromiley and T.F. Torrance (Edinburgh: T. & T. Clark, 1956-77)

—, *Church and State* tr. G. Ronald Howe (London: SCM, 1939)

—, *Community, State, and Church* (Gloucester, MA: Peter Smith, 1968)

—, *Dogmatics in Outline* (1947) tr. G.T. Thomson (London: SCM, 1949, 2001)

—, *Eine Schweizer Stimme 1938-1945* (Zurich: Theologischer Verlag, 1945)

—, *Ethics* tr. G.W. Bromiley (Edinburgh: T & T Clark, 1981)

—, *How I Changed My Mind* ed. J. Godsey (Edinburgh: St Andrew Press, 1969)

—, *The Christian Life* tr. G.W. Bromiley (Grand Rapids: Eerdmans, 1981)

—, *The Church and the Political Problem of Our Day* (London: Hodder & Stoughton, 1939)

—, *The Epistle to the Romans* tr. E.C. Hoskyns 6th edn. (London: OUP, 1933, 1968)

—, *The German Church Conflict* (1956) tr. P.T.A. Parker (London: Lutterworth, 1965)

—, *The Holy Ghost and the Christian Life* (1929) tr. R. Birch Hoyle (London: Frederick Muller, 1938)

—, *Letters 1961-1968* Fangemeier and Stoevesandt eds., tr. G.W. Bromiley (Grand Rapids: Eerdmans, 1981)

—, *The Theology of John Calvin* (1993), tr. G.W. Bromiley (Grand Rapids: Eerdmans, 1995)

—, *The Word of God and the Word of Man* (1925) tr. D. Horton (London: Hodder & Stoughton, 1935)

Barth K. and Brunner E., *Natural Theology comprising 'Nature and Grace' by Professor Dr Emil Brunner and the Reply 'No!' by Dr Karl Barth* tr. P. Fraenkel (London: Geoffrey Bles, 1946)

Bartholomew, C., Chaplin, J., Song, R., Wolters, A. eds., *A Royal Priesthood? The Use of the Bible Ethically and Politically – A Dialogue with Oliver O'Donovan* (Carlisle: Paternoster, 2002)

Bartholomew, C., 'Introduction' in Bartholomew et al. eds., *A Royal Priesthood?* (Carlisle: Paternoster, 2002) 1-45

—, 'A Time for War and a Time for Peace: Old Testament Wisdom, Creation and O'Donovan's Theological Ethics' in Bartholomew et al. eds., *A Royal Priesthood?* (Carlisle: Paternoster, 2002) 91-112

Bauckham, R., ed., *God Will Be All in All: The Eschatology of Jürgen Moltmann* (Edinburgh: T&T Clark, 1998)

Bauckham, R., 'Eschatology in *The Coming of God*' in R. Bauckham ed., *God Will Be*

All in All 1-34

—, 'Jürgen Moltmann's *Trinity and the Kingdom of God* and the Question of Pluralism' in K. Vanhoozer ed., *The Trinity in a Pluralistic Age* (Grand Rapids: Eerdmans, 1997) 155-64

—, 'The Millennium' in R. Bauckham ed., *God Will Be All in All: The Eschatology of Jürgen Moltmann* (Edinburgh: T&T Clark, 1998) 123-148

—, 'Moltmann's Eschatology of the Cross', *Scottish Journal of Theology* 30 (1977) 301-311

—, *The Theology of Jürgen Moltmann* (Edinburgh: T&T Clark, 1995)

—, *The Theology of the Book of Revelation* (Cambridge: CUP, 1993)

—, 'Time and Eternity' in R. Bauckham ed., *God Will Be All in All: The Eschatology of Jürgen Moltmann* (Edinburgh: T&T Clark, 1998) 155-226

—, *Word Biblical Commentary vol. 50: Jude, 2 Peter* (Milton Keynes: Word, 1983)

Berthoud, J-M., *Une Réligion Sans Dieu: Les Droits de l'Homme contre l'Evangile* (Paris: Editions l'Age de l'Homme, 1993)

Bettis, J.D., 'Political Theology and Social Ethics: The Socialist Humanism of Karl Barth', *Scottish Journal of Theology* 27 (1974) 287-305, also in G. Hunsinger ed., *Karl Barth and Radical Politics* at 159-180

—, 'Is Karl Barth a Universalist?', *Scottish Journal of Theology* 20 (1967) 423-36

Bicknell, E.J., *A Theological Introduction to the Thirty-Nine Articles of the Church of England* 2nd edn. 3rd impression (London: Longmans, Green & Co., 1925, 1942)

Biggar, N., ed. *Reckoning with Barth: Essays in Commemoration of the Centenary of Karl Barth's Birth* (London: Mowbray, 1988)

Billings, J.T., 'John Milbank's Theology of the "Gift" and Calvin's Theology of Grace: A Critical Comparison', *Modern Theology* 21 (2005) 87-105

—, 'John Calvin: United to God through Christ' in M.J. Christensen and J. Wittung eds., *Partakers of the Divine Nature: The History and Development of Deification in the Christian Traditions* (Grand Rapids: Baker Book, 2008)

Black, R., *Christian Moral Realism: Natural Law, Narrative, Virtue and the Gospel* (Oxford: OUP, 2000)

Blenkinsopp, J., *Wisdom and Law in the Old Testament: The Ordering of Life in Israel and Early Judaism* revd. edn. (Oxford: OUP, 1995)

Blount, B.K., 'Response to *The Desire of the Nations*', *Studies in Christian Ethics* 11 (1998) 8-17

Bobrinskoy, B., *The Mystery of the Trinity: Trinitarian Experience and Vision in the Biblical and Patristic Tradition* tr. A.P. Gythiel (Crestwood: N.Y.,: St Vladimir's Seminary Press, 1999)

Bonner, G., 'Augustine's Concept of Deification', *Journal of Theological Studies* (1986) 369-86

—, 'Deification, Divinization' in A.D. Fitzgerald ed., *Augustine Through the Ages: An Encyclopedia* (Grand Rapids: Eerdmans, 1999)

Bretherton, L., *Hospitality as Holiness: Christian Witness Amid Moral Diversity* (Aldershot: Ashgate, 2006)

Brunner, E., *The Christian Doctrine of Creation and Redemption* (Westminster, 1952)

Burgess, J.P., 'Recovering a Theology of God's (Gracious) Law', *Theology Matters* 8(4) (2002) 1-16

Burnside, J., 'Inspired Justice', *Justice Reflections* 1 (2002), JR-1

Burrell, D.B., *Freedom and Creation in Three Traditions* (Notre Dame, Ind: University of Notre Dame Press, 1993)

Carl, M., 'Law, Virtue and Happiness in Aquinas's Moral Theory', *The Thomist* 61 (1997) 425-47

Carroll, M.D., 'The Power of the Future in the Present: Eschatology and Ethics in O'Donovan and Beyond' in Bartholomew et al. eds., *A Royal Priesthood?* (Carlisle: Paternoster, 2002) 116-143

Cavanaugh, W.T., 'The City: Beyond Secular Parodies' in Milbank, Pickstock, Ward eds. *Radical Orthodoxy* (London: Routledge, 1999) 182-200

—, 'A Joint Declaration?: Justification as Theosis in Aquinas and Luther', *Heythrop Journal* 41 (2000) 265-280

Cessario, R., 'Aquinas on Christian Salvation' in Weinandy, Keating and Yocum eds., *Aquinas on Doctrine* 117-138

Chaplin, J. 'Political Eschatology and Responsible Government: Oliver O'Donovan's "Christian Liberalism"' in Bartholomew et al. eds., *A Royal Priesthood?* (Carlisle: Paternoster, 2002) 265-308

—, 'Christian Justifications for Democracy', *Ethics in Brief* 11(3) (2006)

Charry, E.T., 'The Crisis of Modernity and the Christian Self' in M. Volf ed., *A Passion for God's Reign* (Grand Rapids: Eerdmans, 1998) 89-112

—, 'The Law of Christ All the Way Down', *International Journal of Systematic Theology* 7 (2005) 155-68

Chenu, M.D., *Toward Understanding St. Thomas* (Chicago: Henry Regnery, 1964) tr. Landry and Hughes

Chester, T., *Delighting in the Trinity: Just why are Father, Son and Spirit such good news?* (Oxford: Monarch, 2005)

Christensen, M.J. and Wittung J.A. eds., *Partakers of the Divine Nature: The History and Development of Deification in the Christian Traditions* (Cranbury, NJ: FDU Press, 2007)

Clarke, A., *A Cry in the Darkness: The Forsakenness of Jesus in Scripture, Theology and Experience* (Oxford: Regent's Park College, 2002)

Colwell, J.E., *Living the Christian Story: The Distinctiveness of Christian Ethics* (Edinburgh: T. & T. Clark, 2001)

—, 'The Contemporaneity of the Divine Decision: Reflections on Barth's Denial of Universalism' in N. M. de S. Cameron ed., *Universalism and the Doctrine of Hell* (Grand Rapids: Baker Book House, 1993) 139-60

—, *Promise & Presence: An Exploration of Sacramental Theology* (Carlisle: Paternoster, 2005)

Cosden, D., *A Theology of Work: Work and the New Creation* (Carlisle: Paternoster, 2004)

Couenhoven, J., 'Law and Gospel, or the Law of the Gospel: Karl Barth's Political Theology compared with Luther and Calvin', *Journal of Religious Ethics* 30(2) (2002) 181-205

Craycraft, K.R., 'Return to Christendom', *The Review of Politics* 60(1) (1998) 204-7

Davies, B., *The Thought of Thomas Aquinas* (Oxford: Clarendon Press, 1992)

de Kruijf, G., 'The Function of Romans 13 in Christian Ethics' in Bartholomew et al. eds., *A Royal Priesthood?* (Carlisle: Paternoster, 2002) 225-237

Delhaye, P., 'La Loi nouvelle comme dynamisme de l'Esprit-Saint' in Elders and Hedwig eds., *Lex et libertas* 265-80

De Lubac, H., *Surnaturel: Etudes historiques* (Paris: Aubier, 1946) 2nd edn (Paris:

Desclée de Brouwer, 1991)

Devlin, P., *The Enforcement of Morals* (Oxford: OUP, 1959)

Diem, H., 'Karl Barth as Socialist: Controversy Over a New Attempt to Understand Him' in G. Hunsinger ed., *Karl Barth and Radical Politics* 121-138

Dodds, M.J., 'The Teaching of Thomas Aquinas on the Mysteries of the Life of Christ' in Weinandy, Keating and Yocum eds., *Aquinas on Doctrine* 91-116

Doumergue, E., *Jean Calvin* vol. IV: *La pensée religieuse de Jean Calvin* (Lausanne: Georges Bridel et Cie. Editeurs, 1910)

Duce, P., and Strange, D. eds., *Getting Your Bearings: Engaging with contemporary theologians* (Leicester: Apollos, 2003)

Dych, W., *Karl Rahner* (London: Continuum, 1992)

Dyson, R.W., ed. and tr. *Aquinas: Political Writings* (Cambridge: Cambridge University Press, 2002)

Edwards, J., 'A Divine and Supernatural Light ...' in *The Works of Jonathan Edwards* Vol. 2 (Edinburgh: Banner of Truth, 1974) 12-17.

Elders, L.J., and Hedwig, K. eds., *Lex et Libertas: Freedom and Law according to St Thomas Aquinas* (Rome: Liberia Editrice Vaticana, 1987)

Ellul, J., *Le Fondement Théologique du Droit* (Neuchâtel: Delachaux & Niestlé, 1946), tr. by Marguerite Wieser *The Theological Foundation of Law* (London: SCM, 1961)

—, *Anarchy and Christianity* tr. G.W. Bromiley (Grand Rapids: Eerdmans, 1991)

Elshtain, J.B., 'Review of *The Desire of the Nations*', *Theological Studies* 58 (1997) 749-51,

Emery, G., 'The Doctrine of the Trinity in St. Thomas Aquinas' in Weinandy, Keating and Yocum eds., *Aquinas on Doctrine* 45-66

—, *Trinity in Aquinas* (Ypsilanti, Michigan: Sapientia Press, 2003)

Fergusson, D., *Community, Liberalism & Christian Ethics* (Cambridge: CUP, 1998)

Fiddes, P.S., *Participating in God: A Pastoral Doctrine of the Trinity* (London: Darton Longman & Todd, 2000)

Figgis, J.N., *The Political Aspects of St. Augustine's 'City of God'* (London: Longmans, Green, and Co., 1921)

Finnis, J., *Aquinas: Moral, Political, and Legal Theory* (Oxford: OUP, 1999)

—, 'Natural Inclinations and Natural Rights: Deriving "Ought" from "Is" according to Aquinas' in Elders and Hedwig eds., *Lex et libertas* 43-55

—, *Natural Law and Natural Rights* (Oxford: Clarendon, 1980)

—, *The Fundamentals of Ethics* (Oxford: Clarendon, 1983)

Forrester, D.B., *Christian Justice and Public Policy* (Cambridge: CUP, 1997)

Forster, R., *Trinity: Song and Dance God* (Carlisle: Paternoster, 2004)

Franks, C.A., 'The Simplicity of the Living God – Aquinas, Barth and Some Philosophers', *Modern Theology* 21 (2005) 275-300

Fuller, L.L., *The Morality of Law*, revd. edn. (New Haven: Yale University Press, 1977)

Furnish, V.P., 'How Firm A Foundation? Some Questions about Scripture in *The Desire of the Nations*', *Studies in Christian Ethics* 11 (1998) 18-23

Geiger, L.B., 'L'homme image de Dieu. A propos de *Summa theologiae*, Ia, 93, 4', *Rivista di Filosofia Neoscholastica* 66 (1974) 511-32

Geisler, N.L., *Thomas Aquinas: An Evangelical Appraisal* (Grand Rapids: Baker Book, 1991)

George, R.P., *In Defense of Natural Law* (Oxford: OUP, 1999)

Gilby, T., *Between Community and Society: A Philosophy and Theology of the State*

(London: Longman Green, 1952)

—, *Principality and Polity* (London: Longman Green, 1958)

Gilson, E., *Le Thomisme* 5th edn. (Paris: Vrin, 1947) tr. L.K. Shook *The Christian Philosophy of St. Thomas Aquinas* (London: Gollancz, 1957)

Goldsworthy, G., *Gospel and Wisdom: Israel's Wisdom Literature in the Christian Life* (Carlisle: Paternoster, 1987, 1995)

Gorringe, T.J., *Karl Barth: Against Hegemony* (Oxford: OUP, 1999)

—, 'Authority, Plebs and Patricians', *Studies in Christian Ethics* 11 (1998) 24-29

Gottwitzer, H., 'Kingdom of God and Socialism in the Theology of Karl Barth' in G. Hunsinger ed., *Karl Barth and Radical Politics* 77-120

Green, B., 'The Proto-modern Augustine? Colin Gunton and the Failure of Augustine', *International Journal of Systematic Theology* 9 (2007) 328-341

Greene, C.J.D., 'Revisiting Christendom: A Crisis of Legitimization' in Bartholomew et al. eds., *A Royal Priesthood?* (Carlisle: Paternoster, 2002) 314-340

Grisez, G., 'The Doctrine of God and the Ultimate Meaning of Human Life' in A.J. Torrance and M. Banner eds., *The Doctrine of God and Theological Ethics* (Edinburgh: T&T Clark, 2006) 125-38

—, 'The First Principle of Practical Reason', *Natural Law Forum* 10 (1965) 168-96

Grisez, Boyle and Finnis 'Practical Principles, Moral Truth and Ultimate Ends', *American Journal of Jurisprudence* 32 (1987) 99-151

Gunton, C.E., *A Brief Theology of Revelation: The 1993 Warfield Lectures* (Edinburgh: T&T Clark, 1995)

—, *Act and Being* (London: SCM, 2002)

—, *The Actuality of Atonement: A Study in Metaphor, Rationality and the Christian Tradition* (Edinburgh: T&T Clark, 1988)

—, 'Augustine, the Trinity and the Theological Crisis of the West', *Scottish Journal of Theology* 43 (1990) 33-58

—, *Becoming and Being: The Doctrine of God in Charles Hartshorne and Karl Barth* (Oxford: OUP, 1978)

—, *Father, Son and Holy Spirit: Essays Toward a Fully Trinitarian Theology* (Edinburgh: T&T Clark, 2003)

—, *The One, the Three and the Many: God, Creation and the Culture of Modernity* (Cambridge: CUP, 1993)

—, *The Promise of Trinitarian Theology* (Edinburgh: T&T Clark, 1991)

—, *The Triune Creator: A Historical and Systematic Study* (Edinburgh University Press, 1998)

Hall, D.C., *The Trinity: An Analysis of St Thomas Aquinas'* Expositio *of the* De Trinitate *of Boethius* (Leiden: E.J. Brill, 1992)

Hall, P.M., *Narrative and the Natural Law: An Interpretation of Thomistic Ethics* (Notre Dame: University of Notre Dame Press, 1994)

Hamilton, J., 'Were Old Covenant Believers Indwelt by the Holy Spirit?', *Themelios* 30 (2004) 12-22

Harrison, N.V., 'Review of *The Ground of Union*', *St. Vladimir's Theological Quarterly* 45 (2001) 418-21

Hart, H.L.A., *The Concept of Law* 2nd edn. (Oxford: Clarendon Press, 1994)

Hauerwas, S., *A Community of Character: Toward a Constructive Christian Social Ethic* (Notre Dame, 1981)

—, *Suffering Presence: Theological Reflections on Medicine, the Mentally*

Handicapped, and the Church (Notre Dame, 1986)
—, 'The Sermon on the Mount, Just War and the Quest for Peace', *Concilium* no.1 (1988) 36-43
—, 'The Truth about God: The Decalogue as Condition for Truthful Speech' in A.J. Torrance and M. Banner eds., *The Doctrine of God and Theological Ethics* (Edinburgh: T&T Clark, 2006) 85-104
—, *Truthfulness and Tragedy: Further Investigations in Christian Ethics* (Notre Dame, 1977)
Hauerwas, S. and Fodor, J. 'Remaining in Babylon: Oliver O'Donovan's Defense of Christendom', *Studies in Christian Ethics* 11 (1998) 30-55
Hauerwas, S. and Wilken, R., 'Protestants and the Pope', *Commonweal* 107 (1980) 80-85.
Haugen, G.A., *Good News About Injustice: A Witness of Courage in a Hurting World* (Leicester: Inter-Varsity Press, 1999)
Healy, N.M., 'Introduction' in Weinandy, Keating and Yocum eds., *Aquinas on Scripture* 1-20
Hegel, G.W.F., *Philosophy of Mind* (Oxford: Clarendon, 1971)
Hemming, L.P., ed. *Radical Orthodoxy? – A Catholic Enquiry* (Aldershot: Ashgate, 2000)
Heslam, P.S., *Creating a Christian Worldview: Abraham Kuyper's Lectures on Calvinism* (Carlisle: Paternoster, 1998)
Hewitt-Horsman, S., 'The Kingdom in Milbank: A Critique', *Theology* (2003) 259-266
Hill, E., *The Works of Saint Augustine – A translation for the 21st Century: The Trinity* (Brooklyn: New City Press, 1991)
Hill, W.J., *The Three-Personed God: The Trinity as a Mystery of Salvation* (Washington DC: Catholic University of America Press, 1982).
Holmes, J., 'Aquinas' *Lectura in Matthaeum*' in Weinandy, Keating and Yocum eds., *Aquinas on Scripture* 73-98
Holmes, S.R., *Listening to the Past: The Place of Tradition in Theology* (Carlisle: Paternoster, 2002)
Honoré, T., 'The Necessary Connection between Law and Morality', *Oxford Journal of Legal Studies* 22 (2002) 489-95
Hood, R.E., *Contemporary Political Orders and Christ: Karl Barth's Christology and Political Praxis* (Allison Park, PA: Pickwick, 1985)
Hoonhout, M.A., 'Grounding Providence in the Theology of the Creator: The Exemplarity of Thomas Aquinas', *Heythrop Journal* 43 (2002) 1-19
Hughes, C., *On a Complex Theory of a Simple God: An Investigation in Aquinas' Philosophical Theology* (Ithaca: Cornell University Press, 1989)
Hughes, D. with Bennett, M., *God of the Poor: A Biblical Vision of God's Present Rule* (Carlisle: OM Publishing, 1998)
Hunsinger, G., ed. *Karl Barth and Radical Politics* (Philadelphia: Westminster, 1976)
'Preface' 7-8, 'Introduction' 9-14, and 'Conclusion: Toward a Radical Barth' 181-234 in the same volume
—, 'Review of Jürgen Moltmann *The Trinity and the Kingdom*', *The Thomist* 47 (1983) 129-139
Hyman, G., *The Predicament of Postmodern Theology: Radical Orthodoxy or Nihilist Textualism?* (Louisville, Kentucky: Westminster John Knox Press, 2001)
Insole, C.J., 'Against Radical Orthodoxy: The Dangers of Overcoming Political

Liberalism', *Modern Theology* 20 (2004) 213-241

—, *The Politics of Human Frailty: A Theological Defence of Political Liberalism* (London: SCM, 2004)

Irenaeus, *Against Heresies* in A.C. Coxe ed., *The Ante-Nicene Fathers vol. 1: the Apostolic Fathers with Justin Martyr and Irenaeus* (Buffalo, NY: Christian Lit. Publ. Co, 1887) 315-467

Izuzquiza, D., 'Can a Gift be wrapped? John Milbank and Supernatural Sociology', *Heythrop Journal* 47 (2006) 387-404

Jackson, B.S., '"Law" and "Justice" in the Bible' *Journal of Jewish Studies* 49 (1998) 218-29

Jaffa, H.V., *Thomism and Aristotelianism* (Chicago: University of Chicago Press, 1952)

Jenson, R.W., *Systematic Theology* vol.1 (Oxford, OUP, 1997)

—, 'The Triunity of Common Good' in Miller and McCann eds., *The Common Good* 333-48

Jowers, D.W., 'The reproach of modalism: a difficulty for Karl Barth's doctrine of the trinity', *Scottish Journal of Theology* 56 (2003) 231-46

Jüngel, E. *Christ, Justice and Peace: Toward a Theology of the State in Dialogue with the Barmen Declaration* tr. D.Bruce Hamill and Alan J. Torrance (Edinburgh: T & T Clark, 1992)

Keating, D.A., '1 and 2 Cor.: The Sacraments and their Ministers' in Weinandy, Keating and Yocum eds., *Aquinas on Scripture* 127-48

—, 'Justification, Sanctification and Divinization in Thomas Aquinas' in Weinandy, Keating and Yocum eds., *Aquinas on Doctrine* 139-58

Kerr, F., *After Aquinas: Versions of Thomism* (Oxford: Blackwell, 2002)

—, ed. *Contemplating Aquinas: On the Varieties of Interpretation* (London: SCM, 2003)

—, 'Doctrine of God and Theological Ethics according to Thomas Aquinas' in A.J. Torrance and M. Banner eds., *The Doctrine of God and Theological Ethics* (Edinburgh: T&T Clark, 2006) 71-84

—, 'The Varieties of Interpreting Aquinas' in *Contemplating Aquinas* 27-40

Kevan, E.F., *The Grace of Law: A Study in Puritan Theology* (London: The Carey Kingsgate Press, 1964)

Kilby, K., 'Aquinas, the Trinity and the Limits of Human Understanding', *International Journal of Systematic Theology* 7 (2005) 414-27

—, 'Perichoresis and Projection: Problems with Social Doctrines of the Trinity', *New Blackfriars* 81 (2000) 432-45

Kirk, J.A., *The Meaning of Freedom: A Study of Secular, Muslim and Christian Views* (Carlisle: Paternoster, 1998)

Kirwan, C., *Augustine* (London: Routledge, 1989)

Klug, F., *Values for a Godless Age: The History of the Human Rights Act and its Political and Legal Consequences* (Harmondsworth: Penguin, 2000)

Kramer, M.H., *In Defense of Legal Positivism* (Oxford: OUP, 1999)

—, 'On the Moral Status of the Rule of Law', *Cambridge Law Journal* 63 (2004) 65-97

Kühn, U., 'Nova lex. Die Eigenart der christlichen Ethik nach Thomas von Aquin' in Elders and Hedwig eds., *Lex et Libertas* 243-47

Kuyper, A., *The Work of the Holy Spirit* tr. H. de Vries (Grand Rapids: Eerdmans, 1900, 1975)

Lactantius, *The Divine Institutes* in A.C. Coxe ed., *The Ante-Nicene Fathers vol. VII:*

Fathers of the Third and Fourth Centuries (Buffalo, NY: Christian Lit. Publ. Co, 1887) 9-328

LaCugna, C., *God for Us: The Trinity and the Christian Life* (New York: Harper Collins, 1991)

Lafont, G., *Structures et méthode dans la Somme théologique de saint Thomas d'Aquin* (Paris: Desclée, 1961)

Lalleman-de Winkel, H., 'The Old Testament Contribution to Evangelical Models of Public Theology', unpublished paper delivered at FEET 2004

Lamb, M.L., 'The Eschatology of St. Thomas Aquinas' in Weinandy, Keating and Yocum eds., *Aquinas on Doctrine* 225-40

Lash, N., 'Not Exactly Politics or Power?', *Modern Theology* 8 (1992) 353-64

Letham, R., *The Holy Trinity: In Scripture, History, Theology, and Worship* (Phillipsburg, N.J.: P&R, 2004)

—, 'The Man-Woman Debate: Theological Comment', *Western Theological Journal* 52 (1990) 65-78

Levering, M., *Christ's Fulfillment of Torah and Temple: Salvation according to Thomas Aquinas* (Notre Dame: University of Notre Dame Press, 2002)

—, 'The Liturgy of the Eucharist' in Weinandy, Keating and Yocum eds., *Aquinas on Doctrine* 183-97

—, 'Reading John with St Thomas Aquinas' in Weinandy, Keating and Yocum eds., *Aquinas on Scripture* 99-126

—, *Scripture and Metaphysics: Aquinas and the Renewal of Trinitarian Theology* (Oxford: Blackwell, 2004)

Lincoln, A.T., 'Power, Judgement and Possession: John's Gospel in Political Perspective' in Bartholomew et al. eds., *A Royal Priesthood?* (Carlisle: Paternoster, 2002) 147-69

Locke, J., *Political Writings* (London: Penguin Classics, 1993)

Lockwood O'Donovan, J., 'The Concept of Rights in Christian Moral Discourse' in M. Cromartie ed., *A Preserving Grace: Protestants, Catholics and Natural Law* (Grand Rapids: Eerdmans, 1997) 143-156

—, 'The Poverty of Christ and Non-Proprietary Community' in A.J. Torrance and M. Banner eds., *The Doctrine of God and Theological Ethics* (Edinburgh: T&T Clark, 2006) 191-200

—, *Theology of Law and Authority in the English Reformation* (Atlanta, GA: Scholars Press, 1991)

—, 'A Timely Conversation with *The Desire of the Nations* on Civil Society, Nation and State' in Bartholomew et al. eds., *A Royal Priesthood?* (Carlisle: Paternoster, 2002) 377-394

Long, D.S., *Divine Economy: Theology and the Market* (London: Routledge, 2000)

Long, S.A., 'Providence, liberté et loi naturelle', *Revue Thomiste* 102 (2002) 355-406

Lovin, R.W., *Christian Faith and Public Choices: The Social Ethics of Barth, Brunner and Bonhoeffer* (Philadelphia: Fortress Press, 1984)

Luther, M., 'Temporal Authority: To what extent should it be obeyed?' tr. W.A. Lambert, revd. W.I. Brandt *Luther's Works* ed. H.T. Lehmann (Philadelphia: Muhlenberg Press, 1955-75) 45:81-129

MacIntyre, A., *Whose Justice? Which Rationality?* (Notre Dame: Ind.: University of Notre Dame Press, 1988)

Maile, J.W., 'The Resurrection in Luke-Acts', *Tyndale Bulletin* 37 (1986) 29-60

Malet, A., *Personne et Amour dans la Théologie Trinitaire de Saint Thomas d'Aquin* (Paris : Librairie Philosophique J. Vrin, 1956)

Mannermaa, T., *Der im Glauben gegenwärtige Christus* (Hanover: Arbeiten zur Geschichte und Theologie des Luthertums, 1989)

Marquardt, F-W., *Theologie und Sozialismus* (Munich: Chr. Kaiser Verlag, 1972)

—, 'Socialism in the Theology of Karl Barth' in G. Hunsinger ed., *Karl Barth and Radical Politics* at 47-76

Marrevee, W.H., *The Ascension of Christ in the Works of St. Augustine* (Ottawa: University of Ottawa Press, 1967)

Marshall, B.D., 'Action and Person: Do Palamas and Aquinas Agree About The Spirit?', *St Vladimir's Theological Quarterly* 39 (1995) 379-408

Marshall, C.D., *Beyond Retribution: A New Testament Vision for Justice, Crime and Punishment* (Cambridge: Eerdmans, 2001)

Marshall, I.H., 'The Biblical Concept of Justice', *Shaftesbury Project Working Paper* (Nottingham: Shaftesbury Project, 1977)

McCabe, H., *Law, Love & Language* (Sheed and Ward, 1968; London: Continuum, 2003)

McConville, J.G., 'Law and Monarchy in the Old Testament' in Bartholomew et al. eds., *A Royal Priesthood?* (Carlisle: Paternoster, 2002) 69-88

McCormack, B. 'Grace and Being: The Role of God's Gracious Election in Karl Barth's Theological Ontology' in J. Webster ed., *The Cambridge Companion to Karl Barth* (CUP, 2000) 92-110

McCurry, J.M., 'Trinitarian Theology After and With – But Not Against – Aquinas', *Modern Theology* 21 (2005) 497-509

McGrath, A.E., *Iustitia Dei: A History of the Christian Doctrine of Justification* 2nd edn. (Cambridge: CUP, 1998)

McIlroy, D.H., *A Biblical View of Law and Justice* (Carlisle: Paternoster, 2004)

—, 'The Holy Spirit and the Law', *Justice Reflections* 3(14) (2003) 1-16

—, 'Oliver O'Donovan and the Christian Tradition on the Death Penalty', *Law & Justice* 156 (2006) 37-47

—, 'A Prophetic Vision of Justice', *Engage* 7 (2004) 4-5

—, 'The Relevance of Old Testament Law for Today: Part One', *Law & Justice* 148 (2002) 21-36

—, 'The Relevance of Old Testament Law for Today: Part Two', *Law & Justice* 150 (2003) 21-37

—, 'Review of Oliver O'Donovan *The Ways of Judgment*', *Political Theology* 8(3) (2007) 373-80

—, 'Subsidiarity and Sphere Sovereignty: Christian Reflections on the Size, Shape and Scope of Government', *Journal of Church and State* 45 (2003) 101-126; *Law & Justice* 151 (2003) 111-136

—, 'Towards a Relational and Trinitarian Theology of Atonement', *Evangelical Quarterly* 80 (2008) 13-32

—, 'A Trinitarian reading of Aquinas's treatise on law', *Angelicum* 84 (2007) 277-92

—, 'The Trinity, Politics and the Law', *Whitefield Briefing* 10(1) (2005)

—, 'What's at Stake in Natural Law?', *New Blackfriars* 89 (2008) 508-21

McInerny, R., 'The Basis and Purpose of Positive Law' in Elders and Hedwig eds., *Lex et libertas* 137-46

—, *Thomas Aquinas: Selected Writings* (Harmondsworth: Penguin, 1998)

Meilaender, G., 'Ethics and Exegesis: A Great Gulf?' in Bartholomew et al. eds., *A Royal Priesthood?* (Carlisle: Paternoster, 2002) 259-64
—, 'Recovering Christendom', *First Things* 77 (1997) 36-42
Metz, J.B., 'Prophetic Authority' in J. Moltmann et al. eds., *Religion and Political Society* (New York: Harper and Row, 1974) 171-209
Milbank, J., *Being Reconciled: Ontology and Pardon* (London: Routledge, 2003)
—, 'The Body by Love Possessed: Christianity and Late Capitalism in Britain', *Modern Theology* 3 (1986) 35-65
—, 'Can a Gift Be Given? Prolegomena to a Future Trinitarian Metaphysic', *Modern Theology* 11 (1995) 119-61
—, 'Enclaves, or where is the Church?', *New Blackfriars* 73 (1992) 341-52
—, 'The Gift of Ruling: Secularization and Political Authority', *New Blackfriars* 85 (2004) 212-38
—, 'Materialism and Transcendence' in Davis, Milbank and Zizek eds., *Theology and the Political: The New Debate* (Durham, NC: Duke University Press, 2005) 393-426
—, 'Postmodern Critical Augustinianism: A Short *Summa* in Forty-two Responses to Unasked Questions' in G. Ward ed., *The Postmodern God: A Theological Reader* (Oxford: Blackwell, 1997) 265-78
—, 'The Programme of Radical Orthodoxy' in L.P. Hemming ed., *Radical Orthodoxy? - A Catholic Enquiry* (Aldershot: Ashgate, 2000) 33-45
—, 'The Second Difference: For a Trinitarianism Without Reserve', *Modern Theology* 2 (1986) 213-34
—, *The Suspended Middle: Henri de Lubac and the Debate concerning the Supernatural* (London: SCM, 2005)
—, *Theology and Social Theory: Beyond Secular Reason* (Oxford: Blackwell, 1990)
—, *The Word Made Strange: Theology, Language, Culture* (Oxford: Blackwell, 1997)
Milbank, J., Pickstock, C., and Ward, G. eds., *Radical Orthodoxy: A New Theology* (London: Routledge, 1999)
Milbank, J. and Pickstock, C., *Truth in Aquinas* (London: Routledge, 2001)
Miller, P.D. and McCann, D.P. eds., *In Search of the Common Good* (London: T&T Clark, 2005)
Mobbs, F., 'Is Natural Law Contained in Revelation?', *New Blackfriars* 85 (2004) 454-58
Moberly, R.W.L., 'The Use of Scripture in *The Desire of the Nations*' in Bartholomew et al. eds., *A Royal Priesthood?* (Carlisle: Paternoster, 2002) 46-64
Molnar, P.D., *Divine Freedom and the Doctrine of the Immanent Trinity: In Dialogue with Karl Barth and Contemporary Theology* (Edinburgh: T & T Clark, 2002)
—, 'The function of the immanent trinity in the theology of Karl Barth: Implications for Today', *Scottish Journal of Theology* 42 (1989) 367-99
—, 'Moltmann's Post-Modern Messianic Christology: A Review Discussion', *The Thomist* 56 (1992) 669-93
—, 'Toward a Contemporary Doctrine of the Immanent Trinity: Karl Barth and the present discussion', *Scottish Journal of Theology* 49 (1996) 311-57
Moltmann, J., *A Theology of Hope: On the Ground and the Implications of a Christian Eschatology* tr. James W. Leitch 5th edn. (London: SCM, 1967)
—, 'The Bible, The Exegete and the Theologian' in R. Bauckham ed., *God Will Be All in All* (Edinburgh: T&T Clark, 1999) 227-32
—, 'Can Christian Eschatology become Post-Modern' in R. Bauckham ed., *God Will Be*

All in All (Edinburgh: T&T Clark, 1999) 259-64

—, 'Christianity and the Revaluation of the Values of Modernity and of the Western World' in M. Volf ed., *A Passion for God's Reign* (Grand Rapids: Eerdmans, 1998) 23-44

—, *The Church in the Power of the Spirit: A Contribution to Messianic Ecclesiology* tr. Margaret Kohl 2nd edn. (London: SCM, 1992)

—, *The Coming of God: Christian Eschatology* tr. Margaret Kohl (London: SCM, 1996)

—, 'The Confession of Jesus Christ: A Biblical Theological Consideration', *Concilium* 118 (1979) 13-19

—, 'Covenant or Leviathan? Political Theology for Modern Times', *Scottish Journal of Theology* 47 (1994) 19-41

—, 'The Cross and Civil Religion' in J. Moltmann et al. eds., *Religion and Political Society* (New York: Harper and Row, 1974)

—, *Creating a Just Future: The Politics of Peace and the Ethics of Creation in a Threatened World* tr. John Bowden (London: SCM, 1989)

—, *The Crucified God: The Cross of Christ as the Foundation and Criticism of Christian Theology* 2nd edn. (Munich: Christian Kaiser Verlag, 1973) tr. R.A Wilson and John Bowden (London: SCM, 1974, 2001)

—, *Experiences in Theology: Ways and Forms of Christian Theology* (Gutersloh: Christian Kaiser, 2000) tr. Margaret Kohl (London: SCM, 2000)

—, *Experiences of God* tr. Margaret Kohl (London: SCM, 1980)

—, *The Experiment Hope* tr. M. Douglas Meeks (London: SCM, 1975)

—, 'The Fellowship of the Holy Spirit – Trinitarian Pneumatology', *Scottish Journal of Theology* 37 (1984) 287-300

—, *The Future of Creation* (Munich: Christian Kaiser Verlag, 1977) tr. Margaret Kohl (London: SCM, 1979)

—, *God for a Secular Society: The Public Relevance of Theology* (Gutersloh: Christian Kaiser, 1997) tr. Margaret Kohl (London: SCM, 1999)

—, *God in Creation: An Ecological Doctrine of Creation* (Munich: Christian Kaiser Verlag, 1985) tr. Margaret Kohl (London: SCM, 1985)

—, *Gospel of Liberation* tr. H. Wayne Pipkin (Waco: Word, 1973)

—, 'Gottesoffenbarung und Wahrheitsfrage' in E. Busch. ed., *Parrhesia: Karl Barth zum Achzigsten Geburtstag* (Zurich: EVZ, 1966)

—, *History and the Triune God: Contributions to Trinitarian Theology* tr. John Bowden (London: SCM, 1991)

—, *Hope and Planning* tr. M. Clarkson (London: SCM, 1971)

—, *How I Have Changed: Reflections on Thirty Years of Theology* ed. J. Moltmann tr. John Bowden (London: SCM, 1997) ix-x, 13-21

—, 'Ich glaube an Gott den Vater: Patriarchalische oder nichtpatriarchialische Rede von Gott?', *Evangelische Theologie* 43 (1983) 397-415

—, *In the End – the Beginning: The Life of Hope* tr. M. Kohl (London: SCM, 2004)

—, *On Human Dignity: Political Theology and Ethics* (London: SCM, 1984)

—, *Jesus Christ for Today's World* tr. M. Kohl (London: SCM, 1994)

—, 'The Liberating Feast', *Concilium* 10 (1974) 74-84

—, 'The Liberation of the Future and its Anticipations in History' in R. Bauckham ed., *God Will Be All in All* (Edinburgh: T&T Clark, 1999) 265-89

—, *Man: Christian Anthropology in the Conflicts of the Present* tr. John Sturdy (London: SPCK, 1974)

—, 'The Messiah in Christianity', *Concilium* 10 (1974) 155-61

—, 'Olympia Between Politics and Religion', *Concilium* 205 (1989) 101-109

—, *The Open Church: Invitation to a Messianic Lifestyle* tr. M. Douglas Meeks (London: SCM, 1978)

—, 'Peace the Fruit of Justice', *Concilium* 195 (1988) 109-20

—, *The Power of the Powerless* tr. M. Kohl (London: SCM, 1983)

—, *Religion, Revolution and the Future* tr. M. Douglas Meeks (New York: Charles Scribner & Sons, 1969)

—, 'Revolution, Religion and the Future: German Reactions', *Concilium* 201 (1989) 43-50

—, *The Source of Life* (Gutersloh: Christian Kaiser, 1997) tr. Margaret Kohl (London: SCM, 1997)

—, *The Spirit of Life: A Universal Affirmation* (Munich: Christian Kaiser Verlag, 1991) tr. Margaret Kohl (London: SCM, 1992)

—, 'Theological Proposals Towards the Resolution of the Filioque Controversy' in L. Vischer ed., *Spirit of God, Spirit of Christ* (London: SPCK, 1981) 164-73

—, *The Theology of Hope: On the and the Implications of a Christian Eschatology* tr. J.W. Leitch (London: SCM, 1967)

—, *Theology & Joy* tr. R. Ulrich (London: SCM, 1973)

—, 'Theology for Christ's Church and the Kingdom of God in Modern Society' in M. Volf ed., *A Passion for God's Reign* (Grand Rapids: Eerdmans, 1998) 45-64

—, 'Theology in the Project of the Modern World' in M. Volf ed., *A Passion for God's Reign* (Grand Rapids: Eerdmans, 1998) 1-22

—, *Theology Today: Two Contributions towards making Theology Present* tr. J. Bowden (London: SCM, 1988)

—, *The Trinity and the Kingdom of God: The Doctrine of God* (Munich: Christian Kaiser Verlag, 1980) tr. Margaret Kohl (London: SCM, 1981)

—, *The Way of Jesus Christ: Christology in Messianic Dimensions* (Munich: Christian Kaiser Verlag, 1989) tr. Margaret Kohl (London: SCM, 1990)

—, 'What Has Happened to our Utopias' in R. Bauckham ed., *God Will Be All in All: The Eschatology of Jürgen Moltmann* (Edinburgh: T&T Clark, 1999) 115-22

—, 'The World in God or God in the World? Response to Richard Bauckham' in R. Bauckham ed., *God Will Be All in All: The Eschatology of Jürgen Moltmann* (Edinburgh: T&T Clark, 1999) 35-41

Moltmann, J. and Moltmann-Wendel, E., *Humanity in God* (London: SCM, 1984)

Moltmann, J., Richardson, H.W., Metz, J. B., Oelmuller, W., and Bryant, M.D. *Religion and Political Society* (New York: Harper and Row, 1974)

Moltmann, J., and Weissbach, J., *Two Studies in the Theology of Bonhoeffer* tr. R.H. and I. Fuller (New York: Charles Scribner's Sons, 1967)

Montgomery, J.W., *Human Rights and Human Dignity* (Edmonton, Alberta: Canadian Institute for Law, Theology and Public Policy, 1986, 1995)

—,'Law and Justice', *Law & Justice* 120 (1994), 12-25

—, 'Law & Morality: Friends or Foes?', *Law & Justice* 122 (1994), 87-106

—, 'Subsidiarity as a Jurisprudential and Canonical Theory', *Law & Justice* 148 (2002) 46-53

—, 'Why a Christian Philosophy of Law?' in P. Beaumont ed., *Christian Perspectives on Human Rights and Legal Philosophy* (Carlisle: Paternoster, 1998), 73-94

Mosser, C., 'The Greatest Possible Blessing: Calvin and Deification', *Scottish Journal of Theology* 55 (2002) 36-57

Müller-Fahrenholz, G. *The Kingdom and the Power: The Theology of Jürgen Moltmann* (Gutersloh: Christian Kaiser, 2000) tr. J. Bowden (London: SCM, 2000)

Murphy, F.A., 'Thomas' Commentaries on Philemon, 1 and 2 Thessalonians and Philippians' in Weinandy, Keating and Yocum eds., *Aquinas on Scripture* 167-96

Neufeld, J., 'Just War Theory, the Authorization of the State, and the Hermeneutics of Peoplehood: How John Howard Yoder can save Oliver O'Donovan from himself', *International Journal of Systematic Theology* 8 (2006) 410-432

Neuhaus, R.J. 'Commentary on *The Desire of the Nations*', *Studies in Christian Ethics* 11 (1998) 56-61

Nichols, A., *Discovering Aquinas: An Introduction to his Life, Work and Influence* (London: Darton Longman & Todd, 2002)

—, '"Non tali auxilio": John Milbank's Suasion to Orthodoxy', *New Blackfriars* 73 (1992) 326-32

Nichols, S.J., *An Absolute Sort of Certainty: The Holy Spirit and the Apologetics of Jonathan Edwards* (Phillipsburg, N.J.: P&R Publishing, 2003)

Novak, D. 'Response to *the Desire of the Nations*', *Studies in Christian Ethics* 11 (1998) 62-68

Oakes, P., ed. *Rome in the Bible and the Early Church* (Carlisle: Paternoster, 2002)

Odell-Scott, D.W., *A Post-Patriarchal Christology* (American Academy of Religion, 1991)

O'Connor, D.J., *Aquinas and Natural Law* (London: Macmillan, 1967)

O'Donovan, O., 'Again: Who Is a Person?' in J.H. Channer ed., *Abortion and the Sanctity of Human Life* (Exeter: Paternoster, 1985)

—, 'Response to Respondents: Behold the Lamb!', *Studies in Christian Ethics* 11 (1998) 91-110

—, *Begotten or Made?* (Oxford: OUP, 1984)

—, 'Christianity and Territorial Right' in Buchanan and Moore eds., *States, Nations and Borders: The Ethics of Making Boundaries* (Cambridge: CUP, 2003) 127-39

—, 'Christian Moral Reasoning' in D.J. Atkinson and D.H. Field eds., *New Dictionary of Christian Ethics and Pastoral Theology* (Leicester: IVP, 1995)

—, *Common Objects of Love*: *Moral Reflection and the Shaping of Community* (Grand Rapids: Eerdmans, 2002)

—, *The Christian and the Unborn Child* 2nd edn. (Nottingham: Grove Books, 1975)

—, 'The Concept of Publicity', *Studies in Christian Ethics* 13 (2000) 18-32

—, 'The Death Penalty in "Evangelium Vitae"' in Hütter and Dieter eds., *Ecumenical Ventures in Ethics: Protestants Engage Pope John Paul II's Moral Encyclical* (Grand Rapids: Eerdmans, 1998) 216-36

—, 'Deliberation, History and Reading: A Response to Schweiker and Wolterstorff', *Scottish Journal of Theology* 54 (2001) 127-44

—, *The Desire of the Nations: Rediscovering the Roots of Political Theology* (Cambridge: Cambridge University Press, 1996)

—, 'Evangelicalism and the Foundation of Ethics' in France and McGrath eds., *Evangelical Anglicans* (London: SPCK, 1993) 96-107

—, 'Freedom and Its Loss: Hopes and Fears for the Political Order', the Gore Lecture 2002, available online at www.westminster-abbey.org/event/lecture/archives

—, *In Pursuit of a Christian View of War* (Nottingham: Grove Booklet on Ethics No. 15, 1977)

—, 'John Finnis on Moral Absolutes', *Studies in Christian Ethics* 6 (1993) 50-66

—, *The Just War Revisited* (Cambridge: CUP, 2003)

—, 'Law, Moderation and Forgiveness', *Gregorianum* LXXXII (2001) 625-636

—, 'Liturgy and Ethics' (Nottingham: Grove Ethical Studies No. 89, 1993)

—, *Marriage and Permanence* (Nottingham: Grove Books, 1978)

—, *Measure for Measure: Justice in Punishment and the Sentence of Death* (Nottingham: Grove Books, 1977)

—, 'The Natural Ethic' in D.F. Wright ed., *Essays in Evangelical Social Ethics* (Paternoster, 1981)

—, *On The Thirty Nine Articles: A Conversation with Tudor Christianity* (Carlisle: Paternoster, 1986)

—, 'Payback: Thinking about Retribution', *Books & Culture* July-August 2000, 16-21

—, *Peace and Certainty: A Theological Essay on Deterrence* (Oxford: Clarendon, 1989)

—, 'Peine' in J.Y. Lacoste ed., *Dictionnaire Critique de Théologie* (Paris: PUF, 1998)

—, 'The Political Thought of the Book of Revelation', *Tyndale Bulletin* 37 (1986) 61-94

—, *The Problem of Self-Love in St. Augustine* (New York: Yale University Press, 1980)

—, 'Responses to Participants' in C. Bartholomew et al. eds., *A Royal Priesthood?* (Carlisle: Paternoster, 2002) 65-68, 89-90, 113-15, 144-46, 170-72, 194-95, 221-24, 238-40,255-58, 309-13, 341-43, 374-76, 395-97, 418-20

—, *Resurrection and Moral Order: An Outline for Evangelical Ethics* 2nd edn. (Leicester: Apollos, 1994)

—, 'Todesstrafe' in G. Müller ed., *Theologische Realenzykopädie* Band 23 (Berlin: Walter de Gruyter, 2002) 639-46

—, *Transsexualism and Christian Marriage* (Nottingham: Grove Books, 1982)

—, 'War and Peace' in A.E. McGrath ed., *The Blackwell Encyclopedia of Modern Christian Thought* (Oxford: Blackwell, 1993) 652-56

—, *The Ways of Judgment* (Grand Rapids: Eerdmans, 2005)

—, 'What Can Ethics Know about God?' in A.J. Torrance and M. Banner eds., *The Doctrine of God and Theological Ethics* (Edinburgh: T&T Clark, 2006) 33-46

O'Donovan, O. and Lockwood O'Donovan, J.,

—, *Bonds of Imperfection: Christian Politics, Past and Present* (Grand Rapids: Eerdmans, 2004)

—, *From Irenaeus to Grotius: A Sourcebook in Christian Political Thought 100-1625* (Grand Rapids: Eerdmans, 1999)

O'Donovan, O. and Sider, R., *Peace and War: A Debate About Pacifism* (Grove Booklets on Ethics No. 56, 1985)

O'Rourke, F., 'Aquinas and Platonism' in F. Kerr ed., *Contemplating Aquinas* 247-79

Otto, R.E., *The God of Hope: The Trinitarian Vision of Jürgen Moltmann* (Lanham, Maryland: University Press of America, 1991)

Paeth, S.R., 'Jürgen Moltmann's Public Theology', *Political Theology* 6 (2005) 215-34

Peura, S., *Mehr als ein Mensch? Die Vergöttlichung als Thema der Theologie Martin Luthers von 1513 bis 1519* (Mainz: Verlag Philipp von Zabern, 1994)

Pesch, O-H., 'Thomas Aquinas and Contemporary Theology' in F. Kerr ed., *Contemplating Aquinas* 185-216

Peters, R., *Hobbes* 2nd edn. (London: Penguin, 1967)

Pinckaers, S., 'Liberté et Préceptes dans la Morale de Saint Thomas' in Elders and Hedwig eds., *Lex et libertas* 15-24

Porter, J., 'The Common Good in Thomas Aquinas' in P.D. Miller and D.P. McCann eds., *In Search of the Common Good*, 94-120

Priel, D., 'Review of Kramer *Where Law and Morality Meet*', *Modern Law Review* (2006) 114-19

Rahner, K., *The Trinity* tr. Joseph Donceel (London: Burns and Oates, 1970)

Rasmussen, A., *The Church as Polis: From Political Theology to Theological Politics as Exemplified by Jürgen Moltmann and Stanley Hauerwas* (Lund: Lund University Press, 1994)

—, 'Not All Justifications of Christendom are Created Equal: A Response to Oliver O'Donovan', *Studies in Christian Ethics* 11 (1998) 69-76

Rawls, J., *A Theory of Justice* revd. edn. (Oxford: OUP, 1999)

—, *Political Liberalism* expanded edn. (New York: Columbia University Press, 2005)

Regan, R.J., *Thomas Aquinas: On Law, Morality, and Politics* 2nd edn. (Indianapolis: Hackett, 2002)

Reno, R.R., 'The Radical Orthodoxy Project', *First Things* 100 (2000) 37-44

Richardson, K.A., *Reading Karl Barth: New Directions for North American Theology* (Grand Rapids: Baker, 2004)

Ricoeur, P., *Le Conflit des Interpretations: Essais d'Hermeneutique* (Paris : Seuil, 1969). tr. *The Conflict of Interpretations: Essays in Hermeneutics* (Evanston, IL: Northwestern University Press, 1974)

—, 'Theonomy and/or Autonomy' in Volf et al. eds., *The Future of Theology: Essays in Honor of Jürgen Moltmann* (Grand Rapids: Eerdmans, 1996) 284-98

Rivers, A.J., 'The Abuse of Equality', *Ethics in Brief* 11(1) (2006)

—, 'Liberal Constitutionalism and Christian Political Thought' in P. Beaumont ed., *Christian Perspectives on the Limits of the Law* (Carlisle: Paternoster, 2002) 11-34

—, 'Public Reason', *Whitefield Briefing* 9(1) (2004)

Rodriguez, P., 'Spontanéité et caractère légal de la loi nouvelle' in Elders and Hedwig eds., *Lex et libertas* 254-64

Rogers, E.F., 'The Mystery of the Spirit in Three Traditions: Calvin, Rahner, Florensky or, You *Keep* Wondering Where The Spirit Went', *Modern Theology* 19 (2003) 243-60

—, 'The Narrative of Natural Law in Aquinas's Commentary on Romans 1', *Theological Studies* 59 (1998) 254-76

Rowland, C., 'Response to *The Desire of the Nations*', *Studies in Christian Ethics* 11 (1998) 77-85

—, 'The Apocalypse and Political Theology' in Bartholomew et al. eds., *A Royal Priesthood?* (Carlisle: Paternoster, 2002) 241-54

Ryan, T.F., *Thomas Aquinas as Reader of the Psalms* (Notre Dame, Ind: University of Notre Dame Press, 2000)

Rybarczyk, E.J., *Beyond Salvation: Eastern Orthodoxy and Classical Pentecostalism on Becoming Like Christ* (Carlisle: Paternoster, 2004)

Saward, J., 'The Grace of Christ in his Principal Members: St Thomas Aquinas on the Pastoral Epistles' in Weinandy, Keating and Yocum eds., *Aquinas on Scripture* 197-222

Schaeffer, F., *Trilogy: The God Who Is There, Escape From Reason, He Is There and He Is Not Silent* (Leicester: IVP, 1990)

Schellong, D., 'On Reading Karl Barth from the Left' in G. Hunsinger ed., *Karl Barth and Radical Politics* 139-58

Schweiker, W., 'Freedom and Authority in Political Theology: A Response to Oliver

O'Donovan's *The Desire of the Nations'*, *Scottish Journal of Theology* 54 (2001) 110-26

Scott, P., '"Return to the Vomit of Legitimation"? Scriptural Interpretation and the Authority of the Poor' in Bartholomew et al. eds., *A Royal Priesthood?* (Carlisle: Paternoster, 2002) 344-73

Scott, P. and Cavanaugh, W.T. eds., *The Blackwell Companion to Political Theology* (Oxford: Blackwell, 2004)

Shaffer, T.L., *Moral Memoranda from John Howard Yoder* (Eugene, Oregon: Wipf and Stock, 2002)

Shanks, A., 'Response to *The Desire of the Nations'*, *Studies in Christian Ethics* 11 (1998) 86-90

Shaw, E., 'Beyond Political Theology' in G. McLeod Bryan ed., *Communities of Faith and Radical Discipleship* (Macon: Mercer University Press, 1986) 33-67.

Simmonds, N.E., *Central Issues in Jurisprudence: Justice, Law and Rights* 2nd edn. (London: Sweet & Maxwell, 2002)

—, *Law as a Moral Idea* (Oxford: OUP, 2007)

—, 'Straightforwardly False: The Collapse of Kramer's Positivism', *Cambridge Law Journal* 63 (2004) 98-131

Skillen, J.W., 'Acting Politically in Biblical Obedience?' in Bartholomew et al. eds., *A Royal Priesthood?* (Carlisle: Paternoster, 2002) 398-417

Smail, T.A., *The Forgotten Father* (London: Hodder & Stoughton, 1980)

—, *Like Father, Like Son: The Trinity imaged in our Humanity* (Carlisle: Paternoster, 2005)

Smith, J.K.A., *Introducing Radical Orthodoxy: Mapping a Post-secular Theology* (Grand Rapids, Michigan: Baker Academic, 2004)

Storkey, A., *Jesus and Politics: Confronting the Powers* (Grand Rapids, Michigan: Baker Academic, 2005)

Strauss, L., *Natural Right and History* (Chicago: University of Chicago Press, 1950)

Sykes, S.W. 'The Dialectic of Community and Structure' in F.B. Burnham, C.S. McCoy, and M.D. Meeks eds., *Love: The Foundation of Hope: The Theology of Jürgen Moltmann and Elisabeth Moltmann-Wendel* (San Francisco: Harper & Row, 1988) 121-22

Tanner, K., *Jesus, Humanity and the Trinity: A Brief Systematic Theology* (Edinburgh: T&T Clark, 2001)

—, 'Trinity' in P. Scott and W.T. Cavanaugh eds., *The Blackwell Companion to Political Theology* (Oxford: Blackwell, 2004) 319-32

Taylor, H., *Human Rights: Its Culture and Moral Confusions* (Edinburgh: Rutherford House, 2004)

Tertullian, *The Apology* in A.C. Coxe ed., *The Ante-Nicene Fathers vol. III: Latin Christianity: Its Founder, Tertullian* (Buffalo, NY: Christian Lit. Publ. Co, 1887) 17-61

—, *To Scapula* 105-108 in the same volume.

Theron, S., 'St Thomas Aquinas and Epieicheia' in Elders and Hedwig eds., *Lex et libertas* 171-82

Torrance, A.J., and Banner, M. eds., *The Doctrine of God and Theological Ethics* (Edinburgh: T&T Clark, 2006)

Torrance, A.J., 'On Deriving "Ought" from "Is": Christology, Covenant and *Koinonia'* in A.J. Torrance and M. Banner eds., *The Doctrine of God and Theological Ethics*

167-89

Torrance, T.F., *Christian Doctrine of God: One Being, Three Persons* (Edinburgh: T&T Clark, 1996)

—, 'Karl Barth and the Latin Heresy', 39 *Scottish Journal of Theology* 461-82

—, *Karl Barth, Biblical and Evangelical Theologian* (Edinburgh: T & T Clark, 1990)

—, 'The Legacy of Karl Barth', 39 *Scottish Journal of Theology* 289-308

—, *The Trinitarian Faith* (Edinburgh: T & T Clark, 1988)

Torrell, J-P., *Saint Thomas Aquinas.* Vol. II, *Spiritual Master* tr. Robert Royal (Washington, DC: Catholic University of America Press, 2003)

Valkenberg, W., *Words of the Living God: Place and Function of Holy Scripture in the Theology of St. Thomas Aquinas* (Leuven: Peeters, 2000)

van der Ploeg, J.P.M., 'Le traité de Saint Thomas de la Loi Ancienne' in Elders and Hedwig eds., *Lex et libertas* 183-99

Vanhoozer, K.J., ed. *The Trinity in a Pluralistic Age: Theological Essays on Culture and Religion* (Grand Rapids: Eerdmans, 1997)

Vaus, W., *Mere Theology: A Guide to the Thought of C.S. Lewis* (Leicester: IVP, 2004)

Vischer, L., ed. *Spirit of God, Spirit of Christ* (London: SPCK, 1981)

Volf, M., ed. *A Passion for God's Reign: Theology, Christian Learning, and the Christian Self* (Grand Rapids: Eerdmans, 1998)

Volf, M., 'After Moltmann: Reflections on the Future of Eschatology' in R. Bauckham ed., *God Will Be All in All* (Edinburgh: T&T Clark, 1999) 233-58

Volf, M., Krieg, C., and Kucharz, T. eds., *The Future of Theology: Essays in Honor of Jürgen Moltmann* (Grand Rapids: Eerdmans, 1996)

Vos, A., *Aquinas, Calvin, and Contemporary Protestant Thought: A Critique of Protestant Views on the Thought of Thomas Aquinas* (Grand Rapids: Eerdmans, 1985)

Wannenwetsch, B., '"Members of One Another": *Charis*, Ministry and Representation: A Politico-Ecclesial Reading of Romans 12' in Bartholomew et al. eds., *A Royal Priesthood?* (Carlisle: Paternoster, 2002) 196-220

Wawrykow, J., 'Aquinas on Isaiah' in Weinandy, Keating and Yocum eds., *Aquinas on Scripture* 43-72

Webster, J., *Karl Barth* 2nd edn. (London: Continuum, 2004)

Webster, J., ed., *The Cambridge Companion to Karl Barth* (Cambridge: CUP, 2000)

Webster, J., and Schner, G.P. eds., *Theology after Liberalism: A Reader* (Oxford: Blackwell, 2000)

Weinandy, Keating and Yocum eds., *Aquinas on Doctrine: A Critical Introduction* (London: T&T Clark, 2004)

—, *Aquinas on Scripture: An Introduction to his Biblical Commentaries* (London: T&T Clark, 2005)

Weinandy, T.G., *Does God Suffer?* (Edinburgh: T & T Clark, 2000)

—, 'The Marvel of the Incarnation' in Weinandy, Keating and Yocum eds., *Aquinas on Doctrine* 67-90

—, 'The Supremacy of Christ: Aquinas' *Commentary on Hebrews*' in *Aquinas on Scripture* 223-44

West, C., *Communism and the Theologians* (London: SCM, 1958)

Williams, A.N., 'Deification in the *Summa Theologiae*: A Structural Interpretation of the *Prima Pars*', *The Thomist* 61 (1997) 219-55

—, *The Ground of Union: Deification in Aquinas and Palamas* (New York: OUP, 1999)

Williams, R. 'Barth, War and the State' in N. Biggar ed., *Reckoning with Barth: Essays in Commemoration of the Centenary of Karl Barth's Birth* (London: Mowbray, 1988) —, 'What does love know? St Thomas on the Trinity', *New Blackfriars* 82 (2001) 260-72

Williams, S.N., 'Review of *God Will Be All in All*', *International Journal of Systematic Theology* 2 (2000) 347-49

Winter, B., 'Roman Law and Society in Romans 12-15' in P. Oakes ed., *Rome in the Bible and the Early Church* (Carlisle: Paternoster, 2002) 67-102

Wolterstorff, N., 'A Discussion of Oliver O'Donovan's *The Desire of the Nations*', *Scottish Journal of Theology* 54 (2001) 87-109

—, *Until Justice & Peace Embrace* (Grand Rapids: Eerdmans, 1983)

Wood, R.C., *The Gospel According to Tolkien: Visions of the Kingdom in Middle-earth* (Louisville: Westminster John Knox, 2003)

Wright, C.J.H., *Living as the People of God: The Relevance of Old Testament Ethics* (Carlisle: Paternoster, 1990)

—, *God's People in God's Land: Family, Land, and Property in the Old Testament* (Carlisle: Paternoster, 1997)

—, *Knowing the Holy Spirit through the Old Testament* (Oxford: Monarch, 2006)

—, *Old Testament Ethics for the People of God* (Leicester: IVP, 2004)

—, *Walking in the Ways of the Lord: The Ethical Authority of the Old Testament* (Leicester: Apollos, 1995)

Wright, D.F., ed., *Essays in Evangelical Social Ethics* (Exeter: Paternoster, 1978)

Wright, N.G., *Disavowing Constantine: Mission, Church and the Social Order in the Theologies of John Howard Yoder and Jürgen Moltmann* (Carlisle: Paternoster, 2000)

—, *Power and Discipleship: Towards a Baptist Theology of the State* The Whitley Lecture 1996-97 (Oxford: Whitley, 1996)

—, *The Radical Kingdom* (Eastbourne: Kingsway, 1986)

Wright, N.T., *The Climax of the Covenant: Christ and the Law in Pauline Theology* (Edinburgh: T. & T. Clark, 1991)

—, *Jesus and the Victory of God* (London: SPCK, 1996)

—, *The New Testament and the People of God* (London: SPCK, 1992)

—, 'Paul and Caesar: A New Reading of Romans' in Bartholomew et al. eds., *A Royal Priesthood?* (Carlisle: Paternoster, 2002) 173-193

—, *What St Paul Really Said* (Oxford: Lion, 1997)

Yeago, D.S., 'Martin Luther on Grace, Law and Moral Life: Prolegomena to an Ecumenical Discussion of *Veritatis Splendor*', *The Thomist* 62 (1998) 163-91

Yocum, J.P., 'Aquinas' Literal Exposition on Job' in Weinandy, Keating and Yocum eds., *Aquinas on Scripture* 21-42

—, 'Sacraments in Aquinas' in Weinandy, Keating and Yocum eds., *Aquinas on Doctrine* 159-182

Yoder, J.H., *Body Politics: Five Practices of the Christian Community before the Watching World* (Scottdale: Herald Press, 2001)

—, *The Christian Witness to the State* (Newton, KA: Faith and Life Press, 1964)

—, *Karl Barth and the Problem of War* (Nashville: Abingdon Press, 1970)

—, *The Politics of Jesus: Vicit Agnus Noster* 2nd edn. (Grand Rapids: Eerdmans, 1994)

—, *The Priestly Kingdom: Social Ethics as Gospel* (Notre Dame: University of Notre Dame Press, 1984)

Other Materials

O'Donovan, O., 'Establishment', document submitted to the Evangelical Alliance Commission of Inquiry on Faith and Nation

—, Transcript of Interview with Paul Avis for the Evangelical Alliance Commission of Inquiry on Faith and Nation

—, Transcript of Interview with the Theological Sub-Group Plenary of the Evangelical Alliance Commission of Inquiry on Faith and Nation 26th September 2003

—, Transcript of Interview with the Constitutional Sub-Group Plenary of the Evangelical Alliance Commission of Inquiry on Faith and Nation 12th March 2004

Index

Aquinas, T. 3, 6, 16, 64, Ch. 4 *passim*, 222, 231-32, 236, 237
Aristotle 191-92
atonement 211, 220
Augustine 9-11, 19, 111, 113, 192, 231-32
autonomy – *see* 'freedom, as autonomy'

Bailleux, E. 159, 190
Barth, K. 26, 114, 166, 210 n. 4
Bauckham, R. 25, 33-35, 41, 58, 73, 222, 238
Bible – *see* 'Scripture'

Carl, M. 186
Cavanaugh, W.T. 156, 163
Chaplin, J. 128, 132, 134, 135, 140, 145
charity 173, 186, 190, 198
Charry, E.T. 63
Church 51-52, 56, 58, 64, 83, 138-39
    and Jesus Christ 118, 134-35
    and mission 117-19, 131, 142-150, 201, 205, 237
    and State 36, 42, 83, 101-2, 117-20, 132, 135, 142-48, 205-6, 230, 233
    See also 'Holy Spirit, and Church'
Colwell, J.E. 114, 229-30
common good 132-35, 164, 192-95, 204, 229
creation 75-79, 93
    new creation 55, 58, 75-78, 94
    See also 'God, and creation'
cross 11-12, 24-26, 28-29, 41, 48, 53, 74, 180-1, 218-19, 226-27, 231

Davies, B. 159-60
deification 16, 188, 214, 223. *See also* 'human beings, glorification'
dignity 65, 76-78
divine essence 161-62
divine persons – *see* 'Trinity, persons in relation'
divine kingship 39-40, 87-92, 100. *See*
also 'Jesus Christ, kingship'
Dych, W. 12

Ellul, J. 8-9
Emery, G. 163-64
eschatology 26, 28-29, 33, 38, 48-58, 78, 93-98, 106-7, 138-40, 146-47, 190
    See also 'human beings, glorification'
eternal good 197-201, 203-5
Eusebius of Caesarea 18

Fall 95, 175, 178, 195, 214. *See also* 'political authority, and Fall'
Fergusson, D. 114 n. 149
Fiddes, P.S. 161
Finnis, J. 134, 198
freedom
    and community 61-63
    as autonomy 60-62
    See also under 'God', 'Holy Spirit', 'human beings'
Furnish, V.P. 94, 126-27

Geiger, L.B. 177 n. 160
Geisler, N.L. 155
Gilby, T. 152, 193, 196
Glorification – *see* 'human beings, glorification'
God
    and creation 28, 49, 74-78, 159, 213
    as Triune 15-16, 24-29, 231, 234
    divine simplicity 160-61, 165
    Father 25-26, 35-36, 39
    freedom 61, 78, 213, 230
    justice 52-57, 82, 166, 231-34
    love 27, 35, 54, 63-64, 159, 213, 222, 230, 233
    righteousness 43, 52-54, 58, 73-74, 238
    self-revelation 97, 156-58, 160, 179
    suffering 26, 40
Gorringe, T.J. 147

grace 77-78, 82, 84-85, 115-16, 148-50,
164, 169, 178-85, 187, 189, 215, 219-
21, 231, 233-34. *See also* 'Holy Spirit,
and grace'
Gunton, C.E. 9-11, 13, 47, 153, 156, 215

Hall, P.M. 167, 169, 174-76, 184, 195
Healy, N.M. 156
holiness – *see under* 'God, righteousness'
and 'Holy Spirit, and holiness'
Holy Spirit 17, 23, 29-35, 64, 74, 110-17,
129, 143, 165, 174, 179, 181-85, Ch. 4
and Ch. 5 *passim*
and Church 49, 111-116, 118, 217
and creation 30-31, 45-46
and freedom 62, 110
and grace 78, 115, 181-84, 186-87,
197-98, 202, 215, 216-17
and holiness 32-33
and justice 4, 70-71, 221, 234. *See
also* 'justice, deep justice'
and new law Ch. 4 *passim*, 209-10,
236
and righteousness 57, 85-86, 227
and sanctification 33, 183, 211, 224-
25
and Torah 30-32, 45, 79, 128, 219-21
as 'Holistic Spirit' 23, 32, 74, 78-79
as mediator 210-11
as personal 182, 187
relation to human beings 34-35, 45,
141
work 32, 45-47, 111-17, 147-51, 202-
3, 212, 215-17, 222-23, 230
Honoré, T. 7
human authority – *see* 'political authority'
human beings
freedom 60-64, 99, 110, 204-5, 222-
23, 229-30
glorification 16, 33, 159, 187-91, 202,
207, 221, 223, 236, 238
history 48-51, 60, 89, 95-98, 167, 212
identity 129-35, 138-39
image of God 37, 76, 177, 182, 189,
229-30
human goods 168, 175-79, 186, 203-6
human rights 7, 58-60, 64-70, 77, 79-81,
84

human community 62-63, 69, 106, 132-35

injustice 52, 70
Irenaeus of Lyons 212

Jaffa, H.V. 176
Jenson, R. 224
Jesus Christ 18, 92-110, 179, 188, Ch. 3
and Ch. 5 *passim*
and eternal law 4, 165, 218
and human law 201-2, 228
and salvation 180-81, 185, 204
and Torah 4, 128-29, 169-74, 218
as mediator 46, 190
kingship 21, 36-39, 93, 104, 106-7,
109, 150, 190, 201, 209, 219
obedience 127, 180, 217-18
Sonship 28-29, 39
two natures 19-20, 109, 217
See also under 'Church', 'judgment',
'political authority'
John of Salisbury 20
judgment 105, 121-23, 141-42, 150, 231
and Holy Spirit 141-42, 210-11
and Jesus Christ 53, 54, 138-40, 226-
27
and justice 120-26
and political authority 105-7, 120-23,
125-26, 130-32, 136-42, 148-51
God's judgment 120, 123, 234
human judgment 4, 9, 122, 125-26,
130, 136-37, 226
See also 'Last Judgment'
justice 52-60, 70-71, 122-23, 125-26, 167,
192-94, 215
deep justice 198, 216, 220-22, 233-34
legal justice 192-95
reconciling justice 53-54
restorative justice 52
retributive justice – *see* 'law, and
retribution'
shallow justice 4-5, 8, 198, 216, 232-
34, 237
social justice 59-60, 128
See also under 'God', 'Holy Spirit',
'law, human law', 'political authority'

Keating, D.A. 184, 187

Kerr, F. 178-79, 186, 188, 189, 191, 203, 224
Kilby, K. 72
Kingdom of God 35-39, 48, 57, 82, 190, 194
kingship, earthly 89-92. *See also* 'political authority'

Last Judgment 4-5, 52-55, 226-27, 231
law 5-9, 40-48, 121, 131, 164-65, 183-84
    and eschatology 51-52, 211
    and grace 9, 78
    and ordering 47, 75-79, 121, 167, 216
    and retribution 43-44, 52-55, 79
    and salvation 164-87, 174, 176
    and virtue 185-87, 200
    as domination 73-75, 84
    divine law 6, 168, 173, 197-99, 200, 205
    eternal law 4, 6, 164-67, 218
    human law 3-9, 54-55, 81-86, 123-29, 191-205, Ch. 5 *passim*
        and justice 5-8, 76, 79, 84-86, 209, 215, 218, 231-34
        and legalism 43-44
        and morality 6-9
        and sin 196-98, 204, 230-31
        as temporal 197-200
        limitations 195-200, 227-33
        See also 'Jesus Christ, and human law'
    Mosaic Law – *see* 'Torah'
    natural law 6, 68, 124-26, 150, 168, 171, 174-80, 186, 195-97, 213-14
    New Law 167-69, 172-74, 180-85, 187
    Old Law – *see* 'Torah'
Letham, R. 12, 19, 224, 234
Levering, M. 3, 154, 155-56, 160, 167, 169-74, 183, 185, 189, 192, 197
liberation 58-64, 79, 81, 236
Locke, J. 147 n. 346
Lockwood O'Donovan, J. 1, 132, 133, 136, 145 n. 334, 147-48, 191
Luther, M. 221

Malet, A. 161-62
MacIntyre, A. 174

McConville, J.G. 128
McGrath, A.E. 182
McIlroy, D.H. 8, 68 n. 367, 79 n. 423, 175 n. 146, 176 n. 156, 208-9, 211, 213 n. 17, 216-20, 228 n. 71, 236
Meilaender, G. 206
Milbank, J. 14, 155 n. 11 and n. 17, 161 n. 56, 223 n. 49
mishpat 8
Molnar, P.D. 72
Moltmann, J. 2, 6, 11-12, 14, Ch. 2 *passim*, 93, 94, 222, 236
Montgomery, J.W. 8-9, 126
moral order 94-98, 112-15, 124-30, 149-51, 175-78
Mosaic Law – *see* 'Torah'
Müller-Fahrenholz, G. 28, 71

natural goods – see 'human goods'
Neufeld, J. 135 n. 276
Nichols, A. 189, 191, 203
Norman Anonymous 19-20

obedience 145-46, 174, 180, 182-83, 213-14, 221-26
O'Connor, D.J. 152
O'Donovan, O. 2-3, 6, 8, 16, Ch. 3 *passim*, 177-79, 191, 216, 222, 228-29, 231, 236
Otto, R.E. 42, 72

Paeth, S.R. 69
panentheism 28, 31-33
parousia 38, 58, 94, 227
peace 56, 70, 122-23, 198-99
perichoresis 27-28, 33-34, 72
political authority Ch. 3 *passim*, 192-95
    and accountability 102-3, 148
    and divine providence 99-100, 106, 116-17, 135, 148-50, 194, 214
    and domination 40-44, 75, 80
    and Holy Spirit 47, 108-9, 116-17, 150-51, 216-17
    and Jesus Christ 100-109, 138-39, 227-28
    and justice 125-26, 136-37, 217
    and Fall 99, 133, 140, 214, 226-27, 232

and use of force 46-47, 79-81, 105-6
legitimacy of 65, 98-103, 121, 149,
  236
relationship to God's authority 145,
  148, 166, 193-94, 214, 227-29, 231-33
  See also 'kingship, earthly'
power – *see* 'political authority'
providence 159, 164-67, 194, 214-17. *See
  also under* 'political authority'

Rasmussen, A. 62-63, 72
reconciliation 52-56, 76
redemption 93-95, 227-29
resurrection 48, 92-98, 137, 180-81, 219,
  227
Ricoeur, P. 63-64
Rivers, A.J. 204
Rowland, C. 132
Ryan, T.F. 185
Rybarczyk, E.J. 223, 238

salvation 55-57, 135, 176-79, 180-81,
  224-25, 227. *See also under* 'Jesus
  Christ', 'law', 'Trinity'
Saward, J. 216 n.25
Schaeffer, F. 153 n.6
Scripture 97, 154-57, 210, 213-14, 235
shalom 55-57, 96, 214
sin 32-33, 47, 74, 166, 168, 176, 196-8,
  220
solidarity 58-60, 74, 84, 132-33
State, *see* 'Church, and State'
Storkey, A. 228

Tanner, K. 14-15, 42, 72
theology
  of law Ch. 1 *passim*, 211, 216, 234,

236-37
  political 17-20, 40, 87-117, 212, 216
  Trinitarian 1-3, 9-21, 210-12
Torah 4-6, 43-44, 91, 126-29, 167-74,
  179, 186, 209. *See also under* 'Holy
  Spirit', 'Jesus Christ', 'Trinity'
Torrell, J-P. 165, 215
Trinity 82-83, 110-11, 141, 207, 208, 235-
  38
  and Church 11
  and creation 158-59, 213-14
  and human community 14-16, 211
  and justice 135-42
  and law Ch. 1 *passim*, 117-148, 213
  and natural law 150, 213
  and providence 214-17
  and resurrection 28-29
  and revelation 28, 170-1, 210-12, 235
  and salvation 12-15, 159-60, 181, 207,
    210, 235
  and the cross 11-12
  and Torah 218, 220-21
  as economic 14-16, 25, 163-64, 212,
    235
  as immanent 14-15, 162-63, 229-30
  persons in relation 13-16, 25-26, 34,
    73, 110-11, 159, 161-64, 185
tsedeq 8, 128, 208-9
Tutu, D. 230

Wawrykow, J. 170
Weinandy, T.G. 156, 165, 181
Williams, A.N. 159, 188-89, 190-91
Williams, R. 162
Wright, N.G. 53, 56

Yeago, D.S. 186

www.ingramcontent.com/pod-product-compliance
Lightning Source LLC
Chambersburg PA
CBHW070910100426
42814CB00003B/125